TAKING EMPLOYMENT DISCRIMINATION SERIOUSLY:
CHINESE AND EUROPEAN PERSPECTIVES

Taking Employment Discrimination Seriously:
Chinese and European Perspectives

edited by

YUWEN LI
and
JENNY GOLDSCHMIDT

Netherlands Institute of Human Rights, School of Law,
Utrecht University, The Netherlands

MARTINUS NIJHOFF PUBLISHERS
LEIDEN / BOSTON

Cover photo: "Job-seekers queue at a job fair in Beijing, China on February 15, 2009. China is finding new ways to get jobs for the country's millions of college graduates, as vacancies are getting slashed under the current financial crisis."

This book is printed on acid-free paper.

Library of Congress Cataloging-in-Publication Data

ISBN 978 9004 17717 8

Copyright 2009 by Koninklijke Brill NV, Leiden, The Netherlands.
Koninklijke Brill NV incorporates the imprints Brill, Hotei Publishing, IDC Publishers, Martinus Nijhoff Publishers and VSP.

All rights reserved. No part of this publication may be reproduced, translated, stored in a retrieval system, or transmitted in any form or by any means, electronic, mechanical, photocopying, recording or otherwise, without prior written permission from the publisher.

Brill has made all reasonable efforts to trace all right holders to any copyrighted material used in this work. In cases where these efforts have not been successful the publisher welcomes communications from copyright holders, so that the appropriate acknowledgements can be made in future editions, and to settle other permission matters.

Authorization to photocopy items for internal or personal use is granted by Koninklijke Brill NV provided that the appropriate fees are paid directly to The Copyright Clearance Center, 222 Rosewood Drive, Suite 910, Danvers, MA 01923, USA.
Fees are subject to change.

PRINTED IN THE NETHERLANDS

This book is dedicated to people who suffer from various forms of employment discrimination, and those who give their support to human dignity and equality.

TABLE OF CONTENTS

ACKNOWLEDGEMENTS	ix
LIST OF CONTRIBUTORS	xi
LIST OF ABBREVIATIONS	xiii

INTRODUCTION TO THE BOOK: ANTI-DISCRIMINATION IN EMPLOYMENT NECESSITATES LAW AND ACTION
Yuwen Li and Jenny Goldschmidt — 1

Part 1 – Chinese Analysis

1. An Analysis of Employment Discrimination in China's Economic and Social Transition
   Yuwen Li — 19

2. A Research Report on Health Discrimination in Employment
   Liu Yang — 49

3. Disability Discrimination in Employment
   Ma Yu'e — 85

4. A Study of Current Employment Discrimination against Women
   Wang Xinyu — 113

5. Identity Discrimination in Employment – Household Registration and Regional Origin
   Yao Guojian — 133

6. A Survey of Employment Discrimination in Ten Major Cities in China
   Constitutionalism Research Institute
   China University of Political Science and Law — 157

Part 2 – European Analysis

7	EU Anti-Discrimination Law: Historical Development and Main Concepts *Susanne Burri*	209
8	Anti-discrimination Law in the Netherlands: A Specific Legal Patchwork, Normative System and Institutional Structure *Jenny Goldschmidt*	239
9	Austrian Law and Practice Regarding Anti-Discrimination in Employment *Ingrid Nikolay-Leitner*	261
10	Comparative Study on Positive Action in Law and Practice *Colm O'Cinneide*	279

ACKNOWLEDGEMENTS

This book is one of the outcomes of a cooperative legal project regarding Anti-Discrimination in Employment in China, funded by the Royal Dutch Embassy in Beijing. We would like to thank Mr. Job van den Berg who was in charge of the Rule of Law Program at the Royal Dutch Embassy. His persistent support to the project enabled a number of Chinese researchers to carry out comprehensive and empirical study on the current situation of employment discrimination in China. In addition, it allowed us to organize an international conference in Beijing, during which European anti-discrimination experts could present their views and share their European legal experiences in this area, with a group of Chinese legislators, legal scholars, civil servants, and NGO representatives.

We owe particular thanks to Professor Cai Dingjian at the China University of Political Science and Law for his stimulating and leading role in organizing a Chinese research team that produced the ground-breaking Chinese book entitled, *The Current Situation on Employment Discrimination in China and Anti-discrimination Strategies* (China Social Science Press 2007). Chapters 2 to 6 of this volume are selected articles from that book.

Employment discrimination is a relatively new social phenomenon in China, which has only attracted a degree of legal academic attention in recent years. We are grateful for the contributions by the Chinese authors, which contain both critical analysis and constructive suggestions. In particular, it is evident that these articles make a common plea to the Chinese government, business community and public at large, to make concerted efforts in the fight against labour market inequality.

Our deep appreciation also goes to the European experts who generously responded to our various requests. As reflected in their articles, employment discrimination exists in any society. Even in Western European countries, where legal systems are relatively developed in the field of equality, employment discrimination, especially indirect discrimination, remains hard to eradicate.

We are also grateful to Xia Yuezhu, who carefully compared the English translations with the originals; and to Gina de Graaff, Daniel Jarrett, Róisín Murphy and Hanneke van Denderen at the Netherlands Institute of Human Rights for their practical help.

Finally, we owe many thanks to Lindy Melman at Martinus Nijhoff Publishers, for her efficient and friendly cooperation, which resulted in the timely publication of this volume.

Yuwen Li
Jenny Goldschmidt

Utrecht
January 2009

LIST OF CONTRIBUTORS

Susanne Burri
Associate professor, Institute of Legal Theory, Utrecht University, Faculty of Law, Economics and Governance, Utrecht School of Law and coordinator of the European Commission's Network of Legal Experts in the Field of Gender Equality.

Jenny Goldschmidt
Professor of human rights law and director of the Netherlands Institute of Human Rights (SIM), Utrecht University, Faculty of Law, Economics and Governance, Utrecht School of Law.

Yao Guojian
Associate professor, China University of Political Science and Law.

Yuwen Li
Associate professor, Netherlands Institute of Human Rights (SIM), Utrecht University, Faculty of Law, Economics and Governance, Utrecht School of Law.

Ingrid Nikolay-Leitner
Director of the Specialised Equality Body in Austria.

Colm O'Cinneide
Associate professor, Faculty of Law at University College London, UK *rapporteur* at the EU Network of Anti-Discrimination Experts.

Wang Xinyu
Associate professor, China University of Political Science and Law.

Liu Yang
Associate professor, China University of Political Science and Law.

Ma Yu'e
Deputy-Director at the Rights Protection Department of China Disabled Persons' Federation.

LIST OF ABBREVIATIONS

ACWF	All China Women's Federation
CDPF	China Disabled Persons' Federation
CEDAW	Convention on the Elimination of All Forms of Discrimination against Women
CERD	Convention on the Elimination of Racial Discrimination
CPCC	Communist Party Central Committee
CPPCC	Chinese People's Political Consultative Conference
CRPD	Convention on the Rights of Persons with Disabilities
ECHR	European Convention on Human Rights and Fundamental Freedoms
EC	European Community
ECtHR	European Court of Human Rights
ECJ	European Court of Justice
EEC	European Economic Community
ETA	Equal Treatment Act
ETC	Equal Treatment Commission
EU	European Union
GDP	Gross Domestic Product
HBV	Hepatitis B Virus
ICCPR	International Covenant on Civil and Political Rights
ILO	International Labour Organization
NGO	Non-Governmental Organization
NPC	National People's Congress
NPCSC	National People's Congress Standing Committee
PRC	People's Republic of China
RMB	*Ren Min Bi* (People's Money)
UN	United Nations

INTRODUCTION TO THE BOOK:
ANTI-DISCRIMINATION IN EMPLOYMENT NECESSITATES LAW AND ACTION

Yuwen Li and Jenny Goldschmidt

Prevalent employment discrimination is a relatively new phenomenon in post-1978 reformist China. Before that, the employment market, as part of the central planned economy, was overwhelmingly regulated and controlled by the government. Millions of young urban people were sent to the countryside, which reduced the governmental burden of finding jobs for them in cities. Farmers in rural areas were under strict household control, which prevented them from moving to cities for employment, and indeed there was also no potential for them to get work anyway due to the extremely weak economy. Those working either in state-owned factories or in administrative and public institutions, enjoyed an 'iron rice bowl' provided by the government, namely, they received a salary, housing and pensions from their work units, although the amount and benefit were only at subsistence level.

The rapid economic reform in the 1980s changed this situation quickly and dramatically. Large groups of urban youths who were sent to the countryside started to return to their home towns and demand that the government find them jobs. Reform of state-owned enterprises resulted in many of them becoming bankrupt and many workers were made redundant, consequently they had to seek new employment. The economics of life in the cities attracted millions of rural men and women into leaving their villages and becoming migrant workers in cities. Responding to the supply and demand of the market, the government relaxed its control on the labour market by allowing employers to exercise autonomy when hiring. While the labour market has expanded, the legal system has not matched the speed of development to protect the rights of workers. In conjunction with the lack of awareness of individuals' rights shown by government officials, the business community, and the public at large, employment discrimination spread swiftly and widely in Chinese society in the 1980s and 1990s without getting much public attention. Individuals who suffered from such discrimination either tolerated it or felt that it was their own incompetence that had caused them to be discriminated against.

In 2003, Zhou Yichao, a young Chinese graduate who had passed the national civil servant examination which qualified him to apply for a job with the government, was rejected by the local civil service recruitment office because he tested positive for hepatitis B. Mr Zhou felt hopeless as a result of this refusal and took revenge on the civil service recruitment officers by killing one and injuring another. This tragic event shocked the country and also generated public and media concern about employment discrimination against carriers of hepatitis B and other groups of disadvantaged people in society.

Against this background, some Chinese legal scholars started to critically examine employment discrimination practice in China, as well as the legal system associated with it. To facilitate Chinese research, the Constitutionalism Research Institute at the China University of Political Science and Law and the Netherlands Institute of Human Rights at Utrecht University School of Law, jointly initiated a research project on anti-discrimination in employment in China. The project aimed to find out how serious the current situation of employment discrimination in China's labour market is, and what legal action can be taken against such discrimination. The project received support from the Royal Dutch Embassy in China with a four-year grant for a series of activities on field study, research, conferences, training, visiting European countries, publications, advocacy, etc. The current book is one of the outcomes of the project's activities. The papers contributed by the Chinese authors delved into the present state of employment discrimination, including the current legal framework, regarding both general discrimination and discrimination on particular grounds of disability, health, gender, household registration and place of origin. Chapters 2 to 6 are translated from the Chinese articles in a book entitled '*The Current Situation on Employment Discrimination in China and Anti-discrimination Strategies*', which was edited by Professor Cai Dingjian and published by China Social Science Press in 2007. The four papers written by the European experts, deal with the state of affairs in the European Union and some specific European countries. They are based on the presentations delivered at the International Conference on Promoting Equal Opportunity in Employment, held in Beijing in 2007.

Yuwen Li provides an overview of current employment discrimination in China both in terms of law and practice. The overview starts with an examination of the Chinese legislation which provides general principles of employment equality amongst all citizens, and which prohibits employment discrimination on the grounds of ethnic group, race, gender and religious beliefs. The author introduces, in particular, the Law on Promotion of Employment which became effective on 1 January 2008. As a reaction to the reality of discrimination, this Law has expanded the grounds of employment discrimination to protect carriers of infectious diseases and migrant workers. Recognizing the legislative progress achieved so far at the national level, Li shares the view expressed by most Chinese scholars that the existing laws are too generally formulated, both in the absence of a legal definition of employment discrimination and also in the lack of legal remedies to address the reality of discrimination. Moreover, some administrative regulations and local rules that contain blatant discriminatory provisions, provide a legal source for numerous discriminatory practices. Consequently, in the author's view, China's legislative bodies and competent government bodies at both the central and local level, need to amend the existing laws, regulations and rules, and abolish provisions that are outdated, discriminatory or have the potential to discriminate against people in employment. To enhance Chinese legislation concerning equal employment, Li expresses her preference for enacting a new equal employment law to harmonize legal protection with the prevailing social need. The introduction of such a law would demonstrate governmental determination to seriously counteract employment discrimination. Although it would be unrealistic to expect that equal employment rules would be fully and voluntarily respected and followed by all employers, it is the responsibility of the state to provide legal instruments for citizens to use when their rights to equal employment are violated.

Apart from the legal issues involved in the discussion on employment discrimination, Li uses Chinese media reports and data from various surveys to illustrate that employment discrimination exists both in the public and the private sectors and in the form of both direct and indirect discrimination, and predicts that, with the growing public campaign against employment discrimination, direct discrimination may be replaced by more indirect discrimination which could render anti-discrimination efforts more difficult. Research has also shown that, in today's China, public awareness of employment discrimination remains rather low. Some officials, economists and businessmen take the view that some critics of employment discrimination have exaggerated the situation and overlooked the rules of the market economy, which permit employers' autonomy in making hiring decisions. Against this view, Li stresses the use of legal remedies, especially the judicial system, to protect one's right of equal employment. By the courts' enforcement of the law, serious and blatant acts of employment discrimination can be corrected, victims can be compensated and, moreover, members of the public can be educated, which contributes to the building-up of a social culture of willingly respecting people's equal employment rights. However, the author points out that the judicial settlement of employment discrimination disputes also has its limitations, in particular, too often this may not result in the individual being hired or being kept in employment by the same employer. Thus one might create a situation in which one wins a lawsuit but loses a job in the end. In addition, the heavy workload of the courts makes it unrealistic to expect that they would be used as the principal way to solve discrimination disputes. As a way of counteracting this drawback, the author draws attention to the experience of Western countries in establishing Equal Treatment Commissions, which provide services to improve public awareness of equal employment as well as handles individual complaints.

Liu Yang's chapter on health discrimination in employment originates from his interview-based research conducted in August and September 2005. The author concentrated his research on the most visible and grave health-based employment discrimination in China, namely against carriers of hepatitis B and HIV, and against those who have recovered from venereal disease, especially syphilis. As rightly indicated by the author, the infectious diseases which these groups of people have cannot be spread through everyday social contact; thus exclusion and isolation of them from the normal job market constitutes employment discrimination.

With regard to employment discrimination suffered by carriers of hepatitis B in employment, according to Liu Yang's findings, almost half of the people interviewed (48.8%) believed that hepatitis B carriers should not have equal access to employment. Similarly, more than half of the enterprise owners interviewed (56%) stated that hepatitis B carriers should not receive equal treatment in employment hence they would be rejected when applying for a job. The discrimination against hepatitis B carriers is manifested in several ways. The author discusses the cases known nationwide of Zhang Xianzhu, Zhou Yichao, and Chen Shunyuan who were refused employment after passing civil servant recruitment examinations. Similar outcomes happened to candidates who applied for jobs with companies. An extremely shocking case is that of Mr Wang, a doctor in a hospital who was infected with hepatitis B during a voluntary blood donation; he was then forced to leave his job and only taken back by the hospital in another position after seven years out of work.

HIV positive people suffer similar employment discrimination to carriers of hepatitis B; however, they experience more serious social exclusion. 55.4% of the interviewees indicated that they would try to avoid people who were HIV positive. 65% of business people interviewed stated that they would not give HIV positive people equality in employment. Such discrimination is partly caused by the lack of knowledge concerning how HIV is transmitted, as well as a confusion between HIV and AIDS. Discrimination is also caused by the widespread moral condemnation of HIV sufferers, who are often assumed to become infected through drug use or promiscuity. Liu reports that:

> Since the majority of people have not come into face-to-face contact with HIV/AIDS sufferers, and HIV/AIDS sufferers rarely dare identify themselves publicly, they maintain an air of mystery and separation. Public opinion and propaganda in the media are the principal means of determining their public image. However, as a result of ceaseless negative reports, HIV/AIDS sufferers live under a cloud of fear, enduring insults and shame and being unable to obtain the same status as other people.[1]

The author's findings and analysis of employment discrimination against syphilis sufferers and those who have recovered from syphilis are even more alarming. Since syphilis is principally transmitted through sexual intercourse, most people view the infection as self-inflicted. 75% of people interviewed declared that they did not think that people who had recovered from syphilis should be given equal treatment in employment. The primary reason for this, as pointed out by the author, is people's contempt for the low moral standards of those who were once infected with syphilis. Compared with HIV/AIDS, there are

---

[1] Liu Yang, 'A Research Report on Health Discrimination in Employment', Chapter 2 of this book, p. 66.

hardly any public awareness campaigns about people who have recovered from syphilis; thus the author concludes that this group of people suffers the most severe discrimination in employment amongst all groups suffering from infectious diseases. People who have a history of syphilis are disqualified from becoming civil servants, reflecting the fact that they are even more excluded by government organizations than HIV positive people and carriers of hepatitis B.

Ma Yu'e presents an in-depth discussion on employment discrimination against disabled persons. According to the statistics in 2006, there were about 82.96 million disabled people in mainland China. Although China's legal system forbids employment discrimination against persons with a disability, there is no precise definition of what disability discrimination in employment actually is, nor is there any protection for victims of discrimination. To the author's knowledge, there has never been a case of a disabled person bringing a lawsuit on disability discrimination against an employer to court, though it is commonly known that such discrimination obviously exists.

In the author's view, it is apparent that disabled people face greater difficulties than non-disabled people in finding employment, as the discrepancy in the employment rates of disabled and non-disabled people clearly illustrates. Apart from analysing the data of various surveys to point out the seriousness of disability discrimination in employment, the author's information on a few cases provides readers with a vivid picture of how appalling it can be in reality for disabled people to find a job that they are capable of doing. A female, disabled postgraduate was rejected by 60 recruiters; a female, deaf mute graduate knelt down to beg for a job at a recruitment fair after being refused by numerous employers. Obviously these students have spent more energy and time than the non-disabled to complete their college education; the success of their education proves their ability to do certain jobs and indeed it could be fairly expected that their knowledge, ability, perseverance and enthusiasm would convince employers to hire them as a privilege. However, the reality is to many people's dismay. If educated disabled graduates suffer such a degree of employment discrimination, one could imagine how much greater the misery is of those disabled people without higher education.

Ma Yu'e's research into disability employment discrimination reveals the following. (1) There are unequal opportunities for disabled people, which is supported by the common argument of employers that there are not even enough employment places for healthy people, so why care about the handicapped? (2) Disabled people are discriminated against at work, by the fact that many of them have no social insurance, and also by the fact that some work units impose higher targets and tasks on disabled workers. (3) The lack of employment services and facilities to accommodate disabled persons in the workplace.

The author discusses the major preferential treatments for disabled people in employment in Chinese law and in policy documents. First, the law provides a quota system for the employment of disabled persons which requires state organizations, social organizations and enterprises to employ a certain proportion of disabled persons in appropriate types of jobs. If the quota is not fulfilled, the work unit must pay into the disability employment protection fund. Secondly, the law encourages the establishment of social welfare enterprises that concentrate on employing large numbers of disabled people: as a reward, such enterprises receive tax exemptions and preferential policies. Thirdly, disabled persons are encouraged to set up their own businesses.

Despite some success by the preferential treatment measures, the author highlights that all of them face problems in practice. The quota system has proved difficult to implement nationwide, and many work units prefer to pay into disability employment protection funds rather than employ disabled people. The restrictions on the qualifications to be a social welfare enterprise are outdated since they exclude many enterprises from the benefits of the tax incentives, regardless of the high numbers of disabled people they employ. It also happens that some work units claim to employ disabled persons in order to qualify for tax exemption but do not actually let them work, since the benefit of tax exemption exceeds the costs of keeping them on. Hence, some disabled people are merely employed 'on paper'; in reality, they are not given proper jobs but merely receive modest living costs. With regard to self-employment, even though a relatively large number of disabled people are employed in this way, they have no security.

In the conclusion the author notes that: 'While there has been rapid economic development, disabled people as a group have faced increasing unemployment. Government policies and laws have been drawn up, but the actual benefits for disabled people have been minimal. Society has progressed, but disability discrimination still exists.'[2] The author suggests that in order to eliminate employment discrimination against disabled people, the existing laws and regulations must be revised to strengthen legal effectiveness of anti-discrimination in employment on the ground of disability. In addition, the author firmly believes that of the utmost importance in combating employment discrimination concerning disability is the need to eradicate traditional prejudices about and concepts of discrimination against disabled persons. If they are commonly referred to as 'cripples', if government institutions and companies refuse to employ them because of the mistaken impression that this would damage an institution's or company's good image, and if disabled people are seen as 'unlucky', employment discrimination against disabled people will not be improved. In the end, the author specifically calls on the government to take disability employment discrimination seriously, since: 'In China, the government has a strong role in setting an example. If the government takes the lead in eliminating disability discrimination, many enterprises and public institutions will in turn emulate this.'[3]

---

[2] Ma Yu'e, 'Disability Discrimination in Employment', Chapter 3 of this book, pp. 109-110.
[3] Ibid., p. 112.

Employment discrimination against women exists in every country, and China is no exception. Since the founding of the People's Republic of China in 1949, the government has continually endorsed the policy that 'men and women are equal' and 'women hold up half the sky' meaning that women's role in society is the same as that of men; however, in the employment market women suffer various sorts of direct and indirect discrimination. Wang Xinyu's chapter on the current state of employment discrimination against women touches upon four issues: various aspects of employment discrimination against women; reasons that caused such discrimination; legal protection aimed at promoting employment equality between men and women as well as legal insufficiency; and measures that need to be taken to improve employment equality and to fight gender discrimination. According to Wang, gender discrimination in employment reflects unequal employment opportunities in which women face more difficulties in finding employment than their male counterparts. This is particularly problematic for female graduates who have followed the same educational route as male graduates but find they are inferior in the labour market. In some sectors, young and good-looking women enjoy the advantage of being the first to be hired, but this is not because they are treated better than men but rather that they are treated as a 'commodity' in a market catering to the interests and tastes of men. Another form of unequal treatment of men and women in employment, both in law and in practice, is that Chinese women's retirement age is lower than that of men. While female workers and civil servants retire at the age of 50 and 55 respectively, men's retirement age is 60. In addition, men and women are paid differently for the same work, showing direct discrimination against women. Moreover, the employment market is characterized by the segregation of the sexes according to the type of work. Women are concentrated in the labour-intensive industries rather than the high-tech industries, and are increasingly rare in higher management posts.

Wang observes that some government officials and business people do not consider certain differences in the hiring of men and women to be discrimination against women. For them, employers have the autonomy to decide who to hire according to their own need. Obviously, Wang disagrees with such a mindset. In her view the reasons that cause gender discrimination in the labour market are manifold. In the first place, the surplus in the labour force puts job-seekers at a disadvantage and allows recruiters to select candidates on the basis of gender. Secondly, due to the lack of a social security system, companies feel that they have to bear the extra costs of female employees if they give birth and take maternity leave. Thirdly, women are also seen as intrinsically less productive and less capable of development, since household concerns also demand their attention. In addition, the lack of an effective guarantee of women's equal rights in law and the inadequate supervision of the labour market by the government, also contribute to the escalation of gender discrimination in employment. Some protective legal provisions based on women's biological nature may in reality have an adverse impact on women's employment. Thus, in the author's view it is time for China to revise the laws and administrative regulations which contain either discriminatory elements against women or outdated protective provisions that result in women actually being discriminated against in employment.

Yao Guojian's chapter on identity discrimination in employment, based on the household registration and regional origin of the job-seeker, reflects a particular problem in China. Such discrimination manifests itself in the government policy to enhance employment opportunities for local urban people by excluding or limiting job-seekers with a rural household registration or without a local household registration. By contrast with employment discrimination on other grounds, identity discrimination is mainly (but not exclusively) perpetrated by government bodies rather than enterprises. Such discrimination is manifested in various ways. In many cases the possession of a local household registration is a mandatory condition for employment. The number of migrant labourers is controlled, and the industries and jobs open to migrants are restricted. Imposing higher standards on migrant labourers than on local workers is also a technique to exclude migrants from employment. In some cases employers even explicitly lay down specific conditions to exclude labourers coming from unpopular areas. When migrants are employed, they receive lower salaries than local employees as well as fewer economic and social benefits in terms of labour insurance, subsidies, allowances, etc.

Yao describes identity discrimination as a 'policy level discrimination in employment' since it is based on, or supported by, government regulations or policy documents. The root of identity discrimination rests on the long-standing household registration system which divides citizens in urban and rural areas into two separate classes. Those with urban household registration enjoy more job opportunities and a social welfare system, while rural people are largely left to take care of themselves. In addition, local government officials do their utmost to promote local people's employment and to reduce the unemployment rate, since they were instructed to do this not only as an economic task but also as a political task to ensure social stability. Consequently, employment rate is used as a benchmark in evaluating the work achievements of local government.

However, the author also indicates that a policy change on migrant workers has been initiated by the central government in recent years, which has resulted in the abolition or revision of some administrative regulations and local rules which contained obvious discrimination against migrants. In his view, China is undergoing a transformation from the discriminatory policies of the past, which bristled with restrictions and controls, to protective policies supporting equality in employment. While applauding this development, the author stresses the necessity for substantive reform and change in legislation, administration and ideology.

The household registration system must be gradually reformed in order to grant citizens freedom of movement. It is also important to generate public awareness and appreciation of contributions made by migrants to society. The author also appeals for a change to the current electoral system, to grant migrants voting rights to elect members of the local people's congress in the place where they work. In this way the interests of migrants could be represented and promoted.

Chapter 6, on the Survey of Employment Discrimination in Ten Major Cities in China, produced by the Constitutionalism Research Institute and the Institute of Sociology of China University of Political Science and Law, offers the outcome of a first-hand investigation of public reaction to various basic issues concerning employment discrimination in China. The data contained in the Survey is based on questionnaires received from 3454 interviewees in Beijing, Guangzhou, Wuhan, Nanjing, Shenyang, Chengdu, Xi'an, Zhengzhou, Yinchuan, and Qingdao. These cities are situated in the East, South, West and North of China, representing different levels of urban economic development.

From sporadic media reports on cases of employment discrimination in China, one could get an impression that such discrimination is serious and pervasive. But to verify how serious it might be and to what degree people are affected, needs comprehensive statistics. Due to the lack of formal information on employment discrimination, which could be provided by authorities or independent fact-finding institutions, the data in the Survey is very useful for us to understand the scope and degree of current employment discrimination in Chinese society. The Survey comprises five parts. Part one provides the background of people interviewed as well as the research methodology. Part two contains the information on what type of discrimination interviewees encountered when they sought employment. The data shows that disability ranks the highest and this is followed by household discrimination. For civil service recruitment, discrimination based on the local resident permit ranks the highest, and disability and health follow. Part three covers different treatment in employment, such as whether employers have requested restrictions on marriage and having children, in what ways migrant workers are treated differently from normal employees, what age restriction was imposed when interviewees took the civil servant examination, and so on. Part four examines the different treatment experienced in social and political life, such as whether women, disabled persons and migrant workers enjoy the same political rights as other employees; whether interviewees felt that they had been looked down upon in expensive places (hotels, shopping malls, etc.). Part five covers individuals' opinions on issues relating to employment discrimination, such as what are reasonable conditions which employers could impose in their hiring practice, what groups are most susceptible to discrimination, if you were an employer, which group of people would you not like to hire, and so on. It is interesting to note that in answering the question whether and to what extent employment discrimination exists in today's China, 85.5% replied 'yes', 50.8% indicated that it was serious, and only 6.6% said 'no' (E4 of the Survey). Part six involves a number of questions on people's attitudes towards employment discrimination. For instance, Table F1 lists 20 controversial issues that are often debated by employers, legal scholars and economists in China, such as whether equality in employment will affect economic development, or whether, for the effectiveness and good image of a work unit, an employer is entitled to employ only those who are of a high calibre, particularly as regards health, good looks and technical expertise. In Table F5, people were asked, if you want to complain about being discriminated against, what institutions do you go to? Interestingly, 25.5% of interviewees chose the option of lodging a case with the courts for settlement. Of course, the Survey is based on interviews with 3454 persons, which cannot be said to be representative of the whole Chinese population of 1.3 billion. However, this Survey, together with other statistics used in the chapters written by the Chinese authors in this book, provides academic research information for readers to understand the general situation of employment discrimination in China.

The European chapters in this book start with a contribution by Susanne Burri who offers an overview of the historical development of EU anti-discrimination law. Since the 1970s, European Community law has been a source of regulations which have been implemented in the member states and which have developed into a comprehensive legal and conceptual system of non-discrimination law. Over the years, many different anti-discrimination provisions and directives have been adopted and it has become a fragmented and complicated body of law. Burri discusses the development of basic concepts such as direct and indirect discrimination, as well as harassment and sexual harassment, emphasizing the important role played by the European Court of Justice (ECJ) in the development of such concepts.

This development has taken about half a century. In the EEC Treaty (1957), only a few anti-discrimination provisions relating to gender and nationality were included. In the Treaty of Amsterdam (1999), the promotion of equality between men and women was designated as one of the essential tasks of the Community, as listed in Article 2 EC. Since 1999, the EU Treaty has promoted action to combat discrimination based on the grounds of gender, racial or ethnic origin, religion or belief, disability, age or sexual orientation.

The European Court of Justice has ruled that the (original) economic aim of Article 141 EC (formerly Article 119 EEC), providing the principle of equal pay for male and female workers for work of equal value, is subordinate to its social aim. This means, amongst other things, that the concept of 'worker' in the sense of the Article must have a Community meaning and cannot be interpreted restrictively. Similarly, the concept of 'pay' has been interpreted broadly and purposively.

The anti-discrimination directives also allow positive action with a view to ensuring full equality in practice, but in the view of the ECJ this possibility must be seen as an exception to the principle of equal treatment, rather than as an integrated part of it. Since Directive 79/207/EEC, on equal treatment of men and women in employment, two more exceptions to the prohibition of direct (sex) discrimination have been included in the law: occupational activities for which the sex of the worker is a determining factor, and the protection of women, particularly as regards pregnancy and maternity. Many provisions on anti-discrimination have a closed system of exceptions as regards direct discrimination. This is the case with most of the sex equality directives, except for Directive 2004/113 EC regulating the principle of equal treatment of men and women in access to and supply of goods and services, which has no closed system of exceptions. Directives 7/79/EEC and 86/378/EEC, on equal treatment of men and women in social security and occupational social security schemes, do have a closed system, which contains many exceptions to the principle of equal treatment.

Directive 86/613/EEC, concerning equal treatment of men and women engaged in an activity, including agriculture, in a self-employed capacity, has not played a significant role in practice so far, due to the fact that the rights conferred are very weak.

Article 13 of the Treaty of Amsterdam has provided the legal basis for two directives: the Race Directive (2000/43/EC) and the Framework Directive (2000/78/EC). Both directives lay down a framework for combating discrimination: the Race Directive on grounds of racial and ethnic origin, and the Framework Directive on grounds of religion or belief, age, disability, or sexual orientation. They introduce new definitions and concepts, e.g. (sexual) harassment (which cannot be objectively justified) and reasonable accommodation for the disabled, and strengthen enforcement mechanisms. However, the scopes of these directives differ. The Race Directive has a broader material scope, giving the impression of a hierarchy in discrimination grounds.

All the anti-discrimination directives differentiate between direct and indirect discrimination. The latter concept has been developed in particular in the ECJ case law regarding indirect sex discrimination in relation to part-time work. As a consequence of this case law, a more specific division of the burden of proof has emerged. The ECJ has ruled that the applicant must establish a *prima facie* case of indirect discrimination; if successful, the defendant must provide an objective justification for the discriminatory practice or criterion. This division also been laid down in the burden of proof directive (97/80/EC).

Effective implementation is an important feature in EU law: member states must ensure that judicial procedures are available to all persons who consider themselves wronged by failure to apply the principle of equal treatment to them, even after the relationship in which the discrimination is alleged to have occurred has ended. They must also ensure that sanctions must be effective, proportionate and dissuasive, and provide protection against dismissal or adverse treatment in reaction to a complaint. In addition, they must designate equality bodies and promote social dialogue between the social partners and with NGOs or stakeholders.

Although every country faces problems concerning discrimination, the method needed to deal with the problem varies from country to country, as the manifestations of discrimination depend on the regional and national context. This is true even in Europe, where the equality legislation of the member states is heavily influenced by European Directives. In her article, Jenny Goldschmidt offers a survey of Dutch equality legislation and a description of the practice of the national equality body, the Equal Treatment Commission (ETC), explaining the relevant concepts and discussing the main problems facing Dutch equal treatment legislation.

One of the features in Dutch equality legislation is the fact that there are three separate sources of non-discrimination law in the Netherlands. Firstly, the Constitution of the Kingdom of the Netherlands of 1984 contains several provisions concerning non-discrimination. In order to clarify further the extent of the third party effect and the clash of fundamental rights, the Equal Treatment Act (ETA) was enacted in 1994. Secondly, international provisions, contained e.g. in the European Convention on Human Rights and UN treaties, also play a role. Thirdly, since the 1970s, European Community law, as described by Susanne Burri, has played an ever more important role. As these sources differ in scope, purpose and context, the resulting laws tend to differ, leading to a patchwork of legislation that is confusing even to experts.

Having discussed this problem, Goldschmidt moves on to a discussion of various relevant concepts. A distinction must be made between direct discrimination, which refers to treatment which is explicitly based on a prohibited ground, and indirect discrimination, which refers to the use of a neutral criterion that nonetheless disadvantages people from a specific group. Intentions are irrelevant in either case. As regards the burden of proof, this has been divided according to the EU law: the claimant must pose facts that raise an assumption of discrimination, whereupon the defendant has to prove that there was in fact no discrimination. Indirect discrimination is less blatant than direct discrimination. To establish its occurrence, it is necessary to demonstrate a detrimental effect. This can be done by referring to statistical evidence or more general information. If this is done, it must be investigated whether the indirectly discriminatory act can be objectively justified, with reference to a proper non-discriminatory objective, which must be proportional. A financial argument will almost never constitute a sufficient justification.

It must be noted that the legal system in the Netherlands is, on the whole, characterised as closed with regards to grounds of discrimination and the scope of, and exceptions to, the prohibition of discrimination. This means that only those grounds, exceptions etc. that are explicitly listed in the provisions are relevant; extra-legal justifications are not admitted. The exceptions roughly fall into four categories: genuine (occupational) requirements, protection of members of the relevant group, exceptions based on other fundamental rights, and preferential treatment. The last mentioned exception is admissible only under very strict conditions and in line with the ECJ case law. On occasion, employers may be expected to fulfil positive obligations. The types of positive obligations include temporary special measures to remedy enduring past disadvantages, positive action, and reasonable accommodation.

The ETC has been established in order to comply with European requirements. Its power is based on specific non-discrimination legislation; it is not competent to give an opinion on cases that are not based on its specific laws. Its primary task is to investigate discrete complaints of individuals or groups on alleged discrimination, give its decision, and afterwards monitor the implementation of the decision. It may also issue (non-binding) opinions (which is a preventive measure and very effective), bring a legal action, or refer parties to alternative dispute resolution. Additionally, the Commission also advises the government and social partners, evaluates the efficacy of relevant laws and works with civic society. It may be concluded that it has developed into an authoritative institution which is useful in combating discrimination. However, it remains a disadvantage that its mandate is restricted by the scope of specific Dutch equality laws and that its opinions are not binding.

Austrian equal treatment law has been in effect for near 30 years now. In her contribution, Ingrid Nikolay-Leitner sketches the development of this legislation and describes the monitoring mechanisms, especially the practice of the Austrian Specialised Equality Body. The first Austrian Equal Treatment Act (ETA), enacted in 1979, transformed the problem of unequal pay from an issue of unfairness to an issue that could be resolved through the use of legal tools. The ETA has been amended many times since, as a result of new international obligations, such as those derived from the International Labour Organisation and the Convention on the Elimination of all Forms of Discrimination against Women. Principally, however, the international obligations stem from European Directives.

The Specialised Equality Body was founded according to the third amendment of the ETA for the private sector in 1990. The reason for its creation was the almost complete lack of complaints brought to the pre-existing Equal Treatment Commission (ETC) relating to equal pay, even though it was quite evident that women were being discriminated against in this field. The main tasks of the Specialised Equality Body are counselling and supporting people who feel discriminated against, and providing information to the public about discrimination and equality issues. Its foundation is a success: many complaints were brought to it when it was founded, and the number of complaints has increased every year since then. The large number of complaints enables it to acquire unique knowledge concerning discrimination. Most complaints relate to unequal pay and sexual harassment.

In 2004, the scope of the ETA was enlarged: grounds now also include ethnic origin, religion or belief, age, and sexual orientation. The fields in which the law applies have also been expanded; the areas of education, social protection and social advantages, and access to and supply of public goods and services are now also included, although ethnic origin is the only relevant ground in these fields.

Unlike the Specialised Equality Body, the ETC is supposed to be an impartial and independent body. Its opinions are not binding, as the legislators of the ETA believed that soft law institutions would make it easier for employees to raise complaints against their employer whilst they are still employed, and hoped that many cases could be solved through reconciliation or joint dispute resolution. NGOs may also play a role in ETC and court procedures as experts, third parties and representatives of the victim. The procedure before the Specialised Equality Body varies. Sometimes, the complainant is satisfied simply with the recognition of possible discrimination and does not require further intervention. At other times, the Specialised Equality Body negotiates a settlement with compensation. The support of the Specialised Equality Body is free and confidential. If the Specialised Equality Body is not successful, it will pass on the case to the Commission. Of course, a complainant may also choose to go straight to the Commission. This procedure may take a year or more. Very few cases make it to court. Hence, in order to eliminate discrimination, it is not enough to rely on individual negotiation and litigation, but structural measures are necessary.

O'Cinneide's chapter discusses the importance of positive action as an element of anti-discrimination law and policy, as well as the types of measures that are used as part of positive action initiatives and the legal controls that exist in this area of law. He emphasizes the fact that positive action comes in a variety of forms, depending on the nature of the disadvantages at issue and the relevant socio-economic and political context, and argues that its use is legitimate.

First, O'Cinneide discusses why the use of positive action may be necessary. Although anti-discrimination law is often an effective tool, it cannot combat discrimination in cases where there is no clear evidence that discrimination has occurred or where individuals are unwilling or unable to complain about the negative treatment they have suffered. Moreover, if an action is successful, its impact is limited to the individual case, whereas often wider changes within the organization are needed. Finally, individuals from disadvantaged groups often lack social capital and role models, and will be underrepresented in forms of government, adding to the structural inequality. It has become clear that anti-discrimination law is not equal to these challenges, hence the necessity to use positive action measures.

Positive action includes all measures that seek, by means of positive steps, to alter existing social practices so as to eliminate patterns of group exclusion and disadvantage. There are five basic categories: the eradication of prohibited discrimination, purposefully inclusive policies which give special assistance on the basis of general criteria (e.g. the poor or unemployed), outreach programmes (attracting applicants from disadvantaged groups for employment or education), preferential treatment, and redefining merit (i.e. redefining criteria so as to ensure greater participation from disadvantaged groups). O'Cinneide also discusses 'mainstreaming' policies, consisting of impact assessments of public policy, as well as participation policies, which encourage these groups to take part in the decision-making process.

Positive action has been widely criticized, and even accused of being 'discrimination in reverse'. O'Cinneide argues that positive action should not be seen as a departure from the principle of equal treatment. The main debate centres around the question of whether 'suspect' characteristics such as gender or ethnicity should be used to decide who benefits from positive action. However, this may be countered by the argument that positive action can provide an effective remedy for the disadvantages of a group and that suspect classifications should only be prohibited if they are used in a negative or harmful manner. However, even strong supporters of positive action generally agree that it should be shown to be objectively justified and may only be maintained for the minimum period necessary to achieve its goals.

EU provisions establish the permissibility of positive action when it is used to compensate for specific disadvantages faced by particular groups. Equally, case law appears to have established that positive action to compensate for past disadvantages is permissible when there is no automatic preference, but it is used to distinguish between more or less equally qualified candidates, provided that an opportunity for individual merit assessment is always available. However, as the European Court of Justice has not clarified what constitutes the forbidden 'automatic preference', the position of the Court remains ambiguous. It should also be noted that EC law generally permits rather than requires the use of positive action. By contrast, the UN Human Rights Committee has recognized that positive action is fully compatible with equal treatment and may in certain circumstances actually be required to give effect to this right. The European Court of Human Rights has recognized the legitimacy of positive action measures, if they can be objectively justified. Hence, there is a broad consensus on the permissibility of temporary and proportionate positive action measures.

The various contributions in this book highlight the challenges in the struggle against employment discrimination, which is a worldwide phenomenon. Despite a large number of international, regional and national provisions, employment discrimination is a persistent feature in every country. The manifestations of this form of discrimination may differ. The situation in China differs in many aspects from the situation in European countries, which, in turn, also have national characteristics. The differences concern both the scale of the problem (the size of China's landmass and its population are hardly comparable with that of a country like the Netherlands) and the occurrence of specific forms of discrimination. For instance, the problems facing hepatitis B infected citizens are more specific for China. Still, despite these differences, China and the countries of the European Union are bound by numerous international, regional and national legal provisions prohibiting employment discrimination. The international instruments can provide a common framework for anti-discrimination law and policies. The International Labour Organisation has enacted various instruments to combat employment discrimination, and the relevant provisions of the United Nations Human Rights Treaties contain similar provisions. The treaty bodies have given extensive interpretations of the implications of these provisions in their General Comments: e.g. General Comment 18(2005) of the Commission on Economic Social and Cultural Rights elaborates the implications of the right to work referring to non-discrimination instruments too. These instruments can be taken as a common starting point and they enable national systems to see how others have faced employment discrimination. They offer a platform where states can learn from each other.

It has to be recognised that most international provisions, even when they allow a certain amount of state discretion, are rather strict when it comes to this specific form of discrimination, in particular on specific grounds such as gender, ethnic origin, disability, sexual orientation, religion and race. But, depending on the national circumstances, the most effective approaches have to be found and on the basis of these findings the system of anti-discrimination can be different. This even applies to the EU countries, where the regional system of EU law has a special compelling supra-national character. While some EU states have a single equality law covering all grounds of discrimination, others such as the UK have different legislation for each ground of discrimination, that is, a separate law applies to gender, race, disability, religion, sexual orientation and age discrimination. In addition, the UK system is heavily based on adversarial individual litigation to enforce rights, while in other European countries case law on discrimination is much less frequent. Despite the difference, the common legal basis has contributed to the development of central concepts that can be applied in all systems.

The development of central concepts, such as direct and indirect discrimination, harassment, preferential treatment and effective remedy, constitutes a first essential condition for the development of a comprehensive system of protection against employment discrimination. These concepts provide safeguards against the intrusion of stereotyped opinions and attitudes in the interpretation of the law. Most employment discrimination is closely linked to these kinds of implicit attitudes, which can only be combated by very strict rules and definitions, leaving no room for such opinions. These aspects are relevant not only to Europe but are also a part of universal international systems, e.g. Article 5 of the CEDAW. In addition, it must be kept in mind that even the most perfect legal system, which is essential, will not be a sufficient measure to combat discrimination. To be effective, the law has to be embedded in a system of measures and policies that contribute to public awareness of the unfairness, costs and disadvantages of discrimination, and an effective system of implementation by accessible, specialised bodies. The existence of a feasible and effective system of implementation and monitoring is a third condition. What, in an exact national context, is the best format for such a structure, including bodies with adequate specialised expertise in the areas of employment discrimination, also depends on the national landscape: which organisations are active and competent to bring cases to court, to support victims, to educate the parties concerned. It must be borne in mind that the realisation of employment equality cannot depend on the victims only: it demands a lot of courage from them to raise their voices from a very vulnerable position, and the state's duty to realise employment equity goes far beyond the possibilities which these victims have. Finally, we want to re-emphasize that the success of non-discrimination law and policy depends on public awareness of the necessity of this form of employment equity: discrimination and marginalisation of large parts of the population entails huge costs, both economically and socially and it is in the interests of all to combat it.

We would hope that China would take Western systems and experience as a reference point (although they are certainly not the only possible reference point), and gradually establish a legal system that is sufficiently effective to uphold the principle of anti-discrimination in employment and, hopefully, a system that would be consistent with internationally recognized principles and standards. In this volume the current legal system on employment discrimination in the EU countries can be seen to serve this aim. The European systems are very much influenced by EU Directives which have been made and expanded since the 1970s. As requested by Directives, member states have enacted their own equality law as well as having established specialised monitoring bodies and systems. China is at the initial stage of tackling employment discrimination: specific law on equal treatment in employment is needed to define and prohibit discrimination in employment, to set out clearly the scope of the grounds of discrimination according to the realities in China, as well as to reflect internationally recognized principles. Moreover, it would be desirable for the law to set out provisions to establish independent bodies at different levels to facilitate implementation of the law, and to handle individual complaints, as well as to educate the public at large. In connection with this, we consider that the legal systems and the work of similar institutions in EU countries could offer some ideas and experience to the Chinese.

Needless to say, discrimination, including employment discrimination, is unfortunately rooted in the culture of any society. Our assessment is that in China employment discrimination remains too often open, obvious and direct, while in the EU countries it is more indirect and difficult to prove. For both China and the EU the goal should be to prevent and prohibit all kinds of employment discrimination and to achieve maximum social justice and human equality.

1

AN ANALYSIS OF EMPLOYMENT DISCRIMINATION IN CHINA'S ECONOMIC AND SOCIAL TRANSITION

Yuwen Li

1   INTRODUCTION

Since the introduction of the market-oriented economic reform and open door policy in 1978, China has become one of the most dynamic and fastest-growing economies in the world. The rapid economic development over the past three decades has been viewed by many as an 'economic miracle'. The World Bank study on poverty reduction showed that the economic progress has lifted approximately 500 million Chinese off the poverty line of earning less than $1.25 per day.[1] The living standard of the majority of Chinese, especially those living in urban areas, has improved considerably. In the course of economic development and restructuring, the Chinese government has made efforts to broaden the range of avenues for employment and maintain a relatively stable employment situation.

Despite government policy, which aims at a balanced positive interaction (*liangxinghudong*) between economic growth and expansion of employment, the outcome is far from satisfactory. A commonly known fact is that the economy has maintained a high rate of growth, while the growth rate of employment is low or even non-existent. Chinese research showed that in 1997 the GDP grew by 8.8%, while employment grew by 1.1%; in 1998 the GDP grew by 7.8%, while employment grew by 0.5%; in 2000 the GDP grew by 8%, while employment grew by 0.8%.[2] The registered unemployment rate in urban areas,

---

[1]   'World Bank and Poverty Debates (II): Poverty Reduction Claims Vindicated?', http://www.brettonwoodsproject.org/art.shtml?x=561848. Last visited December 2008. David Dollar concluded that: 'Wherever you draw the poverty line, China gets the gold medal for poverty reduction.' in 'New Global Poverty Estimates Confirm China's Leading Role in Meeting MDGs', http://eapblog.worldbank.org/content/new-global-poverty-estimates-confirm-china%E2%80%99s-leading-role-in-meeting-mdgs. Last visited September 2008.

[2]   Xie Zhiqiang, 'Three Major Problems concerning Employment Difficulty in China', http://theory.people.com.cn/GB/40764/105054/105055/7002858.html. Last visited September 2008.

according to official statistics, was 3.1% in 2000, and 4.3% in 2003.[3] However, Chinese scholars estimate that the actual unemployment rate has reached 7%.[4]

The sheer magnitude of people entering the labour market, resulting in the demand for jobs far surpassing the supply, has increased competition in the labour market. Taken in conjunction with the establishment of a market-oriented employment mechanism, which allows employers to enjoy hiring autonomy without adequate regulatory restrictions, as well as the lack of legal support for citizens' rights to employment, job applicants are facing increased disadvantages. A resulting phenomenon is that employment discrimination is becoming an ever more serious and pervasive problem on China's road to modernization.[5] According to the survey conducted by the Constitutionalism Research Institute of the China University of Political Science and Law in 2006 (hereafter the Survey),[6] of the 3454 people investigated, 85.5% replied that employment discrimination does exist, 50.8% considered the discrimination to be very serious, and only 6.6% held the view that discrimination does not occur.[7] Discrimination in employment exists in both blatant and latent forms. The Survey illustrated that when asked what requirements employers had stated regarding job applicants, 21% indicated gender, 32.9% indicated age, 13.8% required a certain height, 36.7% required a certain appearance, 28.7% demanded the right resident permits, 47.7% stipulated that there should be no serious illness, 13.6% touched on disability, 18.9% indicated that there should be no infectious diseases, 6.4% required Communist Party membership, and 4.4% barred applicants from an ethnic minority.[8]

This chapter discusses the major characteristics of employment discrimination in China's transition from a centralized planned economy to a socialist market economy. Firstly, from a legal point of view, the Chinese Constitution, the Labour Law and the most recently promulgated Law on Promotion of Employment contain general principle of equality of all citizens and the principle of prohibiting employment discrimination on the grounds of ethnic group, race, gender, religion, disability, infectious diseases and migrant worker. However, these general principles are primarily declaratory in nature, and they lack the legal mechanisms to protect equal employment rights, both of which undermine the role of law in tackling employment discrimination. In

---

[3] *China Statistical Yearbook*, (National Bureau of Statistics of China, 2004), http://www.stats.gov.cn/english/statisticaldata/yearlydata/yb2004-e/indexeh.htm. Last visited September 2008.
[4] Xie Zhiqiang, *supra* note 2.
[5] Prior to 1978, under the 'iron rice bowl' system, those who worked within state-owned enterprises and public sectors (*shiye danwei*) enjoyed guaranteed lifetime job security and other benefits such as housing and medical insurance from the state.
[6] 'A Survey of Employment Discrimination in Ten Major Cities in China', See Chapter 6 of this book.
[7] *Ibid*, E4.
[8] *Ibid*, B1-a to B1-n.

addition, although Chinese laws and regulations also contain protective provisions and positive measures promoting equal access to employment for women and the disabled, there are also some regulations, especially local government rules, containing discriminatory provisions that render discriminatory acts against certain groups of people legitimate. Secondly, as in many other countries, employment discrimination based on gender, disability, and age is widespread in China. At the same time, however, employment discrimination based on infection with hepatitis B, HIV/AIDS, or other infectious diseases, and discrimination on the basis of household registration and regional origin, have shown that China faces particular problems and challenges in tackling wide-scale employment discrimination. Thirdly, the current serious employment discrimination appears both as obvious, direct and as hidden, indirect discrimination, and exists in both the public and private sectors. Fourthly, since employment discrimination is a relatively new social phenomenon, which only emerged in the reform period since the 1980s, the government, employers and the public at large all have a limited awareness of what constitutes employment discrimination, and of the harmful consequences it could have for individuals and society. Some Chinese scholars describe the Chinese attitude to employment discrimination as 'collective ignorance' (*jiti wuyishi*), meaning lack of awareness on the part of the government, employers, and the general public.[9]

However, an encouraging development is that in recent years some Chinese scholars have started to examine employment discrimination critically, both in law and in practice; some lawyers have helped victims of employment discrimination by supporting their cases in arbitration and litigation; some victims have publicized their painful experience through the public media, especially through the Internet, which has generated and is generating wide social response and sympathy; and, responding to the emerging social needs, the government is taking new policy and legal measures to strengthen the opportunities of fair employment for all. These developments demonstrate that employment discrimination is receiving serious attention in China. In the last part of this chapter I will discuss some dynamic ideas put forward by Chinese legal scholars on dealing with the problem of employment discrimination from systematic and institutional perspectives, such as enacting equal employment law and establishing new institutions to handle employment discrimination complaints and disputes.

---

[9] Cai Dingjian, 'A Comprehensive Research Report on Anti-discrimination in Employment', in Cai Dingjian (ed.), *The Current Situation on Employment Discrimination in China and Anti-discrimination Strategies*, (Beijing: China Social Science Press, 2007), p. 4.

2 CHARACTERISTICS OF EMPLOYMENT DISCRIMINATION IN CHINA

2.1 Chinese Laws on Anti-Discrimination in Employment: Legal Principles and Limitations

2.1.1 General Principles of Equality and Prohibition of Employment Discrimination

There is no specific law on anti-discrimination in employment in China, nor is the concept of discrimination defined in any law. However, both the principle of equality of all people and the prohibition of employment discrimination on various grounds are provided in several laws. In the Constitution, Article 33 formulates the fundamental principle that 'All citizens of the People's Republic of China are equal before the law'. Article 42 provides that citizens 'have the right as well as the duty to work. Using various channels, the state creates conditions for employment, strengthens labour protection, improves working conditions and, on the basis of expanded production, increases remuneration for work and social benefits'. These Articles can be viewed as the constitutional source of anti-discrimination in employment. To safeguard equality between men and women, Article 48 asserts that women enjoy equal rights with men in all spheres of life, including the political, economic, cultural and social spheres, and family life. The state protects the rights and interests of women, applies the principle of equal pay for equal work for men and women alike and trains and selects cadres from among women.

The 1994 Labour Law is the basic law protecting the legitimate rights and interests of labourers. Article 3 provides that labourers enjoy the right to equal opportunities of employment and choice of jobs, the right to labour remuneration, the right to rest and vacation, the right to labour safety and health protection, the right to vocational training, the right to social insurance and welfare, the right to settlement of labour disputes and other rights as provided by law. With regard to employment discrimination, Article 12 provides that 'labourers shall not be discriminated against in employment on the grounds of their ethnic group, race, gender and religious beliefs'. This Article is the most frequently cited legal provision on anti-discrimination in employment. However, although discrimination in employment on grounds of gender does occur, employment discrimination on grounds of ethnic group, race and religion does not occur commonly in China.[10] The most serious and widely spread grounds of employment discrimination, namely age, health, and social origin, are not covered by the Labour Law.

---

[10] *Supra* note 6, B1-n. When asked whether an employer had certain ethnic requirement concerning job seekers, 3.4% replied that employers had a Han Chinese requirement; 0.3% an ethnic minority requirement; and 0.7% indicated that employers did not want a certain ethnic minority.

In 2007, the National People's Congress Standing Committee (NPCSC) promulgated the Law on Promotion of Employment,[11] which entered into force on 1 January 2008. Chapter 3 of the Law, on fair employment, contains seven articles. Article 25 requires the governments at all levels to create a suitable environment for fair employment, to eliminate employment discrimination and to formulate policies and take measures to support and assist the hard-to-employ. Article 26 obliges employers and employment agencies to provide workers with equal employment opportunities and fair employment conditions, and obliges them to refrain from discriminating in employment. Article 27 re-emphasizes that employers should not refuse to hire women on the basis of gender unless the job in question is of the kind that the state has specified as being unsuitable for women, nor set standards for the employment of women that are higher than those for men. An employer is not allowed to stipulate restrictions in an employment contract on a woman getting married, having children, etc. Articles 28 and 29 re-emphasize that employers are prohibited from discriminating against ethnic groups and disabled persons in employment. In addressing the widely prevalent employment discrimination against people with infectious diseases, Article 30 requires employers not to refuse to recruit any person on the ground that he or she is a carrier of an infectious disease. However, until a carrier of an infectious disease has undergone a medical test confirming that he or she is cured or cannot possibly spread the disease, he or she should not take up jobs in which they are likely to spread the disease and which are prohibited through laws and administrative regulations and by the health administrative department of the State Council. Finally, Article 31 affirms that rural labourers who go to cities in search of employment should enjoy labour rights equal to those of urban workers. The expansion of the scope of employment discrimination concerning people with infectious diseases and migrant workers represents a new step forward by Chinese law in fighting employment discrimination. However, discrimination on the grounds of household registration, regional location, age and physical appearance, which exists widely in employment, remains uncovered by the Law.

China has a specific Law on Protection of Women's Rights and Interests which was promulgated by the National People's Congress in 1992 and revised in 2005. The Law formulates the protection of women's right to work. It prohibits any work units from raising the employment standards for women or from refusing to employ women on grounds of gender, with the exception of special types of work or posts unsuitable for women. In concluding a labour contract, no restrictions may be imposed on a woman's freedom to marry or bear children (Art. 23). The principle of equal pay for equal work should be applied to men and women alike and women should be equal with men in the enjoyment of

---

[11] The English translation of the Law is available at: http://www.lawinfochina.com/law/display.asp?db=1&id=6382&keyword=labor%20employment%20promotion. Last visited September 2008.

welfare benefits (Art. 24). The principle of equality between men and women should also be applied in promotion, evaluation and determination of professional and technological titles, prohibiting discrimination against women (Art. 25). Any work units should, in line with women's characteristics and according to law, protect women's safety and health during their work or physical labour, and should not assign them any work or physical labour not suitable for women. In addition, women enjoy special protection during their menstrual period, pregnancy, maternity leave and nursing period (Art. 26). Article 27, which was added to the Law in 2005, forbids any work unit to reduce the salary, dismiss, or unilaterally dissolve the contract of a female employee because of marriage, pregnancy, maternity leave or breast-feeding, unless the female employee chooses to end the labour contract. Obviously, this Law stresses the special protection that female workers should be provided with on the grounds of their different biological constitution, but lacks a provision safeguarding the equal right to employment for men and women. Such protective legislation 'provides benefits women workers need, but, ironically, also results in a preference for hiring men in the first place'.[12]

Protection of the rights of disabled persons has been a persistent policy of the Chinese government, and in 1990 the National People's Congress promulgated the specific Law on Protection of Disabled Persons, which was revised in April 2008. This Law contains concrete measures aimed at promoting the right of people with disabilities to work. It highlights three main channels of employment opportunity for disabled persons. One is to set up welfare enterprises for persons with disabilities, massage services by blind people, and other enterprises and institutions of a welfare nature to offer focused job opportunities for persons with disabilities (Art. 32). The second is the introduction of a quota scheme of employment which requires public organizations and enterprises to arrange job opportunities for persons with disabilities. Those who cannot reach the prescribed quota should fulfil other obligations to guarantee job opportunities for persons with disabilities. The State encourages employers to employ more disabled persons than the quota requires (Art. 33). The third is to encourage and support self-employed disabled people. Preferential treatment is rewarded by tax deductions and other such incentives (Arts. 34 and 36).

In sum, the above-mentioned laws provide some general principles of promoting equality of employment opportunities and prohibition of employment discrimination. However, no law has defined what employment discrimination is, or included legal remedies to address discriminatory acts. The scope of the grounds of discrimination is also too narrow to cover various major grounds of discrimination in practice. Moreover, there is no provision for the legal liability of those who violate the anti-discrimination laws. Consequently, these laws do

---

[12] Christine M. Bulger, 'Fighting Gender Discrimination in the Chinese Workplace', (Spring 2000) *Boston College Third World Law Journal*, p. 348.

not lead one to conclude that China has established a functional legal system with sufficient protection against discrimination in employment.

2.1.2 Discriminatory Provisions Reflected in Administrative Regulations and Local Regulations

The sources of Chinese law according to the Law on Legislation, which was promulgated by the National People's Congress (NPC) in March 2000 and became effective on 1 July of the same year, include laws enacted by the NPC and the NPCSC; administrative regulations issued by the State Council; and departmental rules issued by ministries at the national level. At the local level, the sources of Chinese law include local regulations issued by provincial people's congresses and their standing committees; and local rules issued by provincial governments. Local legislation is intended to implement and supplement national laws and regulations. The structure of multi-level and varied legislative powers has resulted in some inconsistencies between national legislation and local legislation. [13] With regard to equal opportunities in employment, discriminatory provisions can be found in rules and regulations originating at various legislative levels.

(1) *Age and health discrimination in recruitment of civil servants*

A number of rules and regulations concerning candidates' qualifications and the physical examination that they need to undergo in order to become civil servants, contain discriminatory conditions. The 1994 Provisional Rules on Recruitment of Civil Servants, issued by the Ministry of Personnel, provided that candidates who wanted to take the civil servant examination to qualify for a position as a civil servant, 'should be healthy and aged below 35' (Art. 14). These Provisional Rules were replaced by the 2007 Rules on Recruitment of Civil Servants (Trial Implementation) issued by the same Ministry. The latter again stipulated that one of the requirements for those registering to take the civil servant examination is to be under 35 years old (Art. 16). Instead of requiring applicants to be 'healthy', the 2007 Rules require candidates with 'physical conditions that guarantee that they will be able to carry out the functions normally'.

The requirement of being younger than 35 for all applicants, no matter which positions they are applying for, obviously constitutes age discrimination. It disqualifies those over 35 from taking the civil servant exam, the first step in applying for a position as a civil servant, which subsequently deprives them of their right to participate in the administration of public affairs as well as their right to take part in government. It should be noted that in 2005 the NPCSC enacted the Law on Civil Servants. Article 11 of the Law lists the qualifications

---

[13] Jianfu Chen, *Chinese Law: Context and Transformation*, (Leiden/Boston: Martinus Nijhoff Publishers, 2008), pp. 187-191.

necessary to become a civil servant, in which the only age restriction is that applicants must be 18 years or older; there is no upper age limit. This raises the question whether the 2007 Rules are contradictory to this Law. In the case of Yang Shijan v Ministry of Personnel, brought to court in 2006, Mr. Yang claimed that the Rules of the Ministry of Personnel, stipulating an upper age limit of 35 years in order to be eligible to take part in the civil servant examination, violated the Law on Civil Servants.[14]

Similar to Article 14 of the old rules, Article 16 of the new rules also allows an adjustment to the age limit with the approval of the personnel department at provincial level. This flexibility has been abused by relevant departments to lower the upper age limits even further. For instance, in 1996 the Ministry of Personnel and the Ministry of Public Security jointly issued the Methods of Recruitment of People's Police which provided that applicants who wanted to take the examination for becoming police officers should be under the age of 25. For special positions or in remote areas, local relevant bodies could relax the age restriction, but could not allow applicants above the age of 30. Research showed that age limits have been stringent for some civil service posts, with random alterations to the age of 33, 32, 28, 26, 25 or 23.[15]

With regard to the requirement that applicants must be healthy, it is rather unclear what is healthy and what is unhealthy. The stereotypical thinking in China labels disabled persons, carriers of HIV/AIDS, hepatitis B and infectious diseases as unhealthy persons. Before the General Standards on Physical Examinations Relating to the Employment of Civil Servants (Trial Implementation) were issued by the Ministry of Personnel and became effective in 2005, nearly all local provincial governments issued their own standards for civil servant physical exams. Most of them rejected all those who tested positive for hepatitis B; and a few accepted only those hepatitis B carriers who were not infectious. No disabled persons qualified for the physical examination to become a civil servant.[16] Moreover, some local standards contained discriminatory requirements concerning height, weight, appearance, visual capacity, hearing capacity and so on. For instance, the 1993 Notice on Recruitment of Cadres at Local People's Courts and People's Procuratorates, issued jointly by the Ministry of Organization and Personnel of the Central Communist Party, the Supreme People's Court and the Supreme People's Procuratorate, requested that, concerning the newly recruited, the 'five facial features must be good-looking'.

The 1996 Methods on Recruitment of People's Police required that applicants be blessed with a 'physically good-looking body'. The 1999 Methods on Civil Servant Physical Examination, issued by the Personnel Bureau of Tianjing Municipality, required that male applicants should be taller than 1.60

---

[14] Xue Xiaojian, 'A Research Report on Age Discrimination', in Cai Dingjian (ed.), *supra* note 9, p. 270. The court did not accept the case, see *infra* note 71.

[15] *Ibid*, p. 272.

[16] See Ma Yu'e, 'Disability Discrimination in Employment', Chapter 3 of this book.

metres and weigh more than 50 kilos. Female applicants were required to be taller than 1.50 metres and weigh more than 40 kilos. If an applicant was shorter than the requirements specified, overweight by more than 35% or underweight by 20%, he or she did not qualify. The 1999 Implementing Rules on Civil Servant Physical Examination, issued by the Personnel Bureau of Guangdong province, disqualified persons with arms and legs with an obvious disability, such as those lacking a hand, an arm, a leg or fingers, or with an arm or leg that could not be used (including an artificial arm or leg).[17] The 2003 'Physical Examination Items and Standards on Recruitment of Civil Servants', issued jointly by the Personnel Bureau and Health Bureau of Hunan Province, provided that in order to be qualified, female candidates should have 'an appearance normal to their gender, balanced breasts, …'. Similar ridiculous requirements also appeared in the rules issued by the government bodies in Jiangsu province.[18] These physical requirements are often not relevant to the work of a civil servant. Imposing these physical conditions excludes many people who are capable of doing civil service work from being able to take the physical examination which is the first step in applying for a job as a civil servant. This infringes the right to equal employment opportunities of many people.

In January 2005 the Ministry of Personnel and Ministry of Health jointly issued General Standards on Physical Examinations Relating to the Employment of Civil Servants (Trial Implementation). The standards listed 50 diseases that disqualify people from a government position. However, with regard to hepatitis B carriers, the General Standards state that an applicant for a civil servant position would be disqualified if the applicant was infected with hepatitis B, but carriers of the virus are qualified so long as a contagious infection can be ruled out through further tests. This Article reflects progress by the law towards recognition of the right of a hepatitis B carrier to be a civil servant, though its practical impact remains limited. Soon after the General Standards were issued, the Personnel Bureau of Zhejiang province imposed more stringent hepatitis B testing on its civil servant applicants.[19]

A physical examination as a qualification to be a civil servant should be linked to and balanced with the concrete requirements of civil service posts. However, China applies a unified standard of physical examination for all civil

---

[17] Liu Shen, 'A Study Report on Administrative Regulations and Rules concerning Employment Discrimination', in Cai Dingjian (ed.), *supra* note 9, pp. 463-464.

[18] *Ibid.*, p. 470. Such direct discriminatory requirements were questioned by female university graduates and criticized by media reports. Legal scholars claimed that they violated women's rights to privacy and human dignity. Under the media pressure, the Personnel Bureau and Health Bureau of Hunan Province deleted the discriminatory provisions. Xue Ninglan, 'A Legal Analysis of Gender Discrimination in the Workplace', in Lisa Stearns (ed.), *Employment Discrimination: International Standards and National Practice*, (Beijing: Law Press China, 2006), pp. 285-286.

[19] 'Tension on Zhejiang Civil Servant Physical Examination Concerning HB Carriers', http://msn.ynet.com/view.jsp?oid=5102688. Last visited October 2008.

service posts at both the central and local level which separates the standards of the physical examination from the requirements of actual posts, giving rise to suspicions of health discrimination.

(2) *Discrepancy Between the Retirement Age of Men and Women*

At the national level, regulations setting up different retirement ages for men and women constitute another source of law in which discrimination against women has generated increasing concern in recent years. According to the regulations issued by the State Council, the mandatory retirement age for female workers is 50, while for men this is 60; similarly, the retirement age is 55 for female civil servants and 60 for male civil servants.[20] Hence, while women employees leave their posts at 50 or 55, their male counterparts do not do so until they are 60.

This compulsory system has been applied since the 1950s, soon after the founding of the People's Republic of China. At that time, Chinese women were burdened with heavy physical labour both at the factory and at home. The policy of imposing an earlier retirement age upon women was intended to protect women's health and to help them. However, in recent years the situation has changed dramatically. Statistics show that the average life expectancy for Chinese women is 71 while it is 69 for men. In some well-off areas such as Shanghai, the figure is nearly 80 for women.[21] Because of their improved health and the reduced amount of household work they are expected to perform, physically women are now fully capable of working longer than before. In addition, as a consequence of economic reform, sources of income for employees in today's China are very different from how they were before. In the past, salary was the only source of income, and the retirement pension was fixed to a certain percentage of the salary. Nowadays, apart from the basic salary which in many cases is not very high, there are various subsidies and bonuses which can only be obtained if one has a job. If female employees retire earlier than men, they cannot enjoy these extra-salary benefits to the same extent as their male colleagues of the same age. Moreover, pensions for retirees depend on the length of service and position at retirement. If women retire earlier than men, they receive lower pensions. Consequently, the financial disadvantage for women is self-evident. Moreover, 'early retirement could possibly render many women ineligible to receive favourable treatment from government policies, which usually require employees to have more than 30 years of service'.[22] The early retiring age means fewer social welfare benefits. For highly educated women this could be a drawback, since under the current Chinese educational system, a

---

[20] The Provisional Regulations Regarding Ageing, Sick and Disabled Cadres and Provisional Regulations on Retirement of Workers. Both Regulations were issued by the State Council in 1978.
[21] 'Chinese Women Want to Keep Their Jobs Longer', People's Daily January 23, 2003, http://www.china.org.cn/english/China/54269.htm. Last visited July 2008.
[22] *Ibid.*

woman is aged about 23 when she finishes her undergraduate college studies, and will spend approximately three years for both a master's degree and a doctoral degree. A woman with a PhD certificate will therefore most likely work for fewer than 30 years if she has to retire at 55. Unsurprisingly, these rules, which have been imposed since the 1950s and were written into various regulations after 1978, have recently been challenged by women, particularly white-collar professionals and civil servants, who are increasingly sceptical about their equity.[23]

Some Chinese experts have argued that the discrepancy in retirement ages for women and men is simply based on their gender and should be viewed as gender discrimination. In 2003 deputies to the First Session of the Tenth National People's Congress discussed potential legislation that would stipulate that men and women retire at the same age. In 2005 the All-China Women's Federation proposed a change in law to the National People's Congress, entailing the same retirement age for male and female civil servants.[24] These efforts have not resulted in any change in law. Some argued that the early age of retirement for women could reduce the pressure in the employment market and allow more female students to find jobs. Others pointed out that women at the age of 55 are undergoing the menopause, which involves biological changes and declining energy, and often reduces women's working capacity and requires employers to take special care of them. A poll in 2003 showed that 100% of female factory workers, 80% of female employees in the non-business sector, and 20% of female civil servants were against the same retirement age for men and women.[25] Ideally, the law should be revised by taking both women's equal employment rights and their personal choices into consideration. However, in view of the current growing rate of unemployment and the economic recession, legislative changes may not receive sufficient support.

(3) *Discrimination Based on Residence and Place of Origin*

At the national level, in 1994 the Ministry of Labour issued the Provisional Rules on Administration of Employment of Rural Labourers Across Provinces, which imposed various restrictions on hiring rural labourers coming from another province. At the local level, regulations and rules leading to employment discrimination on the grounds of social origin are also prevalent. These mainly include the obligation for migrants to obtain an employment certificate; employers may only hire migrants if they cannot employ enough people with a local residence; priority should be given to hiring university graduates with a

---

[23] *Ibid.*
[24] 'Retirement Regulations Reflect Gender Discrimination', http://www.china.org.cn/english/China/146347.htm. Last visited December 2008.
[25] Xue Ninglan, *supra* note 18, p. 294.

local residence; and job-seekers must have a local household registration when applying for a civil service position.

Job-seekers with a rural household registration suffer the most discrimination in the labour market. Since the 1950s, China has operated a strict household registration system, which divides citizens into those with rural residence and those with urban residence. From the 1980s onwards, labourers with rural household registration have moved in order to find work in cities and were called migrant workers. From 1997 to 2000, the number of rural labourers who moved from the countryside to cities increased from about 83 million to 113 million, an average increase of 10 million per year. Employees coming from rural areas constitute about 80% of workers in the mining industry, 60% in textiles and 50% of service sectors.[26] Most large and medium-sized cities have issued regulations limiting the number and range of sectors in which rural people can find jobs. For instance, in 1995 the Labour Bureau of Shanghai issued the Methods in Administrating Non-Local Labourers by Shanghai Work Units, which distinguished three types of jobs. Type A listed the sort of work for which people without local household registration could apply. Type B listed the fields of work for which people without local household registration could be hired, with certain limitations. Type C included the industrial sectors for which people without local household registration would not be permitted to apply. This Shanghai model was soon followed in other cities.[27] In 1996 the Labour Bureau of Beijing issued the Scope of Types of Work that Migrants May Do With and Without Limitations in Beijing, which listed 12 sectors with 204 types of work that migrants were allowed to perform. These mainly covered jobs that were dirty, involved hard labour, were tiring, or involved risks and exposure to poisons.[28] According to a study of 21 local regulations relating to the administration of the taxi industry, issued by the competent local people's congress standing committees, 12 of these regulations set limits on household registration and identity, 6 of them required taxi drivers to have a permanent household registration in the city or a temporary resident permit in the city; 5 required taxi drivers to have a permanent resident permit for that city; 1 required the driver to hold an 'ID card compatible with local rules'; the remaining 9 did not mention household requirements.[29] The different regulations reflect the various opinions of local governments concerning qualifications for taxi drivers. The differences also show that the requirements imposed might not be necessary or rational for the profession of taxi driver. A number of local regulations with

---

[26] Zhou Wei, 'Research on the Legitimacy of Local Legislation on Employment', in *Employment Discrimination in China: Legislation and Reality*, Zhou Wei (ed.), (Beijing: Law Press China, 2005), p. 254.

[27] Lin Yanling, 'Report on Employment Discrimination against Farmer Workers', in Cai Dingjian (ed.), *supra* note 9, pp. 232-233.

[28] *Ibid*, pp. 233-234.

[29] Wu Zeng, 'A Study Report on Local Regulations concerning Employment Discrimination', in Cai Dingjian (ed.), *supra* note 9, pp. 492-493.

household registration requirements were based on the expectation that it would be difficult to maintain control of migrants.[30] Some Chinese scholars take the view that the discrimination against migrant workers in local legislation reflects systematic employment discrimination.[31]

In summary, discriminatory provisions reflected in regulations and rules issued by the competent government bodies constitute legislative discrimination, which is more serious than individual employers' discriminatory hiring practices. Legislative employment discrimination violates the right to equal employment opportunities of a large group of people, and legitimizes prejudicial employment practices. The above examination demonstrate that some regulations containing employment discrimination originated for historical reasons, such as the discrepancy in retirement ages between men and women, the household registration and regional location. Other discriminatory rules, such as those relating to physical appearance, height, weight, and age, reflect a lack of awareness of discrimination on the part of local governments. Thus, the first step for the public campaign against employment discrimination is to call on the government to abolish all such discrimination present in legislation.

2.2 Open and Direct Employment Discrimination in Both Private and Public Sectors

In today's China, a special problem is the fact that employment discrimination on the grounds of gender, household registration, health, age, disability, height and physical attributes is open, direct and largely tolerated by society.[32] Discriminatory hiring practices can be found in both public and private sectors. One might easily find a vacancy advertisement like the following: 'In order to expand the company's business we plan to hire several new employees with the following qualifications: male, household registration in Beijing, under the age of 35, with a Bachelor's degree or higher, good computer skills, Communist Party membership can be an advantage. People from Henan are not employable.'[33] Some vacancy advertisements are outrageous: 'Seeking an office clerk. Female, decent height and appearance. All five facial features must be in the right place (*wuguan duanzheng*).'[34]

In the public sector, as a result of following administrative regulations and rules which contain discriminatory conditions, employment discrimination on the grounds of age, health and social origin, by government departments and public institutions (*shiye danwei*) is rampant; moreover, violation of the law by discriminating against women and the disabled in hiring practices is also a

---

[30] *Ibid.*
[31] Lin Yangling, *supra* note 27, p. 262.
[32] Cai Dingjian, *supra* note 9, pp. 4-5.
[33] *Ibid*, p. 23.
[34] Ronald C. Brown, 'China's Employment Discrimination Laws During Economic Transition', (Spring 2006) *Columbia Journal of Asian Law*, p. 362.

serious problem. Currently, most of the Chinese scholars' research on employment discrimination focuses on discrimination in the public sector. It is logical that if government institutions do not follow the law strictly, one could hardly expect the private sector to abide voluntarily by the law which restricts their autonomy in hiring employees. According to the Survey, when replying to the question whether job-seekers had been discriminated against in applying for a civil service position, 43% replied that they were discriminated against for not having a local resident permit; 40.9% due to their disability, 40.7% for health reasons, 33.9% for their unattractive appearance, 32% for age and gender, and 18.4% for not being a Communist Party member.[35]

2.2.1 Gender-Based Employment Discrimination

It is the consistent policy of the Chinese government to prohibit gender discrimination in employment. Both the Constitution and other laws contain numerous provisions to promote gender equality in the workplace. However, the impact of the law on employers and the public at large remains rather limited. Discrimination against women is viewed as the most prevalent in China's job market.[36] This is also reflected in the decline in the employment ratio of women. A 2000 survey showed the employment rate of urban males had dropped by 8.5 percentage points from the rate in 1990, whereas the rate for urban women fell by 12.6 percentage points.[37] An investigation conducted by the All China Federation of Trade Unions concluded that 'gender discrimination is the norm in today's workplace. The progress made in the early decades of the PRC has in many cases been abandoned in the years since economic reform began.'[38] Bulger describes gender discrimination in the Chinese workplace as having 'taken the form of preferences in hiring men, excessive fines based on alleged violations of family planning regulations, unfair dismissals, periodic employment plans, earlier retirement ages for women, wage discrepancies, and outright sexual harassment.'[39] Job advertisements aimed exclusively at or stating a preference for male candidates are obvious instances of direct discrimination against women. One report revealed that '67% of the work units set gender limits and expressly stipulate in writing that females must not become pregnant or bear children during the term of their employment.'[40]

Female university graduates are facing particular employment discrimination. A survey conducted by the Women's Federation in Jiangsu

---

[35] *Supra* note 6, B3.
[36] Mo Wenxiu, 'Government Urged to Help Women Find More Jobs', http://www.china.org.cn/english/10th/89775.htm. Last visited July 2008.
[37] *Ibid.*
[38] Wang Zhiyong 'Women in the Workplace: A Great Leap Backward', www.china.org.cn/english/2004/Mar/90950.htm. Last visited July 2008.
[39] Christine M. Bulger, *supra* note 12, pp. 345-346.
[40] Ronald C. Brown, *supra* note 34, p. 372.

province illustrates that 80% of the graduates polled had encountered gender discrimination in job-seeking, and 34.3% complained of repeated job refusals. Some foreign companies put terms such as 'no birth for five years' in the labour contract. Many female graduates accepted such terms anyway, for fear of losing the job opportunity.[41] Many of them had frequently witnessed unfair recruitment terms such as 'male graduates only' or 'male students enjoy priority in case of equal competence'. A study by the Research Institute for Population and Development of Nankai University demonstrated that more than half of the employers stated the condition of 'male only' in their recruitment for graduates and postgraduate applicants.[42] This excludes young female students from being qualified to participate in competition. It is a disquieting reality that gender discrimination has resulted in the female student employment rate being lower than that of male students. Statistics from the Student Affairs Office under the Education Department of Heilongjiang province showed that the province's employment rates for female college graduates were commonly lower than those for male graduates. The overall employment rate for male graduates is 9% higher than that of their female counterparts.[43]

In addition, with the growing public awareness of employment discrimination based on gender, employers nowadays are changing their tactics. For instance, if an employer wants to dismiss a female employee because of her pregnancy, the employer will state other reasons, such as bad performance, to justify firing her rather than admitting that she was fired due to her pregnancy. Thus, it has become more difficult for a woman to prove that she was discriminated against, although the reality is that she loses her job as soon as she informs her boss of her pregnancy. In a reported case a female technical engineer was fired from her position at a Qingdao company after her pregnancy became known to her employer. After she sued her former employer in court, she was informed by the company's lawyer that she could return to work but could not have her original position. She was offered the job of cleaning toilets.[44]

2.2.2 Discrimination against Migrant Workers

Direct discrimination against migrant workers is another serious problem. Migrant workers with rural household registration 'are technically not allowed to live and work in the cities and cannot benefit from the social safety net which the

---

[41] Chen Chao, 'Gender Gap, Discrimination for Women University Grads', http://www.china.org.cn/english/2003/Apr/62907.htm. Last visited July 2008.
[42] Ibid.
[43] Ibid.
[44] 'Firing Provokes Debate on Maternity Rights', http://www.china.org.cn/english/features/cw/187611.htm. Last visited July 2008.

Chinese government provides to urban citizens.'[45] In the mid-1980s, as a consequence of economic reform, industrial cities needed workers, and a large quantity of migrant workers moved to cities to find jobs. In 1989 approximately 30 million migrant workers worked in cities and the number increased to 50 million in 1995.[46] These migrant workers have suffered various kinds of open and direct employment discrimination. In order to work in the city, they had to pay to receive various permits, such as the permit for temporary habitation in the city, an employment permit, a certificate of physical health, and so on. Migrant workers are only allowed to take certain types of work in cities. For instance, Beijing regularly issues directives limiting the types of occupations open to migrants. These have to be followed by employers. In addition, the discrimination is reflected in different wage scales. Migrant workers undertake the same jobs as workers from cities, but receive a much lower salary. Moreover, there is an absence of medical insurance, social security, and schooling for their children.

It should be noted that, in recent years, employment of migrant workers has been undergoing gradual improvement. In 2003 the State Council issued the Announcement on Improving Employment Administration and Service to Farmers Seeking Jobs in Cities, which requires local governments to abolish administrative approval for enterprises to hire migrant workers as well as the restrictions on the types of work for which migrant workers may apply. In 2006 the State Council passed the Several Opinions on Resolving Problems Faced by Migrant Workers, in which the central government policy regarding the improvement of employment and working conditions for migrant workers was further elaborated. Local governments have responded to this by revising local regulations and introducing new measures aimed at protecting the rights and interests of migrant workers. Thus, some Chinese scholars have observed that the Chinese government is changing its position from the creator of discrimination against migrant workers to the leader of anti-discrimination.[47] On 12 October 2008, the third session of the 17th Central Committee of the Communist Party passed the Decisions on Several Significant Issues Concerning Pushing Forward Reform and Development in Rural Areas, in which emphasis was placed on the need to strengthen the protection of rights and interests of migrant workers, by a gradual realization of the same treatment for them as for urban citizens in respect of payment for labour, schooling for children, public health, renting and buying houses, etc. One can expect employment discrimination against migrant workers to diminish as a result of this policy change.

---

[45] Zhang Ye, 'Hope for China's Migrant Women Workers', (2002) *The China Business Review*, p. 2. Available at http://www.chinabusinessreview. com/public/0205/ye.html. Last visited 28 March 2008.
[46] Lin Yangling, *supra* note 27, p. 231.
[47] *Ibid*, p. 247.

2.2.3 Health Discrimination in Employment

Employment discrimination based on health can be studied from two aspects. One is the protection of the disabled in employment, for the purpose of which China has applied various positive measures and standards, with a certain amount of success in practice.[48] The other is serious employment discrimination against carriers of HIV/AIDS, hepatitis B and venereal disease.[49]

Discrimination in employment against hepatitis B carriers deserves particular attention. In China there are approximately 120 million hepatitis B carriers, which is nearly 10% of the Chinese population. According to an investigation, 56% of interviewed carriers of hepatitis B indicated that they had experienced refusal by employers: of those who were refused, 72.3% were due to failure to meet the standards of the physical examination and only 11.7% were refused due to other reasons. 32% of those interviewed had experienced dismissal: 70.8% of them indicated that their employers informed them directly that their dismissal was because they were carriers of hepatitis B.[50] For many years, carriers of hepatitis B were excluded from applying for civil servant positions. In 2003, Zhou Yichao, a college graduate who had successfully passed the city's civil servant qualification examination, learned that he had been rejected because his medical examination was positive for hepatitis B. He was deeply offended, lost his self-control and ran to the government office where he attacked two officials in charge of hiring civil servants, killing one and injuring another.[51] However, this tragic event generated a nationwide appeal against the employment discrimination shown to carriers of hepatitis B. A series of protests eventually resulted in the 2005 General Standards on Physical Examination Relating to the Employment of Civil Servants (Trial Implementation), permitting hepatitis B carriers to apply for civil servant positions.[52]

In the private business sector, carriers of hepatitis B still suffer serious discrimination. In 2007 a survey by the China Hepatitis Prevention Fund, based

---

[48] Ye Jingyi and Wei Qian, 'Legal Problems Concerning Health Discrimination in Employment', p. 24, in http://www.humanrights.cn/zt/magazine/200402004921170301.htm. Last visited December (1954)2008. However, some Chinese scholars maintain that discrimination against people with a disability in the public sector, such as in the recruitment of civil servants, remains a serious problem. Some governmental institutions took the position that hiring disabled people would damage the image of their organizations. See Ma Yu'e in Chapter 3 of this book.

[49] For a detailed analysis of employment discrimination based on health, see Liu Yang in Chapter 2 of this book.

[50] Ye Jingyi and Shi Yuxiao, 'Discrimination on the Basis of Health and Disability: An Analysis of Chinese Employment Discrimination Law from the Case of the Hepatitis B Carriers', in Lisa Stearns (ed.), *supra* note 18, p. 319.

[51] He was put on trial by the court, received the death penalty, and was executed in 2004. During his trial, nearly 4000 people, most of them hepatitis B carriers, petitioned the court for leniency.

[52] Ye Jingyi and Wei Qian, *supra* note 48, p. 23.

on interviews with the local representatives of 98 multinationals located in 11 major cities in China, revealed that 77% of these multinationals intended to reject job applicants who were hepatitis B carriers.[53] In a few reported cases in which complainants sued Taiwanese and Hong Kong companies, complainants were openly informed by the companies that they did not get the jobs or were debarred from continuing their work due to the fact that they were hepatitis B carriers.[54]

2.2.4 Age-Based Employment Discrimination

Recently the 'turning 35 phenomenon' has been a much-discussed issue in the Chinese employment market – people older than 35 face particular difficulties in finding jobs. Age-based or age-linked distinctions to discriminate against individuals exist in both the public and the private sector. According to a study of advertisements of vacancies in 70 work units in Chengdu in 2004, at least 80% of work units clearly stipulated age requirements, while some work units did not specify an age limit but did actually apply such requirements. Most age limits were set below 35 (32%) or 40 (25%). The investigation showed that work units were quite arbitrarily setting age limits, since the limits imposed for the same position by different work units were quite different. For instance, some work units did not impose an age limit on the position of accountant, while some required applicants to be under 30 and still others required them to be under 40. IT industries showed the most obvious age requirements: around 85% of the companies required applicants to be under 30. When work units were asked whether they had given an explanation to job-seekers concerning the age limit, 20% of the work units had not offered any explanation; 20% barely explained; 40% had given an explanation, and 20% held the view that there was no need to explain. When asked their opinions on job-seekers above 35 years old, 23% of the work units chose 'lack of energy'; 12% chose 'outdated knowledge'.[55]

Age discrimination in the employment of civil servants by government bodies is public, common and currently developing. Originating from high-level state administrative departments, the view that the upper age limit in competitive exams is a vital condition for the selection of employees in any industry has become legally institutionalized and systematized. It is rooted in the 1994 Provisional Regulations on Recruitment of Civil Servants, which sets the age limit at not more than 35 years. Research on vacancies for national civil servant posts at the central party apparatus and at the administrative bodies of central government from 2002 to 2005 showed that, in 2002, there were 897 posts, 806

---

[53] 'Responding to hepatitis B discrimination in the workplace', China Labour Bulletin, http://www.clb.org.hk/ en/node/46945. Last visited July 2008.
[54] *Ibid*.
[55] Li Jihui, 'Age Requirement in Employment', in Zhou Wei (ed.), *supra* note 26, pp. 81-83.

of which imposed an age limit of 35 and the rest further imposed age to 23, 25, 28, 30, 31, and 33. The statistics from 2003 to 2005 reveal a similar situation.[56]

At the local level, it is also quite obvious that government departments have arbitrarily lowered the age requirement in recruiting civil servants. According to a study of recruitment of civil servants in Sichuang provincial governmental bodies, of 109 positions, 41 required the applicant to be under 30, which is about 37.6% of the total. Age is hardly relevant to these positions, and the methods of calculating the age were also different: some referred to the date on which the applicant registered for the examination, while others referred to the date on which the applicant received permission to take the examination, or to the date on which the applicant took the examination; yet others referred to the applicant's age on 1 January of that year, or on 31 December of that year.[57]

2.3 Low Social Awareness of Employment Discrimination

Chinese scholars have observed that in today's China, many officials and economists are against anti-discrimination in employment. They usually argue that anti-discrimination in employment and the realization of equal opportunities can be expected in industrialized countries. However, China is a developing country, in which economic development should prevail and efficiency should be given priority. In their view, China has a large population with an oversized labour-force, and employment pressure is high. Anti-discrimination will not help to increase employment, and some discrimination by work units is natural. It is only to be expected that they do not want to hire females or disabled people, and like to employ young, tall, beautiful people. Enterprises have autonomy to choose their employees. Anti-discrimination in employment interferes with such autonomy, which may harm an enterprise's overall development.[58]

Under the desperate pressure to find work, some job-seekers even committed illegal acts to meet employers' discriminatory requirements. For instance, a shopping mall in Beijing advertised vacancies for staff 'under the age of 35, with household registration in Beijing'. Some candidates bought fake ID cards and household registration cards in order to qualify for the job. This resulted in 24 people being charged with the crime of forging an identity card and being sentenced to between 6 and 10 months' imprisonment.[59] In some cases, people were discriminated against in the labour market and lost hope of finding a job, which pushed them into taking the risk of violating the law. This resulted in personal tragedy for them and had a harmful effect on others.

---

[56] Xue Xiaojian, 'Research Report on Age Discrimination in Employment', in Cai Dingjian (ed.), *supra* note 9, pp. 271-272.
[57] Li Jihui, *supra* note 55, pp. 85-87.
[58] Cai Dingjian, *supra* note 9, pp. 18-19.
[59] Wu Jihong and Chen Weizheng, 'Employment Discrimination and Reasonable Selection', (No. 2, 2004) *Zhongguo Laodong*, p. 23.

Low social awareness of employment discrimination is particularly visible with regard to health and age discrimination. According to the Survey, when asked what are reasonable conditions for enterprises and other employers to impose in hiring employees and civil servants, a condition pertaining to the applicant's health was viewed as reasonable by 59.8% for hiring civil servants and by 67% for hiring other employees. A condition pertaining to the applicant's age was also considered reasonable by a large percentage: 47.9% for civil servants and 52.3% for other employees.[60] In replying to the question as to which groups of people are vulnerable to employment discrimination, 65.6% chose disabled people, ranking the highest of the listed groups; 62.8% chose AIDS/HIV sufferers; 54.2% chose hepatitis B carriers.[61] We might expect that most of the people interviewed realized the problems that these groups of people face in employment. However, in answering the question as to which groups of people you would not like to hire if you were an employer, 63% answered people with AIDS and HIV carriers; 55.8% named hepatitis B carriers; 52.5% named carriers of sexually transmitted diseases; 31.2% named people with a disability; 33.1% named homosexuals.[62] These figures illustrate that when people are given the choice to make decisions, their prejudices are clear. This reflects a dilemma in people's minds between justifying the good or bad decision on the one hand, and rationalizing their decision on the other hand. According to the Survey, when asked whether they thought that people with HIV/AIDS should be treated the same as healthy people in seeking employment, 42.1% answered yes, 36.2% answered no, and 21.7% did not know. When asked the question whether they thought that people with hepatitis B and sexually transmitted diseases should have the same employment opportunities as healthy people, 32.2% replied yes, 49.7% replied no, and 18% did not know. When asked whether they would work with someone with hepatitis B, 31.9% answered yes, 49.3% no, and 18.9% did not know. When asked whether they would work with someone with HIV/AIDS, 25.8% replied yes, 52.5% replied no, and 21.7% did not know.[63]

Public knowledge of age discrimination in employment is somewhat confusing. A questionnaire investigation showed that 76.9% of job-seekers considered age discrimination to exist and 61.5% answered that they had experienced age discrimination. When asked, however, the causes of discrimination, 92.3% replied that discrimination was due to the contradiction between supply and demand in the labour market; 5.3% believed that it was due to the demand of work units; and 2.3% of job-seekers believed that it was due to the deficiency of the law. When asked whether age discrimination should be kept within bounds, 54.8% of the job-seekers replied that the age limit should be set by national law; 30.8% replied that the age limit should be fully in the hands of

---

[60] The Survey, *supra* note 6, E3-1.
[61] *Ibid*, E5.
[62] *Ibid*, E7.
[63] *Ibid*, F2.

work units; and 14.8% did not know. When asked whether job-seekers have any legal knowledge of equal opportunity in employment, 36.3% replied 'no knowledge' or 'just know a bit'. When asked what attitude the job-seekers had after suffering from age discrimination, 93.3% replied 'never thought to seek legal remedy' or 'thought about it, but felt it was not possible'.[64]

Limited public awareness of employment discrimination is also reflected in the biased views on women's working capacity. Many people are still influenced by the traditional thinking that women's principal responsibility should be taking care of the family. Factors, such as having to spend their time cooking and cleaning, taking care of children, ageing parents and other household work, render women unable to be fully committed to their jobs. By contrast, men were considered to be less burdened by household work and could consequently concentrate more on the workplace. It was reported that in 2002 a job fair for female college students had to be called off because only five out of the five hundred companies invited reacted positively to the invitation. Many companies simply said they were not interested in hiring female graduates.[65] An often-voiced argument against the same retiring age for men and women is that women's earlier retirement would alleviate the competitiveness of the current job market; the withdrawal of women means more job opportunities for men.[66]

Since the Fourth World Conference on Women took place in Beijing in 1995, some Chinese women's organizations and women's rights advocates have become more active in addressing problems facing Chinese women. Taking action against gender discrimination in employment is one of the fields which particular attention has been given to. For instance, in 2007, Li Jin, a congress representative and president of the Guangzhou Municipal Women's Federation, submitted a bill to the People's Congress in Guangzhou municipality which suggested barring 'males only' restrictions in job vacancies, and a maximum fine of RMB 5,000 to be imposed on employers who maintained gender restrictions on jobs that women are capable of doing.[67] Of course, some are also sceptical about whether such a law could make a real difference in practice because employers could always find other reasons to avoid hiring women, and it is extremely difficult for women to prove gender discrimination.[68]

---

[64] Li Jihui, *supra* note 55, pp. 84-85.
[65] Xun Zeng, 'Enforcing Equal Employment Opportunities in China', (Summer 2007) *University of Pennsylvania Journal of Labor and Employment Law*, p. 999.
[66] *Supra* note 21.
[67] 'Provincial Lawmakers Mull Regulation to Boost Job Opportunities for Women', http://www.china.org.cn/english/features/cw/197416.htm. Last visited November 2008.
[68] *Ibid.*

2.4 Lack of Legal Remedies to Handle Complaints of Employment Discrimination

Since China started its legal reconstruction in 1978, in parallel with economic reform and opening up to the outside world, law-making has been a government priority because of the fact that the country scarcely had any laws to apply as a consequence of the lawless period of the Cultural Revolution. The legislative products of the past 30 years are incredibly impressive: the NPC and the NPCSC have enacted 805 laws; the State Council has issued 4156 administrative regulations; various Ministries have issued 58,797 ministerial rules, local people's congresses at the provincial level have issued approximately 115, 369 local regulations.[69] Although the necessity of improving and updating the legislation remains, the main difficulty lies in the implementation of law. This causes particular problems with anti-discrimination in employment.

Firstly, the right of equality among all citizens and the right to work as declared in the Constitution cannot be directly claimed by a citizen in bringing a case to court. Under the Constitution, the NPC and NPCSC have the power to interpret its provisions. Courts, including the Supreme People's Court, are not entrusted with the interpretation of the Constitution. Even though in recent years some Chinese citizens, with the support of indefatigable lawyers, have tried to claim their constitutional rights in front of courts, the latter have managed through various means to avoid directly referring to the Constitution. For instance, in 2001, Jiang Tao brought a case against the Chengdu Branch of the People's Bank of China for height discrimination. Jiang Tao, a law student at Sichuan University, read an advertisement of the Chengdu Branch of the People's Bank of China, which was hiring new staff and which stipulated a minimum height requirement of 168 cm for male candidates and 155 cm for female candidates. Jiang Tao, who is 165 cm in height, alleged that the Bank's 168 cm height requirement for male applicants excluded him from applying for a civil service position at the government bank, which 'violated his constitutional equal right to be employed by a government agency and his political right to participate in the management of state affairs'. The case was filed as an administrative case by the court; after receiving the bill of complaint, the defendant immediately removed the height requirement from the advertisement published in local newspapers and on the Internet. The court consequently dismissed the case because of the defendant's removal of the questionable requirement. The court further suggested that a claimant of such case would fail due to a significant legal barrier: the height requirement would most likely not be 'judicially reviewable'.[70] Another well-known case is Yang Shijan v Ministry of Personnel. In November 2006, Yang Shijian, a master's student in law, brought

---

[69] Zhu Jingwen, ed., *Report on China Law Development: Database and Indicators*, (Beijing: *Zhongguo Renmin daxue chubanshe*, 2007), p. 2.

[70] Xun Zeng, *supra* note 65, p. 992.

an administrative action in Beijing No. 2 Intermediate People's Court because his application to register for the civil servant examination was refused due to the fact that he was over 35. According to the rules of the Ministry of Personnel, candidates who apply to take the civil servant examination must not be over the age of 35. Yang claimed that such a rule is illegal and violated his constitutional rights of 'all citizens are equal' and 'citizens have the right and obligation to work'. However, the court refused to accept the case.[71]

Secondly, the Labour Law only provides that labourers should not be discriminated against in employment on the grounds of ethnic groups, race, gender or religious belief. However, the Law does neither define what constitutes employment discrimination, what the legal penalty is for those who have committed employment discrimination, nor whether labourers could sue employers for the discriminatory acts. The Labour Law mainly regulates the labour relationship that has been established by the labour contract between labourer and employer, while most employment discrimination occurs before this relationship is established. Thus, those suffering at the job application stage could not use the Labour Law to protect their rights. Most Chinese courts do not file cases of employment discrimination. Only a few courts have started to accept cases in accordance with the Administrative Litigation Law in which public institutions are being sued for employment discrimination.[72]

Thirdly, although some existing laws are outdated due to changing attitudes and social reality, courts have to follow the laws in accepting and handling cases. The first discrimination case on retiring age is a typical example of such a situation. In 2005, Zhou Xianghua, brought a case against her employer for the discriminatory mandatory retirement age for women. She was forced to retire at 55, while her male co-workers could retire at the age of 60. Zhou argued that the mandatory age retirement violated her constitutional right to be treated equally, and the discrepancy in retirement ages for women and men is based on their gender, which should be seen as gender discrimination. The Zhaihe District Court in Pingdingshan rejected her claims on the grounds that they lacked a legal basis.[73]

Fourthly, barriers and failures of the judicial system in addressing employment discrimination result in many citizens' reluctance to seek judicial protection of their rights. It is true that with the rising rights consciousness of Chinese citizens, the past decades have shown an expansion of law suits that ordinary people have brought to court. However, generally speaking, Chinese people are exceptionally hesitant to sue employers for employment discrimination. The prevalence of employment discrimination on the one hand,

---

[71] Yang Shijan, 'The First Case of Age Discrimination in Registering for Civil Servant Examination Sues the Ministry of Personnel', http://edu.sina.com.cn/exam/2006-02-19/110228772.html. Last visited October 2008.
[72] Cai Dingjian, *supra* note 9, p. 39.
[73] http://news.xinhuanet.com/legal/2006-02-09/content_4158073.htm. Last visited July 2008.

and the few cases brought to court on the other, proves how inadequate the judicial support has been to victims of such discrimination. The few cases in which the claimants decided to resort to judicial address are largely due to the insistent efforts of their lawyers or legal representatives. In the case of Zhou Xianghua v Pingdingshan Branch of the China Construction Bank, her legal representatives were her son (then a law student) and her son's law professor, Zhou Wei, who is an eminent scholar and a leading lawyer in defending victims of employment discrimination in China. The court first refused to accept the case and asked them to settle the dispute through the labour arbitration committee. The committee ruled that Zhou Xianghua had failed to provide sufficient evidence and legal basis to support her appeal and charged her with the total arbitration fee of RMB 420 (€42). Having failed with the arbitration, Zhou filed the lawsuit at the court.[74] In the case of Gao Jung against the telecommunication company, Gao Jung was uncertain at first as to whether he should sue the company. His lawyer, who came from the Impact Law Firm (a not-for-profit public interest law firm in Beijing), encouraged him to take the case not only for his own sake but also for the thousands of hepatitis B carriers who have had similar experiences but were unable to come to court.[75]

Another fact that discourages citizens in their search for judicial settlement of employment discrimination is that too often the courts cannot offer practical help: even if one were to win a case on paper, there is no guarantee that the claimant would be hired or allowed to retain his or her job. For instance, in 2003 Zhang Xianzhu sued the Personnel Affairs Bureau of Wuhu, in Anhui Province, for refusing him a civil servant job because his physical test showed positive for hepatitis B. As a 25-year-old college graduate, he received the highest score in the Wuhu city civil servant examination. This case was tried at Xinwu District Court, which set the precedent in handling complaints of employment discrimination against hepatitis B carriers. The court was of the opinion that the decision by the defendant to refuse to hire the claimant based on his hepatitis B status lacked sufficient evidence. However, the court could not meet Zhang's request to be reconsidered for the civil servant position, citing conclusion of the recruitment season.[76]

Looking to the near future, we can predict that the number of employment discrimination cases to be handled by courts will surely increase. One encouraging indication is that since the Law on Promotion of Employment entered into effect on 1 January 2008, the number of cases concerning employment discrimination against hepatitis B carriers has risen due to Article 30 of the Law, which clearly states that employers cannot refuse job applicants

---

[74] 'Woman Challenges Regulations', http://www.china.org.cn/english/features/cw/157460.htm. Last visited July 2008.
[75] Interview with lawyers at the Impact Law Firm, August 2008. See *infra* note 78.
[76] Liang Chao, 'Law Drafted to End Hep B Discrimination', http://www.chinadaily.com.cn/english/doc/2004-08/11/content_364055.htm. Last visited July 2008.

on the grounds of infectious diseases. From 2003 to 2007, there were only four or five cases of discrimination against carriers of hepatitis B brought to court each year. However, within six months after the Law on Promotion of Employment was brought into force, an online not-for-profit organization, specializing in helping hepatitis B carriers, assisted in more than 20 cases.[77] The outcomes of some cases are also encouraging. For instance, in May 2008 the Chaoyang District Court in Beijing delivered the judgment of the case of Gao Jung (not his real name) v *Bidechuangzhan* Telecommunication Technology Company in Beijing (hereafter the Company). Gao, a college graduate, worked in a software company in Shanghai from 2005 to May 2007. He was invited by the director of the Company to join the Company in Beijing. Gao resigned from his job in Shanghai and went to Beijing. When he took all the necessary documents to the Company, he was refused the job because his physical examination showed a hepatitis B positive result. The judgment of the court supported Gao Jung's claim by stating that, based on the communication concerning the conclusion of a labour contract between the claimant and the defendant before the claimant took the physical examination, the claimant was entitled to believe that the defendant would hire him. Thus, when the defendant violated the principle of equal employment and refused to hire the claimant, the claimant's financial losses from the time he quit his job until his re-employment, should be covered by the defendant; hence a total of RMB 17,572 should be paid. The judgment also stated that the fact that the defendant refused to hire the claimant because of his hepatitis B positive result must have caused the claimant some psychological stress and emotional pain, thus the court ordered the defendant to provide a written apology to the claimant and pay RMB 2,000 (€ 200) general damages. The court further elaborated that the content of the apology should be approved by the court. If the defendant refused to make the apology, the court would publish the main content of the judgment in newspapers in Beijing, the cost of which would be born by the defendant.[78] The court's decision is extremely encouraging for many people who have suffered and are suffering from employment discrimination based on hepatitis B. It also demonstrates that a few Chinese courts are starting to enforce the newly introduced Law on Promotion of Employment. Although Chinese courts do not have a system of precedence as common law countries do, the way a court handles a new type of case will often influence the way other courts handle subsequent similar cases.

It should be noted that until now, trying discrimination cases has been plagued with ambiguity concerning the courts' jurisdiction. In the case of Gao Jung, since the new Law on Promotion of Employment was at issue, the lawyers

---

[77] Chen Hongwei, 'Beijing Chaoyang District Court Tried Two Cases of Employment Discrimination of HB Carriers', www.imlawyer.org/Article.asp?ArticleID=619. Last visited September 2008. The organization's website is www.HBHB.com.

[78] Judgment delivered on 23 May 2008. A copy is with the author.

who brought the case to court felt that it was not simply a labour case, but concerned the claimant's equal right to employment, and hoped the court could file the case as employment discrimination. However, the court requested that the claimant first appeal for arbitration at the bureau of labour disputes. After refusal by the bureau, the court accepted the case. According to the Chaoyang District Court, the newly published regulations on the classification of civil cases by the Supreme People's Court contained no reference to employment discrimination. Therefore, the Court decided to file the case as a labour dispute case. With the increasing number of such cases brought to court and for the effective enforcement of the Law on Promotion of Employment, it may be expected that the Supreme People's Court will issue judicial opinions to guide courts in dealing with employment discrimination cases.

3. PROSPECTS FOR NEW LEGISLATION AND INSTITUTIONS FOR TACKLING EMPLOYMENT DISCRIMINATION

The 1994 Labour Law outlaws employment discrimination on the grounds of ethnic group, race, gender and religion. The 2007 Law on Promotion of Employment expanded the grounds to include infectious diseases and migrant workers. The scope of legal protection has been gradually increased as discrimination in reality has developed. However, the legal provisions in these Laws remain too general and limited, lack mechanisms to operate in practice, and lag behind the necessity to tackle employment discrimination effectively. Moreover, some administrative regulations and local rules containing discriminatory provisions remain valid. In order to respect and protect citizens' equal rights to employment properly, and to resolve the most serious discrimination problems existing in the labour market, it is necessary to revise the existing laws and abolish those rules and regulations that provide legitimacy for employment discrimination.

There are two approaches to designing the Chinese legal system on anti-discrimination in employment. One is to amend the Labour Law by adopting more provisions on anti-discrimination in employment rather than enacting a new, special law. In the view of proponents of this approach, the procedure to have a special law made by the National People's Congress is complicated and takes a long time, while modification of the Labour Law can be achieved within a short time. The National People's Congress Standing Committee could issue a legislative interpretation, or the Supreme People's Court could issue a judicial interpretation to give a liberal explanation of Articles 3 and 12 of the Labour Law, in order to provide a substantive legal basis for anti-discrimination in employment.[79]

---

[79] Zhang Yan, 'Anti-discrimination in employment and law', (Vol. 8, No. 1, 2006) *Journal of South West University of Political Science and Law*, p. 94.

The other approach, which is advocated by most Chinese legal scholars, is to strengthen anti-discrimination legislation by enacting an Equal Employment Law to safeguard citizens' rights to employment.[80] From 2004 to 2007, Professor Zhou Hongyu, a member of the National People's Congress, presented proposals four times to the NPC to draft a law on anti-discrimination in employment.[81] Despite the fact that the drafting of such a law is not yet on the NPC's legislative agenda, scholars are continuing to make efforts to ensure that such a new law comes about.

In 2008 the Constitutionalism Research Institute of China University of Political Science and Law drew up a complete Draft Law on Anti-Discrimination in Employment.[82] The draft law contains 55 articles, covering general provisions, measures against discrimination in employment, establishment of Equal Treatment Commissions, remedy mechanism, legal liability, and supplementary provisions. Employment discrimination is defined as 'any act of an employer involving a distinction, exclusion of, or preference for a labourer, based on factors that are irrelevant to professional capacity and to the inherent objective requirements of the profession, and which has the effect of nullifying or impairing a worker's equality in employment.' It further divides employment discrimination into both direct and indirect discrimination. Direct discrimination refers to the 'act of an employer involving distinction, exclusion or preference of a worker on the grounds of ethnic group, gender, status, religion, physique, health, age and others, which affect a labourer's equality in employment.' Indirect discrimination refers to a situation in which an employer, without committing direct discrimination as defined above, behaves in such a manner that it results in an unequal adverse effect on a worker. With regard to measures of anti-discrimination in employment, it indicates: the general obligation of the government at various levels to safeguard the implementation of the law on equal access to employment; social organizations, including NGOs, may assist workers to uphold their rights of equal employment; employers should follow the relevant laws to ensure workers' equal employment rights; in hiring practice, an employer should not ask personal information concerning marriage, social relations, child/children and non-infectious diseases, except such information as is directly relevant to a job; an employer should not dismiss an employee on discriminatory

---

[80] See 'The Chinese Legal System in Relation to Employment Discrimination', which is written by the Project Group from the Law Faculty of Renmin University, in Lisa Stearns (ed.), *supra* note 18, pp. 241-245. Liu Xinjie, 'Legal Remedies in Tackling Employment Discrimination', in Zhou Wei (ed.), *supra* note 26, pp. 300-309. Yu Shuhong, 'Comparative Study on the Legal Issues concerning Anti-discrimination in Employment', (No.1, 2005) *Zhongguo faxiu*, pp. 129-136.
[81] 'Member of the NPC Is Calling for Enacting Anti-discrimination Law', http://news.sina.com.cn/c/2007-03-07/032712448007.shtml. Last visited November 2008.
[82] This draft law is a product of the Project on Sino-Dutch Legal Cooperation on Anti-Discrimination in Employment in China, funded by the Royal Dutch Embassy in Beijing. The text of the draft law is with the author.

grounds, nor should he retaliate against a worker because of his or her petition, or on the basis that the worker appeals to, informs, accuses or assists at an investigation and gives evidence regarding an alleged act of employment discrimination.

The draft law proposes to establish Equal Treatment Commissions at four levels: the central level; the provincial and autonomous region level; the level of municipalities directly under the central government; and the level of cities with districts. The first two levels primarily have the functions to study and issue policies and guidelines on anti-discrimination in employment; to investigate and evaluate employment discrimination situations and report annually to the National People's Congress; to facilitate implementation of anti-discrimination laws by governmental bodies, etc. The Equal Treatment Commissions at the level both of the municipalities directly under the central government and of cities with districts would handle individual complaints on employment discrimination, including mediation and making a decision; in serious cases of violation of the law and if deemed necessary, the Equal Treatment Commissions could represent discriminated individuals or groups in bringing the lawsuits to court. With regard to the remedial mechanism, the draft law provides a procedure for the Equal Treatment Commissions to handle complaints; the Commissions have the power to investigate, to mediate, to hold a deliberation, and to make a decision. An appellant should first provide evidence on the basis of which the discrimination of the defendant may initially be presumed with reason. The defendant should provide evidence to prove that these acts do not constitute employment discrimination. If the parties are not satisfied with the decision of an Equal Treatment Commission, either party may bring the case to court.

This draft law can be viewed as taking into account both the reality of employment discrimination in China, such as listing discrimination on the basis of ethnic group, gender, status, religion, physique, health, age and others, and incorporating international experience, for example by setting up Equal Treatment Commissions to handle individual complains. The draft team, which was led by Professor Cai Dingjian at the China University of Political Science and Law, visited the Netherlands in 2006 and has undertaken a careful study of the Dutch Equal Treatment Commission. In the Dutch system, the semi-judicial body of the Equal Treatment Commission and the judicial bodies (courts) co-exist and both deal with disputes of employment discrimination, which has certainly inspired the Chinese scholars in drafting this law. If the draft law is taken seriously by the National People's Congress, and used as an initial draft to be elaborated, one could expect China to enact a modern law on anti-discrimination in employment that will provide a sufficient legal basis for the protection of employees' rights to equal treatment in employment, and enforcement of the law could reduce the rampant practice of discrimination significantly.

4. CONCLUSION

In 2004, the Chinese government stated that in the next 20 years, China's population above the age of 16 would multiply on average by 5.5 million annually. By the year 2020, the total population of working age would reach 940 million. While the working age population keeps expanding, there are about 150 million surplus rural labourers who need to find employment, and over 11 million unemployed and laid-off people who need to be employed or re-employed.[83] There is no doubt that the difficulty of finding employment is now a serious concern for both the government and individuals. The sheer size of the population determines that the severe imbalance between the supply of and demand for labour will further intensify the competition in the labour market. On the other hand, the employment market still shows potential. Up until the present time, the government has taken measures to create more employment opportunities, avoid a high unemployment rate, and arrange re-employment for laid-off workers. However, these measures have been mainly aimed at providing jobs in governmental and business sectors, while the third sector, which is non-governmental and non-profit making, has not been aided in its capacity to absorb employees. One would expect that a more liberal policy aimed at expanding the third sector would help to a certain extent to ease the bottleneck in the labour market. In addition, the growing consciousness of citizens of their rights leads them to demand more equal opportunities in access to jobs. An unavoidable trend seems to be an increased demand for equal and fair competition in the employment market. The government has to respond promptly and effectively to this social reality.

In handling the current blatant discrimination, priority should be given to enacting a law that safeguards citizens' rights to equal employment and that bans various types of employment discrimination. The law should also provide adequate legal remedies for individuals to enable them to seek a legal settlement for violation of their rights; victims of employment discrimination should be compensated, and employers should bear legal liability for their discriminatory actions. Enacting such a law is not only necessary in order to meet domestic requirements, but also in order to fulfil China's international obligations. On 1 December 2006, China ratified the ILO's 111 Convention concerning Discrimination in Respect of Employment and Occupation (1958). Thus the Chinese government is obliged to ensure that its laws comply with the ILO principles and standards. Parallel with its status as a newly emerging economic power, China is under more international scrutiny than ever before, and must upgrade its labour standards, including improving the right of citizens to equal opportunity in employment.

---

[83] 'China's Employment Situation and Policies', issued by the Information Office of the State Council in April 2004, available at: http://www.chinadaily.com.cn/english/doc/2004-04/26/content_326356.htm. Last visited September 2008.

Whilst recognizing that some positive changes in law and policy against employment discrimination have been initiated by the central government, another action that is urgently necessary is to press government agencies to stop discrimination in their own hiring practices. Chinese scholars' research has revealed that at present, employment discrimination by governmental institutions remains prevalent. Anti-discrimination in employment requires governmental bodies to set a good example. Only then could one expect private business to follow. However, the practice of discrimination will not disappear effortlessly. The public at large also needs to utilize the law fully to protect their own rights. Equal opportunity in employment is an essential part of the right to work, which is guaranteed by the Chinese Constitution. Individuals need to fight to ensure that this right is respected. Otherwise, public tolerance of employment discrimination will lead to more serious and widespread discrimination.

2

A RESEARCH REPORT ON HEALTH DISCRIMINATION IN EMPLOYMENT

Liu Yang

1. INTRODUCTION

On 4 September 2003 Zhou Yichao, a student of Zhejiang University, was sentenced to death for murder by the Jiaxing Municipality Intermediate People's Court. Zhou Yichao was 22, and had been due to graduate from the Agriculture Department of the Agricultural and Biological Technology College in 2003. On 23 January 2003 Zhou Yichao registered to take part in an examination which was to be held by the Xiuzhou District Government, Jiaxing Municipality for the purpose of recruiting nine township civil servants. In the written examination Zhou Yichao was placed third and after an interview he was ranked fifth overall. As he had not yet received notification of his employment Zhou Yichao went to enquire at the local personnel and social security department. After speaking to the office manager he discovered that the results of his physical examination had shown that he had tested positive for 'hepatitis B three small positives'[1] meaning he had not passed the physical examination and for this reason would not be employed. In his frustration Zhou Yichao grabbed a fruit knife and stabbed the office manager, seriously wounding him. In the ensuing chaos and confusion he stabbed to death Mr Zhang who worked in the same office.

This murder, which had its roots in discrimination against hepatitis B sufferers, was labelled one of the top ten most influential cases in 2003, drawing the attention of all sectors of society to health discrimination in employment. A relatively large part of public opinion, as conveyed by the media, expressed the view that whilst Zhou Yichao's extreme actions should be punished, illogical regulations governing physical examinations for civil servants, which stipulated that carriers of the 'three small positives' could not be employed, were also a major cause of this tragedy. The relevant data shows that there are about 120

---

[1] A popular distinction is made in China between those with the 'three big positives' for hepatitis B and those with the 'three small positives'. The former test positive for HBsAg (hepatitis B surface antigen), HBeAg (hepatitis B e antigen) and HBcAb (antibodies to the hepatitis B core antigen); the latter test positive for HBsAG, HbeAb (antibodies to the hepatitis e antigen) and HBcAb. The latter result indicates decreased infectivity and, in cases which do not proceed to become chronic, the end of infection. WTO website, http://www.who.int/csr/disease/hepatitis/whocdscsrlyo20022/en /index3. html. Last visited August 2008.

million carriers of hepatitis B in China, approximately 1 million people who are HIV positive, and numerous others suffering from a variety of diseases. How to protect this large group of ill people so that they do not suffer discrimination in employment as a result of their poor health has become a big problem that cannot be ignored in today's China. It is thus an important subject that urgently needs to be investigated by legal experts and social scientists.

Currently there is no clear interpretation of health discrimination in employment in China. Several scholars have put forward their own views. For example, Professor Cai Dingjian, at the China University of Political Science and Law, stated 'employment discrimination means that for some reason unrelated to his or her ability to work, a jobseeker is unable to enjoy equal employment opportunities so that the right to equal treatment in employment is infringed... If limiting conditions are imposed as a result of health problems and if the individual concerned does not represent any risk to others, these limits are unjust and constitute clear discrimination.'[2]

It is necessary to make it clear that not all limits imposed on the sick are discriminatory. As far as the protection of public health and prevention of the spread of infection are concerned, to allow those with infectious diseases to work with the healthy would lead to the spread of infection. It is therefore reasonable both in the public interest and according to cultural need, to impose certain limits on the unhealthy seeking employment. These limits will only be discriminatory if they go beyond what is rational and infringe the rights of unhealthy people to just treatment in employment.

2. CURRENT HEALTH DISCRIMINATION IN EMPLOYMENT

Because those people with infectious diseases, and in particular those with highly infectious diseases, pose a possible threat to others, we have not included those suffering from highly infectious diseases within the scope of our research. This is because quarantining these people appropriately is a means of preventing the spread of infection and protecting public health, and is not in itself intended to be discriminatory. Therefore our research into discrimination against those with infectious diseases in employment is limited to groups infected with diseases which cannot be spread through everyday social contact, such as people who are hepatitis B carriers, or are HIV positive, or people with venereal diseases and so on.

---

[2] Taken from a speech given by Cai Dingjian at Peking University, 'Discussion Forum on Combating Discrimination in Employment', held on 7 December 2003, http://www.hbvhbv.com/forum/arcHIVer/?tid-314861.html. Last visited 3 August 2005.

2.1 Discrimination against Carriers of Hepatitis B in Employment

Hepatitis B is an infectious disease caused by the hepatitis B virus (HBV). Research published by the Ministry of Public Health shows that China has the highest rate of hepatitis B infection in the world; there are about 120 million hepatitis B carriers, 20 million of whom are infected with chronic hepatitis B.[3]

In reality, many Chinese often confuse carriers of hepatitis B with sufferers of the disease, even though there is a medical distinction between the two. Carriers of the disease are those whose symptoms are slight. On 10 October 2005 the Chinese Society of Hepatology and the Chinese Society of Infectious Diseases jointly published Guidance on the Prevention and Control of Chronic Hepatitis B, which state, 'Sufferers of acute or chronic hepatitis B can be treated either at home or in hospital, depending on the severity of their condition. Carriers of chronic HBV and HBsAg (the hepatitis B surface antigen) should not give blood and are prevented from taking certain jobs by law (such as active military service). However, aside from this they can work, study and lead a normal life.'[4] One can see that the physical condition of hepatitis B carriers is basically no different from that of healthy people. The Guidance describes the infectivity of hepatitis B as follows: 'HBV is principally transmitted through blood, blood products, between mother and infant, through broken skin or mucous membranes and sexual contact… Ordinary contact at work or everyday social contact, such as sharing an office, (including sharing a computer and other office equipment), shaking hands, embracing, living in the same dormitory, using the same canteen or sharing a toilet, and other contact where there is no exposure to blood is usually insufficient to transmit HBV.'

Given the physical condition of and danger of infection posed by carriers of hepatitis B, in practice these people are excluded from working in a few fields. (1) Physically demanding employment such as the military, the police, space flight and so on. Due to the particular nature of these types of employment, they require applicants to have a certain level of physical strength; carriers of hepatitis B are not physically capable of taking up these types of employment. (2) Employment in which there is a high risk of contact or exchange of blood and other bodily fluids, for example surgeons, blood donation personnel, those who deal with blood products, food and drink service staff and so on. This is because these particular forms of employment require very high standards of hygiene. (3) Other employment involving the kind of physical contact which may spread the disease, for example working with babies and patients and so on. This is because these professions involve caring for those with weaker immune systems who therefore require more protection than the general population.

---

[3] Zhao Yuhong (ed.), *Combating Hepatitis B*, (*Zhansheng yigan*), (Beijing: *Dongfang chubanshe* 2005), p. 2.

[4] China Medical Association, 'Guidance on the Prevention and Control of Chronic Hepatitis B', www.1689.com.cn/Article/ShowArticle.asp?ArticleID=72&Page=6. Last visited August 2008.

The industries that can impose restrictions on hepatitis B carriers can be counted on the fingers of one hand, and the majority of industries should give carriers equal treatment. Article 7 of the General Standards on Physical Examinations Relating to the Employment of Civil Servants (Trial Implementation) issued in 2005 states that those with any type of chronic liver disease do not meet the standard. Carriers of the hepatitis pathogen whose test results show that they have eliminated hepatitis B meet the standard. This clearly shows that hepatitis B carriers are qualified to be civil servants.

However, misconceptions about hepatitis B are tenacious, in particular as a result of the hepatitis epidemic in Shanghai, which led to several tens of thousands of people being infected. The public's terror of hepatitis has risen to unprecedented levels. Recently, fear of hepatitis B has also spread due to media attention, particularly as a result of several inappropriate medical reports and public statements by healthcare departments. Due to this, discrimination against carriers of hepatitis B in the Chinese labour market is very common.

In August and September 2005, we organized interview-based research into such problems as the level of understanding of hepatitis B, attitudes to hepatitis B carriers in employment and attitudes of interacting with hepatitis B carriers in Beijing, Wuhan, Guangzhou city and certain rural areas in Guangdong province.

With regard to the level of basic understanding of hepatitis B, statistics show that only 49.7% of the people interviewed correctly understand how the hepatitis B virus is transmitted, and more than half (50.3%) have a mistaken or incomplete understanding of how it is transmitted. A total of 68.8% have a correct understanding of the physical condition of carriers of hepatitis B and believe that their physical condition is basically the same as that of a healthy person. However, 27.6% still believe that their physical condition is considerably worse, and 4.6% of people expressed no opinion on this issue.

Research shows that although China has increased education and public awareness campaigns dealing with the prevention and control of hepatitis B and almost half of the population are now aware that, 'everyday social contact such as living together, eating together, sharing a toilet and so on, will not spread hepatitis B', there is still a considerable number of people who have a mistaken understanding of this issue. Below are statistics relating to the public understanding of hepatitis B.

A Research Report on Health Discrimination in Employment 53

Table 1: Public Understanding of Hepatitis B

Research subject		Understanding of hepatitis B		View on the physical condition of hepatitis B carriers		
		Basic understanding	Some errors or do not understand	Basically normal	Uncertain	It's very different
Civil servants: 200	Health department employees: 50	45	5	47	0	3
	Civil servants in other departments: 150	89	61	126	2	22
Employers: 200	State-owned enterprises: 100	51	49	72	5	23
	Private-owned enterprises: 50	23	27	31	3	16
	Foreign funded enterprises: 50	35	15	39	1	10
Other 600	Migrant workers: 200	48	152	95	21	84
	University students: 120	72	48	86	3	31
	Intelligentsia (professors etc): 80	60	20	70	0	10
	Ordinary workers, business people etc: 200	74	126	122	11	67
Total Percentage		497 49.7%	503 50.3%	688 68.8%	46 4.6%	266 26.6%

As to the attitudes to hepatitis B carriers taking part in public activities and employment, research shows that only 43.8% of people are willing to place hepatitis B carriers on an equal footing in employment and almost half, 48.8%, believe that they should not have equal access to employment, while a further 7.4% expressed no view on this issue. When those interviewed were asked how they would behave if they had to work with a hepatitis B carrier, a total of 48% of people said that they would do their best to avoid them, less than half (46.8%) said that they would interact with them normally and a further 5.2% expressed no view on this issue (see Table 2).

Another study carried out at the same time into the lives of hepatitis B sufferers confirmed this result. On 19 November 2005, the Chinese Society of Hepatology and the Chinese Society of Infectious Diseases jointly published a report into the 'Current Situation of Hepatitis Sufferers in China'. This report showed that 50% of hepatitis sufferers said that when friends found out that they were infected, their relationships were affected; 52% of sufferers lost ideal employment or educational opportunities after becoming infected.[5]

The statistics in Table 1 reflect the current situation for hepatitis B carriers in employment. The research shows that discrimination against hepatitis B carriers in employment is caused by the fact that people do not fully understand hepatitis B and in particular the means by which it is transmitted.[6]

It is of particular note that many enterprise owners who were interviewed stated very clearly that they would reject hepatitis B carriers. Amongst the total of 200 employers who were interviewed there were only 89 who approved of hepatitis B carriers receiving equal treatment in employment, whereas 112 opposed this. A further 9 employers were uncertain. This situation is reflected in the recruitment advertisements of many enterprises, the wording of which very often manifests blatant discrimination. For example, on 6 September 2005 the Management and Retail Centre of Beijing Mobile Limited Company hired Beijing Tuanxing Labour and Social Security Services Company to publish in its online recruitment news an advertisement to hire people with these requirements: 'physically healthy, normal liver function and no history of chronic diseases'.[7] On 1 August 2005 the Shanghai Postal Department listed the following conditions in its recruitment for postmen, '... no chronic diseases, liver function test is HA positive'.[8] On 1 June 2006 Xiamen City Vocational College posted a recruitment advertisement for teachers and campus administrators. The physical checks included liver function, routine blood tests, ECG, ultrasound and so on, and those applicants whose liver function was not normal would fail the physical examination.[9]

Recruitment advertisements like those above, which discriminate against hepatitis B carriers, are common in today's China. Under the influence of this type of advertisement a 'hepatitis B terror' is spreading in China. Carriers of hepatitis B are seen as sufferers of infectious diseases, and they are usually

---

[5] China Medical Association, 'Report into Current Situation of Hepatitis Sufferers in China', www.net263.cn/hepatitis/medicine/4893.htm. Last visited August 2008.

[6] Below are representative views of those who discriminate taken from our research: a teacher at Fengxia Middle School, Taihe Township, Qingxin County, Guangdong Province said 'Hepatitis B carriers have an infectious disease, they are too dangerous, no teachers at our school would permit someone with this disease to be in the school.' Hou, a second-year student at South China University of Technology said: 'If you have very close contact with a hepatitis B carrier you will be infected, you should do your best not to touch them and should avoid them.' A manager at Zhihuihuaren Company said: 'Hepatitis B carriers are not in good enough physical condition, they aren't up to the job, and it's possible to be infected by contact with them. If anyone finds out it has an effect on the work of the company.'

[7] Employment News published by Teachers College of Beijing Union University Website, www.sfbys.com/jyxw/show_jyxw.asp?newsid=126. Last visited October 2005.

[8] Employment News published by Yichun City, Jiangxi Province Labour Security News Website, www.yc9y.com/company/index.asp/231. Last visited May 2006.

[9] General Recruitment Regulations published by Xiamen City Vocational College Website, www.xmcu.cn/employ/Updates_pdf/2.1. Last visited October 2006.

unable to pass the employer's physical examinations. Moreover, some employers misunderstand the disease, and there is confusion about the concept of 'normal liver function', so that hepatitis B carriers with normal liver function are often rejected. As a result, most hepatitis B carriers lose their right to just treatment in employment.

Table 2: Attitudes to Hepatitis B Carriers Taking Part in Public Activities and Employment

Research subject		Reaction to working with carriers of hepatitis B			Should hepatitis B carriers have equal access to employment?		
		Normal interaction	Uncertain	Try to avoid them	Yes in normal circumstances	Uncertain	Basically no
Civil servants: 200	In the health departments: 50	45	0	5	43	1	6
	Ordinary civil servants: 150	83	3	64	78	5	67
Employers: 200	Managers of state-owned enterprises: 100	43	5	52	39	5	56
	Managers of private-owned business: 50	20	1	29	19	2	29
	Managers of foreign company: 50	35	0	15	31	2	17
Other: 600	Migrant workers: 200	46	22	132	38	35	127
	University students: 120	70	3	47	68	1	51
	Intelligentsia (professors etc): 80	59	0	21	56	0	24
	Workers, business people etc: 200	67	18	115	66	23	111
Total Percentage		468 46.8%	52 5.2%	480 48%	438 43.8%	74 7.4%	488 48.8%

The following conclusions can be drawn from our research. Firstly, discrimination against hepatitis B carriers is principally caused by a lack of understanding of prevention and control of the disease and in particular a misunderstanding of how the disease is transmitted. Better educated people have a relatively good scientific knowledge of hepatitis B and there is a correspondingly low level of discrimination in this group. Health workers have the greatest understanding of hepatitis B carriers: their levels of misunderstanding of the transmission and symptoms of the disease were the lowest of any professional group. They also had the most rational attitudes to interaction with hepatitis B carriers and hepatitis B carriers in employment (only 10% would choose to avoid hepatitis B carriers and 12% denied their capabilities in employment). By contrast, the least educated people, such as migrant workers, often expressed a lack of understanding, terror or confused attitudes to the questions asked above. Only 24% expressed a correct understanding of the transmission of the disease and only 47.5% expressed a correct understanding of the symptoms. In addition, only 23.3% would interact normally with a hepatitis B carrier and 19.0% were willing for them to have equal access to employment. In this group, the rate of those who did not respond to questions because of a lack of understanding was highest.

Secondly, discrimination against hepatitis B carriers has existed in China for almost thirty years, particularly during the 1980s and 1990s when the transmission of the disease was less understood in medical circles. The idea that hepatitis B can be transmitted by everyday social contact has become deeply ingrained in people's minds. Although health departments and social organisations have begun trying to change this situation, it is very difficult to transform ideas that have already taken hold.

Thirdly, because medical knowledge is not widely known, different levels of understanding existed among all groups interviewed. Even amongst those with the highest level of knowledge of the disease this was the case, and even more so amongst those with the lowest level of education. On an even deeper level, these misunderstandings and the discrimination they cause are a reflection of the failings in our current system, such as insufficient education and public awareness, a lack of action on the part of medical institutions and the government to prevent discrimination, and so on. Consequently, in the face of these misunderstandings, hepatitis B carriers have no means of ensuring an equal position in employment, and when compared with other people, at least 50% had lost employment opportunities. Although their physical condition is nearly the same as a healthy person, they generally suffer social pressure and quite severe discrimination in employment due to their condition.

Cases of Hepatitis B Carriers in Employment

On 30 June 2003, the Human Resources Department of Wuhu city in Anhui Province carried out competitive civil servant recruitment examinations. Zhang Xianzhu, a young man from Wuhu city, applied for the post of Economic Manager of Wuhu County Office, and overall he was ranked first out of almost 100 entrants. Following the procedure, he received a notification to attend a physical examination. The examination result showed that he was positive for hepatitis B and thus the hospital concluded that he did not meet the standard. The conclusion of a repeat test at another hospital was the same. On 25 September, the Wuhu City Human Resources Department published its decision not to employ him because he had failed two physical examinations. Zhang Xianzhu did not accept this decision and brought an administrative litigation case, alleging that the human resources department discriminated against carriers of hepatitis B. The case was handled by the People's Court in Xinwu district, which gave the judgement that the defendant did not have enough evidence to nullify Zhang Xianzhu's employment, as he had met the required standard in the administrative assessment. However, because the examination and recruitment process had been concluded, the court refused to support the plaintiff's request that he should be employed by the defendant in a similar post.[10]

In 2003, in another case of discrimination, which has already been mentioned in the Introduction to this paper, violence resulted in death and severe physical injury. The cause of this incident was the rejection of Zhou Yichao, a hepatitis B carrier, during the civil servant recruitment process, which led him to commit murder. One employee of the human resources department was murdered and another severely injured, and Zhou Yichao was sentenced to death. Because Zhou Yichao was both a perpetrator and a victim, this case attracted discussions from all sectors of society. A considerable number of people felt sympathy for Zhou Yichao and appealed for the death penalty not to be imposed on him. 429 of Zhou's classmates and teachers signed a petition calling for a lesser punishment; 121 Jiaxing city residents wrote to the judge requesting that his life be spared; 208 inhabitants of Pingshan community where Zhou Yichao had lived wrote a letter to the court pleading that he be shown clemency and the death penalty not be imposed. After the death sentence was given by the court of first instance, 1,611 citizens petitioned the Standing Committee of the National People's Congress. A number of distinguished members of the social elite demanded investigations into the unconstitutionality of the regulations on recruiting civil servants which contain restrictions on hepatitis B carriers in 31 provinces and also demanded the strengthening of legislative protection for hepatitis B carriers.[11] The actions led to the issue of new standards relating to hepatitis B carriers in the General Standards on Physical Examinations Relating to the Employment of Civil Servants (Trial Implementation).

Another case is that of Chen Shunyuan who sued the Human Resources Department of Ruian city. In September 2003, Chen Shunyuan came first in the written examination in the civil servant recruitment examination of Ruian city. However, the subsequent physical examination showed him to be a hepatitis B carrier, and tests for the hepatitis B surface antigen (HBsAg) revealed the 'three big positives'. The employer rejected him as a result of this. Subsequently, Chen Shunyuan took the Ruian city Human Resources Department to the Basic

---

[10] 'Focus on the First Hepatitis B Discrimination Case', *Yanzhao dushi bao,* 17 November 2003.
[11] 'University Student Murderer of Civil Servant Executed Yesterday', *Xinwen wanbao*, 3 April 2004.

People's Court, which found, however, that this case was not within the jurisdiction of the court and did not accept the case. On 6 January 2004, Chen appealed to the Intermediate People's Court and was rejected again.[12]

Of course, such cases are not limited to civil servant recruitment. In 2005, Mr. Wang sued Shenzhen Airlines. Mr. Wang had passed the written examination and job interview given by the Beijing Offices of Shenzhen Airlines for a post in sales. Then Mr. Wang was requested to go for a physical examination. A week later the company phoned Mr. Wang to inform him that of five liver tests he had tested positive in three, and therefore the headquarters in Shenzhen had not approved the request from the Beijing Office to employ him. Mr. Wang brought a claim in the Chaoyang District Court in Beijing, requiring Shenzhen Airlines to revoke their decision not to employ him, to remove discriminatory rules in their physical examination system, and also for the Chairman of the Board of Shenzhen Airlines personally to pay him one yuan (about 10 EU cents) as damages for the emotional distress he had suffered. The court found that an employment relationship had not been established between Mr. Wang and Shenzhen Airlines, and the suit did not fulfil the conditions to fall within the scope of labour disputes which the court could accept, so they rejected the case. Mr. Wang did not accept this judgement, so he brought an appeal, which was also refused.[13]

In another case, Doctor Wang Chao was unable to work for seven years because he was diagnosed as a hepatitis B carrier. He was originally an oral doctor in a hospital in Liaoning Province. In 1998, during a voluntary blood donation, it was confirmed that he had been infected with the hepatitis B virus. The hospital then terminated his employment and sent him home to recover. In September 2000, the hospital announced that Wang Chao had resigned voluntarily. In April 2005, Wang made a request to be transferred to another post at the hospital and continue working, which was refused by the hospital. In August 2005, after seven years of suffering, with the support of all sectors of society, Wang Chao returned to the hospital and took up the post of a lead diagnostician.[14]

These cases show that hepatitis B carriers receive unfair treatment, which includes being refused employment after passing civil servant recruitment examinations, being unable to pass standard physical examinations required to enter other organisations, and even being forced out of work. When hepatitis B carriers stand up and protest to protect their right to fair treatment in

---

[12] 'The Story of the First Hepatitis B Discrimination Case in Hunan, Experts Called for Using the Constitution to Protect Rights', 26 December 2005, news.sina.com.cn/c/2005-12-26/17078696555.shtml. Last visited August 2008.

[13] 'Claimant in Beijing Hepatitis B Discrimination Case Loses his Case', *Xinmin wanbao*, 5 October 2005.

[14] 'Liaoning's First Victim of Hepatitis B Discrimination Goes Back to Work', www.xinhuanet.com/chinanews/2005-05/16/content_4235781.htm. Last visited August 2008.

employment, and request judicial assistance, the courts often refuse to accept the cases on the pretext that 'they are not within the scope of administrative litigation' or that 'they are not within the legally defined scope of labour disputes as there is no employment relationship'. This means that their rights cannot be effectively protected by the judicial system.

2.2 Discrimination in Employment against HIV Positive People

According to our interview-based research in 2005, public attitudes to HIV positive people taking part in public activities and employment showed that if people have to interact with those who are HIV positive, a total of 55.9% of people will try to avoid them, and only 38.8% of people will interact with them normally. A further 5.3% of people expressed no opinion on this matter. 47.7% were willing to give HIV positive people equality in employment but more people (48.8%) believed that they should not be given equality in employment, while a further 4.5% of people expressed no opinion on this matter.

Table 3: Public Attitudes to HIV Positive People Taking Part in Public Activities and Employment

Research subject		Reaction to interacting with HIV positive people			Should HIV positive people have equal access to employment?		
		Normal interaction	Uncertain	Try to avoid them	In normal circumstances	Uncertain	Basically no
Civil servants: 200	In health departments: 50	35	0	15	38	0	12
	In other departments: 150	88	2	60	96	1	53
Employers: 200	State-owned enterprises: 100	35	4	61	27	1	72
	Private-owned enterprises: 50	18	2	30	16	1	33
	Foreign funded enterprises: 50	30	1	19	25	0	25
Other: 600	Migrant workers: 200	29	30	141	67	23	110
	University students: 120	48	3	69	84	3	32
	Intelligentsia (professors etc): 80	42	2	36	43	0	37
	Ordinary workers, business people: 200	63	9	128	70	16	114
Total Percentage		388 38.8%	53 5.3%	559 55.9%	477 47.7%	45 4.5%	488 48.8%

In 2004, a research report from the Ministry of Health showed similar conclusions: 58.9% of people said that if they were in a public place with sufferers of HIV/AIDS they would try to avoid them; 59.8% of urban and rural people said that they would be unwilling to work with sufferers of HIV/AIDS; 36.1% of urban and rural people said that sufferers of AIDS and HIV positive people should not have the right to enter employment or education and a further 33% held the extreme view that 'AIDS sufferers and the HIV positive people should be quarantined'.[15]

One can see that the environment in which HIV positive people enter employment does not permit optimism. The rate of those who choose to avoid HIV/AIDS sufferers is very high; less than half of the population are clearly willing to give them equal access to employment. Amongst these people, there are still many who are not willing to work with HIV/AIDS sufferers, and their willingness to give them equal access to employment is rooted solely in pity rather than in the recognition of the need to protect human rights.[16]

When public attitudes to HIV positive people in employment are compared with discrimination against hepatitis B carriers in employment, there are very clear similarities. Following the gradual spread of knowledge about AIDS, the proportion of people who believe that HIV positive people should have equal access to employment is similar to the proportion of people who believe that hepatitis B carriers should have equal access to employment. However, the social exclusion of HIV positive people is far more serious than the exclusion of hepatitis B carriers, and the rate of avoidance is higher.

There is a lack of public knowledge or understanding of HIV, and a group exists who are prejudiced against those who are HIV positive. It is also common to deny the rights of HIV positive people to enter work. Although some people's understanding of HIV has undergone a transformation, there is still an irrational fear of those who are HIV positive.

Employers usually have relatively stringent requirements for employees; this makes the exclusion from employment of people who are HIV positive more severe. Among the 200 enterprise managers interviewed, a total of 130 (65%, Table 3) believe that HIV positive people should not be allowed equality in employment, and this is far higher than in any other groups of people interviewed. Some employers expressed the view that even if HIV positive people were capable of working normally, they would not employ such 'seriously ill people' in their enterprise. This discrimination against those who are HIV positive is clearly reflected in recruitment advertisements for many enterprises, For example, in April 2005, Zhejiang Zhonglida Group posted a recruitment announcement on the company website, which said, 'Recruiting workers…Requirements below: …….3) Healthy, no history of infectious diseases such as liver disease or AIDS'.[17] Guangdong Dongwan Jingbin Engine

---

[15] 'Research Report on the Lives of Hepatitis B Sufferers and Prevention and Control of the Disease', www.moh.gov.com /tlex/2%B1%A8& /doc. Last visited 3 August 2005.

[16] During our interview process an IT worker in Zhongguancun, Haidian District, Beijing expressed the following view: 'It is inhumane to deprive HIV/AIDS sufferers of their right to work completely, but obviously I could not interact with them. I hope that the state can find some social welfare organisation which could provide them with jobs…'.

[17] The online recruitment advertisement of Zhejiang Zhonglida Union, www.zhonglida.com/ html/zld-zxnc.asp. Last visited 10 July 2007.

Management Systems Ltd posted the following recruitment advertisement: 'Position: Research Development Department Design. Requirements: ….. no physical disabilities, healthy, no infectious diseases (including hepatitis B and AIDS etc)'.[18]

Causes of discrimination

Our research showed that there were three principal causes for public discrimination in employment against those who are HIV positive.

Firstly, a lack of understanding of the means of transmission of HIV/AIDS leads to the fear of infection. In recent years, the large volume of scientific publications about the prevention and control of HIV/AIDS produced by the government and social organisations at every level, means that both Chinese rural and urban people have a good grasp of the basic knowledge about prevention and control of HIV/AIDS. In particular, most people (60.8%, Table 4) are clear about the means by which HIV/AIDS is transmitted and it is already common knowledge that 'everyday social contact will not lead to infection'. However, there are still 39.2% (the majority of whom live in rural areas) who believe that 'eating with, swimming with, and sharing a toilet with HIV positive people will lead to infection'. For example, during our research at Jingtang Village, Taihe Township, Qingxin County, Guangdong Province, villager Chen Shengquan expressed the following opinion to us, 'AIDS is an infectious disease, you shouldn't sleep or live with HIV positive people, keeping your distance is the best way to avoid infection'. On 12 April 2003, Li Guoxing, an HIV positive inhabitant of Lipo Village, Houliu District, Pingyu County in Henan killed eight others and then himself because he could no longer bear the discrimination he suffered from the villagers. The cause of this tragedy was the fact that after Li Guoxing was diagnosed as HIV positive, the villagers treated his whole family as if they had a 'plague demon', and tried as hard as they could to avoid them due to their fear of infection, even to the extreme that some villagers requested the local government to quarantine his whole family.[19]

Secondly, discrimination in employment against HIV positive people who have not yet developed AIDS is due to confusion between the physical condition of those who have and have not developed AIDS. From a medical point of view the physical condition of HIV positive people in the latent period and those who have developed full-blown AIDS is very different. In the latent period, particularly in the very early stages of infection, there are very few or no physical manifestations of the disease and these people are able to do the same work as healthy people. The time between infection and development of the full

---

[18] The online recruitment advertisement of Dongwan, www.dgjob.cn/information/ =hhj123. Last visited 10 July 2005.

[19] 'A Henan AIDS Victim Can't Take the Discrimination, He Killed Eight People and then Committed Suicide', *Shenzhen fazhibao,* 12 April 2004.

onset of AIDS depends on the physical health of the patient and can be either short or long. Therefore, whether one considers that having a positive attitude can help fight the disease or whether one looks at it from a purely physical point of view, HIV positive people in the latent period cannot be treated in employment in the same way as those who are suffering from AIDS. To do so would constitute discrimination against those who are in the latent period. Our research showed that 59.5% (Table 4) of people believe that HIV positive people in the latent period are capable of doing the same work as healthy people, 30.2% believe that their physical condition is very inferior to that of healthy people, and a further 12.3% of those interviewed expressed no clear opinion on this point. A lack of understanding of the relevant facts about AIDS and a confusion between the physical condition of those who are in the latent period and those who have fully developed AIDS, have been principal reasons for denying the ability of those with AIDS to enter employment.

Thirdly, some people discriminate against AIDS sufferers on moral grounds. Because HIV infection can be transmitted by promiscuity and drug use, some people have formed the view that HIV/AIDS sufferers are 'evil'. In recent years, stories have emerged throughout the country of HIV positive people deliberately infecting others, or using their HIV positive status to blackmail others. This has led to the image of HIV positive people being distorted. Research showed that 22.6% (Table 5) of those interviewed took the extreme view that HIV positive people are morally damaged; HIV is an 'unclean virus', and only those who have committed 'wrong' or 'unclean' deeds will be infected. 48.6% of interviewees were unclear about HIV positive people's moral quality, and many of them were suspicious of HIV positive people; only 28.8% of those interviewed believed that the HIV infection was not indicative of moral problems and that the specific causes of infection should be analysed in order to judge the morality of the sufferers.

Table 4: Levels of Knowledge about AIDS

Research subject		Understanding of the means of transmission of HIV		View on physical condition of HIV positive people in the latent period		
		Basically understand	Misunderstand some points or don't understand	Basically normal	Uncertain	Different from healthy people
Civil servants: 200	In health departments: 50	47	3	44	0	6
	In other departments: 150	122	28	116	3	31
Employers: 200	State-owned enterprises: 100	67	33	62	5	33
	Private-owned enterprises: 50	32	18	30	4	16
	Foreign enterprises: 50	43	7	34	3	13
Other: 600	Migrant workers: 200	55	145	64	51	85
	University students: 120	95	25	92	8	20
	Intelligentsia (professors etc) 80	71	9	71	1	8
	Ordinary workers, business people and so on: 200	76	124	82	38	90
Total Percentage		608 60.8%	392 39.2%	595 59.5%	123 12.3%	302 30.2%

Table 5: Understanding of the Link between AIDS and Morality

Research subject		Understanding of the link between AIDS and morality		
		Morally destructive	Uncertain	Look at each case on its own merits
Civil servants: 200	In health departments: 50	5	16	29
	In ordinary departments: 150	31	79	40
Employers: 200	State owned enterprises: 100	19	52	29
	Private-owned enterprises: 50	15	26	9
	Foreign enterprises: 50	9	22	19
Other: 600	Migrant workers: 200	72	101	27
	University students: 120	13	62	45
	Intelligentsia (professors etc) 80	4	52	24
	Ordinary workers, business people and so on: 200	58	76	66
Total Percentage		226 22.6%	486 48.6%	288 28.8%

The following conclusions can be drawn from analysis of the above data.

Firstly, discrimination against HIV positive people in employment has similar characteristics to discrimination against hepatitis B carriers in employment. Better educated people usually have a clearer understanding of the disease, and the severity of discrimination is proportionate to their knowledge of the disease. For example, when one compares the levels of understanding of the infectiousness of HIV/AIDS of civil servants in health departments, intelligentsia and migrant workers, the respective levels of basic understanding within the three groups are as follows: 94%, 88.7% and 27.5% (Table 4). Similarly, the percentages of these groups who are willing to let HIV positive people into employment are 76%, 53.7% and 33.5% respectively.

Secondly, discrimination against HIV positive people in employment comes from many sources. In addition to some people's lack of understanding of the relevant facts about HIV/AIDS, ideas that HIV/AIDS sufferers are an evil influence are also an important cause. It is a matter of note that as a result of government publicity campaigns in recent years, people have a better idea what AIDS means, particularly in terms of prevention and control. By contrast, as a result of incidents such as AIDS 'needle revenge' and 'AIDS thieves', the evil image of HIV/AIDS sufferers has persisted.

Thirdly, since the majority of people have not come into face-to-face contact with HIV/AIDS sufferers, and HIV/AIDS sufferers rarely dare to identify themselves publicly, they maintain an air of mystery and separation. Public opinion and propaganda in the media are the principal means of determining their public image. However, as a result of ceaseless negative reports, HIV/AIDS sufferers live under a cloud of fear, enduring insults and shame and being unable to obtain the same status as other people.

Cases of 'AIDS Discrimination' in Employment

Striving to protect equal access to employment for HIV positive people is a requirement for all UN member states in protecting human rights and eliminating discrimination. The Chinese government has consistently emphasised the protection of fair treatment for HIV positive people in employment. However, from the situation which is manifested through our research, one can see that the attitudes of some regional governments and some prejudiced people are still unchanged. In practice there are still many instances of discrimination against HIV positive people in employment. For example, in the civil servant recruitment examination process, there have been no reports of the smooth recruitment of anyone who is HIV positive into the civil service. In January 2005 before the issue of the most recent General Standards on Physical Examinations Relating to the Employment of Civil Servants (Trial Implementation), regional government departments had in reality always excluded HIV positive people from entry into the civil servant examinations. When recruiting civil servants several regional government departments stated clearly in writing that HIV positive people should not register for civil servant examinations. In addition to this, very few HIV positive people dared to attend the exams because of the inferiority they felt as a result of their condition. When faced with clear exclusion from the civil servant recruitment examinations, few people stood up to fight this legally. There have been no reports of HIV positive people being employed as civil servants and until now there have been no administrative litigation cases brought by those who have suffered from such discrimination.

Cases of discrimination against HIV positive people in employment in other areas are by no means rare. It is well-known in China that inhabitants of the 'AIDS Village' are discriminated against in employment. According to a report by the CCTV programme Economics Half Hour on 31 March 2004, Wenlou Village, Shangcai County, Henan is widely known in China as the 'AIDS

Village'. Because of a high incidence of AIDS in Wenshu, people in the surrounding areas are terrified of the village, and many who have close relations in the village have severed ties with them. Several young people left the village to look for casual work but when their colleagues discovered that they were HIV positive they were immediately forced back to the village. While recruiting, several local employers, including Shangcai County government, avoided speaking to any interviewee who came from Wenlou village. As a result, the majority of HIV positive people in Wenlou village have no choice but to stay at home and have no means of finding employment. When healthy people try to find work outside the village they must hide their identity.[20]

On 30 November 2005, a China Economic Times journalist revealed that several people were infected with HIV/AIDS in Xingtai, Hebei through blood transfusions. The report revealed that after being diagnosed as HIV positive, not only were many sufferers forced out of their jobs, but even members of their families and relatives suffered irrational treatment at the hands of their employers. When the journalist was interviewing Liu Xianhong, the first of the infected to be publicly identified, it was discovered that Liu Xianhong's entire family had been isolated by the village, they were seen as a fearful 'plague', and even her healthy husband was fired from his job because his wife was infected and he was unable to find another job in the area. Not only did local employers avoid them, but health workers in the hospital also behaved in a discriminatory manner. The Xingtai-infected were frequently let down and there were instances of them being refused admission and treatment or not being allowed to stay in the hospital. After the members of some families had been diagnosed with HIV/AIDS, they suffered from discrimination caused by fear, and many people were afraid to make their illness known. In order to protect other members of the families, many sufferers were cruelly separated from them. Almost all those interviewed who were publicly known to be sick had the same complaint, 'death would be a release, and those of us who are alive would be better off dead!' Many have lost friends and family because they have been infected with HIV/AIDS. They have become completely isolated and close to collapse.[21]

Another case study showed that people suspected of being HIV positive suffer discrimination in employment in Chongqing. On 23 April 2002 the Fuzhou Evening News reported that a policeman from the Northern Branch of Chongqing Public Security Bureau had been accidentally pricked by a needle used by an HIV/AIDS sufferer during his duties. There is a six-month window for doing an HIV/AIDS test, meaning that you must wait six months after HIV enters the body to establish whether someone has actually been infected. During this six-month period this policeman was shunned by others. He was transferred to the management of household registration and the public security bureau tried

---

[20] 'The Present and Future of the AIDS Village', CCTV 'Economics 30 minutes' report program on 31 March 2004, *Zhongyang Dianshitai Jingji Ban Xiaoshi Jiemu Baodao*.

[21] 'The Truth about AIDS in Xingtai Hebei', *Zhongguo jingji shibao,* 30 November 2005.

as much as possible to keep him separate from other people. He was also prevented from taking part in activities organised by the work unit. His wife worked in the logistics department of a factory, and her colleagues treated her as if she had been infected with HIV/AIDS as well. They did not dare to sit on a chair on which she had sat, or touch anything she had used, and even when speaking to her they would keep a few metres apart.[22] The policeman turned out not to have been infected with HIV/AIDS and his life returned to normal. However, from his experiences during this time one can see that those at high risk of infection who have not even been diagnosed as HIV positive still suffer this type of isolated treatment in everyday life and at work. The discrimination in employment suffered by those who are actually infected is undoubtedly even more severe.

Cases of Discrimination Suffered by HIV Positive People in Education

People's terror of those who are HIV positive is not only reflected in the treatment they receive in employment. It has also spread to education. In recent years the biggest public outcry has been caused by the experiences of an AIDS victim, university student Zhu Liya (an alias), who was broadcast on CCTV publicly calling for opposition to discrimination. Zhu Liya was an excellent student of good character. She was infected with HIV/AIDS because her foreign boyfriend was infected. The news caused uproar from senior staff and the faculty upon discovery and the school immediately called an urgent meeting with the health department. She was quarantined in a hostel. Any disposable chopsticks, plates and other waste she had used were thrown away immediately. The university even sent people to watch her to prevent her having intimate contact with other students and she was urged to give up her studies by several faculty members. Once the news reached other students, students with whom she had been on good terms also kept their distance, and some refused to have any contact with her. Finally, unable to bear the pressure, Zhu Liya left her beloved campus.[23]

The treatment endured by Zhu Liya is simply the tip of the iceberg when it comes to the discrimination suffered by HIV/AIDS sufferers in the Chinese education system. The first HIV/AIDS carrier to be publicly identified, Song Pengfei, found himself in a very difficult situation because he had been publicly identified as HIV positive. Not only was he forced out of his home by his family and neighbours, he was also excluded from the local primary school, and deprived of his right to receive the same education as other children of his age. After he was forced to move to Beijing, he was mistreated in many different ways. Some medical personnel were unwilling to treat him because of their fear

---

[22] 'A Policeman is Accidentally Pricked by an AIDS Needle whilst on Duty', *Fuzhou wanbao*, 23 April 2002.
[23] CCTV program on 'Face to Face', 25 July 2005.

of HIV/AIDS; some landlords evicted him once they discovered that he was HIV positive; and he was unable to find any school which would accept him.[24]

In fact, in some cases, even the family members of HIV positive people have no way of receiving a normal education. A Hebei doctor was accidentally infected with HIV/AIDS whilst he was working for a construction company abroad. When his neighbours and colleagues discovered that he had been infected, almost all of them treated him differently, and did not dare to have any contact with him. Faced with pressure from other parents, the school his children attended forced them to change schools.[25]

It is true that in recent years the Chinese government has taken several measures to eliminate the discrimination suffered by HIV positive children and the offspring of HIV positive people. For example, the government has already provided free education to HIV positive children and AIDS orphans in Wenlou, the Henan 'AIDS Village'. However, as discriminatory attitudes towards and prejudice against HIV/AIDS sufferers persist in society as a whole, the situation in some areas of China for HIV/AIDS sufferers is the same in education as in employment: they still have not received sufficient protection.

In sum, in general terms there are still many people in Mainland China who have an incomplete understanding of the transmission of HIV/AIDS, the latent period and the development of the disease, and there are still misunderstandings about the causes of HIV/AIDS infection on a moral level. The majority of HIV/AIDS sufferers are unable to receive equal treatment in employment, including equal opportunities of employment, and equal opportunities in education which will lead to employment opportunities and so on. They, and their families, are often shunned by others in their daily lives. Even AIDS doctors and nurses are shunned by society on a certain level.[26] This shows that there is still hard work ahead of us before discrimination against HIV/AIDS sufferers in employment can be eliminated.

It is a cause for optimism that the Regulations for the Prevention and Control of HIV/AIDS, which were issued on 1 March 2006, required measures to be taken to protect HIV positive people. At the same time as aiming to control the spread of HIV/AIDS, the regulations also aim to eradicate discrimination against HIV/AIDS sufferers and to protect the rights of HIV positive people and AIDS orphans to marry, enter employment and receive education. At present, the Chinese government has passed measures to expand publicity, education and relief efforts. The Communist Party and the government have given unprecedented weight to protecting the rights and interests of HIV positive people. Social activities to increase the attention which Chinese people pay to

---

[24] *Ibid.*
[25] 'Suzhou Legislates for the First Time to Give HIV/AIDS Sufferers the Right to Education and Access to Employment', http://www.people.com.cn/GB/kejiao/42/152/20021015/ 842144.html. Last visited August 2008.
[26] 'Wholeheartedly Hand in Hand with HIV Patients', *Beijing qingnian bao*, 18 October 2002.

HIV positive people, eradicate discrimination against HIV/AIDS sufferers and encourage them to respect themselves are being developed and becoming increasingly widespread. According to the requirements of the National Treatment Handbook for free HIV Anti-retroviral Drugs, China's current HIV/AIDS prevention targets are: decreasing death rates and the rates of HIV positive people who develop full-blown AIDS, and bringing 95% of patients back into their previous posts or other productive employment within a year of receiving free standardised treatment. One can optimistically believe that with the boost provided by these targets in the future, more and more HIV positive people will be able to return to a normal life and enter the job market together with healthy people in China.

2.3 Current Discrimination against Those Who Have Recovered from Venereal Disease

Venereal disease is the name for more than 20 different sexually transmitted infections, principally meaning infections transmitted through sexual contact. In the past, only syphilis, gonorrhoea, chancroid, lymphogranuloma venereum and donovanosis were contained within the scope of venereal disease. With increases in the number of infections which are transmitted through sexual contact, and the advance of medical science, the concept and scope of venereal disease has expanded and, at present, medicine recognises more than 20 types. Since the 1980s, reported cases of venereal diseases in China have risen year by year; in 2005 there were 180,300 cases of gonorrhoea alone.[27]

Under the influence of China's traditional culture and moral concepts, syphilis, as the classic venereal disease that people have heard most about, and other venereal diseases, are associated with behaviour that is frowned upon by society, such as promiscuity and unchecked sexual activity. Moreover, in comparison with other infectious diseases, the passive infection rate of these diseases is very low; and the majority of cases are caused by the active conduct of the infected person. For this reason, syphilis has become an unclean disease, abhorred and detested by almost everyone. The exclusion suffered by those who have recovered from syphilis and the level of discrimination that they suffer in employment is higher than that suffered by people infected with any other disease, including HIV/AIDS.

Serious Discrimination against Syphilis Sufferers and Those Who Have Recovered from Syphilis in Employment

From our research in 2005, we found there to be very severe discrimination in

---

[27] 'Reported Cases of Venereal Disease in China Rise Year on Year, Gonorrhoea and Syphilis are in the Top Five', www.news.163.com/06/0811/14/2O8I55NG 0001124J.html. Last visited August 2008.

employment against syphilis sufferers and people who have recovered from syphilis. Our research data shows that the majority of those interviewed (71.8%, Table 6) were disdainful of people who had recovered from syphilis and their first reaction was that they were unwilling to interact with them; only 21.9% stated that they would interact normally with someone who had recovered from syphilis. A further 6.3% expressed no opinion on this issue.

When questioned about their attitude to people who had recovered from syphilis in employment, almost 75% of people stated that even if people who had recovered from syphilis were able to work normally, they did not want them to be given equal treatment in employment; only 17.6% stated that as long as someone who had recovered from syphilis was capable of the work, they should not receive discriminatory treatment because they had been infected with the disease. One can see that in everyday life and in employment people who have recovered from syphilis are shunned by others, as became clear in conversations with our interviewees.[28] During our research, we heard many Chinese people expressing resentment, disdain and disgust towards those who had syphilis. This could explain the discrimination and mistreatment which those who have recovered from syphilis encounter in the employment market.

---

[28] Below are some representative quotations: the manager of a timber factory in Taihe Township, Qingxin County said, 'How can we let mixed-up people like that [who have recovered from syphilis] into the factory? They would be better in prison'. A third-year student at the University of Beijing International Business and Trade said, 'If I were close to someone who had recovered from syphilis, I would feel sullied and would try to get as far away as possible'. A third-year student at the Business School at Guangzhou University said, 'Only prostitutes and their customers get infected with syphilis, they have no class and are objectionable on every level, there's no way they should have equal access to employment.' These quotations are taken from records of research interviews.

Table 6: Public Reactions to People who have Recovered from Syphilis and Attitudes to them in Employment

Research subject		Reaction to interacting with people who have recovered from syphilis			Should people who have recovered from syphilis and are able to work normally be given equal treatment in employment?		
		Try to avoid them	Uncertain	Normal interaction	Yes	Uncertain	No
Government civil servants: 200	In health departments: 50	13	0	37	16	0	34
	In other departments: 150	108	2	50	29	3	118
Employers: 200	State-owned enterprises: 100	77	2	21	16	2	82
	Private-owned enterprises: 50	38	1	11	13	2	35
	Foreign funded enterprises: 50	35	0	15	12	1	37
Other: 600	Migrant workers: 200	146	34	20	25	32	143
	University students: 120	94	2	24	25	3	92
	Intelligentsia (professors etc): 80	59	1	20	13	2	65
	Ordinary workers, business people: 200	148	21	31	27	23	150
Total Percentage		718 71.8%	63 6.3%	219 21.9%	176 17.6%	68 6.8%	756 75.6%

Causes of discrimination

From our research we believe that there are two principal reasons for discrimination against people who have recovered from syphilis. Firstly, there are misunderstandings concerning the ways in which syphilis is transmitted and about the disease itself. Research data shows that most interviewees (64.6%, Table 7) know that 'everyday contact with people who have recovered from syphilis will not lead to infection'. 63.2% are sure that 'syphilis is a disease that can be controlled and cured'. However, only 42.8% of interviewees believed that a history of infection would not affect one's ability to work. During our research we discovered that there are still a considerable number of people who believe that 'sharing crockery and cutlery or shaking hands' with someone who has been infected with syphilis can transmit the disease; some people also believe that syphilis is an incurable disease and that infection will lead to decreased fertility or death and so on. Some interviewees believe for these reasons that syphilis is a serious infectious disease and that once someone is infected there is no way they will be able to go to work again.

Secondly, the morality of people who have recovered from syphilis is called into question and deep-rooted hatred of these people is common. Research shows that the vast majority of interviewees (89.6%, Table 8) believe that syphilitics all belong to a morally damaged group; only 10.4% of interviewees believe that syphilis is not necessarily linked to morality. However, in this group, some people felt that if infection occurred as a result of prostitution, it was a punishment that one deserves.

Precisely because syphilis is principally transmitted sexually, and a large number of infected people have used prostitutes, some periodicals and newspapers attach statistics on how many people have been infected with venereal disease and syphilis when they report cases of prostitution. This means that in the minds of many, syphilis and venereal diseases are 'prostitutes' diseases' and 'degenerate diseases'. The moral conduct of those who have recovered from syphilis is therefore criticised by many, and many are also disdainful of the moral value of people who have recovered from syphilis and so want to deny them access to employment.

Table 7: Levels of Public Understanding of Syphilis

Research subject		Everyday contact with infected persons will not transmit syphilis	Syphilis infection can be controlled and cured	People who have recovered from syphilis can work normally
Government civil servants: 200	In health departments: 50	43	35	33
	In other departments: 150	113	120	75
Employers: 200	State-owned enterprises: 100	73	65	43
	Private-owned enterprises: 50	29	34	21
	Foreign funded enterprises: 50	38	36	29
Others: 600	Migrant workers: 200	97	76	61
	University students: 120	85	99	56
	Intelligentsia (professors etc): 80	62	71	42
	Ordinary workers, business people: 200	106	96	68
Total Percentage		. 646 64.6%	632 63.2%	428 42.8%

A Research Report on Health Discrimination in Employment

Table 8: Public Understanding of the Link between Syphilis and Morality

Research subject		Believe that people who have recovered from syphilis are on a lower moral level	Have an unclear view on the moral status of those who have recovered from syphilis
Government civil servants: 200	In health departments: 50	40	10
	In other departments: 150	135	15
Employers: 200	State-owned enterprises: 100	93	7
	Private-owned enterprises: 50	45	5
	Foreign funded enterprises: 50	43	7
Others: 600	Migrant workers: 200	179	21
	University students: 120	104	16
	Intelligentsia (professors etc): 80	75	5
	Ordinary workers, business people: 200	182	18
Total Percentage		896 89.6%	104 10.4%

Table 9: Comparison of Views on the Link between Syphilis and Morality by Gender

Research subject	People infected with syphilis are all immoral	Have an unclear view on the moral status of those who are infected with syphilis
Male: 643	553	90
Female: 353	343	10

From the above research we can draw the following conclusions.

Firstly, no matter what profession the interviewees were in, or their level of education, or what kind of a grasp they have of the pathology of syphilis and its means of transmission, the majority of interviewees still believe that people who have recovered from syphilis should not have equal access to employment. For example, even amongst health department workers, with the greatest understanding of the pathology of syphilis and its means of transmission, 68% (Table 6) would deny equal rights in accessing employment to people who have recovered from syphilis.

Secondly, the reasons for which people deny the right to access employment by people who have recovered from syphilis are different from those reasons concerning sufferers of other infectious diseases. Apart from those who fear infection or believe that the physical condition of people who have recovered from syphilis is such that they will not be capable of working, the principal reason that people who have recovered from syphilis are unable to receive equal treatment is that people cast doubt on their moral fibre. The differences between attitudes towards the moral fibre of those who have recovered from syphilis amongst different interviewees are very small, and those interviewees who cast doubt on the moral fibre of people who have recovered from syphilis were the majority in every group. A far greater percentage of women than men cast doubt on the moral fibre of people who have recovered from syphilis. Among a total of 353 women who were interviewed, a total of 343 believed that someone infected with syphilis is morally damaged; the men who were interviewed were relatively more tolerant, amongst 643 interviewees, a total of 553 responded that people who are infected with syphilis are morally damaged (Table 9). This may be related to the social status of both genders and to their attitudes to sexual activity.

Thirdly, the reason why syphilis has such a bad reputation in the eyes of society is that there is really only one means of transmission. The majority of sufferers are promiscuous, and their sexual behaviour is opposed to Chinese traditional culture and moral philosophies. In comparison to the case of HIV/AIDS, there have been very few public awareness campaigns dealing with sufferers of syphilis and other venereal diseases, instigated by the government or social organisations in the media, because no one is interested in discrimination against such people in employment. This means that amongst all groups suffering from infectious diseases, people who have recovered from syphilis constitute the group which suffers the most severe discrimination in employment.

Actual Instances of Discrimination in Employment against People Who Have Recovered from Syphilis

The fact that syphilis sufferers are commonly excluded from mainstream society means that people who have recovered from syphilis are inevitably discriminated against in employment. Below are some examples of discrimination, which we encountered in our research.

(1) Discrimination against people who have recovered from syphilis in the civil servant recruitment examinations. In the 2005 General Standards on Physical Examinations Relating to the Employment of Civil Servants (Trial Implementation), there is a clear provision that people who are infected with syphilis cannot register for the civil servant examinations. Compared with HIV/AIDS, the diseases have almost identical means of transmission and in the early stages infected persons do not manifest any symptoms; moreover, the development of syphilis can be controlled with treatment and can be completely cured. As soon as AIDS develops, modern medicine cannot control or cure it, and sufferers can only delay the deterioration of their condition. However, in the General Standards on Physical Examinations, there is a clear provision that HIV positive people who show no symptoms can register for the civil servant examinations. By contrast, syphilitics who show no symptoms, either, because they are in the early stages of the disease and it is under control, or, because they are undergoing treatment, are not dealt with in the same way. At the same time, because the General Standards have not explicitly stated whether people who have recovered from syphilis can register for the civil servants examinations, and have clearly stated that people infected with syphilis cannot register for them, it is very easy for people to assume that people who have recovered from syphilis cannot register for the examinations, indirectly creating discrimination.

(2) Discrimination in endorsing teaching eligibility. Article 8 of the Implementation Methods of the Regulations on Teachers Qualification which came into force in 2000, states that applicants for the endorsement of teaching eligibility must fulfil the following criteria: a good physical and mental condition, no infectious diseases, no history of mental illness, etc. According to this provision people who have recovered from syphilis or who have a history of any other venereal disease would be completely excluded. In truth, the original aim of this regulation was to protect students' health and prevent infectious diseases being passed from teachers to students. However, when one considers the means through which syphilis and other venereal diseases are transmitted, and the fact that they can only be transmitted whilst the infected person is ill, people who have recovered are no longer infectious and everyday contact between them and students would certainly not spread the disease or present any threat to a student's health. This kind of provision is not in line with the reasoning of medical science. In reality, such regulation leads people who have been infected with syphilis and other venereal diseases but who have been completely cured, to suffer from discrimination in employment.

(3) Other instances of discrimination. In the science and technology district of Zhongguancun, Beijing, where many people with higher education backgrounds are employed, we interviewed several employers and recruitment personnel. Almost all employers said that they would usually not employ a candidate who had a history of syphilis or any other venereal disease. Only recruiters looking for salespeople where there were clearly not enough applicants, and recruiters of heavy labourers and transport personnel, said that they would assess candidates according to their actual situation.

In some employers' own systems and recruitment advertisements, discrimination against people who have recovered from syphilis is clearly visible on paper. The human resources system of the Beijing Leadership Management Consulting Company clearly states, 'This Company refuses to accept anyone who is not in good physical condition. Applicants must be physically healthy, have no record of infectious diseases, chronic diseases or no incurable diseases (such as hepatitis, pulmonary tuberculosis, syphilis and so on)'.[29]

When the Jiangsu Mudan Auto Group Limited advertised for an enterprise administrator, the advertisement clearly stated that candidates must be healthy, and that those with infectious diseases such as hepatitis B, gonorrhoea or syphilis would not be considered.[30]

In the recruitment news of the Accounts Department of Guangxi Normal University, under 'requirements', it said: 'basic accounts personnel: requirements...under 45, healthy, no history of chronic disease (including hepatitis B, syphilis and so on)'.[31] A condition in the job recommendation system of Xiangda Computing College in Zhuzhou, Hunan province is '...healthy, no history of infectious disease (including hepatitis, pulmonary tuberculosis, venereal diseases and so on)'.[32]

Our researchers met a middle-aged man who had recovered from syphilis at the Centre for the Prevention and Control of AIDS and Sexually Transmitted Infections in Changping district, Beijing. After he was unfortunately infected with the disease, he did not dare to tell anyone, but by chance he had to take a physical examination and was forced to leave his job. He has now recovered but he still does not dare to make his medical history known, because as soon as the truth comes out he feels he will not be able to raise his head in public and will

---

[29] Management system published online by Beijing Leadership Management Consulting Co. on 5 March 2006 www.bj-leadership.com/gsjj.htm#7. Last visited August 2008.

[30] Recruitment advertisement published online by University Employment Union website on 1 August 2006, www.job9151.com/person/ShowJobsAll. asp?id=3821. Last visited August 2008.

[31] Recruitment advertisement published online by Guangxi Normal University on 18 January 2005, www.2.gxnu.edu.cn/personnel/zhaopinwang/20051220_e0185a3fe76fc 9f2d154b5b8c675723d.doc. Last visited July 2008.

[32] Work recommendation regulations published online by Xiangda Computing College in Zhuzhou on 11 September 2005, wjwlp.51.net/tuijian=345=123/c.doc. Last visited 3 October 2005.

not be able even to think about finding employment. This middle-aged man's words reflect the sense of shame and self-imposed isolation suffered by people infected with syphilis or who have recovered from syphilis. This shows the widespread levels of discrimination against these people in employment and in society at large. It also explains why, in the course of our research into discrimination in employment against people suffering from venereal diseases, it was difficult to find individual cases of people who had recovered from syphilis or another venereal disease, bringing litigation as a result of discrimination in employment.

In sum, discrimination against people who have recovered from venereal diseases, with syphilis being the most typical, is more serious than discrimination encountered by sufferers of any other infectious disease. Because most sufferers of syphilis and other venereal diseases have been infected due to unsafe sex, society widely regards these infections as self-inflicted, and believes that discrimination against these people in employment once they have recovered is rational and natural. In China there is no shortage of positive propaganda about the ability of people with infectious diseases, including HIV/AIDS, and the ability of people who have recovered from these diseases to work normally and, in some cases, to establish a fruitful career. Yet positive propaganda reports about people who have recovered from syphilis and other venereal diseases in employment rarely appear outside academic medical journals, and they are almost never printed in other media. People are rarely concerned with the life and employment situation of people who have recovered from syphilis or other venereal diseases. Even social scientists rarely pay attention to this large and genuinely disadvantaged group. In fact, if a person is infected with venereal disease, even if this infection is caused by immoral behaviour, government and society must provide positive assistance, not only to protect the infected person's right to employment, but also as a means of protecting the infected person's basic human rights. Therefore in China, combating discrimination in employment against people infected with venereal diseases, especially those who have recovered, demands immediate attention and efforts to combat such discrimination should be strengthened.

3 Defects in Law and Policy Combating Health Discrimination in Employment

For reasons based on public understanding, legislative technique and legislative ideas, there are several discriminatory regulations governing unhealthy people in employment in China. There is also a lack of necessary systematic measures both to protect the rights of unhealthy people to enter employment and also to provide relief.

3.1 Certain Regulations Are Unscientific Regarding the Nature of Hepatitis B

Article 3 of the Law on Prevention and Control of Infectious Disease promulgated by the National People's Congress in 1989 and amended in 2004, states that 'infectious diseases dealt with by this Law are divided into Class A, Class B and Class C. Class A infectious diseases are: plague and cholera. Class B infectious diseases are: non-classic infectious pneumonia, AIDS, viral hepatitis…'. In this Article viral hepatitis is treated generally as a Class B disease.

The problem with this Article is that hepatitis A and hepatitis B are two different diseases with different means of transmission. Hepatitis A is a highly infectious disease and can be passed by everyday social contact, for example through saliva, food and drink. Hepatitis B is principally transmitted by blood products, from mother to infant and by sexual contact; everyday social contact with infected persons is usually safe. Putting these two diseases in the same category for the purposes of prevention and control by law makes it easy for people to become confused and think that the means of transmission are similar. It has also led to the same mistake being replicated in several subordinate regulations dealing with the prevention and control of infectious diseases.

3.2 Certain Regulations Are Unscientific Regarding the Nature of AIDS

Before the 2004 amendments, the Law on Prevention and Control of Infectious Diseases considered AIDS an incurable infectious disease which could have very harmful consequences; it was classified as a Class A infectious disease along with plague and cholera. The latter two diseases are highly infectious, yet everyday social contact with a sufferer of AIDS is completely safe. Because of this, the 2004 Law on Prevention and Control of Infectious Diseases reclassified AIDS as one of 22 Class B infectious diseases. This designation of AIDS now has a relatively scientific basis.

However, the Law on Prevention and Control of Infectious Diseases still provides for AIDS sufferers, like any sufferer of an infectious disease, to be subjected to 'enforced quarantine and treatment measures'. According to Article 24 when the medical services discover someone infected with an infectious disease, they should immediately take the following measures to control it: 'Sufferers of Class A infectious diseases, or carriers of Class A infectious diseases, sufferers of AIDS and sufferers of pulmonary anthrax should be quarantined for treatment. The quarantine period is to be determined on the results of a medical examination. Those who refuse quarantine and treatment or who leave quarantine before the end of the quarantine period can be forcibly re-quarantined by medical personnel with the assistance of the public security bureau…'.

It must be noted that the Regulations on Prevention and Control of AIDS, issued by the State Council, which came into force on 1 March 2006, clearly eliminate enforced quarantine for AIDS sufferers and definitively state that HIV positive people are to enjoy equal treatment in employment and education. The provisions included in these regulations make it clear that in China the prevention and control of AIDS has become more scientific in both legislation and practice. Positive action has been taken to eliminate the public fear of HIV positive people, raise HIV/AIDS sufferers' quality of life, and enable HIV sufferers to enter normal employment. For this reason, the quarantine provisions in the Law on Prevention and Control of Infectious Diseases should be repealed.

3.3 Defects of the Regulations on Hygiene Management in Public Places and the Implementation Rules

Article 7 of the Regulations on Hygiene Management in Public Places, which were published by the State Council on 1 April 1987, states that: 'People who directly serve customers in public places must hold a certificate of health. Sufferers of dysentery, typhoid, viral hepatitis, active pulmonary tuberculosis, suppurating or oozing skin diseases and any other disease which is a threat to public health cannot do this kind of work.' Article 2 of the Regulations states public places refer to: (1) hotels, restaurants, hostels, youth hostels, coffee shops, bars, tea houses; (2) public baths, hairdressers, beauty salons; (3) theatres, cinemas, recreation rooms, dancehalls, music halls: (4) sports grounds, sports centres, swimming pools, parks; (5) galleries, museums, libraries; (6) shopping centres, bookshops; (7) waiting rooms, public transport.

On 1 June 1991, the Ministry of Health issued the Implementation Rules on the Regulations on Hygiene Management in Public Places. Amongst the main limitations on people working in public places were staff who directly serve customers in the hotel industry, coffee shops, bars, tea houses, public baths, hairdressers, beauty salons and swimming pools. They must have a health check every year; people who directly serve the public in other public places must have a health check every two years. They can continue working once they have obtained a health certificate. New employees must obtain a health certificate before they can start work. Article 6 provides that those with viral hepatitis or who test positive for HBeAg cannot serve customers as hairdressers, beauticians or in public baths.

When the above articles from the Regulations and the Implementing Rules are compared with the Guidance on the Prevention and Control of Chronic Hepatitis which was jointly published by the Chinese Society of Hepatology and the Chinese Society for Infectious Diseases on 10 December 2005, inconsistencies appear. There is a contradiction with the statement in the Guidance on the Prevention and Control of Chronic Hepatitis B that 'everyday social contact which does not involve exposure to blood or blood products, such as working in the same office (including sharing a computer and other office equipment), shaking hands, embracing, sharing a dormitory, eating in the same canteen or using the same toilet will not lead to infection with HBV'. The employment restrictions placed on sufferers of chronic hepatitis B by the Regulations and the Implementation Rules are too severe, and in reality deprive them of their right to work in many public places. In addition, both the Regulations and the Implementation Rules require people who work in public places to hold a certificate of health. According to this regulation, sufferers of illnesses which are not spread by everyday social contact such as HIV/AIDS and venereal disease are directly excluded from employment in public places. This constitutes discrimination in employment against those who have diseases which are not spread by everyday social contact. These provisions in the Regulations and the Implementation Rules should be redefined to fall within the scope of limitations drawn up in light of the most recent medical knowledge, which are placed on people suffering from infectious diseases.

3.4   Irrational Regulations Dealing with Sufferers of Venereal Disease in Employment

Article 18 of the General Standards on Physical Examinations Relating to the Employment of Civil Servants (Trial Implementation) states that those with gonorrhoea, syphilis, chancroid, lymphogranuloma venereum, human papillomavirus, genital warts and HIV/AIDS do not meet the standard. This regulation attracted controversy and in later amendments HIV positive people were allowed to register for the civil servant examinations. However, sufferers of venereal diseases are not allowed to register.

3.5   Defects in the Implementing Rules on Teachers' Eligibility

The Implementing Rules on Teachers' Eligibility which were published by the Ministry of Education on 23 September 2005 limits the conditions for teachers' eligibility as follows: to be in good physical and mental health, not to have infectious diseases, no history of mental illness, they must be suitable for work in education and must undergo a physical examination at a hospital of county level or above designated by the teachers' eligibility endorsement apparatus. Article 13 provides that the content of the physical examination is to be determined by the administrative department of the provincial people's government. It must include 'infectious diseases' and 'history of mental illnesses'.

The above standards for endorsement of teachers' eligibility exclude everyone with an infectious disease and a history of mental illness from the teaching profession. These standards may play a role in protecting the health of students but, considering the way in which these diseases are transmitted and the curability of these diseases, these regulations are clearly insufficiently scientific or rational. In practice because they are understood and implemented very simplistically, they easily cause discrimination in employment.

4 CONCLUSION

In recent years, as the call for protection of human rights has grown stronger, the Chinese legislature has paid increasingly more attention to protecting the employment rights of people with a certain illness. For example, Article 16 of the Law on Prevention and Control of Infectious Diseases clearly provides that the state and society should look after and assist sufferers of infectious diseases, carriers of infectious disease virus, and suspected sufferers of infectious diseases so that they receive prompt treatment. No organisation or individual should discriminate against these people. Anti-discriminatory content is interspersed throughout several other laws and regulations. For example Article 3 of the Regulations on Prevention and Control of HIV/AIDS, which came into force on 1 March 2006, states that 'No organisation or individual should discriminate against HIV positive people, AIDS sufferers and their families. The legal rights of HIV positive people, AIDS sufferers and their families to marriage, employment, medical advice and education are protected by law.'

However, so far the Chinese regulatory system merely establishes anti-discriminatory principles; it lacks systematic, specific, plausible, operational content. There is no clear legal provision dealing with what health discrimination is; who should determine it; how victims of discrimination in employment obtain relief; or what kind of legal burden of proof should be borne by employers that practise discrimination. It is a cause of greater regret that as yet there has been no specific law combating discrimination in employment. The good intentions of legislators who wish to combat discrimination in employment have yet to find expression in the enactment and implementation of specific policies, laws, regulations and judicial interpretation.

In addition, the existing Chinese laws which combat discrimination in employment are really only statements of principle; they can hardly be used in judicial practice. For example, the scope of labour disputes as set out in the Labour Law and other related laws includes only disputes between employers and employees between whom there already exists a contractual employment relationship. This includes disputes in which an actual employment contract has been signed. In most actual health discrimination disputes, the employer has behaved unfairly in the recruitment process, the dispute involves discrimination at this stage and relates to lost employment opportunities. At the same time, the Law on Labour and related laws also provide that in order to be accepted by the relevant tribunal, labour disputes must be between two parties in an employment relationship and arise from differing opinions about the rights and obligations included in the employment contract, including salary disputes, unfair implementation of the contract, and other disputes relating to treatment of employees. However, when health discrimination occurs in a work unit, with the exception of some cases of enforced termination of the employment relationship which are violations of the employment contract, in the majority of cases this behaviour falls outside the scope of the law, and there is no legal remedy.

Besides, the principal function of the labour dispute apparatus, which has been established according to the labour law, is to deal with disputes between employers and employees that relate to salary, treatment and so on. There is no specialised apparatus to protect rights in discrimination cases. This means that when workers suffer from health discrimination, they often find themselves with nowhere to turn. For example, it is not the case that all instances of health discrimination in the civil servant recruitment examination can be remedied through an administrative review, or through bringing administrative litigation. When health discrimination occurs in the civil servant recruitment process, it is usually possible to bring administrative litigation on the basis that the administrative organ's specific administrative act is improper. However, when health discrimination occurs in the civil servant examination recruitment process for non-administrative organs such as the courts and the police, this does not fall within the scope of law.

In addition, victims of health discrimination in employment do not fall clearly within the scope of legal aid. The legal aid system is a means of alleviating severe disparities between stronger and weaker groups in society. According to the Criminal Law, the Lawyer's Law and the Law on Protection of the Rights of the Elderly and related legislation, the scope of legal aid includes: (1) criminal cases; (2) requests for alimony and child support payments; (3) compensation for injuries on job caused other than by deliberate accidents; (4) compensation for infringement of the rights of blind, deaf, dumb and other disabled people, minors and the elderly; (5) cases seeking state compensation; (6) administrative reviews and administrative litigation; (7) requests for compensation payments for the loss of a family member in the line of duty, requests for relief payments; (8) other matters where legal aid is necessary. Thus, the current scope of legal aid in China does not expressly include health discrimination against disadvantaged groups in employment. This means that because they cannot bear the costs of litigation, a large number of people who suffer health discrimination in employment, who are in economic difficulties because they are unemployed and suffer from long-term illnesses which require treatment, are unable to exercise their rights to employment through judicial channels.

Moreover, the public interest litigation system is lacking. Public interest litigation aims at protecting the national and social public interest. It is an effective method of using judicial means to protect the rights and interests of disadvantaged groups. At present, the public interest litigation system in China is facing various obstacles. One of the principal obstacles is the limited eligibility criteria for bringing litigation, because only those who are directly interested can bring a case. Another barrier is a shortage of funds, as individuals who do want to bring litigation do not have capital support.

3

DISABILITY DISCRIMINATION IN EMPLOYMENT

Ma Yu'e

1. INTRODUCTION

People with disabilities and disabled people are two separate concepts. Some people's disabilities do not meet the prescribed standards and therefore they are not considered to be disabled. Consequently, they do not enjoy the same legal protection as a disabled person.

Every country in the world has different definitions and criteria for disability. In some countries and regions, especially in developed countries, every person who suffers discrimination because of his or her disabilities receives legal protection. Some countries, however, have stricter disability criteria, especially developing countries, and therefore the range of disabled people receiving legal protection is relatively small. The Chinese definition of a disability is set down in the Law on Protection of Disabled Persons: 'A disabled person is someone who has a mental, psychological, or physical impairment, someone who has fully or partially lost the ability to carry out activities in a normal fashion'.[1] There are some discrepancies between this definition and that in the Convention on the Rights of Persons with Disabilities, in which social attitudes and environmental factors were not taken into account, particularly from the perspective of disabled people. The Chinese categorization of disabled people in the Law on Protection of Disabled Persons states that 'disabled people include someone who has a visual impairment, hearing disability, speech impediment, physical, mental or nervous disability, multiple disabilities or other disabilities'.[2] At the same time, the Law also stipulates that 'criteria for disability must be set by the State Council'.[3] However, the State Council has yet to draw up any such criteria.

For many years the basic criteria have been drawn from the Disabled People's Practical Evaluation Standards according to testimonial evidence

---

[1] Art. 2 of the Law on Protection of Disabled Persons. The Law was promulgated by the National People's Congress Standing Committee in 1990 and was amended in 2008. Since this Chapter is translated from the article published in 2007 the articles cited in this Chapter are from the 1990 Law.
[2] *Ibid.*
[3] *Ibid.*

released by the China Disabled Persons' Federation (CDPF). These criteria are drawn from the 1987 1st Standard National Disability Survey. The criteria for disability are far stricter than many people in society in general would imagine. Some disabled people may be recognized by society, but if their disabilities do not accord with the Disabled People's Practical Evaluation Standards, they will not be considered to be disabled. From 1987 to the end of 2005, the national percentage of disabled people in China was calculated according to the data of the 1987 survey, which set the percentage at 4.9%.[4] Thus by the end of 2005, the number of disabled people was reckoned to be more than 60 million (not including Taiwan, Hong Kong and Macao).[5] In 2004, the Chinese mainland launched the 2nd National Disability Survey, amending and improving the criteria set in the 1st Standard National Disability Survey. Although in some respects the standards set by the second survey were more relaxed, they remained far stricter than those of many countries and the World Health Organisation. A comprehensive survey was launched on 1 April 2006, and the data was published on 1 December 2006: the number of disabled people on the Chinese mainland up to 1 April 2006 was 82.96 million, or 6.34% of the population.[6] In most countries and within the United Nations (UN), the number was calculated as 10% or even higher (in the US there are more than 15%). The UN announced that the global number of disabled people had reached 600 million in 2000.[7]

The Law on Protection of Disabled Persons, promulgated in 1990, clearly prohibits discrimination against disabled people in employment, stipulating that: 'No discrimination shall be practised against disabled persons in recruitment, employment, obtaining of permanent status, promotion, determining professional titles, payment status, welfare, labour insurance or in other aspects'.[8] However, there are no regulations specifying what disability discrimination is, what kind of behaviour constitutes discrimination, or what the procedure is to initiate a complaint. There are also no regulations specifying disabled people's rights to legal aid. Clearly, although China opposes disability discrimination in principle, no regulatory steps have been taken to put this principle into practice. At the same time, while Chinese law prohibits disability discrimination there is no protection for those who fall victim to it and no way of distinguishing people who commit such discrimination.

---

[4] Xiang Zicheng, *The History of the Issue of the Legal Protection of Chinese Disabled People*, (Beijing: *Zhongguo Fazhi Chubanshe*, 2003), p. 271.

[5] 'Outline Proposals for the Development of China's Disabled Enterprises During the 11th Five Year Plan', http://www.cdpf.org.cn/sytj/content/2007-12/02/content_ 77887.htm. Last visited August 2008.

[6] Legal Daily, 4 December 2006.

[7] 'Resolution of the United Nation 56th General Assembly (agenda item 119(b)) and the New Century Disability Rights Beijing Declaration', 15 January 2002.

[8] Art. 34 (2) of the Law on Protection of Disabled Persons.

People usually recognise that disability discrimination in recruitment refers to deciding against employing someone because of their disabilities. There was one case in particular that sparked great debate over the exact nature of disability discrimination. According to a media report, the Dalang food company in Wanzhou, Chongqing, released a job advert which specified: 'workers wanted, less than 1.4 metres tall, full of spirit though physically disabled, men or women, dwarfs, and those with osteoporosis are all welcome'. The company's number one product was 'Dalang steamed bread', and because of the product's uniqueness and the special characteristics of 'Wu Dalang',[9] the company manager wanted to recruit short persons to help create a distinct restaurant brand. This company believed that by recruiting someone short in stature it would achieve success. For the employee it was a rare employment opportunity, and for the company it was a chance to promote its major product. But could this case of a company employing short persons, disabled person and exploiting them in this fashion – also be regarded as an issue of discrimination? A great number of experts have voiced many opinions, demonstrating the lack of consensus over disability discrimination.

2   THE CURRENT SITUATION OF DISABILITY DISCRIMINATION IN EMPLOYMENT

2.1   Employment Opportunity Discrimination

Disabled people face many more difficulties in finding employment than non-disabled people, and there is always a relatively large difference between the employment rates of the two groups. In 2003, the total Chinese population was 1.292 billion (not including Hong Kong, Macao and Taiwan). This includes a labour force over the age of 16 of 998.89 million, 744.32 million of whom were employees. This included 256.39 million in urban areas, where the employment rate was 34.4%, compared with 65.6% in rural areas. There were more than 60 million disabled people in China, of whom about 24 million were of working age. 20.883 million disabled people were actively employed, 4.031 million in urban areas, which constituted a 19.3% employment rate compared with 80.7% in rural areas.[10] It becomes obvious that the rate of employment in urban areas of disabled people is far lower than that of non-disabled people.

Looking at new employment figures from 2004, the number of disabled people finding employment still lags far behind that of non-disabled people. In 2004 the total number of employed in China reached 752 million, an increase of

---

[9]   Wu Dalang is a character from the Chinese epic novel, *The Water Margin*. *Wu i*s short in stature.
[10] '2005 China Employment Report', www.china.com.cn/zhuanti2005/node6005254.htm. Last visited August 2008.

7.68 million from 2003. This number includes 264.76 million urban employees, 8.37 million more than 2003 and representing 35.2% of the national employees.[11] As for disabled people, by the end of 2004, there were about 4.3 million employed disabled people in urban areas, only 270,000 more than 2003.[12] By the end of 2006, among the 82.96 million disabled people in China, 8.58 million capable of working were unemployed.[13] On 10 May 2005, when the Hubei Provincial Regulation for the Preferential Treatment of Disabled People became effective, Jinchu website published an article based on a survey carried out by the Hubei Provincial Disabled Persons' Federation, showing that the employment rate among disabled people in urban areas throughout the province was less than 50%.[14] According to a survey jointly issued by Fujian province and Fuzhou City Disabled Persons' Federation, the Fuzhou Academy of Social Sciences, and Fuzhou University, 70.9% of disabled people of a legal working age were unemployed. Even after discounting those who are unable to work (33%), 37.8% face unemployment.[15] The same survey showed that 55.57% of the disabled respondents thought that looking for a job was an extremely difficult process; 34.73% of respondents thought it was hard; 7.73% thought it was average; and only 1.97% thought that it was easy.[16]

How hard disabled people find getting a job obviously depends on their physical condition and general social environment. Discrimination in society is one of the main factors causing difficulty for disabled people seeking employment. While disabled people often suffer direct discrimination in employment, indirect discrimination is even more prevalent. Recruiters do not want to hire disabled people, or believe that disabled people are unable to work, and that the costs of accommodating them will be too high. Many work units take the view that there are not even enough positions for healthy people, so why take on a disabled person? It is also thought that taking on a disabled person is bound to affect the image of the work unit. Some units not only do not hire disabled people, but also do not contribute to disability benefits. In order to make their investment environment more attractive, some local governments do not require foreign-invested enterprises and enterprises within development zones to carry out their obligations to employ disabled people or contribute to a disability employment protection fund. In even more serious scale, some industrial sectors

---

[11] *Ibid.*
[12] '2005 Statistical Report of the Development of China Disabled Work' (China Disabled Persons' Federation document 2006. No.7).
[13] Li Li, 'Concerns about 80 Million Disabled People in China', *Legal Daily*, 1 March 2007.
[14] Fan Xiaoyan *et al.*, 'Good News for 3.7 Million Disabled People', http://www.cnhubei.com/200503/ ca752872.htm. Last visited August 2008.
[15] Zhang Baolin (ed.), *Research into the Theory and Practice of China's Disabled People (Humanity Volume)*, *(zhongguo canjiren shiye lilun yu shijian yanjiu rendaojuan)*, (Beijing: *Huaxia chubanshe*, 2007), p. 214.
[16] *Ibid.*

issued documents which restrict or even refuse employment to disabled people. As a result many disabled people are marginalised and become impoverished.

For a long time, disabled people have been placed in the same category as unhealthy people. Those who make health requirements for job applications and recruitment exams, often also specify that they will not take those with disabilities. For example, before the Law on Civil Servants was implemented, when examining civil servant candidates every local department required that those who passed the exams must be healthy. Each local department enforced compulsory physical exams or standard conditions. Disabled people were regarded as unhealthy and were not able to pass the physical exam. Traditionally, health issues surrounding employment discrimination have mainly centred on disability discrimination.[17]

According to a survey undertaken by a relevant government department, the main external factor affecting disabled people's employment is 'disability discrimination'; 51.23% of disabled people chose this item. This suggests that social discrimination greatly affects disabled people's employment chances. The next major factors were thought to be 'intense competition' and 'lack of access to information', selected by 40.7% and 40.35% respectively. Finally, 36.49% chose 'no available employment agencies' as the major reason and 13.68% chose 'other'.[18]

Qingdao City Disabled Persons' Federation carried out an online survey investigating the reasons why disabled people find it hard to gain employment. Out of the 317 participants, 192 people (60.57%) thought that discrimination and prejudice was the main reason; 51 people (16.09%) thought it was due to the lack of skills of disabled persons; 74 people (23.34%) thought that it was because recruiters imposed unreasonable demands.[19]

During the run up to the 2006 15th National Support Disability Day, a journalist from Hunan province investigated the employment circumstances of disabled students at 10 universities and went to numerous recruitment agencies, revealing that 'the disabled students face a far lower rate of employment than normal students'.[20] On 19 May 2006, the journalist carried out an investigation into recruitment processes within 28 work units in Changsha city. 23 work units made it clear they would not recruit disabled students, and only 2 expressed a willingness to give precedence to disabled people. Among the 23 companies, 17 thought that disabled students could not succeed in their work placements and did not possess the necessary ability to adapt to different environments. 4 work

---

[17] Ye Jingyi, 'Research on Legal Issues concerning Health Discrimination in Health Employment', http://www.zgldfl.com/news/zjlt/show.asp?id=33. Last visited August 2008.
[18] '2005 China Employment Report', *supra* note 11.
[19] Qingdao City Disabled Persons' Federation website, http://www.qdpf.org.cn. Last visited 2 November 2006.
[20] 'Hard Road to Seek Job – an Investigation of Difficulties for Disabled Graduates to Find Employment', http://school.csonline.com.cn/fm/200605/t20060522_475698.htm. Last visited August 2008.

units thought that disabled people had limited scope for development and 2 work units believed disabled people would affect the enterprise's image. At one company, the person responsible for recruitment even said: 'at the moment the personnel market is saturated; healthy people can't get a job, let alone disabled people. We're not a social welfare enterprise or a charity'.[21] This investigation revealed that: first, discrimination against disability still exists in employment services; secondly, many recruiters discriminate against disabled people when they are advertising and hiring; and thirdly, a large number of people are prejudiced in their thinking concerning disabled people's working capacity.

Some individual or corporate discrimination against disabled people, or refusal to employ, is quite openly and publicly expressed. For example, the Hunan Disability Federation Labour Employment Service Centre found work for a disabled graduate from the Medical College of Zhongnan University, but in April 2006 discovered the director of personnel department at the provincial capital hospital had refused to employ the disabled person in question or pay employment securities.[22] Another example is the similar experience of a 4th year student of a university in Hunan who had lost his right leg in a traffic accident at the age of 7. In February 2006 he submitted his CV to 12 companies, and 3 invited him for an interview. But when the recruiters saw his empty trouser leg and the fact that he walked with a stick, a look of embarrassment passed over their faces, and he failed to succeed in the interview.[23]

Female disabled students find searching for work particularly harrowing, as they potentially face both gender and disability discrimination. For example, Li Boling, a girl from Xi'an, became a postgraduate student after nearly 20 years of gruelling study, but due to her disability she met the 'cold faces' of more than 60 recruiters, and was refused by more than 200 companies online.[24] In response to this, a media critic[25] said that the fact that a woman with a master's degree was turned down by 60 recruiters shows there is serious disability discrimination in Chinese society, and that China lacks an adequate employment protection system for disabled people. There is no such effective protection for disabled people seeking jobs: their employment is entirely in the hands of recruiting companies. Disabled people thus have absolutely no control over seeking employment and they have no choice but to allow recruiters to 'deal with' them.

---

[21] *Ibid.*
[22] *Ibid.*
[23] *Ibid.*
[24] 'A Female Graduate was Refused for Sixty Times in Looking for Job', http://news.xinhuanet.com/edu/2005-10/23/content_3671335.htm. Last visited August 2008.
[25] Lu Zhijian, 'What are the Real Problems When a Female Graduate was Refused Sixty Times', http://finance1.jrj.com.cn/news/2007-01-29/000001958252.html. Last visited August 2008.

Another example is the case of Xiong Xiaoyun,[26] a deaf mute girl from Chongqing city. She knelt down to appeal for a job, as a result drew a focus on disability discrimination. Xiong Xiaoyun, age 24, graduated in art and design from Changchun University's Special Education Institute. She submitted her CV to nearly a hundred companies, but she was refused employment because she was disabled. In November 2005 Xiaoyun returned to Chongqing and went around to all of the colleges and recruitment agencies giving them her CV in the hope of finding a job. However, from 100 CVs submitted she heard no reply. In September 2006 at Huaxinjie Recruitment Fair, she knelt helplessly before recruiters and finally managed to get 5 companies to accept her CV. The report of this incident attracted widespread attention throughout China. The former President of Changchun University's Special Education Institute, Chen Hong (previously Xiaoyun's tutor) revealed that Xiaoyun had been a successful student, coming among the top five students every term: 'I can say with authority that she is very capable of many different jobs, including teaching'. A media commentator said that this case constituted a blow to a disabled student's dignity and dreams, and was also an unpleasant clash of law and reality. For recruiters, it is very hard to consider that a disabled, strong-willed person and a strong, able-bodied person are of equal status: 'If we can find a university student with all-round moral, intellectual and physical development, then why would we want to hire a disabled person?'[27] Xiong Xiaoyun's father said that he had made contact many times with recruitment departments which had shown genuine interest at first, but once they knew of Xiaoyun's situation they said, one after another, 'we'll think about it and talk later', and then he heard no more. Another media commentator said that Xiaoyun had travelled along a difficult and tempestuous path in pursuit of study, only to have to return to her hometown, and long for the day when she could put her knowledge to good use. Finally for her to have to kneel and beg for work was truly shocking and shameful.

A mute deaf female student forced to go to such an extreme is a wake-up call to society as a whole and epitomises disabled people's difficulties in looking for work. Even though the law forbids disability discrimination, it is clearly a concept deeply embedded in many people's unconsciousness. This is particularly clear among recruiters, who make specific requirements such as: 'healthy, no disabilities' in job adverts everywhere. Some people say that foreigners regard protecting disabled people in employment as 'a basic measure of the protection of human rights', and the Chinese must in the same way gain a deeper understanding of its implication.[28]

---

[26] Zhou Xiyin, 'A Female Deaf Graduate Knelt Down Begging for a Job, the Employer Showed Sympathy but Refused her Eventually', http://news.xinhuanet.com/school/2006-09/07/ content_5059468.htm. Last visited August 2008.

[27] Xiaofeng, 'Debate on Female Deaf Graduate Kneeling Down for Job, a Focus on Fair Treatment for Disabled People in Labour Market', http://www.legaldaily.com.cn/bm/2006-09/08/content_405499.htm. Last visited August 2008.

[28] Zhou Xiyin, *supra* note 27.

These experiences of discrimination by disabled students are truly harrowing. Although the search for employment by disabled university graduates and postgraduates is somewhat less difficult than for other disabled people as the work they seek is more intellectual and less physically demanding, if they even suffer such an extent of discrimination, it is easy to imagine what other disabled people suffer.

2.2 Discriminatory Treatment at Work

Many Disabled People Do Not Enjoy Social Insurance

According to the data published by the National Statistics Bureau, in 2003 out of the 264.760 million employees in urban areas, 163.530 million had social insurance (61.67%).[29] In comparison, 1.13 million urban disabled workers had social insurance, amounting to only 26.26%.[30] By the end of the 10th Five Year Plan (2001-2005), the number of disabled workers covered by social insurance was about 1.252 million,[31] which is to say for every 3.7 disabled people actually working, only 1 has social insurance, leaving the majority unprotected.

Some Disabled People Do Not Enjoy Equal Rights

Some social welfare enterprises employ disabled people on paper in order to receive tax exemption, but in reality the disabled are not given proper jobs, merely receiving modest living costs. Some enterprises do not even pay living expenses or the social insurance for disabled people. One provincial state enterprise employed more than 30 disabled people, but during an annual audit it was discovered that salaries and insurance for disabled workers were very low; moreover, some were laid off and received only living expenses. A social welfare enterprise in the northeast of China did not provide its disabled workers with social insurance for years, which was only exposed when the company subsequently went bankrupt. As a result, tens of disabled workers went on strike. Recently, the main reason for disabled people taking collective action has been due to their work units failing to provide them with social insurance.

---

[29] '2004 Annual Statistical Report on the Development of Labour and Social Security', 19 May 2005.

[30] '2004 Statistical Report on the Development of China's Disabled Work', http://www.cdpf.org.cn/sytj/content/2007-12/02/content_77876_2.htm. Last visited September 2008.

[31] 'Statistical Report on the Outline and Implementation of China's Disabled Work during the 10th Five Year Plan', http://www.cdpf.org.cn/sytj/content/2007-12/02/content_77887.htm. Last visited August 2008.

Some Work Units Draw Up Discriminatory Targets and Tasks for Disabled Workers

An example of this is the experience of a student who graduated in 2005 from a faculty of finance and insurance in a university in Hunan and had contracted polio as a child. The first place she went in search of a job was an insurance company in Changsha, but she was refused employment because she was disabled. Afterwards she went to a start-up insurance company in Shenzhen, but again was dismissed because she would give them a 'bad image'. In March 2006 she worked half a month in a company in Changsha, but because she did not achieve the sales target she received no salary. In that company other people were only required to make RMB10,000 per month in order to pass their probation, but the company ordered her to make RMB30,000.[32] In that case, not only was she refused employment because of her disability, but her employment conditions were unequal. Such unfair standards both constitute disability discrimination.

2.3 Employment Services and Environmental Discrimination

On the first hand, careers services are not yet accessible to disabled people, limiting their opportunities for employment advice. Many recruitment agencies and centres take no measures to support disabled people or to provide accessible facilities. For instance, at a large provincial-level recruitment agency, there are more than 50 steps up to the entrance with no ramp; the building has no toilets suitable for use by disabled people, or any facilities for deaf or blind people.[33] Thus, all disabled people will face difficulties even entering the recruitment centre, let alone accessing the general labour market.

Secondly, many work places, residential buildings, roads and transport services fail to install any services for disabled people, and quite a number of work units refuse to employ disabled people because the units lack the necessary access and services. In 2003, a major supermarket chain in Xining in Qinghai province opened a chain store. The provincial disabled persons' federation, in accordance with the Regulations of Implementation of the Law on Protection of Disabled Persons in Qinghai Province, required a certain quota of disabled people to be employed, and recommended employing three disabled people who had followed a specific training course for the disabled. One disabled woman with two walking sticks applied to be the radio announcer. Her voice was suitable for the post, but the employees' passageway to the broadcasting studio was too narrow for her to get through with her two walking sticks, so the store refused to employ her. The disabled woman's family said they were willing to carry her every day to and from work, not wanting the work unit to take on any

---

[32] *Supra* note 20.
[33] *Ibid.*

extra burden, still the store refused and the woman never managed to get the job.[34]

3 THE LEGAL SYSTEM IN GUARANTEEING EMPLOYMENT FOR DISABLED PEOPLE

In recent years, disability discrimination in employment has attracted a certain amount of attention, and has caused many experts to consider the related legal issues. Thus far, however, the author has never heard of such attention bearing any result, that is to say, a legal solution has yet to emerge. Moreover, it is unknown to the author that a single disabled person has taken his/her employer to court for disability discrimination. It is necessary to examine the reasons behind this from a legal and institutional perspective.

A report in 'Jingbao' on the difficulties of finding employment for Guo Hui, a female disabled PhD student at Peking University's English department, explored different opinions on the matter. Shi Meixia, a professor at the Finance Management Institute at the Northern Transportation University and an expert in labour protection, said that one reason for this situation was the deficiencies in employment law. Current Chinese employment legislation includes some anti-employment discrimination articles scattered within such areas as the Labour Law, the Law on Protection of Women's Rights and Interests and the Law on Protection of Disabled Persons. The major problem of these laws is that they are too 'general' and insufficient to correct employment discrimination.[35]

There was another case that instigated great discussion over why discrimination remains prevalent even though the law forbids it. Xiao Wang, who has a leg disability, was due to graduate from the Nanjing Auditing Institute, and planned to attend a job interview. However, when he got into the car which collected the recruitees, he was informed: 'The Company is greatly concerned with its image' and was asked to get out. The recruiters' explanation was that when they saw him, they immediately knew he would not be successful in the interview, so they did not waste Xiao Wang's energy and emotions. Some commentators online maintain that Xiao Wang was forced to get out of the car because he was disabled. This is a very extreme case of discrimination, clearly in violation of the rights of disabled people.[36]

---

[34] This information was obtained by the author when conducting field study at the Disabled Person's Federation in Qinghai in 2005.
[35] 'A Disabled PhD Student was Refused Several Times', http://big5.xinhuanet.com/gate/big5/news.xinhuanet.com/newscenter/2005-09/05/ content_ 3443667.htm. Last visited August 2008.
[36] 'Who Should be Responsible for Discrimination against Disabled People', http://news.xinhuanet.com/ comments/2005-05/14/content_2953506.htm. Last visited August 2008.

Although the Law on Protection of Disabled Persons formally forbids disability discrimination in recruitment, in reality it is usually practised by recruiters. Although there will be no explicit written rules disqualifying disabled people, recruiters in many companies will find a whole host of reasons not to hire a disabled person capable for the job or provide them with any opportunities. Facing this kind of public discriminatory behaviour, disabled people found it hard to take legal measures to protect their own employment rights. Although the root of corporate disability discrimination lies in society itself, one important reason is still the deficiencies in current laws that protect disabled people.

3.1 China's Legislation Protecting Disabled People's Equal Rights and Prohibiting Disability Discrimination in Employment is Too Generalised

According to the Constitution, all citizens of the People's Republic of China have labour rights and obligations, and to work is the honour and responsibility of all able citizens.[37] However, the Constitution contains no provision prohibiting disability discrimination or upholding equal employment rights of citizens.

China's 1994 Labour Law stipulates that 'labourers shall not be discriminated against in employment on grounds of their ethnic group, race, gender and religious beliefs'; workers must enjoy equal employment rights and the right to choose their own careers. However, the Labour Law only protects employees in established employment relations, i.e. the Law only pertains to employees and employers. There are no provisions that protect job applicants. The Labour Law also rules that men and women enjoy equal rights in employment. When recruiting, unless the state has ruled the work to be unsuitable for women, employers cannot refuse to employ women on account of their gender, or attach extra conditions to their employment. But there are no clear provisions prohibiting disability discrimination as such, only regarding the employment of disabled people, ethnic minority workers, and demobilized soldiers, where special laws and regulations should be followed.[38]

The Law on Protection of Disabled Persons is the most specific law prohibiting disability discrimination. This Law not only provides that the state protects the labour rights of disabled people and that governments at various levels have the responsibility to plan for employment of and the creation of employment conditions for disabled workers, it also provides that there must be no discrimination against disabled people in recruiting, hiring, promotion, evaluation of title, salary and welfare benefit. Enterprises or institutions should not deny graduates assigned by the state from higher education institutes, polytechnics and specialized technical colleges on the ground of their disabilities. Those who do so will be dealt with by the relevant state department,

---

[37] Arts. 42 (1) and 42 (3) of the Constitution.
[38] Arts. 12, 13 and 14 of the Labour Law.

which must ensure that the work unit does accept the person in question. All the work units that employ disabled workers are required to provide suitable labour conditions and labour protection.[39] However, this Law remains too general since there is no clear definition of disability discrimination; no specification of what kind of behaviour constitutes such discrimination. Furthermore, there are no provisions to establish standards of conduct to define the legal responsibility of those who behave in a discriminatory manner, nor for the provision of legal remedies for victims. Therefore, although the Law has been promulgated for more than a decade, there has not been one case of a disabled person bringing a lawsuit against disability discrimination prohibited under the Law.

The Law on Vocational Education stipulates that in order to provide disabled people with vocational education and facilities, every such institute and other educational organisation must admit disabled students according to national law.[40] The 1994 Regulations for the Education of Disabled Persons state that governments at various levels must incorporate the education of disabled workers into their general plans for vocational and educational development, set up a system for disabled employees' vocational education, and implement that system with plans.[41] General vocational education institutes and training organisations must admit qualified disabled students.[42] However, none of the provisions make them legally responsible, and there are no remedial measures for the disabled student who has been refused admission.

In February 2007, the State Council passed the Disability Employment Regulation. This reiterated general provisions prohibiting disability discrimination in employment, and required recruiters to provide a labour environment and labour protection suitable to the physical conditions of disabled workers. Disability discrimination in recruitment was also prohibited. However, the Regulation made no real breakthrough in anti-disability discrimination, as it failed to lay down a system that would make the 'discriminator' legally responsible, or provide legal aid for victims of discrimination.

3.2 Preferential Treatment for Disabled People in Employment Needs to Be Taken a Step Further

China's policies for protecting and encouraging disabled people into employment include national laws, administrative regulations, local regulations and departmental rules.

For example, the Constitution stipulates that 'State and society support blind, deaf, mute and other disabled citizens in work, life and education'.[43] According

---

[39] Arts. 27, 34 and 35 of the Law on Protection of Disabled Persons.
[40] Art. 15 of the Law on Vocational Education.
[41] Art. 23 of the Regulations for the Education of Disabled Persons.
[42] *Ibid*, Art. 26.
[43] Art. 45 (3) of the Constitution.

to the Labour Law, employers cannot cancel the labour contracts of workers who contract a work-related illness, or are injured in accidents at work.[44]

The main piece of legislation is the Law on Protection of Disabled Persons which stipulates measures to encourage and protect disabled people in employment. It includes guidelines that set down preferential measures covering four aspects. (1) The state and society must actively develop disabled people's employment, such as by setting up welfare enterprises, therapeutic massage centres and other enterprises and institutions of welfare nature as a way of providing concentrative employment for disabled persons.[45] Local government and related departments must confirm certain products suitable to be made by disabled people, and assign them to be produced by welfare enterprises. The state offers tax exemption policies or reduced rates for disabled people's social welfare enterprises and provides support for their products, businesses, technology, funds, goods and materials and work spaces.[46] (2) To implement policies regulating the proportion of disabled people in employment and to encourage work units to admit disabled people, under the guidance of government departments. Public sectors, enterprises, urban and rural collectives must set aside a certain quota of jobs for disabled people, decided by the local government according to local circumstances, and provide disabled people with a suitable choice of employment.[47] (3) The state should encourage disabled people to become self-employed or set up their own enterprises.[48] Tax reductions and support are provided for individual rural and urban disabled workers. Precedence must be given to disabled people when issuing business permits. (4) For disabled people in rural areas engaged in all kinds of production labour, the Law requires the relevant government departments to provide such assistance as technical guidance, agricultural materials, and the purchasing of farm products.[49] It is quite obvious that these proposed provisions are too general, impractical and unquantifiable to be effectively implemented.

The state also encourages the development of career training for disabled people. For example, the Law on Vocational Education insists on the adoption of measures to 'support the development of disabled people's vocational education', and states that 'vocational colleges and vocational training centres can charge suitable fees for students receiving secondary level vocational education and training, but must exempt students and disabled students with economic difficulties'.[50] However, the regulations do not specify what special exemptions these students could enjoy or the methods through which disputes could be resolved.

---

[44] Art. 29 of the Labour Law.
[45] Art. 29 of the Law on Protection of Disabled Persons.
[46] *Ibid*, Art. 33.
[47] *Ibid*, Art. 30.
[48] *Ibid*. Art. 31.
[49] *Ibid*, Art. 33.
[50] Arts. 7 and 32 of the Law on Vocational Education.

In light of the above laws and regulations, relevant government departments have issued a series of policy documents which contain some detailed measures to protect and encourage disabled people's employment.

(1) Quota System for the Employment of Disabled People

In order to promote the quota system, in May 1995 the China Disabled Persons' Federation issued Opinions to Increase the Quota of Disabled People in Employment. According to the Opinions, every work unit, whether a government institution, public institution, state-owned or private enterprise, township enterprise, joint-venture or foreign-owned company, must honour national laws, and either fulfil the quota or pay into the disability employment protection fund. It was suggested that the quota of disabled people in employment in each locality should be between 1.5% and 2%. Work units that paid into the disability protection fund because they failed to meet the quota were required to draw up plans for the future recruitment of disabled workers including the number of disabled people to be hired in the next fiscal year, the type of jobs that would be made available and the technical standards required of the disabled person. The Opinions suggested that the quota should include disabled people capable of work and of a legal working age. The mentally disabled would not necessarily be included, but every work unit which did employ such people could include them as part of their quota. Injured soldiers are also recognised as disabled people. People with work-related injuries or illnesses that lead to disabilities, as defined by the Ministry of Labour, the Ministry of Public Health and the All China Federation of Trade Unions, and correspond with the criteria of the 1987 State Council survey, are also counted in the quota. It was proposed that the quota should be calculated from the number of total active staff employed by a work unit (including formal workers, contract workers, and the part-time contract workers used in that year). Employing a blind person, or someone with a severe physical disability, counts as employing two disabled people. For those work units which invest in welfare enterprises, the disabled people they employ are counted when calculating their quota.

In 1999, in order to implement the quota system, the State Council issued the Circular on Proposals to Further the Employment of Disabled People made by the Ministry of Labour and Social Security, State Planning Committee, Ministry of Civil Affairs, Ministry of Finance, Ministry of Personnel, State Tax Bureau, National Bureau of Industry and Commerce, and China's Disabled Persons' Federation. The Circular first required every local government and relevant department to focus on the quota system in their efforts to employ disabled people. All cities or prefectures that failed to reach their target quota had to draw up measures within the period of the 9th Five Year Plan to ensure their implementation of the quota system. Secondly, it required government institutions and other organisations to follow laws and regulations to ensure quotas were met. If quotas were not met, the organisations had to make payments into the disability employment protection fund. Thirdly, it required recruiters to sign labour contracts with disabled employees, carry out the necessary recruitment procedures, and arrange suitable work placements. Fourthly, it was to encourage every work unit to employ more disabled people, and provide spiritual or material reward for work units that exceeded quotas while at the same time criticising, educating and compelling those who did not comply to rectify the situation.

Since then, every region has launched this quota system through legal channels. Every province, autonomous region and municipality has laid down standard quotas and the lowest number of disabled people recruiters can employ, as well as making it clear that if quotas are not met, disability employment protection fund payments must be made. The national implementation of this quota system has already produced visible results, and has become an important channel through which disabled people find employment. Under the efforts of central and local government, the proportion of disabled people in employment has continued to increase. For example, Changzhou is the leading city in the employment of disabled people. By the end of 2004, the city area had 3334 work units which employed disabled people and signed labour contracts and arranged social insurance for them. More than 15,000 work units applied to pay into the disability employment protection fund. 327 work units employed more disabled employees than the required quota. Throughout the city there were 6900 disabled workers employed under the quota system. Urban areas had an employment rate of 92.5% for disabled people capable of working.[51] In 2004, Xinhua district in Shijiazhuang city helped 124 disabled workers find work through a proportional employment policy and 108 laid-off disabled workers managed to find new jobs. In 2004, Korla city in Xinjiang had the work unit with the highest proportion of disabled employees in autonomous areas. In one year, it increased its number of disabled people by 41, including 10 people through the quota, 20 people through collective employment and 12 through self-employment.[52]

Many regions use a portion of the disability employment protection fund to reward work units that have exceeded quotas. For example, Penglai city in Yantai drew up the Temporary Measures for the Support of Disabled People's Employment, and launched a campaign that gave work units with a sufficient proportion of disabled employees a one-off prize of RMB 5,000. For work units whose proportion of disabled employees has exceeded the quota required, a reward of RMB 5,000 is given for every extra person. The prize money was in turn used to develop posts, training and services for disabled employees. The city's Disabled Persons' Federation also provided a fund of RMB 1,000 to 5,000 to support those who helped the urban unemployed and rural impoverished disabled people to engage in individual business.[53] Work units that fail to meet

---

[51] http://www.czcl.org.cn/news/xwlm/ggl/20040413150351.htm. Last visited August 2008.
[52] http://www.cdpf.org.cn/jiuy/node_50232.htm. Last visited August 2008.
[53] http://ytcl.yantai.gov.cn/zcfg/index2_show.jsp?id=17803. Last visited December 2008.

these regulations face punitive measures and must pay into the disability employment protection fund. Currently, disability employment protection funds are overseen by the Finance Department or Tax Services, and in a few places are paid to the Disability Federation or Labour Department. This disability employment protection fund is in turn used as a special government fund to help disabled people find employment, including vocational training and career services.[54]

However, there are still many difficulties in carrying out the quota system. Although these regulations were drawn up more than a decade ago, it has been very difficult to implement them nationwide. A great number of work units prefer to pay into the disability employment protection fund, rather than employ disabled people. At present, the majority of disabled people are forced to become self-employed or find employment in social welfare enterprises, rather than participate in the mainstream labour market. By the end of the 9th Five Year Plan (1995-2000), there were 3.313 million urban disabled people in employment. 961,000 were collectively employed, 970,000 people were employed through the quota system, 1.38 million were self-employed, and the number of self-employed and collectively employed was 2.4 times more than those employed through the quota system.[55] The number of those employed through the quota system has increased, but this increase is minimal. The majority of disabled cadres or workers had become disabled after joining the work unit, rather than before they entered.

The quota system is a traditional welfare measure, based on the logic that it is very difficult for disabled people to compete with non-disabled people. It was put in place after the Second World War. Numerous countries set up this kind of system, each with their own different quotas. The policy is more effective at integrating disabled and non-disabled people and raising the capabilities of disabled people, than the centralised deployment of disabled people or encouraging them to set up their own enterprises. The quota system has been effectively implemented in some countries, while not in others. The difficulty lies in the fact that although it is the obligation of the employers to employ disabled people, such obligations cannot be mandatorily enforced. Some countries now adopt motivational measures, giving rewards and compensation to companies that comply. China should increase the legal responsibility of employers, and payments into disability employment protection funds, while at the same time continuing to search for more motivational measures to increase the benefits of the system.

---

[54] Art. 16 of the Disability Employment Regulations.
[55] 'Statistical Report on the Circumstances of the General Implementation of China's Disability Facilities during the 9th Five Year Plan', http://www.cdpf.org.cn/sytj/content/2007-11/27/content_77375.htm. Last visited August 2008.

(2) Running Welfare Enterprises and Collectively Employing Disabled People

From the 1950s, China started running welfare enterprises which have employed large numbers of disabled people, and such enterprises have been offered tax exemptions and preferential policies.[56]

In 1989 the Ministry of Civil Affairs issued the Temporary Measures for Social Welfare Enterprises Employing Disabled People. Social welfare enterprises employ men from 16 to 45 and women from 16 to 40 who are blind, deaf, mute, physically disabled, mentally disabled or with learning difficulties. Mentally disabled people with a doctor's certificate proving them able to work can be employed in a special department, for example, a rehabilitation workshop in a mental institution. However, the Temporary Measures only apply to state-owned or collectively-owned social welfare enterprises. Private, foreign-owned, joint-ventures and joint-stock companies are not eligible for preferential policies even if they employ disabled people.

To encourage welfare enterprises to employ disabled people, the State Tax Bureau issued the Circular on Collection of Business Taxes for Civil Welfare Enterprises that was implemented on 1 January 1994. On the collection of value added tax (VAT), consumption tax and business tax for civil welfare enterprises, it stipulates: (1) Civil welfare enterprises in which people with the 'four disabilities' (blind, deaf, dumb and physically disabled) make up 50% or more of staff (except under the three conditions listed on this Circular) can receive VAT rebates, after being audited by the revenue office. Civil welfare enterprises must apply for this tax rebate within 10 days of every tax period and include all their tax receipts and 'income refund notices' filled in by the county auditing office, before the duly paid taxes can be fully returned. (2) Civil welfare enterprises in which people with the 'four disabilities' make up more than 35% of staff but less than 50% (except under the three conditions listed on this Circular), can receive a partial or full rebate on their VAT if the enterprise suffers losses. Enterprises must first pay their taxes, and then at the end of the year, they can apply to the local tax administration office and will receive a rebate following approval from their county office. (3) Civil welfare enterprises in which 35% of the staff are people with the 'four disabilities' and whose businesses are within the business tax 'service industries' target, (apart from advertising companies) are all exempt from business tax.

Blind people find it even harder than other disabled people to find suitable careers and jobs. After years of searching and experimentation, China has developed massage training for blind people, and has set up blind people's organizations helping blind people to find new employment. The government encourages hotels, spas, health centres, beauty salons and similar places where provide massage services to give precedence to blind masseurs with the technical

---

[56] Xiang Zicheng, *supra* note 4, pp. 250-251.

skills and particularly those with professional certification. During the 10th Five Year Plan (2001-2005), 1451 medical massage centres and 625 therapeutic massage centres were set up nationwide, and almost 60,000 blind people took part in therapeutic and medical massage training.[57]

However, at present there is a systemic problem with welfare enterprises that adversely affects their social function. The government's preferential policies towards these enterprises do not suit the needs of the market economy. The State Tax Bureau, in its Circular on Collection of Business Taxes for Civil Welfare Enterprises, restricted preferential policies to civil welfare enterprises. A civil welfare enterprise, to be designated as such, must fulfil these two conditions: (1) It must have been set up by the civil affairs department, street committee or township government before 1 January 1994. Foreign invested enterprises are excluded. If it is a civil welfare enterprise established after 1 January 1994, it must have undergone rigorous examination and obtained the approval of the provincial civil government and tax administrations before receiving tax exemption. (2) It must employ over 35% of staff with the 'four disabilities'.

There are two major problems with these preferential policies. Firstly, they are not applicable to new types of enterprises resulting from enterprise reform. In recent years, investment methods have grown increasingly pluralistic: state-run enterprises have been reformed, government and commercial management functions have been separated, private businesses have invested in the former state-owned welfare enterprises and more and more private funds hope to open welfare enterprises. Therefore, there are now fewer welfare enterprises owned by civil affairs departments, street committees or township governments. Currently, government-run welfare organisations are the main beneficiaries of preferential government policies, while other kinds of enterprises do not benefit, no matter how high a proportion of disabled people they employ. This reduces some enterprises' motivation to employ disabled people. Secondly, the conditions laid down by the State Tax Bureau restrict the range of disabled people's enterprises that can benefit from government policies, and conflict with the regulations laid down by the Ministry of Civil Affairs. Mentally disabled people with learning disabilities are excluded; this means that enterprises employing the mentally disabled will not benefit from preferential policies, which adversely affects employment for the mentally disabled. Moreover, there is no regulatory body to control welfare enterprises.

In addition, some work units claim to employ disabled people in order to qualify for tax exemption, but do not actually let them work, since the benefits of tax exemption exceed the costs of keeping them on. This kind of 'business

---

[57] Statistics on the Implementation of the Tenth Five year Plan of China's Disabled People's Work, http://www.cdpf.org.cn/sytj/content/2007-12/02/content_77887.htm. Last visited December 2008.

deal'[58] drains away state taxes, violates government policy towards disabled people and is detrimental to disability employment.

(3) Encouraging Disabled People to Set Up Their Own Businesses

In September 1999, the Ministry of Finance, Ministry of Labour and Social Securities, National Bureau of Industry and Commerce and China Disabled Persons' Federation issued the Circular for Actively Supporting Disabled People, Individuals or Volunteer Groups in Starting up Individual Businesses, which ordered the National Bureau of Industry and Commerce to give priority to disabled individuals or volunteer groups who are starting up a business, during registration and other formal procedures. When disabled people apply for an individual business licence, or permit to start their own business, with the disabled people's certificate and the certificate provided by the local Disability Federation proving the type and severity of the disability, and the personal or family economic circumstances, the National Bureau of Industry and Commerce should carefully consider reducing the individual business licence registration costs and management fees.

Regulations for the Employment of Disabled People stipulate that the nation must encourage and support disabled people in choosing their own career, and setting up their own business. Disabled people who engage in individual businesses must receive preferential tax treatment according to law, and relevant departments must take care of such aspects as finding workplaces, managing tax exemptions, registering, licences and other business fees. Furthermore the state should provide small loans to support disabled people to set up their own businesses.

A great number of places have given priority to disabled people for jobs that disabled people are able to carry out, such as cleaning, protecting green areas, parking management, real estate, repair, housekeeping and recycling, logistics distribution, working at breakfast stalls, newspaper stands and vegetable stalls.

The implementation of the preferential policies described above has resulted in a relatively high number of self-employed among those employed disabled people. However, there are some regions where these preferential policies have not been successfully carried out. As far as disabled people are concerned, self-employment gives them flexibility, but no stability or security.

(4) Setting Up Non-profit Positions for Disabled People

In 2005, the Ministry of Civil Affairs, the Ministry of Education, the Ministry of Public Security, the Ministry of Justice, the Ministry of Labour and Social Security, the Ministry of Construction, the Ministry of Culture, the Ministry of

---

[58] Zhang Fan, 'Welfare Enterprises in Shanxi Have Difficulties in Surviving due to Policies', http://theory.people.com.cn/GB/41038/3941889.html. Last visited August 2008.

Public Health, the State Bureau of Sport, the All China Federation of Trade Unions, the Communist Youth League and the China Disabled Persons' Federation jointly issued the Proposal to Strengthen Disabled People's Work within the Community, stating that community disability groups must be set up with the support of community neighbourhood committees, referred to as 'Community Disability Association'. It is chaired by a member of the community neighbourhood committee, and the deputy head is an outstanding disabled person or a close friend or relative of a disabled person in the community. The major role of a Community Disability Association is to work with the community neighbourhood committee to support the work of disabled people. It works closely with disabled people, represents their interests, listens to their opinions and protects their legal rights. The association advocates a spirit of 'respect, confidence, self-improvement and independence', offers solidarity, promotes education as a way of facilitating disabled people to participate in all areas of social life and makes a great contribution to modern socialism. After this document was published, a large number of disabled people everywhere have been employed by the Community Disability Associations.

The Regulations for the Employment of Disabled People issued in 2007 stipulate that local governments at a county level and above must adopt suitable measures to expand the channels through which disabled people find employment and open up public not-for-profit posts for disabled people (Article 15).

In recent years, since the disability employment protection fund has been implemented with direct collection by tax bureaus, the amount of disability employment protection funds levied has increased dramatically. In some areas, finance departments allow disability employment protection funds to be used to set up posts for disabled people, such as special positions or liaison officer posts within the Community Disability Associations. This kind of work is still in its initial stages and further research is required into how to set up more not-for-profit posts for disabled people. It is also necessary to create a more integrated approach between different localities, using legal standards and regulations.

(5) Developing Vocational Training and Careers Services for Disabled People

Various disability regulations require disability federations to make great efforts to develop training schemes and careers services for disabled workers. The Outline of China's Development for Disabled People during the 11th Five Year Plan (2006-2010) proposed that careers services for disabled people must help disabled people set up individual businesses, and provide training and careers guidance. During this Plan, 50,000 blind people will be trained in massage, 10,000 as medical masseurs and 40,000 as therapeutic masseurs. From 2001 to 2005, 2.58 million urban and rural disabled people received vocational education and training. By the end of 2005, there were 3,048 employment services for disabled people: 33 were provincial, 46 prefecture, 648 city, 1,528 county-level, and 793 in districts.[59]

At the same time, disability federations at every level were authorised by the Ministry of Labour and Social Security to launch registration programmes for unemployed disabled people, providing them with information about recruiters, and making employment and re-employment services a reality for disabled people. For example, in order to help disabled graduates find employment, the Beijing Disabled Persons' Federation's careers services run a specialist careers fair for disabled graduates every year on the Support Disability Day. On 14 May 2005, the Beijing Disabled Persons' Federation, the Labour Department, the Personnel Service Centre, the Beijing Union University's Special Education College and other work units came together to launch the 4th Disabled Graduate Recruitment Fair. Recruiters from 36 well-known domestic and multinational companies were present, including IBM China Corporation, Dajin China Investment Company and Wal-Mart, along with 335 disabled job seekers, including more than 60 from outside Beijing. Hiring companies offered 48 types of jobs and 246 posts in financial management, IT, advertising design, and commercial English. 165 disabled people were provisionally offered jobs and 22 people were offered jobs on the spot.[60]

Even though employment training for disabled people has achieved some progress in recent years, there is still a lack of qualified teachers. In addition, the syllabus and skills taught do not satisfy all disabled people's needs, and the scope of training also needs to expand.

(6) Preventing Unemployment of Disabled People and Helping the Disabled Unemployed to Find New Work

In 1998, in the Circular on State Owned Enterprises' Enforcement of Unemployed Workers' Subsistence Pay and Re-employment Work issued by the Chinese Communist Party Central Committee and the State Council, it was stated that the government must do its utmost to prevent the unemployment of model workers, soldiers and disabled people. It required every region to strengthen macro-economic control in order to: avoid disabled workers becoming unemployed; actively help the disabled unemployed to find new employment; strengthen disability employment services; and develop disability vocational training.

In May 1999, the Ministry of Labour and Social Security and the China Disabled Persons' Federation issued the Announcement to implement the above-mentioned Circular. The Announcement required: (1) Adoption and implementation of measures to prevent disabled workers from being laid-off. If an enterprise has to lay-off disabled workers because it goes bankrupt, it must do

---

[59] *Supra* note 57.
[60] http://www.bdpf.org.cn/bjxwzx/index99.htm. Last visited August 2008.

so in accordance with the formalities set down by the government and report the case to the local labour securities department. (2) Giving disabled people who have been laid-off priority when allocating new employment. (3) Increasing policies to expand vigorously the channels through which disabled people can find new employment: all work units which fail to meet the required quota of disabled people in their employment, must give priority to laid-off disabled people when recruiting. (4) Careers services to help and support laid-off disabled people who become self-employed or find employment in a voluntary group, advise them as to their options and provide training and support in applying for business licences, operating businesses, raising funds and tax exemption.

However, the central government Circular is too generally formulated. The Announcement is more comprehensive and detailed, but has little practical impact. There are no supervisory organizations to oversee the implementation of the documents and no regulations specifying how those who fail to comply will be penalised. Therefore, when State-owned enterprises restructure, large numbers of disabled people are laid-off, and, finding new employment is even harder.

(7) Supporting Rural Disabled Employment

The Outline of China's Development for Disabled People during the 11th Five Year Plan aims to provide 10 million rural disabled people with basic food and clothing and help 1 million impoverished disabled people in central and western parts of China who are capable of participating in production work, to receive technical training.

Relying on central government rehabilitation, poverty alleviation loans and local government funds allocated to poverty relief, rural poverty alleviation centres have been set up that focus on planting, raising animals and agricultural processing. This has helped a large number of rural disabled people out of poverty. For instance, Fujian province set up centres to alleviate poverty amongst disabled people by offering micro loans and providing technical training. This has provided employment for 335,500 rural disabled people. By the end of 2005, 135 bases had been opened offering poverty relief to disabled people throughout Fujian. Distributed throughout 63 districts, these centres placed more than 3600 disabled people in employment. The poverty alleviation base in the Jinan district of Fuzhou city – Fuzhou Tongle Ecological and Agricultural Sightseeing Park – provided employment for more than 30 disabled people, growing fruit, ornamental flowers and trees and rearing fish and ducks. Furthermore, the poverty alleviation centre for disabled people in Pucheng county of Fujian produces bamboo handicrafts and employs 46 disabled people.[61]

However, the main problem is that poverty alleviation loans and funds are operated by commercial banks with commercial incentives. As a result, disabled

---

[61] http://www.1203.org/ShowClass.asp?ClassID=2. Last visited August 2008.

people who are in urgent need of financial support cannot get hold of these loans quickly enough and therefore the majority of the poverty alleviation loans are not being taken up.

4. DISCRIMINATORY REGULATIONS AGAINST DISABLED PEOPLE STILL EXISTS IN CHINA

Before the General Standards on Physical Examinations Relating to the Employment of Civil Servants (Trial Implementation) became effective in 2005, almost all disabled people failed to meet the conditions to take civil servant exams, or failed the physical exam. In 1993, the State Council issued the Temporary Regulations for Civil Servants without specifying any physical conditions for employment. However, the Provisional Rules on Recruitment of Civil Servants issued by the Ministry of Personnel in 1994, prescribed 'physical health' requirements as a qualification for the civil servants exams.[62] Traditionally, disabled people have been considered as 'unhealthy' and therefore those with physical difficulties were disqualified. The Regulations gave authority to local departments to decide who to recruit, according to the job requirements and the applicants' written and physical examination results.[63] According to this document, some departments under the central and local governments set up their own physical exam standards. Most of the standards required that candidates who pass the exam must 'not be disabled' or, if this was not specifically stated, disabled people could not pass the physical test in any event. In this way, the vast majority of disabled people could not pass the civil servant exam.

The 2002 announcement in the national civil servant exam in the field of customs stipulated that successful applicants must be 'physically healthy, having regular features and no psychological deficiencies'. As another example, the Ministry of Public Security's Methods for Recruitment of Public Security Police clearly stipulate that, besides fulfilling the basic conditions required by the national civil servant exams and the Police Law, successful applicants must also be 'physically healthy, of regular build, with no disabilities, stammers, hearing impediments, colour blindness, and with a vision strength of above 1.0. Men must be taller than 1.7 metres and women over 1.6 metres'. The Ministry of Justice issued Standards and Items for the Physical Exam for the Recruitment of Prison and Labour Re-education Police by judicial administrative bodies. Although there are no specific provisions stipulating that disabled people are disqualified, there are many restrictions imposed on them. According to these standards, many physically disabled people and those who are not even officially physically disabled, for example those with arthritis, an incurable spinal

---

[62] Art. 14 (1) of the Provisional Rules on Recruitment of Civil Servants.
[63] *Ibid*, Art. 27.

deformity, a hunchback, or someone whose legs are uneven with a difference exceeding 2cm, or those with another abnormality affecting their abilities and exterior appearances, or those who are flat-footed, or not tall enough, cannot be recruited.

The standards of local governments' personnel departments in different areas are more or less the same – all disqualify a large proportion of physically disabled or unhealthy people and ignore the particular physical requirements of a job.

In addition, out of all types of exams for specialised qualifications, blind people can only take part in psychological counselling, therapeutic massage or piano tuning. As for other disabled people, there are many barriers to passing qualification exams or physical tests. For instance, qualifications for teaching posts contain discriminatory conditions. In 1995, the State Council issued Regulations for Teachers Qualification. The conditions for awarding teaching qualifications rely on the execution of Article 10 (2) of the Teachers Law, which rules that 'those who have the ability to provide educational instruction' must accord with the physical conditions of the State regulations.[64] To approve applications for teaching qualifications, apart from the application form, the proof of teaching qualifications, the proof of identity and the education certificate or teaching qualifications certificate, a medical certificate is also required from the education bureau or a hospital appointed by the higher education institution.[65] In September 2000, the Ministry of Education issued Methods for the Implementation of Regulations for Teachers Qualification, which stipulates that those applying to be approved as teachers are required to be in good physical and mental health, and free from infectious disease, or a history of mental illness. In order to be considered suitable for work in educational institutes, applicants would have to pass a physical test in hospitals designated by the relevant institution.[66]

Most provinces have made standards for physical tests required to be passed by those who wish to qualify as teachers. These standards clearly exclude the majority of disabled people from entering the profession. Even many disabled people who had already been teachers for many years could not get the teachers' qualification.

---

[64] Art. 6 of the Regulations for Teachers Qualification.
[65] *Ibid*, Art. 15.
[66] Art. 8 of the Methods for the Implementation of the Regulations for Teachers Qualification.

5. PROPOSALS FOR ELIMINATION OF DISABILITY DISCRIMINATION IN EMPLOYMENT

If we want to eliminate employment discrimination against disabled people, we must first provide an effective legal system that counters discrimination. This includes enacting national law that clearly prohibits disability employment discrimination. Such law must also contain sufficient provisions against those suspected of disability discrimination. Furthermore, a preferential employment system should be established for all disabled people to encourage their employment. Lastly, disability discrimination should be eradicated in other areas, for example in education.

The eradication of traditional prejudices and concepts of discrimination against disabled people is also of the utmost importance. Discrimination and prejudice against disabled people traditionally came in many guises. Although the 1978 Election Law and the Chinese Constitution used the term 'disability' as early as in 1982, in reality, it was not until the promulgation of the Law on Protection of Disabled Persons in 1990 that the terms 'disability' and 'disabled people' gradually gained widespread usage in society following from the mass propaganda. Throughout China's history, disabled people have been referred to as 'deformed' or 'crippled'. The 1976 UN Resolution declared 1981 'International Disability Year' and the Chinese Postal Service issued a commemorative stamp, with the words 'international cripple year' printed on it. Nowadays, some of the public and media still commonly refer to the disabled as 'cripples'. Even the Criminal Code, General Principles of Civil Law, Conscription Law, Product Quality Law and other legal documents use the term 'cripple'. The term implies an injured person, deformed to the point of being useless. How can useless people talk of being employed?

A huge number of people have a prejudiced view of disabled people's working abilities. For many, disabled people are suitable only for running a stall, hairdressing, bicycle repair, selling newspapers, or maybe some relatively light physical labour. Many people doubt both their working abilities and mental capacities, believing they are unable to manage their own lives, or carry out work effectively. Although the Beijing metro has fixed up Braille signs, some carriages still do not have electronic display devices or voice announcements. 'Passenger instructions' still clearly decree that blind, deaf or mentally disabled passengers must be accompanied. This is a display of a lack of confidence in disabled people's ability to control their own lives. If this ability is doubted they certainly will not believe disabled people are capable of working. Work units generally do not fully understand or recognise disabled people's abilities and value, especially those of the deaf, mildly mentally handicapped, and blind people, and therefore active recruitment of these people is low. While there has been rapid economic development, disabled people as a group have faced increasing unemployment. Government policies and laws have been drawn up, but the actual benefits for disabled people have been minimal. Society has progressed, but the discrimination still exists.[67]

There are also some work units that refuse to employ disabled people because they think this will damage their image and they prefer to pay into the disabled employment protection fund. This is particularly true among state organisations, such as courts, foreign-related institutions and schools which all reject disabled people to protect their own image, or even the national image. Some people equate disabled people with low quality, and this affects a company's reputation. At a conference in which the author took part, an official in the highest judicial body with a master's degree gave a speech voicing his opposition to the quota system for employing disabled people. He believed that this could not be adhered to by courts, because it damaged the image of judges and the sanctity of the law. In another case a nationally renowned provincial organisation offering legal services had a relatively liberal thinker in charge, but he refused to employ disabled people because he was worried that social prejudice would have a detrimental effect on the credibility and professional image of his organisation. The man in charge of one provincial tax organisation said that when he was employing civil servants, he interviewed a graduate who was blind in one eye, but he did not discover this until it was too late. He admitted that if he had discovered the disability earlier, he would definitely have found an excuse not to employ the person.

Some think that disabled people will have a negative effect wherever they go. When governmental officials are visiting a city or local governments are organizing general cleaning in the cities, disabled people are often prohibited from doing business so as not to affect detrimentally the image of the town or city. For example, in 2003, a city in one province going through a 'clean-up', removed the business licence of a disabled person in the market, because he was thought to affect the market's image negatively.[68]

---

[67] Zhou Yunjing and Zhang Xue, 'System and Construction of Disability Protection and Social Harmony', (issue 10, 2006) *Zhongguo canjiren*, p. 34.

[68] Another example of this, in 2004, was when a city in a Western province was smartening itself up and it revoked the business licence of a demobilized disabled soldier who legally ran a stall by the roadside, because he was negatively affecting the city's image. The authorities said that if this disabled person was seen selling on the roadside again, the city surveillance team would 'turn a blind eye', but that the disabled person must work with the city surveillance team in enforcing the law. However, subsequently when the city surveillance team came to clear up illegal pedlars on the roadside, healthy pedlars fled one-by-one, leaving only the man who had a leg disability and who was unable to run. Members of the city surveillance team rushed up at once, and violently beat him. At the time the crowd told the members of the city surveillance team that he was a disabled soldier and that they could not beat him, but they paid no attention. Consequently, this was discovered by a Xinhua journalist, and has been investigated and written up many times, attracting the attention of central government. The city surveillance team members who beat the man up were punished.

Many people believe that dealing with disabled people is unlucky and therefore are not willing to do so; some think that people have become disabled through some fault of their own or their family and therefore they must be responsible for the consequences. Some people even believe that people are disabled as a retribution for some sin committed in a previous generation, and so are unsympathetic.

These traditional discriminatory views and prejudices towards disabled people urgently need to be rectified. In the first place, humanitarian values must be promoted throughout society. Valuing social and individual diversity will give rise to a greater respect and understanding of disabled people, and a civilised spirit of compassion towards them. Social awareness must be raised and greater respect should be given to the dignity and human rights of disabled people, in every aspect of life. Prejudice against disabled people must be eradicated and a greater recognition must be given to disabled people's skills and contributions. Secondly, the wilful discrimination of companies and individuals against disabled people must be exposed and legal action must be taken. It must be ensured that there is public awareness that disability discrimination is wrong, illegal and encroaches on disabled people's individual rights. Thirdly, employment for disabled people must be widely promulgated, along with the achievements and independent strengths of disabled people, so that society can recognise their ability to work, discriminatory attitudes towards disabled people in employment can be eliminated, and the value of disabled people will be fully acknowledged.

Needless to say, the government must set a good example. The main responsibility for the quota system for employment for disabled people, as written in the Law on Protection of Disabled Persons, falls upon 'institutions'. However, whether central or local, the majority of party, government and judicial bodies have failed to employ the specified quota of disabled people, or to pay the stipulated amount into disability employment protection funds. The responsibility for the quota system for employing disabled people is shared by the whole of society. Some aspects of the Law on Protection of Disabled Persons contain clear instructions on how party and government organizations must implement the quota system. Some internet research has been carried out on local state institutions' implementation of the quota system, but as yet, no one has discovered the specific required quota of disabled people employed at each level of party and government organizations. News reports have revealed that many local government and party organizations neither employ any disabled people nor make payments into the disability employment protection fund. Disabled peoples' employment conditions reflect the social care for disabled people. The degree of respect for and recognition of disabled people's abilities is a good way to measure a country's level of democracy, civilisation, rule of law and modernity. If party and political organizations cannot set an example and implement these legal regulations, why should other work units place importance on employment for disabled people?

Government institutions should honour the law and set an example for its enforcement. If the government does not comply with legal regulations, how can it supervise the implementation of these legal regulations by other organizations and work units? Government departments must abandon the prejudiced view that 'disabled civil servants affect the government's image', and display more humanity in recruiting civil servants, open their doors wide and give priority to a disabled person if he or she has the same quality as a non-disabled person. In China, the government has a strong role in setting an example. If the government takes the lead in eliminating disability discrimination, many enterprises and public institutions will in turn emulate this. Every local government department must draw up a plan to implement effectively the quota system of employing disabled people as quickly as possible, while actively promoting and earnestly supervising the work of enterprises and public institutions.

In the wake of the construction of socialism and a harmonious society, the creation of a strong and comprehensive legal system, and the emergence of civilized society, as the spirit of humanitarianism seeps deeper into the hearts of the people, China will continue its work to eradicate disability discrimination in employment, and thus fundamentally improve the employment conditions of disabled people.

4

A STUDY OF CURRENT EMPLOYMENT DISCRIMINATION AGAINST WOMEN

Wang Xinyu

1. INTRODUCTION

In the wake of China's rapid economic development and social transformation, employment competition has intensified. The saturated employment market has become a breeding ground for different kinds of employment discrimination. Employment discrimination against women has become a particularly serious issue.

A bizarre kind of phenomenon exists in China's employment market today: it is preferable to recruit men, while women are the first to be laid off. Men are given priority for the important positions in society, while in the home the majority of the housework is left to women. Even women who have received a higher education find it hard to escape this predicament. Central China Television's *Time for the East*, in collaboration with Zhaopin.com − China's specialist recruitment website − conducted a large-scale survey of graduate recruitment in 2006. The survey revealed that 74% of those looking for work faced employment discrimination. Out of the 111 companies that took part in the survey, 51% admitted that they had at some time refused an applicant on account of his or her sex, age, appearance. 75% of companies that discriminated in the recruitment process did not tell the applicant the real reason for the rejection.[1]

Although in the last ten years the number of Chinese female employees has risen, gender disparity and segregation within employment have intensified. According to a survey in 2000 on the social position of Chinese women, although there has been a drop in employment rates since 1990 among men and women alike from an urban background, the number of women in employment has fallen by a greater degree than the number of men. Among women aged 18-49 in urban areas, the employment rates have dropped by 16.2%. Women make up 56.2% of the unemployed population, a disproportionately high number when compared with the 37.8% of women that make up the whole urban employed population. 21% fewer women than men are currently re-employed. Women also

---

[1] Xu Zhaosheng, 'One Can't Rely on Identification', *Zhongguo jiaoyubao*, 8 January 2006.

account for 21% less of the current re-employment rate.[2] The '2003 Chinese Labour Statistics Yearbook' showed that, since 1997, the number of urban women in employment has been falling every year, while their proportion of the employed population has also decreased. In 2002 women made up 37.8% of the working population, 24.4% less than men.[3]

The aim of this paper is to both describe the phenomenon of employment discrimination against women in China, and to analyse the reasons that lie behind this situation. At the same time this paper will examine the existing legal framework relating to employment discrimination against women. The paper also proposes feasible solutions to resolve such discrimination.

2. EMPLOYMENT DISCRIMINATION AGAINST WOMEN

In reality, discrimination against women varies in different fields, at different positions, and at different stages of employment. The particularly prominent aspects are as follows.

2.1 Employment Opportunities Are Unequal

Despite statistics clearly demonstrating that in China females make up 44% of students in higher education, and on the whole 'hold up half the sky'[4] in universities, their employment opportunities fall far below those of male students. In 2002, Xiamen University carried out a survey on the employment situation of more than 1,000 recent graduates. The survey revealed that, under the same conditions, female employment opportunities were only 87% of those of men.[5] According to the survey of women's employment issues by the Shanghai Women's Association, women with high academic qualifications find it harder to find employment than their male counterparts with the same qualifications. Women's rate of successful employment is on average 10% lower. Among female university graduates aged 20-29, the rate of successful employment is 14.4% lower than that of me.[6] Female postgraduates, just as female graduates, find themselves treading a difficult path. For females with a doctorate, finding

---

[2] He Dawei and Wang Xinya, 'Various Employment Discrimination: a Lasting Pain for Job-seekers', in http://www.51labour.com/protect/show.asp?id=7310. Last visited December 2008.
[3] Ren Zhengying, 'The Law on Promotion of Employment Needs Gender Awareness', http://www.women.org.cn/allnews/04/170.html. Last visited December 2008.
[4] Mao Zedong's famous statement that 'women hold up half the sky' marked a new recognition of Chinese women's contributions to their society.
[5] Ren Zhengying, *supra* note 3.
[6] Shi Hong, 'Female 'Capital' and Beautiful Women's Economy', http://www.bass.gov.cn/common/bookcontent2.jsp?type=104&id=194. Last visited November 2006.

employment becomes an even greater uphill battle. Recruiters refuse such women on the grounds that, having studied at university for 10 years on top of 12 years of schooling, a female doctoral student must be aged at least 28 or 29, and so will have children very soon after starting work.

It is not just companies that refuse to employ female students on these grounds; the same kind of gender discrimination exists in the civil service and public sector. According to the Survey of Employment Discrimination in Ten Major Cities in China (hereafter the Survey), when asked 'Have you suffered discrimination while applying for a civil servant position?', 32% of those interviewed replied that they suffered gender discrimination.[7] The same Survey revealed that the main disadvantages of women in the workplace are pregnancy (26.4%), maternity leave (24%) and breastfeeding (20.5%).[8]

Discrimination, during and after pregnancy[9] has become a major problem for women seeking work. Some employers prefer to employ men rather than women, and younger rather than older people. When recruiting workers, companies prefer to employ adolescents, and when signing contracts, they prefer to avoid issues such as pregnancy, maternity leave and breastfeeding. It is now understood that many employers recruiting women often demand supplementary conditions, including an agreement that they will not become pregnant within a certain period; this is the latest form of gender discrimination. Some firms even stipulate a five-year period within which women cannot become pregnant; the reason being that women leave work to have and raise children, and this continually affects a firm and increases its costs. Some companies have no explicit regulations, but once a woman has a child, her chances of promotion or a higher salary will be greatly affected. This forces the majority of women to take measures to postpone parenthood.

From businesses to governmental institutions, gender discrimination in employment exists in different degrees. Pregnancy, giving birth and breastfeeding are major causal factors. Apart from this, some traditional sexual prejudices cause employers to refuse women. Procreation is by its nature a social problem, and it is highly unfair that women have to bear the burden of its unfavourable consequences. If many young women put off pregnancy or do not become pregnant from fear that they will face dismissal or demotion, this will affect the balance of family relationships. There have been cases of victims of sexual discrimination committing suicide, violent acts or even murder. This can exacerbate social tensions, and may eventually develop into a grave social

---

[7] 'A Survey of Employment Discrimination in Ten Major Cities in China', B3, in this book.

[8] *Ibid*, F-12.

[9] A woman from Shenyang called Qing Yi (an alias) passed recruitment tests and interviews for a job, but to her surprise the company then asked her and other two female university graduates to undergo a mandatory test to prove that they were not pregnant. Only those who were not pregnant could join the workplace. *Zhongguo funu bao,* 14 December 2006.

issue.[10]

2.2 Retirement Age and Pensions Are Unequal

Men and women retire at different ages. This is both a social and a legal problem for gender discrimination in China. The relevant retirement law dates from 1951, when the central government issued the 'Labour Insurance Regulations' with Art. 15, stipulating, that male workers and female workers should retire at 55 and 50, respectively. In 1958, the State Council issued the 'Interim Regulations for Handling the Retirement Age of Workers and Civil Servants' which provided for female workers to retire at age 50 and female officers (civil servants) to retire at age 55. In 1978, the Standing Committee of the National People's Congress approved the State Council's Regulation to fix the retirement age for male and female workers at 60 and 50 respectively. All subsequent related laws, regulations and documents have followed the principles set by this regulation.

In 2001, the issue of the unequal retirement age of men and women became the focus of a group of female scholars, who believed that this issue was sufficient to constitute gender discrimination.[11] The unequal retirement age has had three major detrimental effects on women.

Firstly, it impairs the right of women to partake equally in the development of society. Under China's current education system, by the time women take up a job after studying at University for a master's degree or even for a doctorate, they are already nearly 30. If they retire at 55, then they do not even have 30 years to contribute to society through work. A women's career is aborted five years earlier than a man's. This means that at any level, women have far fewer opportunities for training, vocational development and promotion than men. Some places limit the age of female cadres to below 40 at a county level, and below 45 at a prefecture level, resulting in a smaller number of women reaching high-level administrative positions. The fact that high-level female cadres of about 50 years old cannot be promoted any further seriously damages their ability to contribute to national and social affairs and directly affects the promotion of senior women. This leads to a great waste of talent. As for other female workers, they are forced to retire at the age of 50, when their work is at

---

[10] 10 female workers at an electricity and water company filed for divorce together at the local court. Some of these women were happily married, and some even newly-weds, so why did they want to divorce their husbands on paper? The company had a regulation that stipulated that only workers with no partner could sign a work contract. In order to obtain the contract, the 10 female workers had no choice but to file for divorce and together protest the 'marriage discrimination'. See Mao Lei, 'Employment Discrimination has Become a Disease in our Harmonious Society and the Power of Law must Prevent it', http://www.chinacourt.org/html/article/200506/ 15/165479.shtml. Last visited August 2008.

[11] 'The Issue of Equal Retirement for Men and Women Rises to the Surface', (14 March 2005), *Laioning ribao*.

its most mature. Economists believe it is a waste of national assets to force women to retire at an age when they can still contribute to society, especially when the state invests so much in their professional development.[12]

Secondly, early retirement damages women's economic interests. Apart from hindering individual development, early retirement for women results in economic inequalities. Pensions are calculated by the amount of years worked and since women join the workforce at the same time as men, but retire 5 years earlier, their pensions are generally lower than men's. As for the pay structure, the present pay structure has adapted to the structural reform, which has made considerable changes compared to a few decades ago. Previous pay structures focused on basic wages and therefore the income disparity between those who were retired or working was not great. However, now pay structures are more complicated and there are many factors influencing income. For example, bonuses and subsidies constitute a large part of wages. Therefore, when one is retired, one's income can be significantly lower. Female university graduates very rarely collect 35 years' worth of wages and if women hold a master's or a doctorate degree, they enjoy even fewer years' worth of wages. Thus the phenomenon of 'the higher the academic qualifications, the shorter the time worked, the smaller the pension' has emerged.

Thirdly, there were difficulties in implementing the policies related to female cadres. In order to solve the issue of unequal retirement ages for men and women, the Ministry of Personnel released a notice specifying that high-level female specialists and cadres at *Chu* level (head of department) could retire at 60. However, this was conditional upon 'the necessity of the work' and an 'internal document, which should not be publicized or advocated', as well as other conditions, and so the policy was difficult to implement.[13] In 2003, 66 members of the National People's Congress (NPC) and the Chinese People's Political Consultative Conference (CPPCC), put forward a motion to amend the issue of unequal retirement ages. In the years since then, the same motion has continually been put forward but has never achieved any results. The outdated legislation in place also seriously affects judicial practice. In 2005, Zhou Xianghua, the deputy chief of the cashier's department at the Pingdingshan branch of the China Construction Bank, brought a labour dispute to arbitration because she did not accept her office's requirement to retire at 55. The Pingdingshan City Labour Dispute Arbitration Committee rejected Zhou Xianghua's appeal. Subsequently, Zhou sued her work unit in court. On 9 December 2005, the case was tried by the Zhanhe district court of Pingdingshan. After hearing both sides of the argument, the collegiate panel delivered the verdict: Zhou lost her case.[14]

---

[12] 'Women Retire Earlier: Discrimination or Special Care?', http://www.ycwb.com/gb/content/2003-01/30/content_486562.htm. Last visited December 2008.
[13] 'The Retirement Age for Men and Women in the Civil Service should be Equal', http://www.chinatalent.com.cn/gjrc4/open/dt03.html. Last visited August 2008.
[14] Niu Zhonghan and Zhang Chunyang, 'The Case of Discrimination on Retirement Age: the First Instance Judgment Rejected the Claim of Zhou Xianghua'.

Since the reform and opening up to the outside world took place, the state of female health and literacy levels in China have improved. In China, the life expectancy for women has reached 73 years, higher than the life expectancy for men. In 2004, the White Paper, 'Current Situation of Sex Equality and Women's Development in China', issued by the State Council, showed that the number of female students in the nation's higher education institutions had reached 6.09 million, amounting to 45.7% of all students; and the percentage of female postgraduates and doctoral students reached 44.2 % and 31.4% respectively. Female cadres accounted for 40% of the cadre ranks. Once the one child policy was put into practice, women's responsibilities at home were reduced. Therefore, women aspired even more to enjoy the same lawful retirement age as men, or at least to be allowed to choose for themselves at what age they retire.[15]

Confronted with the appeal for the equal retirement age, the government was cautious and low-key in dealing with the issue. Article 27 of the 2005 revised Law on Protection of Women's Rights and Interests provides that when implementing the retirement system, work units must not sexually discriminate against women. However, this Article does not constitute a concrete regulation allowing men and women to retire at the same age. In reality, the question of whether men and women can retire at the same age has still not been decided.

On 15 December 2005, the State Council held a press conference. Jiao Kaiping, a senior official at the Ministry of Labour and Social Security, said to the media that the time was not ripe for revising the issue of retirement age. He said that some problems concerning the retirement age exist, such as the fact that the retirement age was too low, the age for men and women was unequal, and the standard retirement age for cadres and workers was not the same. Calls for reform were loud. However, he pointed out that since the Chinese population is huge and so many places are implementing structural readjustment and company reforms, employment conflicts are enormous. Moreover, employment involves the vital interests of every worker and opinions are sharply divided, a strategic decision must be arrived at cautiously. When consensus is reached the matter will be decided.[16]

We cannot deny that the original intention of the disparity in retirement ages for men and women was to take care of women, and was considered a symbol of the protection of women's interests. However, it also cannot be denied that with social development and the continuous improvement of standards of science and technology, and also the continuous improvement of women's culture and conduct, the old regulations have gone from offering protection to becoming a mandatory restriction. In modern society women's horizons are ever expanding,

---

http://news.sina.com.cn/c/2006-02-10/03508166571s.shtml. Last visited December 2008.
[15] Dai Dunfeng, 'Is Early Retirement a Benefit or an Obligation?', *Nanfang zhoumo*, 13 October 2005.
[16] Bai Tianliang, 'Retirement Age will not be Adjusted at Present', http://www.people.com.cn/GB/paper464/16419/1448319.html. Last visited August 2008.

and earlier legislation has now fallen behind. How to rectify this situation through legislation which provides women with a suitable work environment and legal protection, in order to support women's self-development, should become a major task of any new legislation. The data from the 2006 Survey revealed that 37.9% of people thought that women should retire earlier than men, 22.2% thought that men and women should retire at the same age and 18.6% thought women should be able to choose.[17] Thus it can be seen that 40.8% of people believe in an equal retirement age, or that at least women should be able to choose. This exceeds the number of people who think women should retire earlier than men.

If we are protecting women's interests, should we differentiate between retirement ages or give individuals the right to choose? Because there are different work environments and groups of employees, there are different requirements around retirement. Some believe that those who advocate equal retirement ages speak for female cadres and white-collar workers, and that these demands do not reflect those of the majority of female workers. We cannot confirm exactly how many people advocate or speak against equal retirement ages, but there are certainly a growing number of voices opposing an unequal retirement age, even to the point of taking legal action. Thus, taking into account the variety of opinions, the best method is to allow women to choose their own retirement right: a way truly and genuinely to respect and protect women.

Men and women should retire at the same age, and we should allow women to decide for themselves whether they wish to retire 5-10 years earlier than men. Only when individual decisions are respected at every level or in every government department and retiring at the same age is considered normal, does 'equality among men and women' exist in the true sense of the phrase. We should assume that allowing women and men to retire at the same age does not mean rigidly fixing the age of retirement, but takes into consideration both the equal right to retirement for men and women and gives women the flexibility to choose.

2.3 Men and Women Receive Different Pay for the Same Work

According to the Ministry of Labour and Social Securities' 2002 statistics on the average annual salaries in enterprises, the percentage of men and women's salaries in different professions are as shown below.

---

[17] The Survey, *supra* note 7, F7.

Table 1:[18]

Profession	Average wage		Women's average salary as a percentage of men's
	Women	Men	
Agriculture, forestry, husbandry and fishing	12,177	14,002	87.0
Mining	8,578	11,488	74.7
Manufacturing	13,544	16,652	81.3
Electricity, coal, gas and water production and supply	16,665	18,912	88.1
Construction	15,396	17,400	88.5
Transport communications, storage or telecommunications	17,993	20,895	86.1
Wholesale retail, trade and catering	13,385	16,705	80.1
Real estate	23,186	27,437	84.5
Social services	17,336	23,267	74.5
Other professions	13,937	17,141	81.3

In all professions the pay gap between men and women has become a cruel reality. Many people put this form of unequal pay down to the fact that men and women have different educational qualifications, believing that men's wages are higher because they tend to receive a higher level of education than women. However, the data below from a survey shows that the issue of unequal pay exists at every level of education.

Table 2:[19]

Number of years in education	Average annual wage	
	Men	Women
Under 6 years	5,213.62	2,681.87
6-9 years	6,469.28	4,554.23
9-12 years	9,091.94	6,585.00
12-16 years	13,237.24	9,430.32
Over 16 years	12,948.34	10,455.61

Although the data clearly shows that better-educated men and women earn higher incomes, men have a higher income than women even when they have received the same education, and there is a clear trend towards a widening of the gender pay gap.

Generally speaking, apart from education, it should be an individual's capabilities that decide his or her income level. Specialised research has shown that female students are self-disciplined, diligent and tenacious, and that female employees are not less competitive in going for promotion and pay increases

---

[18] 'Men and Women in Chinese Society – Facts and Figures (2004)', published by the Bureau of Population, Social Science and Technology of the National Statistics Bureau, p. 51.
[19] *Ibid.*

than men. China's 2002 survey on the status of women showed that society already commonly recognised the capability of women: 82% of women were 'confident about their ability', 80% of women 'refused to accept that they cannot achieve anything', and the majority of people (66%) surveyed could not agree with the statement that 'a man's innate abilities are greater than a woman's'.[20] But perhaps the 34% who could agree with that statement determine the fate of most women, and have made unequal pay for men and women an objective reality.

2.4 Segregation of the Sexes at Work

Influenced by traditional concepts, employers choose applicants on the basis of sex. This is clear when looking at the respective situations of men and women at work, and the result is a segregation of the sexes in the workplace. Looking at employment structure, the majority of women are employed in labour-intensive industries, such as clothing or textiles. The ratio of women in high-tech industry is comparatively low, with the tendency for women to be marginalised.[21] Looking at the distribution of women in different professions, the number of women exceeds the number of men in areas such as retail, social services, education, culture and health, while the number of women is close to the number of men in the financial sector, insurance, scientific research, polytechnic services, political institutions and non-governmental organisations. Generally speaking, the higher the management level, the fewer the number of women. The Director of Beijing Zero Survey Company, Yuan Yue, said: 'Based on what I know from all the research and consultancy work on professions that I've done, women have made up 70% of personnel, but at a managerial level in businesses, men account for 70%.'[22] In a survey carried out by Zhilian Recruitment Company the question was asked: 'Have women hit a ceiling in the development of their career?' 53.73% of women believed that the number of women was obviously smaller at higher position in the employment; 15.38% had no opinion; and only 15.27% thought that ability was more important, and that their ability matched their position. Different people in different professions had different experiences. 12.70% thought that in some professions women were more successful than men, and only 2.91% felt that men and women were promoted in the same way.[23]

This so-called 'ceiling'[24] does not only exist in entrepreneurial environments,

---

[20] *Ibid*, p. 104.
[21] Ren Zhengying, *supra* note 3.
[22] Zhang Xin, 'The Sexual Characteristics of the Chinese Economy', http://news.sina.com.cn/c/2005-08-30/05036814010s.shtml. Last visited August 2008.
[23] 'Zhilian Recruitment Report on a Survey Taken on International Women's Day 2005', http://info.food.hc360.com/2005/03/11131351320.shtml. Last visited August 2008.
[24] The 'ceiling phenomenon' means barriers caused by one's sex. Although women may achieve a managerial level position, they subsequently face some invisible obstruction that stops them from getting a further promotion.

but also in government offices. Statistics showed that from 2000 to 2002, the ratio of the sexes among the cadres at a national level reflected the results of the survey previously described. Women accounted for 36.2% of cadres in 2000, 36.7% in 2001 and 37.2% in 2002. The more senior the cadre, the smaller the percentage of women was. From 1995 to 2002, the percentage of female judges grew from 16.7% to 21.6%. In the same period the percentage of female public prosecutors (including chief prosecutors, deputy chief prosecutors and assistant prosecutors) grew from 17 to 22.1%, and the percentage of female lawyers went from 18.4 to 14%.[25] Comparing educational backgrounds, 82.5% of those who held a master's degree or above thought that 'men and women do not have equal opportunities for advancement or promotion', a higher percentage than those with lower education standards. 82.1% of those with 'bachelor degrees' and 68.0% of those with a junior high school education agreed.[26]

This information compels us to explore the reasons for this situation. Since the People's Republic of China was established in 1949, the principle that men and women are equal has always been upheld by law and policy: why then is the reality so vastly different? According to experts at Zhilian Recruitment Company, women's qualities of subtlety and caution can also act as an obstacle to promotion. A prejudicial opinion is that women are less decisive and lack promptness and in-depth consideration when making decisions. Such prejudice has certainly created the ceiling for their promotion. Moreover, men, already surrounded by high-level men, find themselves in the 'know', while women are left out in the cold.[27]

3. REASONS FOR EMPLOYMENT DISCRIMINATION AGAINST WOMEN

It should be indicated that even though employment discrimination against women exists as a serious problem, it has not been largely recognised as such throughout society. Some people believe that, considering the nature of labour distribution, marketisation and companies' operations, what certain people unanimously claim to be 'discrimination' cannot in fact fundamentally be called discrimination. Companies are profit-making economic entities with certain capital, produce the products and have to operate on market principles. The labour force is just one production factor that companies buy from the market, and thus is a kind of commodity. A company buying labour from the market is just like a consumer going shopping, in that there are no essential differences in motivations and behaviour: the purchase is voluntary and self-determined; there

---

[25] 'Men and Women in Chinese Society – Facts and Figures (2004)', *supra* note *18*, pp. 87, 92, 93.
[26] 'A Survey of Men and Women's Economic Lives: 80% Believe that Unequal Pay is Unjust', http://news.xinhuanet.com/fortune/2005-06/23/content_3125355.htm. Last visited August 2008.
[27] *Supra* note 23.

is complete freedom of choice; in each case the buyer hopes to buy the 'best value' product with a low price. Moreover, they argued that companies have freedom of choice which makes it nearly impossible to avoid 'discrimination', and therefore the applicant really cannot say it is unfair.[28]

Some take the view that the employment rate is an important guiding factor in the discrepancy between male and female graduates who find employment; however, the results of the survey show that this discrepancy is not very obvious. According to the Ministry of Education's statistics on the employment rate of graduates from universities, from 2000-2001 the employment rate of female graduates was somewhat lower than men's, but the discrepancy was not distinct. Taking individual degree subjects separately, in courses with a relatively large number of graduates such as engineering and law, the number of male graduates finding employment was found to be relatively high, but among students who had studied subjects like literature, psychology or medicine, the employment rate for women was in fact higher. However, these kinds of discrepancies are not great, and do not shed light on the more serious discrepancies that do exist. Considering all the factors including rates of employment, workplaces, starting salary and applicants' expenditures, the discrepancy between the employment situations of male and female graduates, is not overwhelmingly obvious and one cannot clearly discern a bias of favouring men over women. The discrepancy in the starting salary of men and women depends on the subject that they studied and the profession they have chosen. The best observation is to recognise that female graduates face particular difficulties in finding employment, and some work units do favour males when recruiting new people. On the other hand, one must not exaggerate cases of sex discrimination.[29]

Some do not consider it discrimination when these companies employ people on account of their gender, and even if a discrepancy in the employment rate between the genders exists, it is not worth making a great fuss about. Moreover, because there are realistic factors affecting women finding employment, many mistakenly think of employment discrimination solely on grounds of gender.

The Survey into the reasons for employment discrimination revealed that the most frequently cited reason was the surplus labour force (24.3% of people).[30]

---

[28] Liu Yibing, 'Analysing China's Employment Discrimination', *Zhongguo jingji shibao*, 16 June 2005.

[29] Wen Dongmao, 'Questioning of Sexual Discrimination against Graduates in Employment', (Issue 6, 2003) *Zhongguo daxuesheng jiuye*. The article notes that, according to the 1998 Graduate Survey, looking at the different professions that graduates undertake, it is clear that far fewer women than men engage in the high-tech industry (20.6% lower), while a higher proportion of women become teachers (10.9% more). Looking at the type of work unit, a lower proportion of women join state organizations or state-owned companies (2.5% and 8.8% fewer than men) while a relatively high proportion of women work in schools or foreign invested enterprises (11.1% and 3.8% more than men).

[30] The Survey, *supra* note 7, F6.

The surplus in the labour force market allows recruiters to include requirements based on gender in their standard requirements. At present, competition in China's labour market, and the restructuring of government and public institutions and state-owned enterprises all directly influence the number of women absorbed into the workforce. The second most popular reason chosen was that social security structures have not been fully established (16.3%).[31] Lack of social security means, the financial burden of employees who have children falls on individual companies, which feel the pressure of additional invisible costs on them. With this on top of other factors, many women are turned down by recruiters, or face time restrictions on when they can have children once starting work. Therefore, it can be said that ultimately, the cost of having children is a primary reason why employment discrimination against women occurs.[32] Women suffer the brunt of the challenges faced during this current period of economic transition, particularly with marketisation and reforms of labour mechanisms. As soon as women find themselves unemployed, it becomes difficult to survive. In contemporary China, there are different retirement and social security systems for men and women. The relatively high retirement welfare costs (since women retire 5-10 years earlier and live for longer, they generally get more pension money) and other such issues can all become latent factors contributing towards employment discrimination against women. The third reason was that efficiency and productivity come first and 16% of people chose this.[33] This choice is perhaps influenced by traditional concepts of the productivity of the labour force market. Some recruiters have a prejudiced view of women's abilities and value, believing their productivity levels are lower than men's: women's energy is divided between their employment and their household role, and so they lack the potential for development. Exaggeration of the negative effects of childbirth and parenting on women at work has intensified the disadvantages for women when competing for jobs.

According to Liu Liqun, a notable economist in the State Council Development Centre, the difficulty for women finding work and re-employment is closely linked with the contradictions of supply and demand in the labour force market. Moreover, women having children and doing housework result in added costs for companies looking to maximise profits and so companies are naturally unwilling to suffer the 'sex deficit' of employing female workers. By

---

[31] *Ibid.*

[32] Jiang Junlu, who has a Ph.D in Labour Law, stated that women are limited in their employment because of the disparity compared to men in terms of costs of their labour. The major issue is childbirth. Women workers cannot work while they are pregnant, on maternity leave and nursing (at the longest a year), but a work unit must still pay them. Moreover, naturally a woman expends more energy than a man on looking after children and doing housework. If one is thinking of the interests of a business, then female workers will be more costly than a man. See Mao Lei, *supra* note 10.

[33] The Survey, *supra* note 7, F6.

contrast, there are no limitations on the investment in men, with their superior physical and mental strength and other factors, and it is no surprise that they are commonly lauded as the front-runners in the employment market.[34]

There are a few other influential elements of gender employment discrimination. Firstly, although the law has stipulated equal employment rights for men and women, implementation is weak and legal liability is lacking. Effective methods to limit employment discrimination have yet to emerge.

Secondly, there is no strong supervision and management of the labour force market, particularly for small or medium-sized private companies and informal employment, where supervisory structures do not yet exist. There is a complete lack of coherency between government departments such as industry and commerce, tax administration, civil administration, labour security and health and city management. Both overlapping management and lack of supervision exist. In some places, local government's negligent control of both foreign investment and small to medium-sized private companies means that women are more likely to lose their jobs.

Thirdly, it is more difficult for women to be self-employed, since they lack the skills, training and access to services to start up a business. Women face restrictions from many different angles and, as a result, their education levels or trained skills are generally insufficient. According to the 2002 national survey of eight major cities that covered 4,000 laid-off women, 54.9% did not take part in re-employment training schemes once they had been laid off.[35]

The fourth reason is a social and historical one. Thousands of years under the feudal despotism of the Confucian code of conduct has given rise to the deep-seated traditional belief that men are superior to women. Although modern society has become highly civilised, prejudice against women and the belief that they should stay at home is still prevalent. Governmental institutions have set up all kinds of restrictive policies to limit women's entry into the workplace, while private sectors have tried to solve the employment issue by recruiting beautiful women and forcing them to become 'commodities' for the privileged and elite within society.

The fifth reason is the family. Since ancient times, women have been considered household 'slaves'. The employment level of Chinese women is relatively high compared with many countries. They normally take on full-time work and the strain is no less than on men. However, housework in China has not yet become shared by men, women and society, and therefore working women have to carry the burden of all the housework as well as looking after children and parents. Eventually this either completely exhausts women, or they experience a conflict of roles. This has become the employment dilemma for women. Moreover, from certain quarters there are calls for women to go back into the home. Data from the Survey on factors that influence promotion for

---

[34] Zhang Xin, *supra* note 22.
[35] Ren Zhengying, *supra* note 3.

women revealed that the top three factors chosen by respondents were biological reasons, traditional concepts and conflict with private issues at home, 30.5%, 29.3% and 27.9% respectively.[36] In this way, therefore, all the work which women contribute both to society and to their family becomes a barrier to their own development.

4. CHINA'S CONTEMPORARY LEGAL FRAMEWORK AND MEASURES TO COUNTER DISCRIMINATION

China's current legal framework does not lack relevant provisions to protect women's employment rights. However, they seem like a simple public declaration. There is a lack of enforcement provisions and legal liability for violation of law and, as a result, laws often exist only on paper and their actual use is extremely limited. Legal scholars think that current laws are too theoretical. For example, Article 12 of the Labour Law states: 'Labourers seeking employment must not be discriminated against on grounds of their ethnicity, race, sex, or religious beliefs', but in practice, the nature of discrimination is constantly changing. The specific limitations which employers set up when recruiting are very hard to draw into the scope of the Labour Law. The Law on the Protection of Women's Rights and Interests and the Law on the Protection of Disabled Persons both contain general provisions forbidding employment discrimination. However, there are no clear provisions that specify how to distinguish discrimination. Thus, no legal responsibility has been established, meaning no liability clauses and therefore no legal deterrents and no way to punish acts of sexual discrimination.

Despite this, we can still consider that these statutory provisions reflect legislative progress and we hope that such progress could have a substantive practical impact. Thus, it is worthwhile examining the existing laws, analysing the nature of these legal provisions and exploring how they can be implemented.

4.1 Protective Provisions on Women's Employment Rights

(1) Protecting women's equal employment rights. Labourers (including women) enjoy equal employment rights and the right to choose their own career; labourers should not be discriminated against for reasons of race, ethnicity, sex and religious beliefs;[37] the state guarantees that women and men enjoy equal labour rights.[38] Women enjoy the same employment rights as men. When employing workers, apart from jobs or posts that are not suitable for women as stipulated in national law, one cannot refuse to employ someone for being a

---

[36] The Survey, *supra note* 7, F14.
[37] Arts. 3 and 12 of the Labour Law.
[38] Art. 21 of the Law on Protection of Women's Rights and Interests.

woman or stipulate specific conditions for her employment.[39]

(2) Protecting women's rights to equal development. Laws provide for the prohibition of discrimination against women as regards promotion (in terms of position or salary) or the allocation of titles of specialised technical positions.[40]

(3) It is prohibited to dismiss a female worker without reason. No work unit can dismiss a woman or break a contract because a woman marries, becomes pregnant, or takes maternity or nursing leave.[41] Article 95 of the Labour Law provides that if there is an infringement of women's lawful rights, the work unit should be instructed to rectify the matter, and if harm has been caused, the work unit should pay compensation. Article 50 of the Law on Protection of Women's Interests and Rights stipulates that an organization or higher-level authorities should demand a correction, and may take administrative disciplinary action against the persons to blame for any violations of women's lawful rights and interests. Furthermore, Article 52 states that 'whoever infringes upon women's lawful rights and interests and has caused property or other losses to women should compensate for the losses or bear other civil responsibility according to law'.

(4) Special labour protection. The law has made two distinctions directed at the particular biological condition of women. Firstly, there are general restrictions for female workers. Women are prohibited from taking part in mining, or other work that is stipulated by national law to be level four physical labour[42] and other forbidden work.[43] Secondly, there is the female workers' 'four period' protection. This is otherwise known as 'menstrual period' protection, and it arranges for a woman not to work in high places, low temperatures, or cold water or to carry out work stipulated to be of level three, physical labour intensity under national regulations, during her period. 'Pregnant period' protection means that female workers who are more than seven months pregnant are not allowed to partake in work of extended hours or night shifts. 'Maternity leave' protection provides women with no fewer than 90 days of maternity leave and ensures that they do not receive lower wages for this period or have their labour contract cancelled. 'Nursing period' provides that while women have a child under the age of one year old, not yet weaned, they must not undertake work that is stipulated to be of level three intensity of physical labour, and nursing mothers

---

[39] Art. 13 of the Labour Law, and Art. 22 of the Law on Protection of Women's Rights and Interests.
[40] Art. 24 of the Law on Protection of Women's Rights and Interests.
[41] Art. 26 of the Law on Protection of Women's Rights and Interests.
[42] Level four intensity of physical labour involves onerous physical labour, according to the regulation of the national standard on analysis of the intensity of physical labour, which means that it costs 2,700 calories per day for 370 minutes of labour.
[43] Art. 59 of the Labour Law.

cannot work extended hours or night shifts.[44]

Recruiters who violate the above regulations and fail to protect female workers or who infringe their lawful rights, will be instructed to rectify the situation, and will be fined. If harm has been caused to female workers, employers will have to pay compensation.[45]

As for people or work units that infringe female workers' labour protection rights, managers of the relevant department must carry out administrative sanctions according to the severity of the incident, and instruct the work unit to give the female worker sufficient economic compensation. For incidents that constitute a crime, the person responsible must be tried by a court (Article 13 of the Regulations on Protection of Female Workers).

Particular compensation methods are provided in Article 3 of the Methods for the Compensation for Violating the Labour Contract according to the Labour Law issued by the Ministry of Labour on 10 May 1995: those who have caused women workers a loss in salary must pay the women workers their salary as well as a compensatory fee of 25% extra. If a woman's health has suffered, her medical costs must be paid and compensation should be paid at 25% on top of the medical costs.

4.2 Discriminatory Provisions in Law and Regulations

The main discrimination is the unequal retirement age for men and women. This is reflected in the Provisional Regulations Regarding Ageing, Sick and Disabled Cadres and the Provisional Regulations on Retirement of Workers issued by the State Council in 1978 and which are still valid today. Under the Regulations the full retirement age for employees is 60 for men and 50 for female workers, and 55 for female cadres and 60 for male cadres. Originally, this legislation was to protect women and so the discrepancy in the retirement age must in essence be defined as a kind of right. However, nowadays this has become an obligation and women lack the ability to choose their own retirement age.

Moreover, the system of policy and law has not been fully established and has in reality gone adrift, leaving no method of paving the way for women's employment. This has become an important contributing factor to the difficulty of female employment. For example, much of the important content of the 1988 Regulations on Protection of Female Workers is no longer in sync with contemporary conditions. Some experts[46] maintain that prohibiting all women from certain work has already curtailed a part of a woman's right to choose her employment. Special protection is necessary for women because they have different requirements from men, both for physical and for reproductive reasons.

---

[44] Arts. 60-63 of the Labour Law.
[45] Art. 95 of the Labour Law.
[46] Liu Minghui, 'A Discussion of the Blind Spots Existing in Labour and Social Security Legislation in Relation to the Sexes', (issue 3, June 2006) *Zhonghua nuzi xueyuan xuebao*.

However, apart from the 'four periods' regulations, that prohibit women from engaging in certain occupations, other protective regulations have already produced negative effects. After market economy mechanisms came into effect, the traditional centralised allocation of labour by state department changed to allow the labour market to be deployed optimally, supply became greater than demand in the labour market, and gender discrimination gradually caused the marginalisation of women. Under these circumstances, labour legislation made certain relatively highly-paid posts were forbidden to women, which diminishes women's employment opportunities and curtails a large part of women's rights to choose their own employment. There are women who do not want to have children or have already finished giving birth to children, and as long as they have sufficient ability to cope with heavy labour and high-risk jobs, the law should offer them the right to choose such employment. Indiscriminate, prohibitive rules impinge on the principles of equality in law. If there is a failure to consider all the aspects of the issue and women are merely regarded as objects of protection while their individual rights are neglected, the result will run counter to what was intended.

5   CONCLUSION: ABOLISHING DISCRIMINATIVE LEGAL PROVISIONS AND CREATING GENDER EQUALITY

Whatever methods are used to eliminate existing employment discrimination against women, it will be a comprehensive and complicated process. As this article has described, women's employment discrimination is not only a social problem, but a legal problem too. Effectively protecting women's employment rights involves every profession, and it is necessary for the legal system to provide support. Only by using legislative measures to change perceptions, can public awareness of the equality of men and women be improved. Only by implementing laws can it be guaranteed that the strict implementation of institutional measures to protect women's employment rights will achieve tangible results.

Firstly, current legislation should be revised and legal obligations strengthened. Current legal provisions that do not benefit female employment must be revised, the scope of women's employment opportunities must be expanded and a system of equal retirement ages for men and women be introduced. In addition, legal obligations must be strengthened. For instance, provisions should be added to ensure Article 12 of the Labour Law can be enforced. Due to economic development and social progress, the physical strength required for much production work has decreased, while intellectual requirements continue to grow. As a result, the biological differences between men and women have gradually diminished in importance. Therefore, we need to adjust specifications for the different labour intensity levels according to current conditions, to change legislation that bans women from certain employment, and to declare more jobs appropriate for women. At the same time, legislative regulations could state that recruiters are to employ a specified ratio of women, in order to expand the scope of their careers. We also need to make equal rights as practical as possible. A woman should be able to bring a lawsuit if she feels that her employment right is discriminated against and require recruiters and work units to pay material and non-material compensation.

Secondly, we must enact special legislation to implement Article 11 of the Convention on the Elimination of All Forms of Discrimination against Women which relates to the legal protection of women's labour employment rights. In enacting such law, we could use other countries' legislation as a reference, such as the relatively mature legislation of the EU Equal Treatment Directive, to enable the introduction of a series of supplementary orders to provide equal protection for women in the following areas: equal pay; social employment insurance; pregnancy and maternity leave; social security; freelance work and care of partners; receipt of material goods and services.

Thirdly, there should be a balanced corporate responsibility in promoting a maternity insurance system. At present, China's social security system, including its provision for the elderly and the unemployed, and the provision of medical treatment and accident insurance is all relatively successful; maternity insurance, however, remains insufficient. The key to defending women's employment rights is the establishment of an effective maternity insurance system. A woman who gives birth is making a contribution to society. We cannot treat it as an institutional or corporate problem, and the burden of giving birth should not fall upon women; rather, a woman who gives birth should be compensated by society. Without a doubt, enterprises must take social responsibility, but in the end enterprises are essentially profit-making groups and it is hard to rely purely on the virtue of each company's director to implement such a system. Moreover, looking at current laws, it is almost impossible to find any concrete, clear systems in place. A complete system of legislation, along with a fully established social security system, is the only realistic and practical course. This is the way to resolve the question of women's employment and the problem of female graduates' employment. We must gradually set up a complete maternity insurance system, so that the state, society and individuals all share responsibility. Trials for a maternity insurance scheme began in 1994, but the initiative has faced a sea of troubles. Due to the fact that there is no existing nationally enforced insurance system, many local authorities have not implemented the policy.

Fourthly, we must increase regulatory strength and the power of monitoring. In the past, the work of China's labour supervisory department has focused on monitoring women's health, safety and protection in the workplace, but has failed to deal with recruiters' open gender discrimination, and no system exists to handle women's employment, dismissal, training and promotion. The labour supervisory department should use its effective administration to prohibit or redress any unlawful discrimination. In the future, related government policies need to be strengthened and systems set up to involve the labour supervisory bureau effectively. At the same time, the law enforcement bureau must make active efforts to listen to the complaints of gender discrimination, take the initiative in supervising and monitoring such discrimination, make sure that those who violate regulations are made to bear legal responsibility, and increase the penalties and compensation charged. There is also a need for regulations that offer support to the victims of discrimination.

Fifthly, positive action regulations are necessary. We must consult other countries' legislative experience in order to encourage recruiters to adopt positive action. The experiences of EU countries are particularly useful.

Sixthly, we should give serious thought to the role of non-governmental organisations in anti-discrimination. Some countries have established Equal Treatment Commissions, and these provide a very good model. Although in China the All China Federation of Women is considered to be a spokesperson for women, and the organisation plays a great role in protecting and safeguarding women's rights, the Federation only has particular supervisory rights or the power to make recommendations, and has no jurisdiction or powers to penalise.

Eradicating employment discrimination for women requires long-term support and dedication. It is not a fleeting task calling only for the efforts of individuals, but instead requires the whole of society to unite and do its utmost to strive together to improve and transform both the institutional systems and individual beliefs at every level. Public opinion must be actively channelled into giving the green light to women's full employment. We need to guide families and society actively in their concern for the needs of contemporary women. Most importantly however women need to make efforts themselves to improve their capacities, in order to prepare themselves fully for the world of work, to change others' preconceptions and to live their own independent lives.

5

IDENTITY DISCRIMINATION IN EMPLOYMENT – HOUSEHOLD REGISTRATION AND REGIONAL ORIGIN

Yao Guojian

1. INTRODUCTION

Of the various types of discrimination in employment which occur in today's China, identity discrimination (*shenfen qishi*) has frequently become a focus of society's attention. Discrimination based on regional origin and household registration means using regional background or household registration, which usually have no bearing on the nature of the job, as conditions for employment, rather than a worker's ability to work or the requirements of a specialist technical post. Workers with a household registration from a different region are excluded or, if not entirely excluded, they are not treated the same as workers with a local household registration. In reality, discrimination based on regional origin and household registration is discrimination directed against people with rural household registration or without a local household registration. The aim of the discrimination is to enhance employment opportunities for local urban people as much as possible and raise the local urban employment rate. Basic methods include limits placed on workers who come from elsewhere by every level of regional government. As supply exceeds demand in the employment market, the position of jobseekers can only get weaker. In addition, there is a lack of effective remedies and jobseekers are unable to question identity discrimination. Therefore they have no option other than passive acceptance, which in turn seems to increase the legitimacy and reasonableness of the discrimination.

2. TYPES OF IDENTITY DISCRIMINATION IN EMPLOYMENT

Identity discrimination against migrants in employment is more noticeable than discrimination based on other factors. According to research carried out in China's ten major cities by the Constitutionalism Research Institute of the China University of Political Science and Law, 28.7% of those interviewed had the experience that employers imposed household registration as a condition of employment, and among these 22.3% required a local household registration.[1] It is of particular note that identity discrimination is strongly connected with public authorities; indeed many of the perpetrators of this type of discrimination are not enterprises and similar employers but the government and principally administrative bodies. Indeed in certain circumstances enterprises and other such employers are not perpetrators of this form of discrimination, but are the victims and opponents, because some governmental discriminatory behaviour is disadvantageous for them. Discrimination against migrants in China has relatively strong systematic characteristics, and in many cases constitutes systematic discrimination. Of course, discrimination based on regional background and household registration does not only come from the government, and in certain cases enterprises are also the perpetrators, but overall they are not the principal proponents of discrimination. Generally speaking, identity discrimination can be identified in employment opportunities, payment and employment service.

2.1 Discrimination in Employment Opportunities

In China there is currently a surplus of labour, which makes the employment market an employers' market, with employment opportunities a scarce social resource. Against this background, creating employment opportunities for the urban workforce should fall within the scope of government responsibility, yet, in order to solve this problem, some regional governments use regional origin and household registration as conditions for employment, implementing policies designed to prevent migrants entering employment or placing stricter conditions on them compared with local workers. In putting these government policies into practice, enterprises and other employers either actively or passively become perpetrators of discrimination. In this way, the loss of employment opportunities by workers who do not hold a local household registration does not result from a natural selection mechanism in the employment market. It is the result of the privileges afforded to local household registration holders which exclude those who do not hold such registration, and maintains the monopoly the urban workforce holds over the 'trinity' of employment, the social security system and the household registration system. Although this is an embodiment of the care and assistance that city governments provide to disadvantaged urban groups, this policy has the effect of depriving other groups, who do not have a local household registration, of their rights to employment. Discrimination in employment opportunities is visible in various ways.

---

[1] See 'A Survey of Employment Discrimination in Ten Major Cities in China', B1-j, Chapter 6 of this book.

Making Local Household Registration a Mandatory Condition of Employment

This is the situation whereby employers make a local household registration or origin a mandatory condition of employment. A requirement for local origin is aimed at higher education graduates. Students from certain large and medium-sized cities such as Beijing and Shanghai are usually unwilling to apply for universities elsewhere when they sit their university entrance exams. In order to encourage them to apply for other universities, the education and human resources departments in these cities have promised that, after graduation, these students will have a priority right to return to the location of their initial household registration. In these cities many employers have clearly made local origin a condition for employment. Such students have an advantage because they previously held a local household registration. This constitutes discrimination against students who come from other areas.

Making a local household registration a condition for employment can be the result of enterprises or other employers acting on their own, but it can also derive from government regulations. For example in the four years between 2002 and 2005 the recruiters in central governmental bodies all required that those applying to become civil servants must hold a Beijing household registration, and that those holding another city's household registration had no right to apply to become civil servants in central government bodies. This system only ended in 2006. However, when some districts and counties in Beijing recruit civil servants, some posts still require that the applicant should hold a Beijing household registration or have origins in Beijing as a prerequisite for entering recruitment examinations. For example, in 2006, amongst the 123 civil servants recruited by Chaoyang District, Beijing, 57 (46%) posts made holding a Beijing household registration or a Beijing origin an additional special condition. This means that students who do not hold a Beijing household registration or a Beijing origin cannot apply for almost half of the posts.[2]

To make a local household registration a condition for employment is very common: government bodies and state owned enterprises emphasise household registration more than private business. In 2004, among 5708 posts recruited for by state owned enterprises directly under the State Council, 142 had requirements linked to household registration, 129 of which required a Beijing household registration. Amongst the 2822 posts recruited for by private enterprises only 15 specified requirements linked to household registration.[3]

Within industry, taxi driving companies have clear requirements as to household registration. From December 1994 to August 2005, 40 large and

---

[2] The 2006 recruitment news posted on Beijing Chaoyang District Government website, http://rsj.bjchy.gov.cn/ sub/newsMore.action. Last visited March 2006.

[3] Zhou Wei (ed.), *Employment Discrimination in China: Legislation and Reality*,(Beijing: Law Press China, 2006), pp. 169-171.

medium-sized cities, including Beijing, Shanghai and Tianjin, set down regional regulations to regulate the taxi driving industry. Statistics relating to 28 cities, which have the right to pass regional legislation, show that 16 cities legislated that only those holding a local household registration could become taxi drivers.[4] Whether or not city taxi drivers hold a local household registration has no relationship to their ability to do this job, and this legislation excludes from this industry those who do not hold a local household registration. This is clearly discrimination in employment.

Restricting Outsiders in Employment

In order to raise local employment rates regional governments use all available measures to impose macro-controls on migrants employed in their city, so that more employment opportunities are left open for local people. There are four specific means of restricting migrants in employment.

(1) Controlling the number of migrant labourers

This refers to restricting on a macro level the possibility of those who do not hold a local household registration finding employment. This form of discrimination usually originates with the government and has many systematic characteristics. An example is Art. 4 of the Beijing Migrant Labourers Management Regulation (*Beijingshi waidi laijing renyuan wugong guanli guiding*), issued in 1995 and amended in 1997. It states that: 'This municipality imposes controls on the numbers of migrant labourers entering the capital. Industries which employ migrant labour and requirements such as educational level and technical skill will be published by the Municipal Labour Department and other relevant departments according to their determination of demand in the municipal workforce.' Qingdao Municipal Government of Shandong Province has limited recruitment of migrants in enterprises under municipal control to 14%. It has also passed regulations requiring payment of 50RMB to employ migrant labour and awarding compensation of 3000RMB to anyone who employs a local who has been looking for work for more than six months (women over 35 and men over 40). Article 13 of the Regulations of Wuhan Labour Market Management of Hubei Province issued on 22 January 1999 affords preferential taxation and administrative treatment to employers who employ an unemployed or redundant local.

Another important method used by large and mid-sized city governments to control migrant labour is to limit the number of graduates from local universities in local employment. Large cities such as Beijing, Shanghai, Guangzhou and Xi'an all have many universities and colleges. They are also areas which are relatively developed economically and therefore remain the first choice locations

---

[4] *Ibid*, p. 249.

of employment for local graduates. In order to impose macro-controls on the numbers of graduates from local universities and colleges entering employment locally, the municipal governments of large and mid-sized cities use allocation targets. In this way, only those graduates who have attained the target will be able to obtain local household registration after they have found employment. Those graduates who have not met the target will not be able to obtain a local household registration even if they find employment locally, and they will also have no access to benefits provided by the local government to those who hold a local household registration.

(2) Restricting the industries and jobs open to migrants

Restricting the industries and jobs open to migrants is a form of discrimination practised by many local governments. In order to guarantee local workers sufficient labour opportunities, they lay down normative documentation listing the industries and jobs in which migrants can work. In reality this means governmental public authority splits the employment market in two: one section only open to local people; the other section allowing migrants to compete with local people for employment. Migrants are only allowed to seek employment in certain sectors, which are usually the sectors and jobs in which local people do not wish to work. They principally involve dirty, menial, poorly salaried physical work such as cleaning, being a security guard or working in transport.

These methods first emerged in Shanghai. On 13 February 1995, as an important means of promoting the re-employment project, the Labour Bureau of Shanghai issued the Methods in Administrating Non-local Labourers by Shanghai Work Units (*Shanghaishi danwei shiyong he pinyong waidi laodongli fenlei guanli banfa*). It divided industry sectors into three categories: category A industry sectors which are able to employ migrant labour; category B industry sectors which should regulate their use of migrant labour; and category C industry sectors which are not permitted to employ migrant labour. After this the first approved category C industry sectors were published. According to this regulation there are 20 specific industries which impose restrictions on migrant labour in Shanghai, including finance, insurance and all types of management. The industries in which migrant rural workers can find employment are physically demanding construction work, municipal cleaning, gardening, and nannying at home, and so on.

The successful experience of using this method to encourage re-entry into employment has since been widely imitated by several large and mid-sized cities. For example, the Wuhan Migrant Labour Management Regulation (*Wuhanshi shiyong wailai laodongli guanli guiding*) separates industries and jobs into those open to migrant labour, those whose use of migrant labour is controlled, and those which are forbidden to use migrant labour. According to this regulation, party and government bodies cannot employ migrants who do not hold a local household registration; leading industries, management, personnel and other highly technical jobs are closed to workers who do not have a local household registration. In commerce, and some technical work in factories, use of those who do not have a local household registration should be controlled, whereas dirty, tiring and dangerous jobs such as construction, industrial cleaning and catering fall within the scope of those jobs open to migrant labour. Consequently these jobs are almost entirely filled by migrant labourers, particularly migrant labourers from rural areas. In 1996, the Labour Bureau of Beijing issued rules governing the scope of employment open to migrant labour in Beijing. Of a total of 204 types of employment, only 12 were open to migrant labourers. The first employment listed by the rules is 'undertaker, crematorium work and grave maintenance'.[5] Since 1996 the Labour Bureau of Beijing has published new limits every year on the use of migrant labour. These jobs and industry sectors increased from 12 in 1996 to 34 in 1997, 36 in 1998 and 103 in 2000. At the same time as these discriminatory policies were implemented, strict public security measures were also put into place. In addition, certain industries and jobs were explicitly closed to migrant labour. Among these were managers, professionals in finance and insurance, accountants, dispatchers, front desk staff in starred hotels, cashiers, telephone operators, valuers and taxi drivers.

Controls on the employment of migrant labour are usually instigated by the government, whilst enterprises and other employers put these discriminatory policies into practice. Of course, in addition to explicit government regulations, some enterprises have their own unwritten rules about not employing migrant labour to do certain jobs involving cash-handling or security. These often include accountants, cashiers, drivers, security guards and so on.

(3) Requiring higher standards from migrant labourers

Although some regional governments, enterprises and other employers have no explicit prohibition on migrants competing for employment, in order to limit the number of people without a local household registration in employment and attract higher quality workers, they have laid down regulations that provide that if migrants need to seek employment in their area they must have a higher level of education than local workers. This has the effect of reducing the employment opportunities for migrants who are in fact treated differently from local jobseekers. For example, Art. 2 of the Guangdong 2003 Examination for the Employment in Government Bodies and the Civil Service Implementation Programme (*2003 xiabannian kaoshi luyong jiguan gongzuorenyuan he guojia gongwuyuan shishi fangan*) provides that applicants who do not have a Guangdong household registration (or origin) must have a degree above undergraduate level from an ordinary university. In 2006 Dongguan Municipality, in Guangdong province, stipulated that applicants who had a local household registration only needed a diploma from a vocational technical

---

[5] The document is with the author.

college, whereas applicants who did not have a local household registration needed an undergraduate degree.

(4) Explicitly regulating to exclude labourers coming from certain areas

As a result of certain social prejudices and negative customs, some enterprises believe that workers who come from certain areas are of a lower quality and easily cause trouble. They believe that employing these people will cause difficulties in their own enterprises and are therefore unwilling to do so. For example, employees at the Guangdong Dongguan Central Talent Market noticed that a recruitment advertisement for security guards had been stuck to several factory entrances in the local area which contained a condition stating that 'people from Henan and Hunan are excluded'. It is reported that the reason for this was that there had been a fight at the recruiting factory involving people from Henan and Hunan, and the factory had therefore decided to include this condition which it felt would deal with the matter once and for all.

2.2 Discrimination in Remuneration Packages

A remuneration package is the compensation that workers receive for their work. It includes salary and other welfare benefits provided by the employer. Discrimination in remuneration packages means that when a migrant undertakes the same work as a local person he or she either receives a lower salary or does not enjoy or only partly enjoys any other benefits provided. In theory enterprises should provide the same remuneration package to all workers who have done the same work, regardless of whether the worker holds a local household registration. However in practice migrant workers frequently suffer discrimination of many forms in their remuneration packages. Discriminatory behaviour is both direct and indirect. Direct discrimination relates to salary and indirect discrimination relates to other benefits, insurance and promotion opportunities.

Firstly, discrimination in terms of salary. So-called 'salary discrimination' refers to workers with the same production capacity earning differing amounts, and manifests itself in practices such as paying different money for the same work and the owners of privately-owned enterprises docking the pay of workers who do not have a local household registration or falling behind in paying them, with the overall effect of paying less money for the same work. Taking an example from Changchun, a city in northeast China, where for cleaning windows for one family, a person holding a local household registration can earn RMB10, whereas a person without a local household registration can only earn RMB 5. It is even more common for the owners of privately run enterprises to dock pay or fall behind with the payment of wages. According to relevant statistics from the Ministry of Labour and Social Security between January and October 2002, RMB 30 billion of salary was owed to rural migrant workers nationally.

According to Hunan provincial labour and social security statistics in the second half of 2002, there were over 487 collective strikes of more than 30 people in Hunan. Among these, 335 strikes which is about 68.8%, were related to delay of paying salary [6]

Secondly, discrimination in terms of benefits, insurance and promotion opportunities. Discrepancies in salary are an obvious means of paying different money for the same work, but more subtle means can also be used. Salary is only one part of the remuneration package provided by Chinese enterprises and other such employers, and sometimes it is only a small part. In addition, other benefits are provided such as subsidies, allowances, insurance and housing. However, these benefits are usually only provided to workers with a local household registration and workers without it do not enjoy these benefits or enjoy them only partially.

2.3 Discrimination in Employment Services

This principally refers to regional governments imposing stricter administrative controls on workers who do not hold a local household registration and charging higher costs for services, thereby increasing the extra costs of employment, and putting migrant labourers at a competitive disadvantage. This constitutes another form of discrimination against migrant workers. For instance, children of migrants have to pay more for education. The household registration barrier not only marginalises migrant workers in the city, it also affects their children. According to national law, all children in rural and urban areas have the right to receive nine years of compulsory education. The wide divide between children holding rural and urban household registrations has become a cause for anxiety when the children of migrant workers enter education. Currently, there are three main ways in which they are educated: entering a municipally run public school after normal contributions of temporary study fees or donations; attending a relatively expensive fee paying, government approved private school; attending an illegal school only for migrant children. If the children of migrant workers wish to enter the public school system they must pay out large donations and other extra costs.

Another example is that after migrant workers come to a city they have to pay fees to obtain several permits, including employment administration fees, temporary resident administration fees and employment regulation fees. This artificially inflates the costs for migrants seeking employment, affecting a migrant's predicted income and eventually limiting their employment goals. In addition to this, migrant workers usually do not have the right to buy economic housing in the city where they are working and neither do they have the right to government assistance. Moreover, migrants not only have to pay various fees when looking for work in cities, but on occasion they do not even have any sense

---

[6] The documents are with the author.

of personal security. Even though the system of round-up and repatriation has been eradicated since 2003, and therefore migrant workers do not have to worry that they will be repatriated for no reason, they are still closely watched by local governments upholding public security. Whenever any incidents occur they are the first object of suspicion and are more likely to be investigated than local people. This is also a reason why some enterprises and other employers do not want to employ them.

2.4 Discrimination in Employment Security

From the point of view of security in the employment process, employers should provide employees with a labour contract in order to give them relative stability. Employers should not arbitrarily amend the terms of the contract, terminate the contract or let the employee go. Even if they dismiss the employee legally they should provide him or her with some form of economic compensation. However at present in China, when it comes to job security there are clear discriminatory practices. The majority of urban workers enjoy job security, and the government has provided detailed regulations and ensures that employers implement them. However the majority of migrants do not have job security in any real sense.

2.5 Migrant Workers Receive Different Treatment

In order to provide 'talent' for local social and economic development, all regional governments have gradually unveiled policies which afford preferential treatment to qualified people. This allows them to attract talent from elsewhere. One means of doing this is to make it easier for these people to obtain a local household registration in comparison with other employees. As soon as they obtain a local household registration they have access to all the facilities and security provided by regional governments to holders of a local household registration.

In 2005 the Shenzhen Party Committee and the Shenzhen Municipal Government published a document which widely reformed household registration, permitting 'talented people' who satisfied certain conditions to go individually to the household registration department and go through the procedure of registration. Talented people include those who hold an undergraduate degree from a well-known overseas university or a nationally accredited major university, those with intermediate or above technical titles or professional qualifications in industries in which Shenzhen is traditionally strong, or technicians who have made at least two years social security contributions in Shenzhen and those who fulfil the Shenzhen industry development requirements and other basic conditions. [7]

---

[7] The document is with the author.

Other examples of the different treatment afforded to migrant workers include certain municipal regulations that only allow graduates from nationally accredited major universities to enter the city to work, barring graduates from normal universities. This is a form of indirect discrimination. For example, according to Beijing municipal regulations, with the exception of those who held a Beijing household registration before they entered university, only the graduates of nationally accredited major universities who comply with certain conditions are able to come into Beijing to work.

3 LEGISLATION SUSPECTED OF IDENTITY DISCRIMINATION IN EMPLOYMENT

In China the Labour Law is the most important law governing labour and employment relationships. Articles 12 and 13 prohibit discrimination. However, these provisions only forbid discrimination in employment based on ethnicity, race, gender and religion, and they do not prohibit discrimination based on household registration or regional origin. This is clearly narrower than the scope of the International Labour Organisation (ILO) Convention (No. 111) concerning Discrimination in Respect of Employment and Occupation, which includes discrimination based on social origin.[8] It is because of a lack of clear prohibitive legislation that all levels of government including central labour department and in particular regional governments have produced a large quantity of legislation and normative documentation which discriminates on the basis of household registration and regional origin. These laws and normative documents provide the legal basis for the existence of most discriminatory behaviour. Governmental discrimination is even more dangerous than discrimination by enterprises and other employers. Such discrimination is usually based on regional legislation, normative documents and policies, and for this reason it is both common and enforceable. Discrimination originating from within the government can be called 'policy level discrimination in employment', which results in existing employees being unable to enjoy equal opportunities in employment, salary, allocation, promotion, training and job security as a result of government policy. This damages equality in employment. Policy level discrimination in employment has left a deep institutional mark. The government is both an opponent of discrimination and an instigator of it.

4 CAUSES OF IDENTITY DISCRIMINATION IN THE EMPLOYMENT MARKET

Identity discrimination is the most serious form of discrimination in the employment market in China. Of course, this form of discrimination has not

---

[8] Art. 1 of the ILO Convention (No. 111).

come about by chance; it is an unusual by-product of the integration of the market economy with the household registration system, which has been a characteristic of communist China for 50 years. There are deep-seated reasons for the occurrence of this type of discrimination.

4.1 Existence of Household Registration System Allows for Policy Level Discrimination

The household registration system is a vitally important system for the control of urban population established by the Chinese Communist Party under the planned economy. In 1954 China published and implemented its first Constitution, providing that citizens had the freedom of movement and residence. In June 1955 the State Council published the Directive for the Establishment of Ordinary Household Registration System (*Guanyu jianli jingchang hukou dengji zhidu de zhishi*), which stated that cities, towns and villages nationally should all establish a system of household registration which started to unify urban and rural household registration. In 1956 and 1957 the state published a series of four documents restricting and controlling the migration of the rural population into cities. In January 1958 the Standing Committee of the National People's Congress passed the Regulations on Household Registration (*Zhonghua renmin gongheguo hukou dengji tiaoli*), which for the first time divided the population into holders of a rural household registration and holders of a non-rural household registration. Ever since the Chinese government has implemented strict restrictions and government controls over population movement, thereby effectively repealing the provisions in the 1954 Constitution, which had granted freedom of movement. The 1975 Constitution formally repealed all provisions relating to freedom of movement and these have not been reinstated since.

In the era of the planned economy, at the same time as imposing restrictions on population movement and migration, the state also instituted several statutory and non-statutory systems complementing the household registration system. These gave preferential treatment to the cities. Household registration entered into all areas of social life. For example, the provision of everyday consumer goods, production resources, education, employment, housing, labour and social security and other benefits were all decided by household registration and a dualistic urban/rural structure took shape. The registration system diverged from its resource allocation function and became another restriction for the rural population, preventing them from entering the cities.

Since the household registration system was formally established in 1958, Chinese citizens have been fixed in one place by their household registration and have lost the freedom of movement. This has carved the Chinese labour market up into innumerable independent markets; Chinese workers could only seek employment in the area in which they hold a household registration. Although in recent years the government has reacted to the need for a reform of the household registration system, and the increasing calls for a renewal of citizens' freedom of movement, the limited reforms to date have been insufficient to satisfy the need for equality among workers. The social inertia of the household registration system is still strong. Under this system the division created between rural household registration holders and non-rural household registration holders made it feasible to define urban and rural residents and treat them differently; the regional administration of urban household registration allowed regional governments to discriminate against workers coming from other cities.

4.2   Discrimination against Migrants in Employment Market is a Vestige of Planned Economy

Policy level discrimination in employment is a continuation of the employment policies from the era of the planned economy. Its protection of urban residents acts to safeguard particular vested interests. After the communists came to power China operated a highly focused, planned economic system and the state imposed tight controls on all resources including the employment market, with regional governments controlling regional employment markets. This formed a fragmented employment policy, whose basic units were industry sectors and regions, and which was strongly coloured by the planned economy; resources were also allocated on the basis of this. In order to prevent too many inhabitants of rural areas and small cities from migrating to large cities and taking employment opportunities and social resources from urban people, in 1953, 1954, 1955 and 1957 the central government published directives discouraging rural people from migrating to the cities. In December 1957 the Central Committee of the CCP and the State Council published the Directive on Control of Arbitrary Rural Migration (*Guanyu zhizhi nongcun renkou mangmu wailiu de zhishi*) which wholly prevented rural people from moving into the cities. In this way a dualistic social structure came into place in China with the rural in opposition to the urban. In this social structure the urban and the rural were kept at an isolated distance from each other, and gradually over time rural people became fixed in the countryside, frozen into their rural identity. During the reform period this rigid dualistic social structure has started to change, becoming another type of social structure in which the rigid and the fast changing are polarised. The boundaries between urban and rural areas, between large and small cities, are no longer clear. The workforce is beginning to move between urban and rural areas and between large and small cities. However this has not changed the dualistic social structural model. The employment, medical, education, labour protection and social security systems formed by this dualistic structure cannot be transformed immediately. When a large quantity of migrant labour comes into conflict with the inertia of the planned economy, it forces regional governments to use administrative intervention rather than the market to solve the urban unemployment problem. A major characteristic of administrative intervention is that it uses public authority to restrict migrants in, or exclude migrants from, local employment, thus reducing the competitive pressures on local unemployed people. From this viewpoint the government-led discriminatory employment policies, are a continuation of the planned economic systems in employment. They are a historical inheritance whose basic starting point is the protection of the vested interests obtained by urban people under the planned economy.

4.3 Raising Local Employment Rates and Reducing Social Security Burden on Government

Regional employment rates are an important indicator when assessing government achievements. Therefore, lowering the unemployment rate is an aim of government work at every level. From the point of view of the local government, using any means to create employment opportunities and jobs for urban unemployed people and lowering the unemployment rate is not only an economic task, it is also a political obligation which is directly related to social stability and evaluation of government achievement. Therefore, all levels of government not only impose controls on migrants when they recruit civil servants, but they also regulate to limit enterprises and other employers recruiting migrants. These discriminatory policies mean that enterprises and other employers are not able to employ migrants according to market norms and are forced to follow the 'first local, then migrant; first urban, then rural' principle. The operation of this system means that migrants either find it difficult to enter the urban employment market, or are able to enter but must pay higher employment costs which, in the grand scheme of things, preserve more opportunities for local people. This effectively lowers the local unemployment rate.

In addition, the Chinese household registration system is not just simple registration system; its economic implications cannot be neglected. China's economic development is severely imbalanced, together with the general system deficiency, some big cities have large quantities of public resources which can be used to benefit to residents. Therefore, in the planned economy, social benefits such as housing, medical care, unemployment benefit, education and old age care were principally enjoyed by urban people, and rural people were not able to enjoy such benefits. When migrants come into the cities there is, necessarily, an influx into the local employment market increasing its competitiveness meaning that more urban workers will be unemployed and the newly increased urban workforce will find it more difficult to find appropriate employment. According to statistics for 2003, the total number of laid-off workers in China was approximately 14 million; 10 million new young people were entering the urban workforce and higher education graduates reached a peak of 2.8 million. In accordance with the current social system the cost of providing a guaranteed minimum wage and other benefits is borne by the government. Therefore as the number of unemployed urban residents increases, the social security payments paid out by the government will also increase, thereby increasing the financial burden on regional governments. Using administrative intervention to reduce the number of migrants seeking employment can effectively increase the local employment rate and thereby reduce the guaranteed minimum wage and other such payments. This should eventually decrease the financial burden on local government.

4.4 Reducing Urban Development Costs, Enterprise Production and Management Costs

Since the beginning of the reform era the rapid development of the cities and large-scale construction has created huge demands on the workforce. This demand cannot be satisfied in the cities and requires a labour movement driven by market forces. Only in a freely moving labour market will outside labour be found to allow the continued development of the urban economy. As is the case in economics, if this goal can be reached at a low cost then the cities will lower costs without hesitation. Carving up the labour market using the household registration system and, on this basis, lowering the costs to the government of employing migrant workers, can effectively reduce the costs of urban development. For this reason the household registration system provides a systematic means of lowering urban development costs. In this sense, rapid urban development has benefited from the household registration system. The system not only means that urban administrators are able to access sufficient cheap labour, they do not have to pay out current benefits which might harm the city's interests. It is profit that motivates regional governments to make use of their public authority to instigate policies which discriminate against migrants in employment.

Governmental profit chasing will provide a model for enterprises. As the national labour market is fragmented, when migrants seek employment in the cities they are dispersed. They act as individuals with no corresponding organisation to protect their rights and interests; in addition, supply outstrips demand in the employment market and in dialogue with employers migrants have lost the right to set the agenda. All levels of government have excluded them from the urban protection system so that migrants have only a limited recourse to assist them when employers reduce or dock wages or fall behind in wage payments. In recognition of this point employers wish to employ migrants, and moreover discriminate against them in salary and other benefits.

4.5 Loss of Rights to Take Part in Politics Means Migrants Have No Rights to Participate in Formation of Labour and Employment Policies

In a democratic system, electing a person from one's own group as a representative to take part in political decision-making is an effective way of protecting one's own interests. Thus, for representatives in regional political congresses to be elected from amongst migrant labourers is an effective way of protecting their right to employment. However, according to the current NPC election system and the urban residents' autonomous election system, citizens can only be elected to the NPC or the Residents Committee in the area where they hold their household registration. In this way, migrants lose their right to political participation in the area in which they work, they have no right to take part in the formation of employment policies, and can only accept passively the discrimination they suffer at the hands of the regional government in the area in which they work. For this reason it is difficult to change regional governments' migrant employment policies even though they are highly discriminatory.

5   PROGRESS IN THE GOVERNMENT'S EFFORTS TO ELIMINATE IDENTITY DISCRIMINATION IN EMPLOYMENT

Following the expansion of reforms, discrimination based on household registration and regional origin has increasingly attracted attention and criticism. The discriminatory positions held by all levels of central and regional governments have started to transform, and different means have been used to eliminate discrimination and pursue equality in employment. The responsibility of both central and regional government is to eliminate discrimination and not to create it. These efforts are therefore a return to the correct function of government.

On 1 May 2003 the General Office of the State Council issued the Notice on Providing Effective Management and Services for Rural Migrants Entering the Cities to Work (*Guanyu zuohao nongmin jincheng wugong jiuye guanlii he fuwu gongzuo de tongzhi*), which pointed out that the movement of the large rural workforce to non-rural industries and urban areas is a necessary part of industrialisation and modernisation. The entry of rural people into the cities to work pushes forward an increase in rural people's incomes, enhances the adjustment of agriculture and the rural economy, moves forward the development of urbanisation and the enrichment of the urban economy and society. Therefore, each province, municipality, district and related department must abolish the requirement for administrative approval for enterprises to employ migrants, must abolish restrictions on rural migrant workers entering the cities to work, and must not interfere in enterprises making lawful autonomous decisions to employ rural migrant workers. The administrative bodies must examine and organise procedures for rural migrant workers to enter cities to work and abolish registration programmes geared towards rural migrant workers, gradually putting into practice a single temporary residence permit structure. The technical skills and health conditions required by industry sectors and jobs, in particular specialist industries and jobs, should be equal for both rural migrant workers and urban residents. In areas such as school entry requirements, education departments in all provinces and municipalities and all schools must treat the children of migrant rural workers receiving their compulsory education in the same way as local students, and they must not charge arbitrary fees in breach of national regulations. They must promote the reform of the household registration system in large and mid-sized cities and relax the conditions for rural migrant workers to enter cities for work and in the application for a household registration permit. They must investigate housing problems of rural migrants who have come into cities for employment.[9]

It has been shown that there has been a transformation in the thinking behind central government's policies towards migrants in employment, from the discriminatory policies of the past which emphasised norms and controls, to protective policies promoting equality in employment. Although this protection is specifically geared towards rural migrant workers, such discrimination is undoubtedly the most serious form of identity discrimination in the employment market, therefore elimination of discrimination against rural migrant workers undoubtedly has wide-ranging significance on anti-discrimination in employment in general.

In June 2003, motivated by the Sun Zhigang incident, the State Council repealed the 1982 Measures on Round-up and Repatriation of Urban Vagrants and Beggars (*Chengshi liulang qigai renyuan shourong qisong banfa*). This demonstrates that it is no longer possible for any level of government to use the vagaries of the law to demonstrate the correctness and necessity of imposing a temporary resident permit system on migrant workers.

In August 2003 the Standing Committee of the NPC passed the Administrative License Law (*Xinzheng xuke fa*), Article 15 of the Law provides that no local regulation or government rule of the provinces, autonomous regions and municipalities directly under the Central Government may establish any administrative license for the qualifications of the citizens, legal persons or other institutions that shall be determined by the state; no administrative license and pre-administrative license may be established for the establishment and registration of enterprises or other institutions. The administrative licenses established thereby shall not hinder the individuals or enterprises of other regions from dealing in production and business and providing services in one region, shall not restrict the commodities of other regions from entering into the market of the local region. In accordance with this Law, regulations from all departments and committees of the State Council, and provincial and municipal regulations which have established administrative licenses which restrict the migrant workforce, are now unlawful.

Article 83 of the Administrative License Law provides that in accordance with the Law, the legislative organs should clean up the relevant regulations prior to the implementation of the Law; those inconsistent with the Law should be abolished from the day when it is implemented. The old system, by which

---

[9] 'Notice on Providing Effective Management and Services for Rural Migrants Entering the Cities to Work', http://www.nxsjy.com.cn/show.asp?id=172. Last visited September 2008.

documents from the General Office of the State Council and Regulations from State Council Departments and Committees provided a legal basis for provinces and municipalities to regulate for employers' license for the employment of migrant labour and employment license for migrant workers, no longer exists.

After the Administrative License Law became effective, local regulations have changed the old regulations which had imposed an employer's license to employ workers and a migrant worker's permit to work into a system in which employers and migrant workers conclude a labour contract, which then report to local government for keeping in record. All regional regulations requiring an employment permit, employer's permit, health certificates for migrants in employment, restrictions on industries and job types, levying administrative charges and so on, are actually repealed.

At the same time, in recent years central and regional governments have been continuously exploring reform of the household registration systems, so as to eliminate discrimination against migrants in labour and employment. In addition to this, before full reform of the household registration system is implemented, all levels of government are taking measures which strive to reduce employment discrimination based on household registration.

On 26 October 2005 the Legal Daily reported that the Vice Minister for Public Security, Liu Jinguo, had revealed that the Ministry of Public Security was currently closely investigating ideas for reform of the household registration system, and planning to abolish the distinction between rural and non-rural household registrations. The Ministry was also exploring the establishment of a unified urban and rural household registration system. This policy is intended to set the correct precedent for thoroughly resolving the out-of-date dualistic urban/rural household registration system.

At the end of 2006, 14 State Council Departments organised a working group to conduct investigations in 12 provinces into the reform of the household registration system. The working group believed that at present the conditions have been improved for advancing reform of the household registration system. They also indicated that, whilst household registration was not in itself complex, the policies which have been appended to household registration and the structures for the allocation of social and economic benefits which have formed as a result are complex and intricate. [10] However complicated it is, the irrationality of the household registration system is patently obvious. One could expect that following the reform of the household registration system, discrimination in employment which has its roots in the household registration system will be gradually eliminated.

---

[10] '14 State Council Departments Investigate the Household Registration', *Xinjing bao*, 31 January 2007.

6 SUGGESTIONS FOR COMBATING IDENTITY DISCRIMINATION IN EMPLOYMENT

The arrival of migrant workers may increase the competitiveness of the urban employment market, but we cannot restrict migrants coming into the cities to work for this reason. We cannot curtail the freedom of movement and sacrifice migrants' interests simply to protect the interests of urban residents. Discrimination against migrants in employment not only harms their interests, it also has a negative influence on the development of the cities themselves. In a nation ruled by law, such discrimination clearly violates the principle that all are equal before the law; in a market economy discrimination against migrants is not conducive to the formation of a single labour market. Therefore, by establishing the rule of law and the market economy, we must take effective measures to eliminate discrimination against migrant workers in employment, thereby protecting the equal rights of all citizens and better serving economic development.

As stated above, identity discrimination based on household registration and regional origin has already attracted wide-ranging attention, and all levels of central and regional government are making use of legislative and administrative means to reduce these levels of discrimination. However, as regards the current situation, these measures are still in their infancy and have not been fully implemented. To eradicate discrimination completely, we must start to push forward broader reforms of relevant systems from an ideological, legislative and administrative standpoint in order to establish a comprehensive mechanism for protecting equality in employment.

6.1 Further Reform of the Household Registration System

During the reform period, there has been a marked clash between the household registration system, formed in the planned economy, and the need for a freely moving workforce as a central part of the market economy. Therefore reform of the household registration system had already started and was gradually moving forward during the 1980s. In October 1984 the State Council published the Notification on the Problem of Rural People Gathering in Towns and Applying for Household Registration (*Guanyu nongcun jinru jizhen luohu wenti de tongzhi*) which allowed rural people to provide for their own grain rations and move into towns and apply for household registration. In July 1985 the Ministry of Public Security published the Urban Population Management Temporary Regulation (*Guanyu chengzhen renkou guanli zhanxing guiding*) which determined that the internal target for rural household registrations becoming non-rural was fixed at 0.0002% per year. At the same time, against a similar background, the Standing Committee of the NPC announced that the national identity card system, which was to be the basis for the modernisation of population management, would be implemented in September 1985. In 1992 the

14th National Congress of the Communist Party of China stated that the aim of China's economic reforms was to establish a socialist market economy. In response to this, in June 1997 the State Council approved and promulgated the Public Security Ministry's Opinion on Pilot Policy for Household Registration Reform in Small Towns and the Perfection of Rural Household Registration Management (*Xiao chengzhen huji guanli zhidu gaige shidian fang'an he guanyu wanshan nongcun huji guanli zhidu de yijian*). The Opinion provided that all rural people who go to small towns to labour in secondary and tertiary industries, management personnel or technical personnel employed by small town bodies, groups, enterprises or undertakings, who buy commodity housing or own legally self-built housing and their close relatives living with them, can apply for a small town residents' household registration. In July 1998 the State Council approved and promulgated the Public Security Ministry's Opinion on Resolving Prominent Problems in the Current Household Registration System (*Guanyu jiejue dangqian hukou guanli gongzuozhong jige tuchu wenti de yijian*) which provided that the following can be approved to apply for household registration in a city: newborn infants applying for the same household registration as their parents; husbands and wives living apart; elderly people being cared for by their children; people who have invested in the city, are setting up industry and commerce, who have purchased commodity housing and their close relatives living with them; anyone who has a fixed, legal abode in that city and is in stable, legal employment or has a stable, legal livelihood and has lived in that city for a fixed period, and complies with relevant local regulations. In 2001 the State Council approved and promulgated the Public Security Ministry's Opinion on Pushing Forward Reform in Small Town Household Registration (*Guanyu tuijin xiaochengzhen huji guanli zhidugaige de yijian*), which no longer imposed family planning targets on people applying for small town residents' household registration.

One can see that since the reform period began, reform of the household registration system has been carried out consistently. However, these reforms have not yet been able to touch the core content of the household registration system, and the diversified structure of the labour market remains basically unchanged. Therefore, it is now necessary to take more decisive measures to reform the household registration system, so that all types of employment are open to all workers as quickly as possible. In particular in order to eliminate discrimination against migrants in employment we must eliminate employment limits appended to the household registration system, in accordance with the general trend of abolishing the political, social and economic function of household registration, so that household registration is no longer an obstacle to employment.

Of course, because the dualistic urban/rural household registration system has been in force for so long, many systems of social management have been built on this foundation. Difficulties may arise in the sudden wholesale elimination of population migration controls and, for this reason, reform cannot happen suddenly but must be carried out gradually. The first step in reforming household registration is a complete reorganisation of the relevant legislation and a thorough elimination of deliberate social injustices based on differences in household registration. The second step is to disconnect the relevant social organisation systems from the household registration system, thereby reducing the adhesion of the household registration system itself to other systems; in other words, disconnecting labour, human resources, salary, education, and health from the household registration system in order to speed up reform in each respective area. In this way we can ensure that household registration reform is unlikely to cause reverberations throughout the entire system. We can also reduce concentrated, cross-departmental, cross-regional decisions. This will obviously reduce barriers to, and costs of, reform. The third step is to unify the social welfare system dealing with migrant workers' employment, housing, education, labour insurance, health care problems and so on, continuously expanding the scope covered by the social security system and gradually forming a system of equality between urban and rural workers. After employment relationships have been genuinely separated from the household registration system, all workers who have reached working age, who have the ability to work, proof of marital and fertility status and the appropriate training certificates, will be able to seek work in the employment market nationally irrespective of where they come from. Enterprises will then be able to recruit employees in the market irrespective of where they come from and will not have to bear the burden of administrative tasks on behalf of the regional government.

In large cities such as Beijing and Shanghai, not only is there a problem of equality for migrants in employment but there is a significant expansion in the number of migrants in the employment market, it will cause considerable difficulties for the administration and public services, which will be detrimental to the effectiveness of city administration. Therefore, finding a balance between justice and effectiveness is very important in such cities. However, difficulties for the city administration and local employment are, in any event, not an appropriate reason for discriminating against migrants in employment.

6.2   Changing Awareness of Migrants in Employment in Cities

Household registration reform is a long-term process which cannot happen overnight. Even if at some point the household registration system were to be completely reformed, discrimination in employment based on regional origin could still continue. China's total workforce has reached 740 million, which is equivalent to the total workforce of all developed countries. Each year 20 million new workers join the Chinese workforce, but only 10 million workers retire. This vast workforce will be sustained for 20 to 30 years, the problem of the tough employment market cannot be solved within a short timescale, and the number of migrants in large and mid-sized cities will only increase. As a result regional governments, in particular large and mid-sized city governments, are most concerned at present with transforming their awareness of migrants in employment. Urban governments must realise that the migrant workforce is an important resource for urban construction and development. Migrant workers do dirty, tiring and dangerous jobs in the cities, they reduce the costs of, and contribute towards, urban development and should be treated fairly rather than discriminated against. When drawing up employment programmes and policies and implementing related measures, regional governments must reform the traditional structure which separates urban and rural areas. They must eliminate all obstacles to the free movement of the workforce and abolish the practice of only considering the local or urban working population. Furthermore they must genuinely combine the local workforce, holding a fixed local household registration, and the migrant workforce in a unified labour market and provide administration and services for the unified labour market.

6.3 Improving Legislation and Establishing a System of Labour Laws which Combat Identity Discrimination

Of course, we should respect freedom of contract in the employment market. However, there are considerable differences between freedom of contract in the employment market and freedom of contract in other civil agreements. This is because the prospective employer is in a stronger position than the applicant which means that simply following this principle will necessarily lead to discrimination. However, there is a lack of legislation prohibiting discrimination in the current Chinese legal system. At present in China the only basic law which protects the rights of employees is the Labour Law. This legislation, however, does not provide an effective remedy for jobseekers who encounter discrimination because there are no provisions prohibiting discrimination against migrants in employment. Of course, the Chinese Labour Law provides for equality in employment in principle, and from the point of view of statutory interpretation one could understand this as including equality between migrants and locals in employment. However because there is a lack of appropriate legal support and no provisions clearly detailing legal responsibility for violations, the present law on equality in employment is ineffective in practice. Therefore, the first step is to follow the guidance of the principle enshrined in the Constitution that all people are equal, to amend the Labour Law or enact an Anti-Discrimination in Employment Law which prohibits discrimination against migrants in employment that is based on factors such as household registration or regional origin, and including detailed implementation provisions which deal in particular with the legal consequences for violation. In addition to improving the law itself, it is necessary to establish a complete implementation mechanism. These enforcement mechanisms and legislation must be established at a national level, within the framework of the basic national laws, which specifically protect migrants in employment, and should set out a single, national standard for the protection of migrants in employment. This is to prevent regional governments using their own legislative powers to provide a legal basis for their own discriminatory practices. In addition to this, it is necessary to establish and perfect a legal assistance mechanism for migrants that provides support and guidance to lawyers and legal professionals who provide necessary legal aid when migrants encounter discrimination in employment.

6.4   Establishing a Mechanism for a Single Labour Market

At present Chinese policies relating to the labour market come from many sources. Governmental departments, such as human resources departments, labour and social security departments, construction departments, agriculture departments, and education departments all take part in the formulation and enforcement of employment policies. This type of system means that each department takes its own interests as their point of departure. Such a system easily creates employment policies containing elements of discrimination. Therefore it is necessary to establish a unified mechanism for administration and services to the employment market, gradually uniting the administration concerning the employment of specialist technicians, graduates of technical colleges and discharged military personnel currently carried out by administrative human resources departments, the administration concerning the employment of industrial workers carried out by labour and social security departments, and the administration concerning the employment of the rural population carried out by agriculture departments, under the Labour and Social Security Ministry. To create an equal labour market we must establish a single mechanism for urban and rural employment administration and services and abolish the system which differentiates between locals and migrants. Workers should be able to choose their employment freely and equally according to their working ability rather than their identity or regional origin.

6.5   Carrying out Reform of the Electoral System to Protect the Rights of Migrants to Political Participation

The nature of a democratic system requires every social group to have its own representative in the democratic representative body, who will reflect their interests in democratic debate, policy formation and in decisions beneficial to its members. Migrants do not have the right to vote or to stand for election in the area to which they have moved, and this is one reason why they suffer policy level discrimination. Therefore, reform of the electoral system is necessary to permit migrants who have lived in an area for a certain amount of time (for example six months or a year) to take part in the elections of the regional people's congress, giving them both the right to vote and to stand for election. When local democratic bodies include representatives of the migrant population, they will be able to vote and have a voice in order to influence the formation of local labour policies and, through supervision of administrative bodies, will be able to gradually eliminate all the city government's discriminatory policies.

6

A SURVEY OF EMPLOYMENT DISCRIMINATION IN TEN MAJOR CITIES IN CHINA[1]

*Constitutionalism Research Institute,
China University of Political Science and Law*

1. AN OVERVIEW OF THE SURVEY (PART A)

From May to October 2006, we carried out a survey exploring employment discrimination in ten major cities in China. We used the method of structured questions. Our researchers followed strict guidelines when questioning the interviewees and noting down their answers. We planned to carry out 3500 questionnaires, but in reality completed 3454 98.7%.

The questionnaire was composed of six parts: part A explored individuals' circumstances; B explored discrimination while seeking employment; C looked at other discrimination within the domain of work; D dealt with discrimination in social and political life; E explored individuals' subjective view and judgment of employment discrimination; and F looked at individuals' identification with and attitude towards discrimination. Through this survey we hope to bring employment discrimination to the fore. We aim to provide an objective and comprehensive understanding of the current situation on discrimination in employment, so as to provide a reliable foundation for anti-discrimination measures; promote law-making on equal employment opportunities; and implement laws to protect people's equal opportunity rights effectively.

Definitions of statistical terminology used:
1. Case: corresponds to an individual's circumstances.
2. Frequency: the number of individual cases (number of answers).
3. Percent: frequency divided by the number of cases.
4. Total Cases: the total number of case samples, that is to say the total number of cases (people) in the survey. This survey has 3454 cases in total.
5. Valid Cases: the total number of properly recorded answers.

---

[1] This survey is based on a social investigation that the Institute of Sociology of China University of Political Science and Law was commissioned to carry out. Professor He Shanjun designed the questionaire and Li An was responsible for the statistics.

6. Missing Cases: the difference between the total number of cases and valid cases. Cases are normally missing because interviewees do not answer, or researchers make mistakes filling in the answers etc.
7. Valid Percent: frequency divided by the number of valid cases.
8. Mean: the average amount. The value of valid cases divided by the number of cases. For example, average height, weight etc.
9. Standard Deviation: the spread of a distribution around the mean of valid cases. The larger the value, the further the case is from the mean. To give an example, suppose the average height of a group of people was 170cm. If most of the persons in this group were taller than 170cm, then the standard deviation would be relatively large, but if the majority were around 170cm in height, then the standard deviation would be relatively small. If everyone in the group was 170cm tall then the standard deviation would be 0.
10. Responses Number: this only appears in the multiple choice questions, when interviewees can choose more than one option. The responses number resulted from adding all the choices from the valid cases. For example, supposing a multiple choice question has 5 options and 3000 people answer it. On average, each person selects 2 options, so the total responses number is 2×3000 = 6000.

The distribution of areas surveyed: [2]

Area Surveyed	Beijing	Guangzhou	Wuhan	Nanjing	Shenyang	Chengdu	Xi'an	Zhengzhou	Yinchuan	Qingdao	Total
Questionnaires returned	600	390	388	300	300	294	296	300	290	296	3454
Percent of total samples	17.4	11.3	11.2	8.7	8.7	8.5	8.6	8.7	8.4	8.6	100

Employment discrimination is everywhere, but in major cities it is even more prevalent and serious. Therefore we chose to carry out our survey in ten major cities throughout China. In selecting the ten cities, we have taken into account the disparities between north, south, east and west, and peculiarities of different cities.

We adopted a random approach in conducting our survey in order to collect a multilayered range of samples. Firstly, we chose our ten major cities according to region, and for both their common and distinctive characteristics. Then, in

---

[2] Out of the questionnaire forms sent out, 600 were distributed in Beijing, 400 to Guangzhou and Wuhan and 300 to the other cities. In total there were 3500 forms, but in reality only 3454 were completed (98.7%).

order to guarantee that the survey was sufficiently random and fully comprehensive, within these cities we chose samples from every area, and distributed the number of questionnaires according to population size. Finally, within each area we selected one high and one low income residential district. The number of samples taken from a residential district corresponded with the number of households in it and we would proceed, for example, by starting from the second flat on the third floor and go from household to household, systematically from right to left.

In addition we considered the particular groups of people who were especially likely to face employment discrimination. If we used random samples, we might find that very few or none of these people had experienced discrimination and therefore it was necessary to send a number of interviewers to penetrate and assess groups of specially designated people in relatively busy places. This investigative method is called the '*run into*' style sample.

The different groups of people questioned in the survey were as follows:

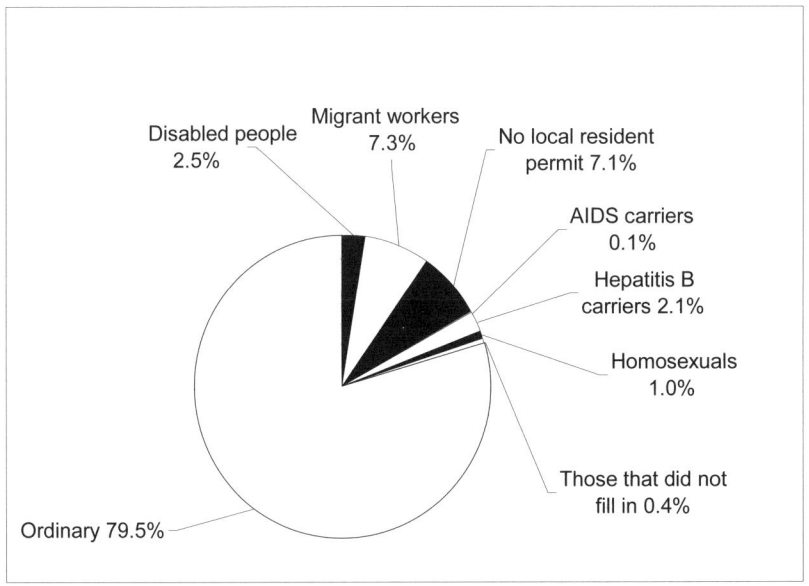

A1: Distribution of sexes:

Sex		Frequency	Valid percent	Total percent
Valid cases	Female	1543	44.8	44.8
	Male	1900	55.2	100
	Subtotal	3443	100.0	
Missing cases	Subtotal	11		
Total		3454		

As shown in A1, out of the 3443 responses to the questionnaire, 55.2% were male and 44.8% were female. This closely reflects the population's male: female ratio as a whole and confirms the successful random nature of the survey.

A2: Age distribution:

Age group		Frequency	Valid percent	Total percent
Valid cases	Under 20	157	4.6	4.6
	21 - 40	2205	64.1	68.7
	41 - 60	1050	30.5	99.2
	Over 61	28	0.8	100
	Subtotal	3440	100.0	
Missing cases		14		
Total		3454		

As shown in A2, out of the interviewees the age group with the most number of people was the 21-40 age group (64.1%), followed by the 41-60 age group (30.5%) and the under 20 group (4.6).

A3: Type of resident permit:

Place of registration		Frequency	Valid percent	Total percent
Valid cases	Local city resident permit	2249	65.4	65.4
	Rural resident permit	700	20.4	85.8
	Resident permit from another city	486	14.1	99.9
	Other	4	0.1	100
	Subtotal	3439	100.0	
Missing cases	Subtotal	15		
Total		3454		

In this survey, 65.4% of those interviewed were residents registered in their respective cities, 20.4% held rural resident permits and 14.1% were registered in other cities. This more or less corresponds with the actual ratio of permanent residents and migrants in large cities throughout China. Moreover, analysing the data on birth places shows that only 55.5% of the interviewees were locals, while the rest had migrated from elsewhere.

A4: Education background:

Education background		Frequency	Valid percent	Total percent
Valid cases	Never gone to school	29	0.8	0.8
	Primary school	109	3.2	4.0
	Junior high school	643	18.7	22.8
	Middle and secondary school	1035	30.1	52.9
	College	718	20.9	73.9
	Undergraduate college	810	23.6	97.5
	Postgraduate	87	2.5	100
	Subtotal	3431	100.0	
Missing cases	Subtotal	23		
Total		3454		

From A4 it can be seen that 52.9% of people had not received a university education and 47% had a college diploma or above. This shows that the number of people with high level educational qualifications in major cities is relatively large.

A5: Health:

Health		Frequency	Valid percent	Total percent
Valid cases	In good health	3073	89.7	89.7
	Ill	337	9.9	99.5
	Unanswered	16	0.5	100.0
	Subtotal	3426	100.0	
Missing cases	Subtotal	28		
Total		3454		

89.7% of interviewees stated they were in good health.

A6: Political affiliation:

Political affiliation		Frequency	Valid percent	Total percent
Valid Cases	Communist Party member	869	25.3	25.3
	Democratic Party	26	0.8	26.1
	Communist Youth League member	598	17.4	43.5
	Non-partisan	1937	56.5	100.0
	Subtotal	3430	100.0	
Missing cases	Subtotal	24		
Total		3454		

Members of the Chinese Communist Party, Communist Youth League and Democratic Party accounted for 43.5% of those interviewed.

A7: Employment status:

Employment status		Frequency	Valid percent	Total percent
Valid cases	Employed	2799	81.8	81.8
	Laid off or unemployed	308	9.0	90.8
	Retired	143	4.2	94.9
	Never been employed	52	1.5	96.5
	Other	121	3.5	100.0
	Subtotal	3423	100.0	
Missing cases	Subtotal	31		
Total		3454		

From A7 we can discern that 81.8% of people were employed and 10.5% had been laid-off or were never employed. The average career span of interviewees was about 14 years.

A8: Present occupation:

Present occupation		Frequency	Valid percent	Total percent
Valid cases	Civil servant	200	6.0	6.0
	Employee in a state-owned units	648	19.3	25.3
	Business manager	456	13.6	38.9
	Professional and technician[3]	453	13.5	52.4
	Service or salesperson	529	15.7	68.1
	Mediating sector	71	2.1	70.3
	Owners of privately owned enterprises	171	5.1	75.4
	Worker	619	18.5	93.8
	Freelance	102	3.0	96.8
	Never been employed	27	0.8	97.6
	Other	79	2.4	100.0
	Subtotal	3355	100.0	
Missing cases	Subtotal	99		
Total		3454		

A8 reveals that employees of state-owned units, workers and those in the service industry or sales made up 19.3%, 18.5% and 15.7% of the interviewees respectively.

A9: Salary level:

Salary in RMB		Frequency	Valid percent	Total percent
Valid cases	Under 800	767	22.9	22.9
	800 – 2000	1762	52.7	75.6
	2000 – 5000	673	20.1	95.7
	5000 – 10000	108	3.2	98.9
	Over 10000	25	0.7	100.0
	Subtotal	3335	100.0	
Missing cases	Subtotal	119		
Total		3454		

---

[3] Professional and technician refer to engineers and technicians in companies as well as teachers, doctors, accountants and such personnel with professional titles.

A9 shows that half of the people interviewed earn between RMB 800-2000 (52.7%), 22.9% earn under RMB 800, 20.1% earn RMB 2000-5000 and a total of 95.7% earn under RMB 5000.

A10: Comprehensive table: welfare and benefits:

Do you receive the following welfare benefit?	Receive		Do not receive		Unclear	
	Frequency	Percent	Frequency	Percent	Frequency	Percent
Health insurance	2120	62.4	1135	33.4	140	4.1
Old-age pension	1899	56.0	1313	38.7	179	5.3
Unemployment benefits	1427	42.2	1657	49.0	298	8.8
Housing benefits	1281	37.9	1841	54.4	260	7.7
Children's schooling	424	12.6	2524	75.3	404	12.1

The least provided benefit was children's schooling. 75.3% of interviewees indicated that employers did not pay for children's schooling. 54.4% of people did not receive housing benefits, and 33.4% of people were not receiving health insurance. The benefit that was provided the most was health insurance (62.4%) followed by old-age pension (56%), with only 12.6% receiving children's schooling.

2. DISCRIMINATION WHILE JOB SEEKING (PART B)

B1-a: When you sought employment, has a work unit (public sector) or private business employer had gender requirements?

Gender requirements		Frequency	Valid percent	Total percent
Valid cases	Male	477	13.9	13.9
	Female	245	7.1	21
	Either fine	1105	32.2	53.3
	Unspecified	1602	46.7	100.0
	Subtotal	3429	100.0	
Missing cases	Subtotal	25		
Total		3454		

B1-a shows that those work units specifically requiring men stood at 13.9%. 7.1% specifically required women, while almost half (46.7%) did not specify. Evidently 21% had clear gender requirements.

A Survey of Employment Discrimination   165

B1-b: When you sought employment, has an employer had age requirements?

Age requirements		Frequency	Valid percent	Total percent
Valid cases	From between the ages of a-b	613	18.1	18.1
	Under age c	499	14.8	32.9
	Unspecified requirements	2269	67.1	100.0
	Subtotal	3381	100.0	
Missing cases	Subtotal	73		
Total		3454		

The statistical data results of a, b, and c are shown in B1-c. As B1-b shows that 32.9% of work units had age requirements and 67.1% had no specific requirements.

B1-c: Age requirements: youngest age a, oldest age b, below required age c:

	Number of cases	Mean	Standard deviation
Youngest age a	676	22.0	7.80
Oldest age b	566	34.5	9.62
Under what age c	390	36.5	8.28

B1-d: When you sought employment, has an employer had specific height requirements?

Height requirement		Frequency	Valid percent	Total percent
Valid cases	Requirements	464	13.8	13.8
	No specific requirements	2896	86.2	100.0
	Subtotal	3360	100.0	
Missing cases	Subtotal	94		
Total		3454		

B1-d shows that 13.8% of interviewees thought their employers had height requirements.

B1-e: When you sought employment, did an employer have specific weight requirements?

Weight requirement		Frequency	Valid percent	Total percent
Valid cases	Requirements	93	2.8	2.8
	No specific requirements	3276	97.2	100.0
	Subtotal	3369	100.0	
Missing cases	Subtotal	85		
Total		3454		

From B1-e it seems that employers rarely have explicit weight requirements (2.8%).

B1-f: When you sought employment, has an employer had requirements related to appearance?

Appearance requirements		Frequency	Valid percent	Total percent
Valid cases	An appropriate appearance	1253	36.7	36.7
	No specific requirements	2164	63.3	100.0
	Subtotal	3417	100.0	
Missing cases	Subtotal	37		
Total		3454		

36.7% of people thought recruiters had appearance requirements.

B1-g: When you sought employment, have employers required educational qualifications?

Educational requirements		Frequency	Valid percent	Total percent
Valid cases	Junior high or above	429	12.5	12.5
	Middle school or above	599	17.5	30.0
	College or above	549	16.0	46.0
	Undergraduate degree or above	538	15.7	61.7
	Masters or above	30	0.9	62.6
	Studied abroad	2	0.1	62.7
	No specific requirements	1282	37.4	100.0
	Subtotal	3429	100.0	
Missing cases	Subtotal	25		
Total		3454		

A Survey of Employment Discrimination   167

B1-g reveals that 62.7% had educational requirements, and among those 32.6% specifically required a college level education and above (this includes undergraduate and postgraduate students). 37.4% had no specific requirements.

B1-h: When you sought employment, has an employer required certificates to prove qualifications?

Certificates of qualifications		Frequency	Valid percent	Total percent
Valid cases	Junior high	361	10.6	10.6
	Middle school	440	12.9	23.5
	Higher education	100	2.9	26.4
	No specific requirements	2506	73.6	100.0
	Subtotal	3407	100.0	
Missing cases	Subtotal	47		
Total		3454		

We can learn from B1-h that 26.4% of people replied that they were asked for certificates to prove qualifications. 73.6% of interviewees had not been asked for certificates to prove their qualifications.

B1-i: When you sought employment, has an employer required work experience?

Work experience		Frequency	Valid percent	Total percent
Valid cases	Yes	678	20.2	20.2
	No	2681	79.8	100.0
	Subtotal	3359	100.0	
Missing cases	Subtotal	95		
Total		3454		

20.2% of people being employed found they needed on average two years of work experience to be employed.

B1-j: When you sought employment, has an employer had requirements related to resident permits?

Resident permits requirements		Frequency	Valid percent	Total percent
Valid cases	Local city resident permit	761	22.3	22.3
	Non-rural resident permit	220	6.4	28.7
	No specific requirements	2435	71.3	100.0
	Subtotal	3416	100.0	
Missing cases	Subtotal	38		
Total		3454		

When recruiting, 28.7% of employers had explicit resident permit requirements, 22.3% wanted people to have resident permits in that city and 71.3% had no specific requirements.

B1-k (Multiple choice questions): When you applied for a job, what health requirements have employers expressed?

Health requirements	Frequency	Percent of valid cases
No serious illness	1632	47.7
No disabilities	464	13.6
No infectious diseases	648	18.9
No history of recurring illness	273	8.0
No specific requirements	981	28.7
Total	3998	116.9

There were 3420 valid cases and 34 missing cases, a total of 3454 cases. This was a multiple choice question, in which 47.7% of people replied that employers specified there were to be no serious illnesses.

B1-l: When you applied for a job, has an employer made requirements related to sexual orientation?

Sexual orientation		Frequency	Valid percent	Total percent
Valid cases	No homosexuals	209	6.2	6.2
	No specific requirements	3179	93.8	100.0
	Subtotal	3388	100.0	
Missing cases	Subtotal	66		
Total		3454		

6.2% of employers were clear that they would not employ homosexuals.

B1-m: When you applied for a job, has an employer had political requirements?

Political requirements		Frequency	Valid percent	Total percent
Valid cases	Communist Party member	221	6.4	6.4
	No specific requirements	3210	93.6	100.0
	Subtotal	3431	100.0	
Missing cases		23		
Total		3454		

Looking at B1-m, only 6.4% of interviewees were asked to meet concrete political requirements, while 93.6% replied there had been no specific requirements as regards politics.

B1-n: When you applied for a job, has an employer had certain ethnic requirements?

Ethnic requirements		Frequency	Valid percent	Total percent
Valid cases	Chinese (Han)	118	3.4	3.4
	Ethnic minority	12	0.3	3.7
	Does not want a certain ethnic minority	23	0.7	4.4
	No specific requirements	3277	95.5	100.0
	Subtotal	3430	100.0	
Missing cases		24		
Total		3454		

Looking at B1-n, 4.4% of interviewees answered that employers had specific ethnic requirements. Making ethnic requirements clearly constitutes discrimination; however ethnic discrimination within the ten major cities does not appear to be prevalent.

B2 Comprehensive table: When applying for a job, have you been turned down on account of any of the following reasons? How many times? What number proportionally?

	No		Cannot remember		Yes			
	Frequency	Percent	Frequency	Percent	Frequency	Percent	Number of incidents	Ratio
Female	1183	75.0	220	13.9	175	11.1	2.7	43%
Disabled	130	60.2	39	18.1	47	21.8	3.7	64%
Resident permit registered elsewhere	520	61.8	168	20.0	154	18.3	2.6	46%
Migrant worker	298	64.4	106	22.9	59	12.7	2.8	39%
Age	641	76.7	94	11.2	101	12.1	2.5	46%
Ungainly appearance	172	77.5	29	13.1	21	9.5	2.9	35%
Low educational qualifications	717	63.9	195	17.4	210	18.7	2.7	44%
Health reasons	211	72.5	41	14.1	39	13.4	2.1	39%
Political beliefs	1266	91.3	73	5.3	47	3.4	2.5	16%

Among the options, the highest proportion of people said disability was the reason they had been turned down for a job, with 21.8% of disabled interviewees stating that they had been turned down on account of their disability. The second most prevalent reason was lack of educational qualifications (18.7%). The third most common reason was not having a local resident permit (18.3%), and the least prevalent option was political beliefs (3.4%). Correspondingly, out of the options not chosen, the most common was political beliefs (91.3%) and the least common was disability (60.2%).

B3 Comprehensive table: Have you suffered discrimination while applying for a civil servant position?

	Yes		No		Don't remember	
	Frequency	Percent	Frequency	Percent	Frequency	Percent
Female	168	32.0	334	63.6	23	4.4
Having a disability	47	40.9	58	50.4	10	8.7
Not having local resident permit	125	43.0	158	51.8	22	7.2
Migrant worker	64	37.8	113	59.8	12	6.3
Age	85	32.0	168	63.2	13	4.9
Unattractive appearance	39	33.9	66	57.4	10	8.7
Education	142	45.0	161	50.9	13	4.1
Health reasons	46	40.7	60	53.1	7	6.2
Political stance	83	18.4	351	78.0	16	3.6

During civil servant recruitment, a low educational standard was the number one factor for being discriminated against (45%), since government institutions have clear educational requirements. Of course, making educational requirements does not constitute discrimination. Not having local resident permits came in at second place with 43%. This is the most serious discrimination. Disabilities and health reasons came in third and fourth respectively. Correspondingly, among the options not chosen, the first three were political stance, being female and age: 78%, 63.6% and 63.2% of people respectively did not choose these factors.

B4-1 (Multiple choice): What kinds of discrimination have you suffered while looking for employment?

	Frequency	Percent answered	Percent of valid cases
Never	1620	28.9	49.3
When getting a job	578	10.3	17.6
When arranging a job or post	748	13.4	22.7
Working conditions and environment	446	7.9	13.6
Wages or welfare benefits	1015	18.1	30.8
Promotion and getting professional title	698	12.5	21.3
Technical training	112	2.0	3.4
Medical insurance and accident cover	249	4.4	7.5
Dismissal and retirement	72	1.3	2.2
Other	86	1.6	2.6
Total	5624	100.0	171

Note: there were 3306 valid cases and 148 missing cases, with 3454 cases in total.

According to the proportion of valid cases, 49.3% of interviewees said they had suffered no discrimination, putting this option in first place. 30.8% of interviewees believed they had been discriminated against in relation to pay and benefits. 22.7% of people interviewed believed that they were discriminated against when arranging a job or post. 21.3% were discriminated against while being up for promotion or getting their professional title.

B4-2: Degree of discrimination:

Degree of discrimination		Frequency	Valid percent	Total percent
Valid cases	Serious	137	4.3	4.3
	Relatively serious	364	11.4	15.6
	Average	887	27.7	43.3
	Relatively light	372	11.6	54.9
	None	1444	45	100.0
	Subtotal	3204	100.0	
Missing cases	Subtotal	250		
Total		3454		

A Survey of Employment Discrimination 173

It is visibly clear that we face serious discrimination in our society. 55% of people thought that they had suffered some kind of discrimination, 15.7% thought that they had suffered serious levels of discrimination, while 45.1% of people had not suffered discrimination at all.

3. DIFFERENT TREATMENT IN THE SPHERE OF EMPLOYMENT (PART C)

C1-a: When you signed a contract, has an employer laid down restrictions on marriage and having children? (Female answers)

Restrictions on marriage and having children		Frequency	Valid percent	Total percent
Valid cases	None	1299	84.6	84.6
	Verbally	183	11.9	96.5
	Written	54	3.5	100.0
	Subtotal	1536	100.0	
Missing cases	Subtotal	1918		
Total		3454		

15.4% of women faced restrictions on getting married and having children. 84.6% of women said they had not had such problems.

C1-b (Multiple choice): Has your work unit already implemented measures to protect women's rights and interests?

	Frequency	Percent answered	Percent of valid cases
Pregnancy	699	21.5	52.4
Maternity leave	972	29.8	72.8
Nursing period/leave	657	20.2	49.2
Special biological leave	233	7.2	17.5
Labour and safety protection	606	18.6	45.4
Other	91	2.8	6.8
Total answers	3258	100.0	244.0

Note: there were 1335 valid cases, 2118 missing cases and a total of 3454 cases.

52.4% of interviewees said their work unit had implemented pregnancy rights, 72.8% said their work unit had implemented maternity leave, 49.2%

mentioned nursing leave, 17.5% said biological leave, 45.4% said labour and safety protection. Expressing this in another way, 47.6% of work units had not implemented women's pregnancy rights.

C2-a: Do you enjoy rights provided by the law? (Disabled people's answers)

Disability rights		Frequency	Valid percent	Total percent
Valid cases	Enjoy full rights	19	15.2	15.2
	Partly enjoy	56	44.8	60.0
	Do not enjoy	24	19.2	79.2
	Unable to say	22	17.6	96.8
	Did not reply	4	3.2	100.0
	Subtotal	125	100.0	
Missing cases		3329		
Total		3454		

15.2% of people enjoy full rights, 44.8% enjoy partial rights, 19.2% have no rights and 17.6% could not say. The number of people who thought that they had no rights exceeded those who enjoyed full rights.

C2-b (Multiple choice): What preferential treatment have you received in a small individual business? (Disabled people's answers)

Preferential treatment and care	Frequency	Percent of answers	Percent of valid cases
Production services	23	17.8	29.5
Technical instruction	27	20.9	34.6
Supply of agricultural materials	6	4.7	7.7
Agricultural by-products purchasing tax	6	4.7	7.7
Business administration fee	29	22.5	37.2
Issuing business licences	25	19.4	32.1
Other	13	10.1	16.7
Total answers	129	100.0	165.4

A Survey of Employment Discrimination

Note: there were 78 valid cases, 3376 missing cases, with a total of 3454 cases.

Of the disabled people interviewed, 37.2% enjoyed preferential treatment in industrial and commercial administration fees, 34.6% got technical instruction and care, 32.1% got preferential treatment in issuing business licences, 29.5% received production services, 7.7% were supplied with agricultural materials and enjoyed agricultural by-products purchasing tax.

C3-a (Multiple choice): In what aspects does your treatment compare unfavourably with normal employees? (Migrant workers' answers)

	Frequency	Percent of answers	Percent of valid cases
Restrictions on employment sector	145	12.1	35.3
Work arrangements (dirty, heavy, or rough)	349	29.0	84.9
Discrepancy in work and living conditions	369	30.7	89.7
Pay	149	12.4	36.2
Medical insurance and accident protection	115	9.6	27.9
Contents of labour contract	27	2.2	6.6
Length of probationary period and training	35	2.9	8.5
Other	14	1.2	3.4
Total answers	1203	100.0	292.7

Note: there were 411 valid cases, 3043 missing cases, and 3454 cases in total.

The most common answers were, first, a discrepancy in working and living conditions (89.7%); second came discrimination in work arrangements (dirty, heavy, or rough) (84.9%); third was pay discrimination (36.2%); fourth was restrictions on sector (35.3%).

C3-b1 (Multiple choice): What issues would employees report to employers in order to improve treatment? (Migrant workers' answers)

	Frequency	Percent of responses	Percent of valid cases
Restrictions on employment sector	26	6.5	11.9
Work arrangements (dirty, heavy, or rough)	110	27.6	50.4
Discrepancy in work and living conditions	184	46.1	84.5
Pay	74	18.6	33.9
Medical treatment and accident protection	5	1.3	2.3
Total answers	399	100.0	183.0

Note: the number of valid cases was 218, with 3236 missing cases, and a total of 3454 cases.

The three answers with the highest percents were discrepancies in working and living conditions (84.5%), work arrangements (dirty, heavy, or rough) (50.4%), and then pay (33.9%). From the data in C3-b1 it could be argued that migrant workers usually report an issue to their work unit when they consider the issue could readily be resolved. For issues such as vocational restrictions, healthcare and accident insurance, which are institutional problems, migrant workers would hardly raise them with their employers knowing that they could not be solved anyway.

C3-b2 (Multiple choice): On what issues would you go to management and demand improvements? (Migrant workers' responses)

	Frequency	Percent of answers	Percent of valid cases
Sector restrictions	18	7.9	12.5
Work arrangements (dirty, heavy, rough)	41	18.0	28.4
Discrepancy in work and living conditions	50	22.0	34.7
Pay	81	35.5	56.2
Medical treatment and accident protection	36	15.8	25.0
Contents of labour contract	2	0.9	1.4
Total answers	228	100.0	158.3

Note: 144 valid cases, 3310 missing cases, total cases 3454.

Pay issues are the main concerns reported to management (56.2%). Healthcare and accident protection issues are also increasingly reported to the management. Compared with C3-b1, these numbers have increased from 1.3% to 15.8%. 34.7% of people reported discrepancies in working and living conditions, 28.4% reported work arrangements (dirty, heavy, rough). This shows that migrant workers are clear about the responsibilities of work units and management.

C3-b3 (Multiple choice): Under what conditions would you seek legal aid? (Migrant workers' responses)

	Frequency	Percent of responses	Percent of valid cases
Vocational restrictions	10	5.4	7.6
Work arrangements (dirty, heavy, or rough)	14	7.5	10.7
Discrepancy in work and living conditions	14	7.5	10.7
Pay	49	26.4	37.4
Medical treatment and accident protection	86	46.3	65.7
Contents of labour contract	12	6.5	9.2
Length of probation	1	0.5	0.8
Total answers	186	100.0	142.0

Note: 131 valid cases, 3323 missing cases, a total of 3454 cases.

From the data C3-b3 it can be seen that, if migrant workers require medical treatment or accident protection (65.7%) or have pay issues (37.4%), then they will appeal to the law.

C3-b4: Do you believe it is natural for migrant workers to be treated differently from regular workers?

		Frequency	Valid percent	Total percent
Valid cases	Yes	113	35.4	35.4
	No	206	64.6	100.0
	Subtotal	319	100.0	
Missing cases	Subtotal	3135		
Total		3454		

35.4% of migrant workers believe that discrimination is natural. 64.6% think it is not right.

C3-b5: Do you complain in private, but tolerate in practice?

Complain in private		Frequency	Valid percent	Total percent
Valid cases	Yes	217	64.8	64.8
	No	118	35.2	100.0
	Subtotal	335	100.0	
Missing cases	Subtotal	3119		
Total		3454		

The majority of migrant workers (64.8%) will just complain in private while 35.2% are not willing to tolerate discrimination.

C4-a (Multiple choice): When you apply for jobs, what educational requirements have recruiters wanted? (College graduates and above)

Education	Frequency	Percent of answers	Percent of valid cases
Public university graduates	327	19.8	24.5
Major university graduates	310	18.8	23.2
Bachelor degree	609	36.8	45.7
Studied abroad	45	2.7	3.3
No educational requirements	362	21.9	27.1
Total answers	1653	100.0	123.9

Note: 1334 valid cases, 2120 missing cases, total number of cases 3454.

45.7% of work units asked that the first degree should be at the bachelor level, while 24.5% of work units require graduates from public universities and 23.2% of work units require students to be from major universities.

C4-b: Have you ever been turned down for a job because your educational qualifications were not suitable?

		Frequency	Valid percent	Total percent
Valid cases	Yes, told directly	455	44.9	44.9
	Yes, but not directly informed	205	20.2	65.1
	Not clear	81	8.0	73.1
	Hard to say	272	26.9	100.0
	Subtotal	1013	100.0	
Missing cases		2441		
Total		3454		

65.1% of people answered that they had been turned down because of their educational qualifications. It is clear that during recruitment the highest percent of people were turned down for educational reasons. 44.9% of people were informed of the reason directly, revealing that at present direct discrimination is prevalent.

C5-a: If an employer discovers an illness during a physical check-up, has this influenced whether or not they hire you? (Responses of people in ill health)

		Frequency	Valid percent	Total percent
Valid cases	Definitely influenced	95	39.6	39.6
	Perhaps influenced	57	23.8	63.4
	No influence	18	7.6	70.8
	Hard to say	70	29.2	100.0
	Subtotal	240	100.0	
Missing cases	Subtotal	3214		
Total		3454		

63.4% of people said illness would definitely influence or perhaps influence their chances of employment. Health is obviously very important to recruiters.

C5-b: If you were dismissed on account of illness, were you informed of the reason?

Were you informed of the reason		Frequency	Valid percent	Total percent
Valid cases	Definitely not	40	18.0	18.0
	Sometimes	46	20.7	38.7
	Normally	68	30.6	69.4
	Hard to say	68	30.6	100.0
	Subtotal	222	100.0	
Missing cases	Subtotal	3232		
Total		3454		

From the data in C5-b, 18% said they were definitely not informed of the reason, 20.7% said sometimes, 30.6% said normally, and in total 51.3% said they were told the reason for dismissal. This shows that this kind of discrimination is still relatively public.

C5-c: Has your health affected your career?

Health reasons have affected finding employment		Frequency	Valid percent	Total percent
Valid cases	No	139	65.3	65.3
	Yes	74	34.7	100.0
	Subtotal	213	100.0	
Missing cases	Subtotal	3241		
Total		3454		

34.7% of interviewees replied that their health had influenced their career, but 65.3% replied it had not.

C6-a: When you are taking the civil service exams, what age requirements have been specified? (Age 40 and above)

Age requirements		Frequency	Valid percent	Total percent
Valid cases	Under 30	87	42.0	42.0
	Under 35	120	58.0	100.0
	Subtotal	207	100.0	
Missing cases	Subtotal	3247		
Total		3454		

42.0% were required to be under 30 and 58.0% under 35. It appears that more than half of work units required applicants to be under 35.

C6-b: Age requirements for taking exams for other professions:

Age requirements		Frequency	Valid percent	Total percent
Valid cases	Under 30	95	22.4	22.4
	Under35	152	35.8	58.1
	Under 40	178	41.9	100.0
	Subtotal	425	100.0	
Missing cases	Subtotal	3029		
Total		3454		

41.9% were required to be under 40 years old, 35.8% under 35 years old and 22.4% under 30 years old. This suggests that the older the person, the more likely he or she is to suffer discrimination.

A Survey of Employment Discrimination
181

C-7: Have you been turned down by an employer because you do not hold a local resident permit? (Responses of people with rural of non-local resident permits)

Resident permits		Frequency	Valid percent	Total percent
Valid cases	Refused for not being locals	212	27.6	27.6
	Refused for holding a rural household registration	36	4.7	32.3
	Never experienced this	520	67.7	100.0
	Subtotal	768	100.0	
Missing cases	Subtotal	2686		
Total		3454		

27.6% of interviewees said they had been turned down because they did not hold a local resident permit, 4.7% had been turned down because they had rural household registration. 67.7% had not experienced this kind of discrimination.

4. DISCRIMINATION IN SOCIAL AND POLITICAL LIFE (PART D)

D-1 (Multiple choice): Apart from employment discrimination, what other kind of discrimination have you suffered from?

Other discrimination suffered	Frequency	Percent of answers	Percent of valid cases
Never been discriminated against	2053	53.9	63.6
Education	521	13.7	16.1
Healthcare	454	11.9	14.1
Housing	711	18.7	22.0
Others	69	1.8	2.1
Total answers	3808	100.0	117.9

Note: 3229 valid cases, 225 missing cases, 3454 total cases.

22% thought that they had suffered housing discrimination, 16.1% said they had been discriminated against in education, 14.1% in healthcare and 63.6% thought that they had never been discriminated against.

D2-a (Multiple choice): Have you faced discrimination when going to expensive places (shops, hotels, restaurants, etc.)?

	Frequency	Percent of responses	Percent of valid cases
Never been	1077	31.3	32.5
Been, but faced no discrimination	1635	47.5	49.4
Yes, faced discrimination	177	5.1	5.4
Discrimination in service	440	12.8	13.3
Other	4	0.1	0.1
Don't remember	111	3.2	3.4
Total cases	3444	100.0	104.0

Note: 3310 valid cases, 114 missing cases, a total of 3454 cases.

It seems that discrimination in expensive places is rare (5.4%), but 13.3% of people thought that they had been discriminated against through the service.

D-3: Comprehensive table: In your work unit do you enjoy the same political rights as other people?

	Comparatively unfavourable		The same		Impossible to say	
	Frequency	percent	Frequency	Percent	Frequency	Percent
Women	596	40.0	480	32.3	412	27.7
Disabled people	68	57.2	23	19.3	28	23.5
No local resident permit	360	51.6	106	15.2	232	33.2

A comparatively high percent of women do not think that they have equal political rights compared with others (40%) while 32.3% thought that they did. 57.2% of disabled people thought that their political rights were not the same as those of healthy people, while 19.3% thought they were the same. 51.6% of people without a local resident permit thought that their political rights were not as good as those of local people, while 15.2% thought that they were equal. Clearly, political discrimination against people who are not local is quite serious. For example, people from other places cannot vote, and are not treated equally in civil servant exams. Of the three groups of people, disabled people think that they suffer the most severe discrimination (57.2%), followed by people whose registered permanent residence is elsewhere (51.6%), and then women (40%).

A Survey of Employment Discrimination 183

5. INDIVIDUALS' OBJECTIVE OPINIONS AND EVALUATION (PART E)

E1: Have you ever taken the civil servant exams?

Experience of the civil service exams		Frequency	Valid percent	Total percent
Valid cases	No	2936	86.7	86.7
	Once	333	9.8	96.5
	Twice or more	119	3.5	100
	Subtotal	3388	100.0	
Missing cases		66		
Total		3454		

86.7% of interviewees had not taken the civil service exams and 13.3% had.

E1-1: Do you think that the civil servant recruitment and employment process is discriminatory?

Was there discrimination?		Frequency	Valid percent	Total percent
Valid cases	Yes	498	65.9	65.9
	No	72	9.5	75.4
	Do not know	186	24.6	100.0
	Subtotal	756	100.0	
Missing cases	Subtotal	2698		
Total		3454		

It is very clear that the majority of interviewees (65.9%) thought that civil servant recruitment and employment was discriminatory, while only 9.5% thought it was not.

E1-2 (Multiple choice): At which stages did you think there was discrimination?

Stages of discrimination	Frequency	Percent of responses	Percent of valid cases
The written stage of the civil service exam	166	16.1	27.0
Second examination stage	406	39.3	66.0
Physical examination	181	17.5	29.4
Promotion stage	220	21.3	35.8
Retirement	60	5.8	9.8
Total answers	1033	100.0	168.0

Note: valid cases 615, missing cases 2839, total cases 3454.

The majority of people do not trust the second stage of examinations, with 66% of people believing it to be discriminatory. 35.8% thought there was discrimination when it came to promotion. 29.4% thought there was discrimination during the physical checks and 27% believed there was discrimination in the written exams.

E2: Do you think the electoral system of the people's congress is discriminatory?

Is there discrimination?		Frequency	Valid percent	Total percent
Valid cases	Yes	1060	31.3	31.3
	No	549	16.2	47.5
	Do not know	1780	52.5	100.0
	Subtotal	3389	100.0	
Missing cases	Subtotal	65		
Total		3454		

31.3% of people thought that the electoral system was discriminatory, 16.2% did not and 52.5% did not know. This reveals that the majority of interviewees were not aware of this issue.

E2-1 (Multiple choice): If you do believe that the people's congress electoral system is discriminatory, in what aspects?

Aspects of discrimination	Frequency	Percent of responses	Percent of valid cases
Rural/urban	596	23.5	52.1
Gender	423	16.7	37.0
Political standpoint	748	29.5	65.4
Educational	564	22.2	49.3
Health	125	4.9	10.9
Other requirements	79	3.1	6.9
Total answers	2535	100.0	221.6

Note: 1144 valid cases, 2310 missing cases, 3454 total cases.

65.4% of people thought that there was political discrimination in the elections for the people's congress. 52.1% thought there was discrimination between rural and urban areas, 49.3% thought there was educational discrimination and 37% thought there was gender discrimination.

E3-1 (Multiple choice): What are reasonable requirements that employers could ask in recruiting practice?

	Frequency		Percent of answers		Percent of valid cases	
	Civil service	Enterprises and institutions	Civil service	Enterprises and institutions	Civil service	Enterprises and institutions
Gender	308	331	5.3	6.7	16.5	21.4
Resident permit	298	246	5.1	5.0	15.9	15.9
Education	1508	1218	26.0	24.8	80.7	78.6
Political standpoint	773	440	13.3	9.0	41.4	28.4
Age	895	810	15.4	16.5	47.9	52.3
Height	262	254	4.5	5.2	14.0	16.4
Health	1117	1038	19.2	21.1	59.8	67.0
Appearance	209	204	3.6	4.2	11.2	13.2
Disability	395	362	6.8	7.4	21.1	20.4
Religious beliefs	45	12	0.8	0.2	2.4	0.8
Total	5810	4915	100.0	100	310.9	317.1

Note: 1869 valid cases, 1585 missing cases, total cases 3454.

80.7% of people believed that an educational requirement is reasonable when recruiting civil servants. In second place, 59.8% of people believed that a health requirement was reasonable, and in third place, 47.9% believed that an age requirement was reasonable. It would seem that in general people are happy with the civil servant recruitment procedures, which select applicants by their education, and more than half of people think that health conditions are reasonable. As for reasonable conditions required by companies when recruiting, most people agreed with education requirements (78.6%), then health (67%) and thirdly age (52.3%). This corresponds with the opinions of the civil servant recruitment procedures.

E3-2 (Multiple choice): Unreasonable conditions in the recruitment processes of the civil service, enterprises and institutions:

	Frequency		Percent of responses		Valid percent	
	Civil service	Enterprises and institutions	Civil service	Enterprises and institutions	Civil service	Enterprises and institutions
Gender	1200	940	18.1	16.6	67.7	63.0
Resident permit	1176	1004	17.7	17.7	66.3	67.2
Education	223	208	3.4	3.7	12.6	13.9
Political standpoint	737	798	11.1	14.1	41.6	53.4
Age	589	443	8.9	7.8	33.2	29.7
Height	1060	813	15.9	14.4	59.8	54.5
Health	193	112	2.9	2.0	10.9	7.5
Appearance	841	661	12.7	11.7	47.4	44.3
Disability	361	320	5.4	5.7	20.4	21.4
Religious belief	266	358	4.0	6.3	15.0	24.0
Total	6646	5657	100.0	100.0	374.8	378.9

Note: valid civil service cases 1773, missing cases 1681, total cases 3454. Valid cases for institutions and enterprises 1493, missing cases 1961, total cases 3454.

67.7% of people put gender discrimination in first position for unreasonable conditions demanded by the civil servant recruitment procedures. Second was resident permit (66.3%), third was height (59.8%), fourth was appearance (47.4%) and fifth was political standpoint (41.6%).

As for unreasonable conditions demanded by enterprises and institutions, number one was resident permits (67.2%), second was gender (63%), third was height (54.5%), fourth was political beliefs (53.4%), and fifth was appearance.

A Survey of Employment Discrimination

E4: Do you think that the world of employment is currently discriminatory? To what extent?

What extent?		Frequency	Valid percent	Total percent
Valid cases	Very serious	445	13.4	13.4
	Fairly serious	1245	37.4	50.8
	Exist, but not serious	1155	34.7	85.5
	Hardly exist	219	6.6	92.1
	Do not know	264	7.9	100.0
	Subtotal	3328	100.0	
Missing cases	Subtotal	126		
Total		3454		

85.5% thought that there was discrimination, 50.8% thought that it was serious or fairly serious and 6.6% thought that it did not exist.

E5 (Multiple choice): Which groups are most susceptible to discrimination?

Susceptible to discrimination	Frequency	Percent answered	Percent of valid cases
Female	965	6.7	28.5
Disabled persons	2224	15.4	65.6
Non-locals	1177	8.2	34.7
Migrant workers	1524	10.6	45.0
unattractive appearance	1253	8.7	37.0
HIV/AIDS carriers	2129	14.7	62.8
Homosexuals	904	6.3	26.7
Hepatitis BV carriers	1839	12.7	54.2
Uneducated	1644	11.4	48.5
Over 40s	726	5.0	21.4
No employment discrimination	50	0.3	1.5
Total cases	14435	100.0	425.8

Note: valid cases 3390, missing cases 64, total cases 3454.

Most people (65.6%) thought that disabled persons were most likely to be discriminated against. 62.8% of interviewees thought that it was people with HIV/AIDS and 54.2% of people thought that hepatitis B sufferers were most likely to face discrimination.

33% of interviewees thought that HIV/AIDS sufferers were the group most likely to be discriminated against. 19.3% of interviewees thought that disabled employees were the most likely to be discriminated against and 9.3% thought that migrant workers were the most likely to suffer discrimination. 17.1% thought hepatitis B carriers were the second most likely group to suffer discrimination, while 15.5% believed that it was disabled employees, with 13.2% thinking that it was HIV/AIDS sufferers. 17.5% thought that hepatitis B carriers were the third most likely group to suffer discrimination, 14.9% thought that it was disabled employees, and 10.9% thought that those with a low education were the third most likely group to suffer discrimination.

E6 Comprehensive table: Different groups in order of how susceptible they are to discrimination:

	First		Second		Third		Fourth		Fifth	
	Frequency	%	Frequency	%	Frequency	%	Frequency	%	Frequency	%
Female	305	9.1	145	4.5	137	4.5	162	6.2	206	9.4
Disabled employees	649	19.3	499	15.5	453	14.9	399	15.2	221	10.1
Non-locals	207	6.2	269	8.3	298	9.8	205	7.8	194	8.9
Migrant workers	311	9.3	328	10.2	315	10.4	322	12.3	248	11.3
Unattractive appearance	99	2.9	240	7.4	324	10.7	297	11.3	285	13.0
HIV/AIDS sufferers	1111	33.0	427	13.2	261	8.6	199	7.6	132	6.0
Homosexuals	60	1.8	376	11.7	218	7.2	143	5.4	112	5.1
Hepatitis BV sufferers	222	6.6	552	17.1	532	17.5	319	12.1	225	10.3
Low education	294	8.7	281	8.7	330	10.9	410	15.6	342	15.6
Over 40s	73	2.2	108	3.3	164	5.4	170	6.5	223	10.2
No employment discrimination	31	0.9	0	0.0	0	0.0	2	0.1	0	0.0

Overall, the three groups most likely to suffer serious discrimination were thought to be: HIV/AIDS sufferers (46.2%), disabled employees (34.8%), while hepatitis B carriers came highest in both the second and third groups with a total of 34.6%.

E7 (Multiple choice): If you were an employer, would you want to employ the following people?

Unemployable people	Frequency	Percent answered	Percent of valid cases
Hepatitis B carriers	1837	18.2	55.8
HIV/AIDS carriers	2077	20.6	63.0
Carriers of venereal diseases	1730	17.2	52.5
Homosexuals	1092	10.8	33.1
Disabled people	1029	10.2	31.2
Female	60	0.6	1.8
Over 40s	197	2.0	6.0
Unattractive appearance	709	7.0	21.5
Obese	123	1.2	3.7
Non local household registration	99	1.0	3.0
Low education	297	2.9	9.0
Those competent	585	5.8	17.8
No answer	236	2.3	7.2
Total cases	10071	100.0	305.6

Note: valid cases 3295, missing cases 159, total cases 3454.

63% of interviewees would not employ HIV/AIDS carriers, 55.8% would not recruit hepatitis B sufferers and 52.5% would not recruit carriers of venereal diseases. Subjectively, many people would not discriminate against women, or people without local household registration.

E8: Views on institutions and companies not employing these specific people:

Views		Frequency	Valid percent	Total percent
Valid cases	Legitimate	640	18.9	18.9
	Not good, but understandable	1582	46.6	65.4
	Not right, it's discrimination	781	23.0	88.5
	Don't know	392	11.5	100.0
	Subtotal	3395	100.0	
Missing cases	Subtotal	59		
Total		3454		

A comparatively large number of people could understand institutions and companies not employing these specific people (46.6%), but 23% of people thought it was discrimination. 18.9% thought it was an employer's legitimate right to refuse employment to someone.

E9: Some people bring a lawsuit against their employer, what is your opinion of this?

Your opinion of bringing a lawsuit		Frequency	Valid percent	Total percent
Valid cases	Do not agree	274	8.1	8.1
	Hard to say	1605	47.5	55.6
	Agree	1116	33.0	88.6
	Cannot say	385	11.4	100.0
	Subtotal	3380	100.0	
Missing cases	Subtotal	74		
Total		3454		

33% firmly supported taking issues to court, 47.5% felt it was hard to say, and 8.1% were firmly against bringing a lawsuit.

E10: Have people you know been treated unfairly at work because of the reasons described in E5?

Unfair treatment		Frequency	Valid percent	Total percent
Valid cases	Yes, many times	692	20.8	20.8
	Yes, but not many	1521	45.7	66.5
	Rarely	441	13.2	79.7
	None	273	8.2	87.9
	Do not understand	402	12.1	100.0
	Subtotal	3329	100.0	
Missing cases	Subtotal	125		
Total		3454		

A total of 66.5% of people thought that they knew people who had been treated unfairly, 13.2% said they thought that this occurred rarely and 8.2% thought they did not know anyone who had been so treated.

E11 Comprehensive table: What is your opinion of the present situation concerning discrimination in society?

	Unacceptable (%)	Bad (%)	Normal (%)	Preferable (%)	Very good (%)	Don't know (%)
Gender discrimination	29.8	39.3	21.6	4.3	1.2	3.9
Disability discrimination	26.2	44.6	21.0	3.1	0.6	4.5
Age discrimination	18.2	42.1	31.5	3.8	0.9	3.4
Height discrimination	18.1	39.9	31.9	5.1	1.1	4.0
Appearance discrimination	17.7	37.8	33.5	5.6	1.4	4.1
Educational discrimination	17.2	37.7	32.7	7.8	1.3	3.2
Resident permit discrimination	26.4	39.3	23.8	4.6	1.4	4.4
Household registration discrimination	26.2	35.6	24.1	6.1	2.4	5.5
Health discrimination	12.3	32.4	37.8	10.5	2.4	4.5
Homosexual discrimination	14.0	30.7	24.8	8.0	4.1	18.5
Work experience discrimination	17.0	39.4	30.5	6.2	1.7	5.2
Political standpoint discrimination	22.7	31.4	27.3	6.7	3.4	8.5

Out of the options deemed unacceptable, the highest percent of people chose gender discrimination. 29.8% of those interviewed thought that the present degree of gender discrimination was unacceptable. The lowest percent, only 12.3%, chose health discrimination. Out of the 'bad' options, the highest percent chose disability discrimination (44.6%); the lowest was homosexual discrimination (30.7%). This reveals that people do not agree with gender and disability discrimination, but find health and homosexual discrimination more acceptable.

E12 (Multiple choice): Methods of improving employment discrimination:

Methods to improve employment discrimination	Frequency	Percent of answers	Percent of valid cases
Prohibition through government legislation	2134	23.7	62.7
Public policy and regulations	2220	24.7	65.2
Non-governmental organizations	1565	17.4	46.0
Mass media	2012	22.4	59.1
Campaign run by victims of discrimination	777	8.6	22.8
Don't know	260	2.9	7.6
Other	26	0.3	0.8
Total cases	8994	100.0	264.3

Note: valid cases 3403, missing cases 51, total cases 3454.

The most popular choice was to use public policy and regulations to prohibit recruiters from using discrimination (65.2%). The second option was to prohibit discrimination through government legislation (62.7%) and the third was to use the tool of the mass media (59.1%). Only 22.8% had confidence in campaigns launched by victims of discrimination.

A Survey of Employment Discrimination

6. IDENTIFICATION WITH AND ATTITUDES TOWARDS DISCRIMINATION (PART F)

F1 Comprehensive table: Do you agree with the statements and degrees below?

Statements	Strongly agree (%)	Agree (%)	Don't agree (%)	Strongly disagree (%)	Can't say (%)
1. When illness, disability, age, education, resident permit, gender, appearance and other such factors affect normal work, employers have the right not to employ or to dismiss someone. This is a company's autonomous right, not discrimination.	13.2	45.6	29.4	5.8	6.0
2. When a person is competent and physically fit for a job, employers must not refuse someone on the grounds of their appearance, resident permit, education, disabilities, age, gender or other factors outside the special requirements of a particular job. This constitutes discrimination.	31.0	52.9	10.8	1.4	3.9
3. In considering the work unit's effectiveness and image, employers naturally have the right to select an applicant who is of a high calibre, particularly healthy, good looking, and who has technical expertise.	21.6	57.8	13.6	1.8	5.1
4. Every employer should pay staff the same wage for the same work.	30.2	35.9	24.2	3.9	5.8
5. China has a surplus of workers, but scant skilled labour. If requiring high standards from their employees by work units, in turn helps improve workers' skills, then it is quite fitting they do so.	12.4	45.0	28.0	4.6	10.0
6. Young, healthy graduates find it hard to secure employment, so why should people want to hire the old, the sick, or disabled people with low education qualifications?	5.9	19.7	47.9	13.6	12.9
7. Compared with young, healthy graduates, disadvantaged groups of people need society's care and consideration even more to find employment.	19.8	49.2	19.3	3.1	8.6
8. 'Employment equality' is a basic labour right bestowed by national law. Employers must respect this.	45.2	41.6	6.5	0.8	5.9
9. Equal employment will affect economic development.	6.2	17.4	46.5	14.7	15.2

10. Not to provide retirement age will mean young people will not be able to find work.	11.4	31.2	35.8	8.9	12.7
11. Regulations on age limits restricting the promotion of cadres, such as the stipulation that 40-year-olds cannot become section chiefs, 45-year-olds cannot become department heads and 55-year-olds cannot become director generals, all constitute age discrimination.	15.2	34.0	30.1	4.6	16.2
12. Different regulations governing the retirement ages for men and women is a kind of gender discrimination.	11.6	26.6	45.0	6.5	10.4
13. Having VIP rooms in airports, train stations etc. is a kind of discrimination.	14.8	34.4	35.7	5.0	10.2
14. To demand a local resident permit when buying a flat or installing a telephone is a kind of household registration discrimination.	25.9	48.1	16.1	3.0	7.0
15. To address someone as a 'Henan Person' constitutes regional discrimination.	14.7	28.6	36.8	6.5	13.4
16. Universities adopting different entry scores or quotas for different regions constitutes regional discrimination.	27.3	32.5	26.0	4.4	9.8
17. To give ethnic minority candidates taking college entrance exams extra points is not fair to Han Chinese candidates.	18.7	30.9	34.5	5.2	10.6
18. Blue collar workers' education levels and technical skills are low and so their incomes should be low as well.	5.5	22.3	49.2	13.5	9.5
19. To use the terms blue collar and white collar workers is a kind of employment discrimination.	11.0	34.0	37.3	4.6	13.2
20. For government, enterprises and social organizations to set up specific conditions for recruitment presents the most harmful kind of employment discrimination.	17.8	35.4	26.7	3.6	16.4

We can see from F1 that the general public has a basic idea of employment discrimination. For example, nearly everyone agreed with statement 8 (86.8% agreed or basically agreed). The majority of people acknowledged discrimination as a concept. For example, 83.9% of people agreed or basically agreed with the concept described in statement 2. 61.2% of people disagreed with statement 9 that 'equal employment will affect economic development'.

74% agreed with statement 14. But many still had a somewhat hazy understanding of discrimination. For example, those agreeing with statements 1 and 3 accounted for 58.8% and 79.4% respectively. Many people magnify the powers of employers in hiring people. Such a view is incorrect. Companies must respect the law and bear corporate social responsibility. The comparison between those who agree and those who disagree with statements 11, 12, 13, 15, 16 and 17 shows that these issues are more controversial.

F2 Comprehensive table: Answers to the questions below:

Questions	Yes (%)	No (%)	Don't know (%)
1. Do you think when seeking employment, people with HIV/AIDS should be treated the same as healthy people?	42.1	36.2	21.7
2. Do you think people with hepatitis B and sexually transmitted diseases should have the same employment opportunities as healthy people?	32.2	49.7	18.0
3. Do you think homosexuals should have the same employment opportunities as heterosexual people?	54.2	26.1	19.7
4. Do you think that the three groups mentioned above should be treated the same as others in daily life?	45.0	32.8	22.2
5. Would you work with someone who has hepatitis B?	31.9	49.3	18.9
6. Would you work with someone with a venereal disease?	25.9	51.6	22.5
7. Would you work with someone with HIV?	25.8	52.5	21.7
8. Would you work with a homosexual?	39.3	37.8	22.8
9. Do you think that a work unit not to give disabled people rights at work amounts to discrimination?	80.4	10.9	8.7
10. Do you think needing a local resident permit when buying a flat or having a telephone installed is a kind of discrimination?	73.4	15.5	11.1

More than half of people (54.2%) agreed that homosexuals should be treated equally, and more people thought that people with HIV/AIDS should be treated equally compared with those who disagreed. However, when asked whether they were willing to work with people with hepatitis B, carriers of venereal diseases and homosexuals, only 25% to 30% of people agreed, while more than half were unwilling. This demonstrates that although many people objectively consider it wrong to discriminate against certain groups, this is not actively reflected in their behaviour. The majority of people (80.4%) thought that not giving disabled people the rights they should have was discrimination, and agreed that requiring a local resident permit when buying houses, having telephones installed and using other public services amounted to discrimination.

F3: Do you think that people from other places have the right to participate in local elections?

Right to participate in elections		Frequency	Valid percent	Total percent
Valid cases	Yes	2161	62.9	62.9
	No	584	17.0	79.9
	Can't say	689	20.1	100.0
	Subtotal	3434	100.0	
Missing cases	Subtotal	20		
Total		3454		

62.9% of people thought that people from other places should have the right to vote; only 17.0% thought that they should not.

F4: If you are suffering from discrimination, what action would you take to protect your own legal rights?

Measures to protect your right		Frequency	Valid percent	Total percent
Valid cases	Endure it yourself	532	15.5	15.5
	Petition the relevant department	1476	43.0	58.6
	Plead one's case on the spot	957	27.9	86.5
	Don't know	464	13.5	100.0
	Subtotal	3429	100.0	
Missing cases		25		
Total		3454		

15.5% of people would endure discrimination themselves, 43% would choose to petition the relevant department about the incident, 27.9% would choose to defend themselves on the spot, and finally 13.5% said they didn't know.

F5: If you chose to lodge a complaint to the relevant department, which institution would you choose?

To which institution would you lodge a complaint?		Frequency	Valid percent	Total percent
Valid cases	Judicial authority	475	25.5	25.5
	Relevant arbitration authority	408	21.9	47.5
	Neighbourhood committee	72	3.9	51.3
	Relevant government institution	401	21.6	72.9
	The discriminator's work unit or supervisory department	328	17.6	90.5
	Can't say	176	9.5	100.0
	Subtotal	1860	100.0	
Missing cases	Subtotal	1594		
Total		3454		

The most popular method to lodge a complaint was through the judicial authority (25.5%). Second was through an arbitration authority (21.9%), third was through the relevant government institution (21.6%), and fourth was to complain to the discriminator's work unit or supervisory body (17.6%).

F6 (Multiple choice): Reasons for employment discrimination:

Reasons for employment discrimination	Frequency	Percent answered	Percent of valid cases
Scarcity of social resources	1552	15.8	45.2
Surplus labour force	2381	24.3	69.4
Traditional cultural reasons	1407	14.4	41.0
Efficiency is paramount	1566	16.0	45.7
Weak social security system	1600	16.3	46.6
It is so pervasive	811	8.3	23.6
Common sense	239	2.4	7.0
Don't know	239	2.4	7.0
Other	3	0.0	0.1
Total cases	9798	100.0	285.7

Note: valid cases 3430, missing cases 24, total cases 3454.

69.4% agreed with the statement that employment discrimination is caused by a surplus workforce, 46.6% thought it was because of a weak social security system and 45.7% thought that it was because efficiency is of paramount importance.

F7: As for regulations governing male and female retirement, which of the methods below is better?

Method of retiring		Frequency	Valid percent	Total percent
Valid cases	Women retire earlier than men	1296	37.9	37.9
	Men and women retire at the same age	760	22.2	60.1
	Women are free to choose	637	18.6	78.8
	Can't say	726	21.2	100.0
	Subtotal	3419	100.0	
Missing cases	Subtotal	35		
Total		3454		

37.9% of people thought that women should retire before men, 22.2% thought men and women should retire at the same age. 18.6% thought women should choose for themselves. 40.8% advocated that men and women should retire at the same time or that women should choose.

F8: Have you been in the situation where an employer does not make it clear that they will not employ a woman, but no women are employed?

Does not employ women		Frequency	Valid percent	Total percent
Valid cases	Never experienced	2863	85.1	85.1
	Experienced	502	14.9	100.0
	Subtotal	3365	100.0	
Missing cases	Subtotal	89		
Total		3454		

85.1% of people had never experienced this, while 14.9% had.

F9: If you are or once were an employee in a state-owned or collectively owned enterprise, have you been discriminated against because of your worker's status? How did you feel?

Discriminated against because a worker		Frequency	Valid percent	Total percent
Valid cases	No	1838	60.7	60.7
	Yes, very depressed and hurt pride	555	18.3	79.0
	Yes, very angry	382	12.6	91.6
	Yes, but it passed	130	4.3	95.9
	Yes, but it didn't matter	124	4.1	100.0
	Subtotal	3029	100.0	
Missing cases	Subtotal	425		
Total		3454		

39.3% of people had been discriminated against. Among these, 18.3% felt very depressed and had hurt pride whilst 12.6% felt very angry. 60.7% of workers believed that they had never been discriminated against.

F10: Have you been discriminated against in a social situation because you were a worker?

Suffered discrimination in a social situation		Frequency	Valid percent	Total percent
Valid cases	No	2040	63.6	63.6
	Yes, rarely	653	20.3	83.9
	Yes, normally	270	8.4	92.3
	Yes, often	96	3.0	95.3
	Don't know	151	4.7	100.0
	Subtotal	3210	100.0	
Missing cases	Subtotal	244		
Total		3454		

31.7% said yes, 63.6% said no. This shows that discrimination against workers in social situations is not that frequent.

F11 (Multiple choice): What are the most important factors for females when seeking a job? (Answers of the entire questionnaire contrasted with those of women with a college education)

Most important thing for women in finding a job	Frequency		Percent of answers		Percent of valid cases	
	Entire questionnaire	Women	Entire questionnaire	Women	Entire questionnaire	Women
Appearance and demeanour	2399	524	30.7	29.3	70.1	70.3
Education	2298	541	29.5	30.2	67.2	72.6
Skills in public relations	2078	483	26.6	27.0	60.7	64.8
Household registration	188	40	2.4	2.2	5.5	5.4
Regional origin	106	29	1.4	1.6	3.1	3.9
Family background	657	157	8.4	8.8	19.2	21.1
Other	77	15	1.0	0.8	2.3	2.0
Total answers	7803	1789	100.0	100.0	228.1	240.1

Note: within the entire questionnaire, valid cases 3421, missing cases 33, total cases 3454; among college educated women, valid cases 745; missing cases 2.

From the entire questionnaire, the most important factors chosen were appearance and demeanour, education and public relations. 70.1%, 67.2% and 60.7% of people chose these factors respectively. Fourth in the list was family background. It appeared that the majority of men answering the questionnaire thought that appearance was important for women when seeking employment.

From the responses of the 745 women with a college education, the three main concerns were education, appearance and skills in public relations, with 72.6%, 70.3% and 64.8% of these women choosing these factors respectively. It is clear from these answers that highly educated women consider education to be even more important than do the other interviewees.

F12 (Multiple choice): The disadvantages of women in the workplace:

Disadvantages of women in the workplace	Frequency	Percent of answers	Percent of valid cases
Pregnancy	2776	26.4	81.6
Maternity leave	2518	24.0	74.0
Nursing period	2153	20.5	63.3
Special biological leave	1518	14.5	44.6
Physical strength	1485	14.1	43.6
Other	48	0.5	1.4
Total cases	10498	100.0	308.5

Note: valid cases 3403, missing cases 51, total cases 3454.
The top three disadvantages chosen were pregnancy, maternity leave and nursing leave: 81.6%, 74% and 63.3% of people chose these options respectively.

F13 (Multiple choice): Advantages of women in the workplace:

	Frequency	Percent of answers	Percent of valid cases
Diligence	2943	32.8	86.3
Take responsibility seriously	2132	23.8	62.5
Strength of public relations	1501	16.7	44.0
Patience	2322	25.9	68.1
Other	65	0.7	1.9
Total cases	8963	100.0	262.9

Note: valid cases 3409, missing cases 45, total cases 3454.

The number one advantage of women was their diligence (86.3%), second was their patience (68.1%) and third was their earnest sense of responsibility (62.5%).

F14 (Multiple choice): Factors that influence women's promotion (entire questionnaire compared with women with a college level education or above):

Factors that influence women's promotion	Frequency		Percent of cases		Percent of valid cases	
	Entire questionnaire	Women	Entire questionnaire	Women	Entire questionnaire	Women
Biological factors	2006	461	30.5	31.3	58.9	62.0
Traditional thinking	1929	513	29.3	34.8	56.7	69.0
Household obligations	1836	378	27.9	25.6	54.0	50.9
Weak work abilities	722	108	11.0	7.3	21.2	14.5
Other	86	15	1.3	1.0	2.5	2.0
Total answers	6579	1475	100.0	100.0	193.3	198.5

Note: Responses of the entire whole questionnaire: valid cases 3403, missing cases 51, total cases 3454. Responses of highly educated women: valid cases 743, missing cases 4.

From the answers from the entire questionnaire, the three main factors that affect women getting promoted were biological reasons (58.9%), traditional thinking (56.7%) and their household obligations (54%). Only 21.2% thought that work abilities were a factor.

From the answers of the 743 highly educated women, the three main factors chosen were traditional thinking (69%), biological reasons (62%) and household obligations (50.9%). However, educated women do not have the same opinion as the majority. The educated women thought that the major factor affecting women's promotion was traditional values, rather than biological factors. Compared with the entire respondents of the questionnaire, 7% fewer women thought work ability was a factor.

7. FEMALE EMPLOYMENT DISCRIMINATION (SPECIAL ANALYSIS)

Basic introduction:
(1) Female employment discrimination has two dimensions and requires statistical analysis and comparison between four types of people. The first dimension is gender and the second is whether they have a college education or

not. From here, we get four types of people: women who do not have a college education, female college graduates, men without college educations, and male graduates. Comparing these four groups we can discover various differences.
(2) This report is therefore divided into four parts:
   1. Basic overview;
   2. Comparison between male and female employment discrimination;
   3. Comparison between college educated women and women without a college education; and
   4. Comparison between male and female graduates.

7.1 Basic Overview

Basic overview:

			Education		Total
			Not college educated	College and above	
Sex	Female	Frequency	789	747	1536
		Percent	51.4%	48.6%	100.0%
	Male	Frequency	1022	866	1888
		Percent	54.1%	45.9%	100.0%
Amount		Frequency	1811	1613	3424
		Percent	52.9%	47.1%	100.0%

Note: valid cases 3424, missing cases 30, total cases 3454.

It can be seen that out of 3424 valid cases, there were 1536 women and 1888 men. Of the women, 747 had a college education (48.6%). That is to say, out of the women surveyed 48.6% were college educated or above.

7.2 Comparing Employment Discrimination among Men and Women

B1-f: Has an employer made requirements about appearance and temperament?

			Appearance and temperament requirements			Numbers
			Correct appearance	Refined appearance	No specific requirements	
Gender	Women	Frequency	524	117	887	1528
		Percent	34.3%	7.7%	58.0%	100.0%
	Men	Frequency	519	90	1272	1881
		Percent	27.6%	4.8%	67.6%	100.0%
Numbers		Frequency	1043	207	2159	3409
		Percent	30.6%	6.1%	63.3%	100.0%

From the 3409 respondents to this question, there were 1881 men and 1528 women. The B1-f shows that employers require different appearance and temperament for men and women: the requirement is 5.7% more for women than men with regard to good appearance, and 2.9% more women than men were required to have a refined appearance.

E1-1: If you have taken the civil servant exams, do you think the civil servant recruitment and employment process is discriminatory?

			Is it discriminatory?			Numbers
			Yes	No	Don't know	
Gender	Women	Frequency	202	23	78	303
		Percent	66.7%	7.6%	25.7%	100.0%
	Men	Frequency	295	49	108	452
		Percent	65.3%	10.8%	23.9%	100.0%
Amount		Frequency	497	72	186	755
		Percent	65.8%	9.5%	24.6%	100.0%

Out of the 755 interviewees who had taken the civil servant exams there were 303 women and 452 men. 66.7% of the women thought that the process was discriminatory and 65.3% of men did – more or less the same.

E5: Do you think that the contemporary world of employment is discriminatory? To what extent?

			Do you think that the contemporary world of employment is discriminatory? To what extent?				Amount
			Yes, severe	Yes, but not serious	Not at all	Don't know	
Gender	Women	Frequency	775	486	91	129	1481
		Percent	52.3%	32.8%	6.1%	8.7%	100%
	Men	Frequency	910	666	128	135	1839
		Percent	49.5%	36.2%	7.0%	7.3%	100%
Amount		Frequency	1685	1152	219	264	3320
		Percent	50.7%	34.7%	6.6%	8.0%	100%

Among the 3320 people who answered this question, 1839 were men and 1481 were women. 2.8% more women than men thought that employment discrimination was severe.

7.3 A Comparison between Women with a University Education and Those without (Female Answers)

B1-a: When looking for work, have you been rejected for being a woman? (Female answers)

			Have you been rejected for being a woman?			Amount
			No	Can't remember	Yes	
Women	Not college educated	Frequency	564	115	73	752
		Percent	75.0%	15.3%	9.7%	100.0%
	College educated and above	Frequency	531	91	97	719
		Percent	73.9%	12.7%	13.5%	100.0%
Amount		Frequency	1095	206	170	1471
		Percent	74.4%	14.0%	11.6%	100.0%

1471 women answered this question. 752 were not college educated and 719 had a college education or above. 13.5% of women with a college education or above were turned away because they were women, 3.8% more than those who were not college educated. This reveals that university graduates are more likely to be discriminated against than non-university graduates.

B3-a: Have you been discriminated against for being a woman while taking the civil servant exams? (Female answers)

			Have you been discriminated against for being a woman while taking the civil service exams?			Amount
			Yes	No	Don't remember	
Women	Non-college educated	Frequency	72	121	13	206
		Percent	35%	58.7%	6.3%	100.0%
	College educated and above	Frequency	94	212	10	316
		Percent	29.7%	67.1%	3.2%	100.0%
Amount		Frequency	166	333	23	522
		Percent	31.8%	63.8%	4.4%	100.0%

522 women answered this question. 206 did not have a college education and 316 did. 5.3% more women with a low education were discriminated against than highly educated women, amounting to 35% of women with a low education. This proves that the civil service has very high education requirements.

C1-b: Has your work unit already implemented measures to ensure women's rights and interests? (Multiple choice)

			Implemented measures to ensure women's rights and interests						Amount
			Pregnancy	Maternity leave	Nursing period	Special biological leave	Labour and safety protection	Other	
Women	Non-college education	Frequency	340	471	322	122	300	60	671
		Percent	50.7	70.2	48.0	18.2	44.7	8.9	50.4
	College education and above	Frequency	358	499	333	110	305	30	660
		Percent	54.2	75.6	50.5	16.7	46.2	4.5	49.6
Amount		Frequency	698	970	655	232	605	90	1331
		Percent	52.4	72.9	49.2	17.4	45.5	6.8	100.0

1331 women answered this question, including 671 women with no college education (50.4%) and 660 with college education or above (49.6%). Studying C1-b, it can be seen that lower educated women clearly had fewer rights when it came to issues such as pregnancy, maternity leave and such like.

D3-a: Do you have the same political rights as men? (Female answers)

			Do you have the same political rights as men?				Total amount
			Clearly fewer than men	Fewer than men	The same as men	Don't know	
Women	No college education	Frequency	143	137	224	250	754
		Percent	19.0%	18.2%	29.7%	33.2%	100.0%
	College educated	Frequency	133	182	253	161	729
		Percent	18.2%	25.0%	34.7%	22.1%	100.0%
Total		Frequency	276	319	477	411	1483
		Percent	18.6%	21.5%	32.2%	27.7%	100.0%

From the data D3-a it can be seen that 40.1% of women thought that their political rights compared unfavourably or very unfavourably with men. 32.2% believed they had equal rights.

7.4 A Comparison of Female and Male Graduates (Graduate Responses)

B1-a: While you have been job seeking, has a work unit had gender requirements?

			Gender requirements				Amount
			Require men	Require women	Both acceptable	No specific requirements	
University education	Women	Frequency	18	81	305	339	743
		Percent	2.4%	10.9%	41.0%	45.6%	100.0%
	Men	Frequency	146	10	302	405	863
		Percent	16.9%	1.2%	35.0%	46.9%	100.0%
Amount		Frequency	164	91	607	744	1606
		Percent	10.2%	5.7%	37.8%	46.3%	100.0%

A Survey of Employment Discrimination

1606 people with college educations or above answered this question, 863 men and 743 women. From the data B1-a, it appears that gender requirements for female and male university students are not common.

B1-f: When you have been seeking employment, did an employer have requirements related to appearance or temperament?

			Requirements of appearance and temperament			Amount
			Appropriate appearance	Refined appearance	No specific requirements	
University education	Women	Frequency	294	64	383	741
		Percent	39.7%	8.6%	51.7%	100.0%
	Men	Frequency	304	51	506	861
		Percent	35.3%	5.9%	58.8%	100.0%
Amount		Frequency	598	115	889	1602
		Percent	37.3%	7.2%	55.5%	100.0%

1602 people with a college education or above answered this question, 861 men and 741 women. From the data in B1-f, work units had different appearance and temperament requirements for men and women.

E4: Is the sphere of employment discriminatory? To what extent?

			Is the sphere of employment discriminatory? To what extent?				Amount
			Yes	Yes, but not serious	Certainly not	Don't know	
University education	Women	Frequency	390	239	42	50	721
		Percent	54.1	33.1	5.8	6.9	100.0
	Men	Frequency	421	323	61	45	850
		Percent	49.5	38.0	7.2	5.3	100.0
Amount		Frequency	811	562	103	95	1571
		Percent	51.6	35.8	6.6	6.0	100.0

1571 people had a college education or above, 850 men and 721 women. 4.6% more women than men thought that employment discrimination existed.

7

EU ANTI-DISCRIMINATION LAW:
HISTORICAL DEVELOPMENT AND MAIN CONCEPTS

Susanne Burri

1. INTRODUCTION

EU anti-discrimination law is of growing importance to individuals in the Member States of the European Union (EU). While only a few such provisions were included in the European Economic Community (EEC) Treaty some 50 years ago, now many directives prohibit discrimination, in particular on the grounds of gender, race and ethnic origin, religion and belief, disability, age and sexual orientation. These directives have to be transposed into national law and Member States have to take the necessary measures to ensure that provisions contrary to the principle of equal treatment in laws, regulations, administrative provisions, collective agreements or individual contracts are declared null and void, or are amended. The European Court of Justice (ECJ) ruled that Member States have to adopt all the measures necessary to ensure that a directive is fully effective, in accordance with the objective that it pursues. The transposition of directives is often not easy, as the national provisions might not reflect the same kind of approach to equal treatment and anti-discrimination as the Community law.[1] However, due to the supremacy of EU law, the anti-discrimination provisions of the EC Treaty and directives prevail in case of conflict between national and Community law.[2] Moreover, some provisions have direct effect and can be applied by national courts in proceedings.[3] The ECJ furthermore ruled that the principle of effectiveness requires that the national courts must interpret

---

[1] See for example: S. Burri and F. Dorssemont, 'The Transposition of the Race Directive (2000/43/EC) and the Framework Directive on Equal Treatment in Employment (2000/78/EC) into Dutch and Belgian Law. At the Crossroads between an Open and Closed Avenue for Justifying Unequal Treatment', (2005) 21/4 *The International Journal of Comparative Labour Law and Industrial Relations*, pp. 537-570.

[2] ECJ 15 July 1964, Case 6/64, *Flaminio Costa v E.N.E.L*, ECR 1964, p. 585 (*Costa/ENEL*).

[3] This doctrine of direct effect was also developed by the ECJ; the first case is ECJ 5 February 1963, Case 26/62, *NV Algemene Transport- en Expeditie Onderneming van Gend & Loos v Netherlands Inland Revenue Administration*, ECR 1964, 1 (*Van Gend and Loos*).

their national law in the light of the wording and the purpose of the directive.[4] Under some conditions, a Member State might even be held liable for damage suffered by individuals due to the fact that a directive has not been transposed on time into national law.[5] The European Court of Justice has played a very important role, in particular in the field of equal treatment for men and women, in ensuring that individuals could effectively invoke and enforce their fundamental right to equality. National courts have the right (and the highest courts sometimes have the obligation) to ask the ECJ for preliminary rulings (Article 234 EC). In the field of equal treatment, the ECJ has issued several hundred binding judgments.

This chapter offers an overview of the historical development of EU anti-discrimination law, including references to some landmark cases of the ECJ (Section 2). The main concepts of direct and indirect discrimination, harassment and sexual harassment are discussed in Section 3. In Section 4, the mechanisms of enforcement are described. This Chapter ends with concluding that EU law imposes far-reaching obligations on the Member States, not in the least due to the dynamic interpretation of legal anti-discrimination provisions by the European Court of Justice.

2. HISTORICAL DEVELOPMENT OF EU ANTI-DISCRIMINATION LAW

In the Treaty of the European Economic Community,[6] adopted in 1957, only a few provisions were included to combat discrimination. The first one prohibits discrimination based on nationality within the scope of the European Community Treaty.[7] This Article is particularly relevant for the free movement of workers within the European Union.[8] The freedom of movement of workers entails the abolition of any discrimination based on nationality between workers of the Member States as regards employment, remuneration and other conditions of work and employment (Article 39(2) EC). Both direct and indirect discrimination are prohibited under this Article.[9]

---

[4] ECJ 10 April 1984, Case 14/83, *Sabine von Colson and Elisabeth Kamann v Land Nordrhein-Westfalen*, ECR 1984, 1891 (*Von Colson*), at para. 26.

[5] ECJ 19 November 1991, Cases C-6/90 and C-9/90, *Andrea Francovich and Danila Bonifaci and others v Italian Republic*, 1991, I-5357 (*Francovich*).

[6] This Treaty (EEC Treaty) was renamed after the Maastricht Treaty (which entered into force in 1993) in European Community Treaty (EC Treaty or TEC).

[7] The former Article 6 of the EEC Treaty, now Article 12 EC. When the Treaty of Amsterdam (ToA) came into effect on 1 May 1999, all the Articles, titles and sections of the Treaty of the European Union (TEU) and the European Community Treaty (EC Treaty) were renumbered.

[8] The prohibition of discrimination on grounds of nationality is therefore discussed only very shortly in this overview.

[9] See for an overview of relevant case law: P. Craig and G. De Búrca, *EU Law. Text, Cases and Materials*, 4th edition, (Oxford: Oxford University Press, 2008), pp. 758-764.

The second provision included in the EEC Treaty in 1957 concerns the principle of equal pay for men and women for equal work.[10] The meaning of this principle in practice has been developed in many cases of the ECJ since 1971. The European Court of Justice has played a very important role in improving the possibilities of women and men receiving equal pay for equal work or work of equal value by invoking this Article.[11] On 8 April 1976, the ECJ ruled that this Article had direct horizontal effect.[12] This means that Article 119 can be relied on by individuals before national courts not only against (bodies of) the state, but also against individuals such as private employers. The ECJ also ruled that respect for fundamental personal human rights is one of the general principles of Community law which the Court has the duty to ensure and that there is no doubt that the elimination of discrimination based on sex forms part of those fundamental rights.[13]

Since 1975, many directives have been adopted in order to implement the principle of equal treatment of men and women in the Member States, and national courts have asked the ECJ many preliminary questions about the interpretation of provisions of these directives (see Sections 2.1 and 2.2).[14]

With the entry into force of the Treaty of Amsterdam (ToA) in 1999, the promotion of equality between men and women throughout the European Community has become one of the essential tasks of the Community (Article 2 EC). Furthermore, the Community will aim to eliminate inequalities, and to promote equality, between men and women in all the activities listed in Article 3 EC (Article 3(2) EC).[15] This obligation of gender mainstreaming means that Member States will actively take the objective of equality between men and

---

[10] The former Article 119 of the EEC Treaty, now Article 141 EC, see Section 2.1.

[11] See also E. Ellis, *European Community Sex Equality Law*, 2nd edition, (Oxford: Oxford University Press, 1998), pp. 59-167 and S. Prechal and N. Burrows, *Gender Discrimination Law of the European Community*, (Aldershot-Vermont: Dartmouth, 1990), pp. 48-103.

[12] ECJ 8 April 1976, Case 43/75, *Gabrielle Defrenne v Société Anonyme Belge de Navigation Aérienne Sabena*, ECR 1976, 455 (*Defrenne II*), at para. 24.

[13] ECJ 15 June 1978, *Gabrielle Defrenne v Société Anonyme Belge de Navigation Aérienne Sabena*, ECR 1978, 1365 (*Defrenne III*), at para. 26-27. See further: C. Barnard, 'Gender Equality in the EU. A Balance Sheet', in P. Alston, M. Bustelo and J. Heenan (eds.), *The EU and Human Rights*, (Oxford: Oxford University Press, 1999), pp. 215-279 and S. Burri, 'The Position of the European Court of Justice with respect to the Enforcement of Human Rights', in: I. Boerefijn and J. Goldschmidt (eds.), *Changing Perceptions of Sovereignty and Human Rights. Essays in Honour of Cees Flinterman*, (Antwerpen-Oxford: Intersentia, 2008), pp. 311-326.

[14] See for a recent overview: S. Burri and S. Prechal, *EU Gender Equality Law*, (Luxembourg: Office for Official Publications of the European Communities, reference KE-80-08-432-EN-C, 2008).

[15] See for information on gender equality the website of the European Commission: http://ec.europa.eu/employment_social/gender_equality/index_en.html (accessed 2 June 2008).

women into account when formulating and implementing laws, regulations, administrative provisions, policies and activities.[16]

Since 1999, furthermore, the Community has had the competence to take appropriate action to combat discrimination based on gender, racial or ethnic origin, religion or belief, disability, age or sexual orientation (Article 13(1) EC).[17] This Article has provided a legal base for three anti-discrimination directives: the directive on the principle of equal treatment between persons irrespective of racial or ethnic origin (2000/43/EC),[18] the framework directive on equal treatment in employment and occupation (2000/78/EC)[19] and the directive on the principle of equal treatment between men and women in the access to and the supply of goods and services (2004/113/EC).[20]

2.1 Equal Pay for Male and Female Workers

2.1.1 Article 119 EEC Treaty (now 141 EC)

The gender pay gap was one of the first problems addressed by the European Economic Community in 1957, but the principle of equal pay between male and female workers for work of equal value was also already established in other international law instruments.[21]

The original text of the former Article 119 EEC Treaty provided that:

---

[16] See Directive 2006/54/EC of the European Parliament and of the Council of 5 July 2006 on the implementation of the principle of equal opportunities and equal treatment of men and women in matters of employment and occupation (recast), OJ 2006, L 204/23, Article 29.

[17] See for further information on anti-discrimination legislation and policies the website of the European Commission: http://ec.europa.eu/employment_social/fundamental_rights/index_en.htm (accessed 2 June 2008).

[18] Council Directive 2000/43/EC of 29 June 2000 implementing the principle of equal treatment between persons irrespective of racial or ethnic origin, OJ 2000, L 180/22, see Section 2.4.

[19] Council Directive 2000/78/EC of 27 November 2000 establishing a legal framework for equal treatment in employment and occupation, OJ 2000, L 303/16, see Section 2.5.

[20] Council Directive 2004/113/EC of 13 December 2004 implementing the principle of equal treatment between men and women in the access to and the supply of goods and services, OJ 2004, L 373/37, see Section 2.2.5.

[21] See for instance the ILO Equal Remuneration Convention Nr. 100, which was adopted in 1951. The first Article of this Convention concerns equal remuneration for men and women workers for work of equal value: see http://www.ilo.org/ilolex/english/convdisp1.htm, accessed 21 May 2008.
See for an overview of the application of the principle of equal pay between men and women in the European Union: S. Prechal, S. Burri, I. van Seggelen and G. de Graaff, Legal Aspects of the Gender Pay Gap. Report by the Commission's network of legal experts in the fields of employment, social affairs and equality between men and women, (2007) Luxembourg: European Commission, at: http://ec.europa.eu/employment_social/gender_equality/legislation/report_equal_pay.pdf. (accessed 2 June 2008).

> 1. Each Member State shall ... ensure and subsequently maintain the application of the principle that men and women should receive equal pay for equal work.
> 2. For the purpose of this Article, 'pay' means the ordinary basic or minimum wage or salary and any other consideration, whether in cash or in kind, which the worker receives directly or indirectly, in respect of his employment, from his employer.
> Equal pay without discrimination based on sex means:
> a) that pay for the same work at piece rates shall be calculated on the basis of the same unit of measurement;
> b) that pay for work at time rates shall be the same for the same job.

The background of this provision was purely economic; the Member States wanted to eliminate distortions in competition between undertakings established in different Member States. France had adopted provisions on equal pay for men and women much earlier. This country was afraid that cheap female labour available in other countries would lead undertakings to avoid investment in France.[22] However, according to the ECJ, this Article has not only an economic, but also a social aim. The ECJ ruled in 1976 that the principle of equal pay forms part of the social objectives of the European Economic Community, which is not merely an economic union, but is at the same time intended, by common action, to ensure social progress and to strive towards the constant improvement of the living and working conditions of its people. This double aim, which is simultaneously economic and social, shows that the principle of equal pay forms part of the foundations of the Community.[23] More recently, the ECJ even ruled that the economic aim is secondary to the social aim, which constitutes the expression of a fundamental human right.[24]

The fundamental importance of the principle of equal pay between male and female workers also means that the concept of 'worker' in Article 119 (now 141 EC) has a Community meaning and that it cannot be interpreted restrictively. A worker is a person who, for a certain period of time, performs services for and under the direction of another person in return for which he or she receives remuneration.[25] The concept of worker does not include independent providers of services who are not in a relationship of subordination to the person who receives the services. However, provided that a person is a worker within the meaning of Article 141(1) EC, the nature of his or her legal relationship with the other party to the employment relationship is of no consequence as regards the application of that article. Therefore, the formal classification of a person as self-employed under national law does not exclude the possibility that a person must

---

[22] See for a discussion of the adoption of Article 119: C. Hoskyns, *Integrating Gender*, (London-New York: Verso, 1996), pp. 43-59.
[23] See *Defrenne II supra* note 12, at paras 10-12.
[24] ECJ 10 February 2000, Case C-50/96, *Deutsche Telekom AG, formerly Deutsche Bundespost Telekom v Lilli Schröder*, ECR 2000, I-743 (*Schröder*), at para. 57.
[25] ECJ 3 July 1986, Case 66/85, *Deborah Lawrie-Blum v Land Baden-Württemberg*, ECR 1986, 2121 (*Lawrie-Blum*), at para. 17.

be classified as a worker within the meaning of Article 141(1) EC if his or her independence is merely notional, thereby disguising an employment relationship within the meaning of Article 141(1).[26]

Article 119 does not only prohibit direct discrimination based on gender in the field of pay, but also indirect discrimination. Indirect discrimination refers to discrimination which is the result of the application of a sex-neutral criterion, which particularly disadvantages persons belonging to one gender as compared with persons of the other sex. The concept of indirect discrimination has been developed in the case law of the ECJ in the first place in the field of pay and now belongs to the main concepts in EU law (see Section 3.2).

Article 119 should have been implemented before 1 January 1962, but Member States were unable or unwilling to implement this Article.[27] Even after recommendations by the European Commission and the adoption of a new timetable, this Article had not been transposed into national law. The implementation of the principle of equal pay became one of the priorities of the social programme that was agreed upon in 1974, and the Member States decided to adopt a new directive on equal pay for men and women.[28]

2.1.2 Directive on the Principle of Equal Pay for Men and Women

The Directive on the application of the principle of equal pay for men and women – the so-called first Directive – was adopted in 1975.[29] Many of the general provisions of this directive can also be found in the anti-discrimination directives which have subsequently been adopted. The directive defines the obligations of the Member States. The Member States have to abolish all discrimination between men and women arising from laws, regulations or administrative provisions which are contrary to the principle of equal pay (Article 3). The Member States also have to take the necessary measures to ensure that provisions in collective agreements, wage scales, wage agreements and individual employment contracts that are contrary to the principle of equal pay must be or may be declared null and void or may be amended (Article 4). Furthermore, they have to ensure the application of the principle of equal pay by the adoption of laws, regulations and administrative provisions (Article 8(1) of Directive 75/117/EEC).

---

[26] ECJ 13 January 2004, Case C-256/01, *Debra Allonby v Accrington & Rossendale College, Education Lecturing Services, trading as Protocol Professional and Secretary of State for Education and Employment*, ECR 2004, I-873 (*Allonby*), at paras 65-71.

[27] S. Prechal and N. Burrows, *Gender Discrimination Law of the European Community*, (Aldershot-Vermont: Dartmouth, 1990), p. 81.

[28] Council Resolution of 21 January 1974 concerning a social action programme, OJ 1974, C 13/1.

[29] Council Directive of 10 February 1975 on the approximation of the law of the Member States relating to the application of the principle of equal pay for men and women (75/117/EEC), OJ 1975, L 45/19.

According to Article 1 of the directive, the principle of equal pay for men and women as outlined in Article 119 means, for the same work or for work to which equal value is attributed, the elimination of all discrimination on grounds of sex with regard to all aspects and conditions of remuneration. In particular, where a job classification scheme is used for determining pay, it must be based on the same criteria for both men and women and must be drawn up to exclude discrimination on grounds of sex.

This Article makes it clear that the principle of equal pay also applies to work of equal value. According to the ECJ, the principle of equal pay in Article 119 does apply to equal work and work of equal value and also, *a fortiori*, to work of higher value. The Court adopted this view, stating that otherwise the employer would easily be able to circumvent the principle of equal pay by assigning additional or more onerous duties to workers of a particular sex, who could then be paid a lower wage.[30] However, the Article 119 does not require that a worker is paid more according to the higher value of his or her work compared to the work of his or her colleague of the other sex. Commentators pointed out that this might leave open the possibility that employers might grade women's jobs as being superior in value, while their wages were classified at the level of the lower-paid men.[31]

The first Directive does not alter the meaning of Article 119 EEC, which is a primary source of community law. The ECJ stated in *Worringham* that although the directive explains that the concept of same work in Article 119 includes work to which equal value is attributed, this in no way affects the concept of pay as laid down in Article 119.[32]

Article 2 of Directive 75/117/EEC puts the obligation on Member States to introduce in their legal systems such measures as are necessary to enable all employees who consider themselves wronged by failure to apply the principle of equal pay, to pursue their claims by judicial process after possible recourse to other competent authorities.

The Member States also have to take the measures necessary to ensure that the principle of equal pay is applied and that effective measures are available to ensure the observation of the principle of equal pay (Article 6). This principle of access to justice is firmly established in other directives as well[33] and has been further developed by the ECJ (see Section 4). Provisions adopted in the field of equal pay have to be brought to the attention of employees, for example in their workplace (Article 7).

---

[30] ECJ 4 February 1988, Case 157/86, *Mary Murphy and others v An Bord Telecom Eireann*, ECR 1988, 673 (*Murphy*), paras 9-10.
[31] S. Prechal and N. Burrows, *supra* note 27, p. 81.
[32] ECJ 11 March 1981, Case 69/80, *Susan Jane Worringham and Margaret Humphreys v Lloyds Bank Limited*, ECR 1981, 767 (*Worringham*), para. 21.
[33] See for example Article 6 of Directive 76/207/EEC, Article 6 of Directive 79/7/EEC, Article 10 of Directive 86/378/EEC and Article 9 of Directive 86/613/EEC.

Furthermore, the Member States have to take the necessary measures to protect employees against dismissal by an employer in reaction to a complaint within the undertaking or to any legal proceedings aimed at enforcing compliance with the principle of equal pay (Article 5).

The European Commission has to monitor and analyse whether the Member States fulfil their obligations regarding, for example, the implementation of Treaty provisions and directives. Two networks of independent legal experts provide the necessary information to the European Commission in the fields of gender equality and anti-discrimination.[34] According to Article 226 EC, the European Commission can start an infringement procedure if it considers that a Member State has failed to fulfil an obligation. The Commission first sends the State a reasoned opinion on the matter after giving the State concerned the opportunity to submit its observations. If the Member State does not comply with the opinion within the period laid down by the Commission, the Commission may bring the matter before the ECJ. If the ECJ considers that the Member State has failed to fulfil an obligation and the Member State does not take the necessary measures to comply with the judgment of the ECJ in time, sanctions may even be imposed upon the Member State (see Article 228 EC).

2.1.3 The Concept of Pay

The potential impact of Article 119 has been strengthened by a large body of case law of the ECJ on the concept of pay. The ECJ adopted a broad and purposive interpretation of this concept.[35] This Article applies not only to sex discrimination arising out of individual contracts, but also to collective agreements and legislation.[36] Pay includes not only the basic pay, but also, for example, overtime supplements,[37] special bonuses paid by the employer,[38] travel facilities,[39] compensation for attending training courses and training

---

[34] There exists the European Commission's European Network of Legal Experts in the field of Gender Equality. See the publications of this network on the website of the European Commission: http://ec.europa.eu/employment_social/gender_equality/legislation/bulletin_en.html (accessed 21 May 2008). There also exists the European Commission's European Network of Legal Experts in the non-discrimination field, see: http://ec.europa.eu/ employment_social/fundamental_rights/policy/aneval/legnet_en.htm (Last accessed 21 May 2008).

[35] See for example E. Ellis, *EU Anti-Discrimination Law*, (Oxford: Oxford University Press, 2005), pp. 121-158.

[36] See *Defrenne II, supra* note 12, at paras 21-22.

[37] See for example ECJ 6 December 2007, Case 300/06, *Ursula Voß v Land Berlin*, ECR 2007, I-10573. (*Voß*).

[38] See for example ECJ 21 October 1999, Case C-333/97, *Susanne Lewen v Lothar Denda*, ECR 1999, I-7243 (*Lewen*).

[39] See for example ECJ 9 February 1982, Case 12/81, *Eileen Garland v British Rail Engineering Limited*, ECR 1982, p. 359 (*Garland*).

facilities,[40] termination payments in case of dismissal [41] and occupational pensions.[42]

In *Defrenne I* the Court had to differentiate between the concept of pay as laid down in Article 119 and social security systems. The ECJ ruled that although a consideration in the nature of social security benefits is not alien to the concept of pay, this concept does not include social security schemes or benefits, in particular retirement pensions, which are directly governed by legislation without any element of agreement within the undertaking or the occupational branch concerned, which are obligatorily applicable to general categories of workers. These schemes assure the workers the benefit of a legal scheme, which is financed by workers, employers and possibly the public authorities less by way of the employment relationship between the employer and the worker than through considerations of social policy.[43] In the famous *Barber* judgment, the Court ruled that Article 119 of the Treaty prohibits any discrimination between men and women with regard to pay, whatever the system giving rise to such inequality.[44] In this case, there was a close relationship between the occupational and the statutory pension scheme. The Court further explained that with regard to equal pay for men and women, genuine transparency, permitting an effective review by the national court, is assured only if the principle of equal pay must be observed in respect of each of the elements of remuneration granted to men and women, and not on a comprehensive basis in respect of the overall consideration granted to men and women.[45]

2.1.4 Recent Developments

Article 119 EEC Treaty was amended when the Treaty of Amsterdam came into force on 1 May 1999 and was renumbered as Article 141 EC. The first two paragraphs remained nearly the same; however, the provision in Article 141(1) now explicitly states that:

> Each Member State shall ensure the principle of equal pay for male and female workers for equal work or work of equal value.

---

[40] See for example ECJ 4 June 1992, Case C-360/90, *Arbeiterwohlfahrt der Stadt Berlin e.V. v Monika Bötel*, ECR 1992, I-3589 (*Bötel*).

[41] See for example ECJ 27 June 1990, Case C-33/89, *Maria Kowalska v Freie und Hansestadt Hamburg*, ECR 1990, I-2591 (*Kowalska*).

[42] See for example ECJ 13 May 1986, Case 170/84, *Bilka-Kaufhaus GmbH v Karin Weber von Hartz*, ECR 1986, 1607 (*Bilka*) and ECJ 17 May 1990, Case C-262/88, *Douglas Harvey Barber v Guardian Royal Exchange Assurance Group*, ECR 1990, I-1889 (*Barber*).

[43] ECJ 25 May 1971, Case 80/70, *Gabrielle Defrenne v Belgian State*, ECR 1971, 445 (*Defrenne I*), at paras 7-8.

[44] See *Barber*, *supra* note 42, at para. 32.

[45] *Ibid*, at paras 33-34.

The addition 'work of equal value' only confirms what had already become clear through the case law of the ECJ. The European Community legislator has thus codified this case law in the Treaty provision. The case law of the ECJ regarding the concept of equal pay in Article 119, in particular the *Barber* judgment and subsequent judgments on occupational social security schemes, has also led to amendments of the so-called fourth Directive on occupational social security schemes.[46] This shows the great influence of the binding judgments of the ECJ on developments in the field of equal pay for male and female workers.

The second section of Article 141 contains the same definition of 'pay' as the former Article 119. Two new paragraphs have been added. According to Article 141(3), the Council can adopt measures to ensure the application of the principle of equal opportunities and equal treatment of men and women in matters of employment and occupation, including the principle of equal pay for equal work or work of equal value.[47]

Article 141(4) allows positive action. It stipulates that:

> With a view to ensuring full equality in practice between men and women in working life, the principle of equal treatment shall not prevent any Member State from maintaining or adopting measures providing for specific advantages in order to make it easier for the underrepresented sex to pursue a vocational activity or prevent or compensate for disadvantages in professional careers.

The scope of the so-called second Directive on equal treatment of men and women in access to employment, vocational training and promotion, and working conditions (see Section 2.2.1) now also includes pay, as provided for in Directive 75/11/EEC.[48] A very similar provision is included in the Recast Directive (see Section 2.2.6), with a reference to Article 141.[49]

---

[46] Council Directive of 24 July 1986 on the implementation of the principle of equal treatment between men and women in occupational social security schemes (86/378/EEC), OJ 1986, L 225/40. This Directive has been amended by Council Directive 96/97/EC of 20 December 1996, OJ 1997, L46/20 (the so-called *Barber* Directive). Directive 96/97/EC has been now incorporated in Directive 2006/54/EC (recast) with some other directives, see footnotes 48 and 49, and Section 2.2.6.

[47] Since the entry into force of the Treaty of Amsterdam, Article 13 provides a legal basis to take appropriate action to combat discrimination based on different grounds, including gender.

[48] Directive 2002/73/EC of the European Parliament and the Council of 23 September 2002 amending Council Directive 76/207/EEC on the implementation of the principle of equal treatment for men and women as regards access to employment, vocational training and promotion, and working conditions, OJ 2002, L 269/15, Article 3(c).

[49] Directive 2006/54/EC of the European Parliament and of the Council of 5 July 2006 on the implementation of the principle of equal opportunities and equal treatment of men and women in matters of employment and occupation (recast), OJ 2006, L 204/23, Article 14(c).

2.2 Equal Treatment of Men and Women

2.2.1 Equal Treatment of Men and Women in Employment

In 1976 a second directive was adopted on the implementation of the principle of equal treatment between men and women in employment.[50] With this directive, the principle of equal treatment between men and women also came to apply to access to employment, vocational training and promotion, and working conditions, including the conditions governing dismissal (Articles 1(1) and 5(1)). The directive prohibits both direct and indirect discrimination (see Sections 3.1 and 3.2). Article 2(1) defines the principle of equal treatment. This principle means that: '... there shall be no discrimination whatsoever on grounds of sex either directly or indirectly by reference in particular to marital or family status.'

In the first draft of this Article, indirect discrimination was not mentioned explicitly. However, the idea of positive action was included in the definition of equal treatment, which was defined as: 'The elimination of all discrimination based on sex or on marital or family status, including the adoption of appropriate measures to provide women with equal opportunity in employment, vocational training, promotion and working conditions.'

During the negotiations on this draft Article, the reference to appropriate measures was deleted.[51] Positive action has since then been framed in EC law as an exception to the principle of equal treatment, instead of as an integrated part of it. The final text of Article 2(4) of Directive 76/207/EEC on positive action stipulates that: 'This Directive shall be without prejudice to measures to promote equal opportunity for men and women, in particular by removing existing inequalities which affect women's opportunities in the areas referred to in Article 1(1).'

The directive contains two more exceptions to the prohibition of direct sex discrimination. One concerns occupational activities for which the sex of the worker is a determining factor. This is for example the case when an actor in a play or a film has to be a man. Article 2(2) reads: 'This Directive shall be without prejudice to the right of Member States to exclude from its field of application those occupational activities, and where appropriate, the training leading thereto, for which, by reason of their nature or the context in which they are carried out, the sex of the worker constitutes a determining factor.'

The ECJ ruled that the exception of occupational activities in Article 2(2), as derogation from an individual right laid down in the directive, must be interpreted strictly.[52] However, according to the ECJ, the exclusion of women

---

[50] Council Directive of 9 February 1976 on the implementation of the principle of equal treatment for men and women as regards access to employment, vocational training and promotion, and working conditions, OJ 1976, L 39/40.
[51] C. Hoskyns, *supra* note 22, p. 103.
[52] ECJ 15 May 1986, Case 222/84, *Marguerite Johnston v Chief Constable of the Royal Ulster Constabulary*, ECR 1986, 1651 (*Johnston*), at para. 36.

from some military units of the Royal Marines did fall within the scope of this exception and therefore did not breach the second Directive.[53] On the other hand, Germany infringed the directive by adopting the position that the composition of all armed units in the *Bundeswehr* (the federal defence force) must remain exclusively male. The Court ruled that the derogations provided in Article 2(2) can only apply to specific activities and that such a general exclusion was not justified by the specific nature of the posts in question or by the particular context in which the activities in question are carried out.[54]

One more exception in the directive concerns the protection of women, particularly as regards pregnancy and maternity (Article 2(3)). This exception allows the adoption of national provisions which guarantee women specific rights concerning pregnancy and maternity, such as maternity leave. Interpreting this exception, the Court ruled that Article 2(3) of the directive recognises the legitimacy, in terms of the principle of equal treatment, firstly, of protecting a woman's biological condition during and after pregnancy and, secondly, of protecting the special relationship between a woman and her child over the period which follows pregnancy and childbirth.[55] These rights are intended to ensure implementation of the principle of equal treatment for men and women regarding access to both employment and working conditions. Therefore, the exercise of the rights conferred on women under Article 2(3) cannot be grounds for unfavourable treatment regarding their access to employment or their working conditions. In that light, the result pursued by the directive is substantive, not formal, equality.[56] In 1992, the Member States adopted a specific directive regarding pregnant workers (Directive 92/85/EEC, see Section 2.2.4).

The second Directive has what is called a closed system of exceptions as regards direct discrimination; the derogations to the principle of equal treatment are limited to these three exceptions.[57] Therefore, direct sex discrimination in employment is prohibited, unless one of these three exceptions is at issue.

In 2002, Directive 76/207/EEC was amended with the aim of modernising and harmonising its provisions.[58] Elements of the case law of the ECJ have been

---

[53] ECJ 26 October 1999, Case C-273/97, *Angela Maria Sirdar v The Army Board and Secretary of State for Defence*, ECR 1999, I-07403 (*Sirdar*).

[54] ECJ 11 January 2000, Case C-285/98, *Tanja Kreil v Bundesrepublik Deutschland*, ECR 2000, I-69 (*Kreil*).

[55] ECJ 12 July 1984, Case 184/83, *Ulrich Hofmann v Barmer Ersatzkasse*, ECR 1984, 3047 (*Hofmann*), at para. 25.

[56] ECJ 30 April 1998, Case 136/95, *Caisse nationale d'assurance vieillesse des travailleurs salariés (CNAVTS) v Evelyne Thibault*, ECR 1998, I-2011 (*Thibault*), at paras 24-26.

[57] ECJ 8 November 1990, Case C-177/88, *Elisabeth Johanna Pacifica Dekker v Stichting Vormingscentrum voor Jong Volwassenen (VJV-Centrum) Plus*, ECR 1990, I-03941 (*Dekker*), at paras 22-24.

[58] Directive 2002/73/EC of the European Parliament and the Council of 23 September 2002 amending Council Directive 76/207/EEC on the implementation of the principle of equal treatment for men and women as regards access to employment, vocational training and

incorporated in some of the new and amended provisions. The provisions of (the amended) Directive 76/207/EEC have been brought together with other provisions on equal treatment for men and women in the single text of the Recast Directive (Directive 2006/54/EC, see Section 2.2.6).

2.2.2 Equal Treatment of Men and Women in Social Security Matters

In 1976, the Member States could not reach an agreement on the equal treatment of men and women in social security matters. However, Article 1 of Directive 76/207/EEC made it clear that the intention of the directive was also to implement the principle of equal treatment for men and women in social security matters and that Member States would adopt provisions dealing with social security. Directive 7/79/EEC, the third Directive on equal treatment between men and women, covers the field of social security.[59]

The directive prohibits both direct and indirect sex discrimination (Article 4(1)). The personal scope is broadly defined in Article 2, which reads: 'The Directive shall apply to the working population, including self-employed persons, workers and self-employed persons whose activity is interrupted by illness, accident or involuntary unemployment, and persons seeking employment and to retired or invalided workers and self-employed persons.'

The material scope is defined in Article 3. The directive applies to statutory schemes which provide protection against the following risks: sickness, invalidity, old age, accidents at work and occupational diseases, and unemployment. The directive also applies to social assistance, in so far as this is intended to supplement or replace the statutory schemes covering the abovementioned risks. Provisions concerning survivors' and family benefits are excluded, except in the case of family benefits granted by way of an increase of benefits due in respect of the risks mentioned above.

This third Directive contains many more exceptions than the second Directive. Article 4 (2) provides for an exception for provisions relating to the protection of women on the ground of maternity. In Article 7 more exceptions are listed, such as the determination of different pensionable ages for men and women in old-age and retirement pensions.

It was not until 1986 that the Member States adopted a fourth Directive (86/378/EEC) on the principle of equal treatment in occupational social security

---

promotion, and working conditions, OJ 2002, L 269/15. See A. Masselot, 'The New Equal Treatment Directive … plus ça change…'. (2004) 12 *Feminist Legal Studies*, pp. 93-104.

[59] Council Directive of 19 December 1978 on the progressive implementation of the principle of equal treatment for men and women in matters of social security (79/7/EEC), OJ 1979, L 6/24.

schemes.[60] According to Article 2 of the directive, occupational social security schemes are schemes which are not covered by Directive 79/7/EEC. Directive 86/378/EEC contains many exceptions to the principle of equal treatment (see Article 5). However, since the ECJ interpreted the concept of pay in Article 119 as including occupational social security schemes, the significance of the fourth Directive was consequently rather limited. The case law of the ECJ has been incorporated in the amended fourth Directive.[61] This directive is part of the recasting exercise (Directive 2006/54/EC, see Section 2.2.6).

2.2.3 Equal Treatment of Men and Women Engaged in an Activity, Including Agriculture, in a Self-Employed Capacity

The fifth Directive on equal treatment was also adopted in 1986.[62] The aim of Directive 86/613/EEC is to ensure the application of the principle of equal treatment between men and women engaged in an activity in a self-employed capacity, or contributing to such an activity, as regards those aspects which are not covered by Directives 76/207/EEC and 79/9/EEC (Article 1). The personal scope of the directive covers self-employed workers and their spouses, not being employees or partners (Article 2). This directive has played a very small role in practice up to now, due to the fact that the rights conferred are very weak.

2.2.4 The Pregnancy Directive

Directive 92/85/EEC, regarding pregnant workers and workers who have recently given birth or are breastfeeding, was adopted in 1992.[63] Its main aim is to implement measures to encourage improvements in the safety and health at work of pregnant workers and of workers who have recently given birth or who are breastfeeding (Article 1). Some provisions of this directive are closely linked to the principle of equal treatment between men and women in employment. Article 8 of this directive stipulates, for example, that Member States have to ensure that women enjoy a period of at least 14 weeks maternity leave. During

---

[60] Council Directive of 24 July 1986 on the implementation of the principle of equal treatment between men and women in occupational social security schemes (86/378/EEC), OJ 1986, L 225/40.

[61] Council Directive 96/97/EC of 20 December 1996 amending Directive 86/378/EEC on the implementation of the principle of equal treatment of men and women in occupational social security schemes, OJ 1997, L46/20 (the so-called *Barber* Directive).

[62] Directive 86/613/EEC of 11 December 1986 on the application of the principle of equal treatment between men and women engaged in an activity, including agriculture, in a self-employed capacity, and on the protection of self-employed women during pregnancy and motherhood, OJ 1986, L 359/56.

[63] Council Directive 92/85/EEC of 19 October 1992 on the introduction of measures to encourage improvements in the safety and health at work of pregnant workers and workers who have recently given birth or are breastfeeding (tenth individual Directive within the meaning of Article 16 (1) of Directive 89/391/EEC), OJ 1992, L 348/1.

this period they are entitled to the maintenance of payment and/or to an adequate allowance (Article 11 (2)(b)). Furthermore, pregnant women are protected against dismissal from the beginning of their pregnancy until the end of the maternity leave (Article 10). The provisions of this directive have often been interpreted jointly with provisions of Directive 76/207/EEC.[64] A proposal to amend this directive and extend maternity leave to 18 weeks is pending.[65]

2.2.5 Equal Treatment of Men and Women in the Access to and the Supply of Goods and Services

In 2004, the material scope of the principle of equal treatment of men and women was broadened with the adoption of Directive 2004/113/EC, implementing the principle of equal treatment between men and women in the access to and the supply of goods and services.[66] This is the first directive addressing gender equality issues outside the field of employment. The preamble of this directive recognises that discrimination based on sex, including harassment and sexual harassment, also takes place in areas outside the labour market and can be equally damaging, acting as a barrier to the full and successful integration of men and women into economic and social life. In the preamble, a reference is made to the Race Directive (2000/43/EC), adopted in 2000, which also has Article 13 EC as a legal base and which applies to many areas outside employment (see Section 2.4).[67]

Directive 2004/113/EC applies to all persons who provide goods and services that are available to the public both in the public and private sectors, including public bodies, and which are offered outside the area of private and family life and the transactions carried out in this context (Article 3(1)). Goods and services should be taken to be those within the meaning of the relevant provisions of the EC Treaty.[68] The Directive does not apply to the content of the media and advertising and education (Article 3(3)). The initial proposal[69] had the same broad scope of application as Directive 2000/43/EC, but during the negotiating process the scope became much more limited. There is now a difference in material scope and thus level of protection between the Race Directive (2000/43/EC) and the gender equality directives (and the Framework

---

[64] See for example ECJ 30 June 1998, Case C-394/96, *Mary Brown v Rentokil Ltd.*, ECR 1998, I-4185 (*Brown*), at para. 18.
[65] COM 2008 (637) final.
[66] Council Directive 2004/113/EC of 13 December 2004 implementing the principle of equal treatment between men and women in the access to and the supply of goods and services, OJ 2004, L 373/37. See E. Caracciolo di Torella, 'The goods and services directive: limitations and opportunities', (2005) 13 *Feminist Legal Studies*, pp. 337-347.
[67] Council Directive 2004/113/EC, Preamble, at paras 9-10.
[68] *Ibid*, at para. 11.
[69] COM 2003 (657) final.

Directive 2000/78/EC). This might give the impression that some discrimination grounds are considered to be more important than others.[70]

The principle of equal treatment means that there is to be no direct discrimination based on sex, and this includes less favourable treatment of women for reasons of pregnancy and maternity (Article 4(1)(a)). More favourable provisions concerning the protection of women as regards pregnancy and maternity are not contrary to the principle of equal treatment (Article 4(2)). Positive action is allowed (Article 6). The directive further prohibits indirect sex discrimination (Article 4(1)(b)), harassment and sexual harassment (Article 4(3)) and an instruction to discriminate (Article 4(4)).

Definitions of direct discrimination, indirect discrimination, harassment and sexual harassment are included in the anti-discrimination directives which have been adopted since 2000 (Directives 2000/43/EC, 2000/78/EC and 2002/73/EC, see Section 3). Similar definitions are to be found in Article 2 of the goods and services directive. However, this last directive allows more exceptions to the principle of equal treatment, even in cases of direct sex discrimination. Article 4(5) stipulates that the directive is not to preclude differences in treatment, if the provision of the goods and services exclusively or primarily to members of one sex is justified by a legitimate aim and the means to achieve that aim are appropriate and necessary. Unlike the other sex equality directives, the directive has thus no closed system of exceptions in cases of direct discrimination and therefore offers less protection against direct sex discrimination.

The directive also contains specific provisions regarding actuarial factors in insurance. Insurance is often offered on different terms both as regards the premiums and the benefits to men and women, in particular in private pension schemes. These differences are based on the fact that, on average, women live longer than men and that the insurance therefore runs a higher financial risk in insuring women than in insuring men. Article 5(1) therefore stipulates that: 'Member States shall ensure that in all new contracts (…) the use of sex as a factor in the calculation of premiums and benefits shall not result in differences in individuals' premiums and benefits.'

In any event, although Member States have the possibility of derogating from this provision (Article 5(2)), costs related to pregnancy and maternity may not result in differences in an individual's premiums and benefits (Article 5(3)).

2.2.6 Recasting

In 2006, a new directive was adopted in which existing provisions of different sex equality directives were brought together and some case law of the European Court of Justice was incorporated (Directive 2006/54/EC).[71] The aim of this so-

---

[70] L. Waddington and M. Bell, 'More Equal than Others: Distinguishing European Union Equality Directives', (2001) 38 *Common Market Law Review*, pp. 587-611.
[71] Directive 2006/54/EC.

called recasting was to clarify and bring together in a single text the main provisions regarding access to employment including promotion, and to vocational training, as well as working conditions, including pay and occupational social security schemes.[72] This Recast Directive had to be implemented by 15 August 2008 and the directives which are brought together in this directive (Directives 76/207/EEC as amended by Directive 2002/73/EC; 86/378/EEC as amended by Directive 96/97/EC; 75/117/EEC and 97/80/EC) are to be repealed one year later (Article 34). Of course, the Member States had to fulfil the obligations arising from all these directives before the end of the diverse implementation periods. Nearly all the Articles in the Recast Directive correspond to existing Articles in one or more of the abovementioned directives.

The Recast Directive is divided into four titles. The first title, on general provisions, includes a description of the aim of the directive and definitions of various concepts, such as direct and indirect discrimination, harassment and sexual harassment. These definitions are similar to those found in other recent anti-discrimination directives (see Section 3). The second title includes provisions on equal pay (Chapter 1) and on equal treatment as regards access to employment, vocational training, promotion and working conditions (Chapter 2). In the third title, provisions are brought together regarding remedies, the burden of proof, and the promotion of equal treatment through equality bodies, social dialogue and dialogue with NGOs. This title also includes general provisions on, for example, victimisation and penalties. In the fourth title, the final provisions concern for example the obligations for the Member States to report on the application of the directive, the review by the European Commission of the directive and its implementation.

2.3 Non-Discrimination of Part-Time Workers and Fixed-Term Workers

Two specific directives in which the principle of non-discrimination is also enshrined apply to part-time workers[73] and fixed-term workers.[74] Both directives are meant to implement a framework agreement of the European social partners (ETUC, UNICE and CEEP), which forms the annex of the directives.[75]

The framework agreement on part-time work is aimed in the first place at eliminating discrimination against part-time workers and improving the quality of part-time work. A second aim is facilitating the development of part-time work on a voluntary basis and contributing to a flexible organisation of working

---

[72] Preamble at para. 1 and Article 1.
[73] Council directive 97/81/EC of 15 December 1997 concerning the framework agreement on part-time work concluded by ETUC, UNICE and CEEP, OJ 1998, L 14/9.
[74] Council Directive 1999/70/EC of 28 June 1999 concerning the framework agreement on fixed-term work concluded by ETUC, UNICE and CEEP, OJ L 1999, L 175/43.
[75] The European Trade Union Confederation (ETUC), the Union of Industrial and Employers' Confederations of Europe (UNICE) and the European Centre of Enterprises with Public Participation (CEEP).

time in a manner which takes into account the needs of employers and workers (clause 1). However, the provisions relating to this second aim are rather vague and do not grant clearly defined rights to employees (clause 5).

The part-time worker is defined as an employee whose normal hours of work are less than the normal working hours of a comparable full-time worker (clause 3(1)). The principle of non-discrimination applies only to working conditions. Clause 4(1) stipulates that part-time workers are not to be treated in a less favourable manner than full-time workers solely because they work part-time, unless different treatment is justified on objective grounds. The agreement also specifies that where appropriate, the principle of *pro rata temporis* is to apply (clause 4(2)). Case law regarding this directive is still scarce, but the concept of 'objective grounds' in clause 4(1) will probably be interpreted by the ECJ in the same way as in the fixed-term directive (see below).

The framework agreement on fixed-term work is framed very similarly to the framework agreement on part-time work. The twofold aim of this agreement is to improve the quality of fixed-term work by ensuring the application of the principle of non-discrimination and to establish a framework to prevent abuse through the use of successive fixed-term employment contracts or relationships (clause 1). The principle of non-discrimination is defined in comparable wording to that in clause 4 of the framework agreement on part-time work. The ECJ has ruled that the concept of objective grounds in this clause requires 'the unequal treatment at issue to be justified by the existence of precise and concrete factors, characterising the employment condition to which it relates, in the specific context in which it occurs and on the basis of objective and transparent criteria in order to ensure that that unequal treatment in fact responds to a genuine need, is appropriate for achieving the objective pursued and is necessary for that purpose.'[76] The test therefore is quite similar to the objective justification test in cases of indirect discrimination (see Section 3.2).

The use of successive fixed-term employment contracts or relationships has to be justified by objective reasons (clause 5(1)(a)). This concept is not defined in clause 5 of the framework agreement. The ECJ ruled that 'the concept of 'objective reasons' (...) must be understood as referring to precise and concrete circumstances characterising a given activity, which are therefore capable in that particular context of justifying the use of successive fixed-term employment contracts. Those circumstances may result, in particular, from the specific nature of the tasks for the performance of which such contracts have been concluded and from the inherent characteristics of those tasks or, as the case may be, from pursuit of a legitimate social-policy objective of a Member State.' A national provision which merely authorises recourse to successive fixed-term

---

[76] ECJ 13 September 2007, Case C-307/05, *Yolanda Del Cerro Alonso v Osakidetza-Servicio Vasco de Salud*, ECR 2007, I-7109 (*Del Cerro Alonso*), at para. 58.

employment contracts in a general and abstract manner by a rule of statute or secondary legislation does not meet with these requirements.[77]

2.4 Equal Treatment between Persons Irrespective of Racial or Ethnic Origin

In 2000, two directives were adopted with Article 13 EC as a legal basis. The aim of the first directive (Directive 2000/43/EC, the so-called Race Directive) is to lay down a framework for combating discrimination on the grounds of racial and ethnic origin.[78] The second directive (Directive 2000/78/EC, the so-called Framework Directive) has the same objective regarding discrimination on the grounds of religion or belief, disability, age or sexual orientation (see Section 2.5).[79] Both directives were adopted in a context of increasing manifestations of racism in Europe and electoral successes of right-wing movements.[80] These directives and those adopted afterwards regarding sex equality have a similar structure and similar definitions (see Directives 2000/73/EC, 2004/114/EC and 2006/54/EC). New definitions and new concepts have been introduced, such as harassment and the requirement to provide reasonable accommodation for disabled persons (see Section 3.5).[81] Furthermore, the enforcement mechanisms have been strengthened (see Section 4). However, the scope of these directives differs.

The Race Directive has the broadest scope of all the anti-discrimination directives adopted thus far and applies to all persons, both in the private and public sector. However, the directive does not cover difference of treatment based on nationality, nor does it cover provisions and the conditions relating to the entry into and residence in a Member State of so-called third-country nationals (persons with a nationality other than that of a Member State of the European Union) and stateless persons (Article 3(2)).

The material scope covers access to employment, to self-employment and occupation, including selection criteria and recruitment conditions; and access to promotion (Article 3(a)) and vocational training, including practical work experience (Article 3(b)). The directive applies to working conditions, including dismissals and pay (Article 3(c)) and membership of and involvement in an organisation of workers or employers (Article 3(d)). The directive further covers

---

[77] ECJ 4 July 2006, Case C-212/04, *Konstantinos Adeneler and Others v Ellinikos Organismos Galaktos (ELOG)*, ECR 2006, I-6057 (*Adeneler*), at paras 69-71.
[78] Council Directive 2000/43/EC of 29 June 2000 on equal treatment irrespective of race or ethnic origin in employment and regarding access to and supply of goods and services, OJ 2000, L 180/22.
[79] Council Directive 2000/78/EC of 27 November 2000 establishing a general framework for equal treatment in employment and occupation, OJ 2000, L 303/16.
[80] L. Waddington and M. Bell, *supra* note 70, p. 610.
[81] See for a discussion: D. Schiek, 'A New Framework on Equal Treatment of Persons in EC Law?', (2002) 8/2 *European Law Journal*, pp. 90-310.

the access to and supply of goods and services (Article 3(h)). The Race Directive applies to social protection, including social security and healthcare (Article 3(e)); social advantages (Article 3(f)) and education (Article 3 (g)). It has been submitted that there is a clear hierarchy of discrimination grounds and that sex equality has been displaced by racial equality, in particular in the light of this broader material scope of the Race Directive.[82]

The Race Directive has a closed system of exceptions in cases of direct discrimination, similar to the structure of the sex discrimination directives in the field of employment. Direct discrimination based on race or ethnic origin is prohibited, unless an exception can be proved. The first exception concerns genuine occupational requirements. Member States may provide that a difference of treatment which is based on a characteristic related to racial or ethnic origin will not constitute discrimination where, by reason of the nature of the particular occupational activities concerned or of the context in which they are carried out, such a characteristic constitutes a genuine and determining occupational requirement, provided that the objective is legitimate and the requirement is proportionate (Article 4). The ECJ has not yet interpreted this provision, but it seems likely that the case law regarding the similar exception when sex is a determining factor will provide guidance.

Positive action is also explicitly allowed. Article 5 stipulates that with a view to ensuring full equality in practice, the principle of equal treatment must not prevent any Member State from maintaining or adopting specific measures to prevent or compensate for disadvantages linked to racial or ethnic origin.

2.5 Equal Treatment on the Grounds of Religion or Belief, Disability, Age or Sexual Orientation

For most of the discrimination grounds covered by this directive, the structure of the Framework Directive (2000/78/EC)[83] is similar to the structure of the Race Directive. The same is true for the definitions of the concept of discrimination (see Section 3). However, there are some marked differences between the directives covering the grounds of race and ethnic origin and gender on the one hand and the Framework Directive on the other hand, in particular regarding the material scope, exceptions to the principle of equal treatment and enforcement mechanisms.

The Framework Directive only applies to (access to) employment and does not cover the access to and supply of goods and services (Article 3(1)(a-d)). Nor does the directive apply to payments of any kind made by state schemes or similar, including state social security and social protection schemes (Article 3(3)). The Member States may furthermore exclude the armed forces from the

---

[82] L. Waddington and M. Bell, *supra* note 70, p. 610.
[83] Council Directive 2000/78/EC of 27 November 2000 establishing a general framework for equal treatment in employment and occupation, OJ 2000, L 303/16.

scope of the Framework Directive in relation to discrimination on grounds of age and disability (Article 3(4)). A general exception further includes measures laid down by national law which, in a democratic society, are necessary for public security, for the maintenance of public order and the prevention of criminal offences, for the protection of health and for the protection of the rights and freedoms of others (Article 2(5)). No other EU anti-discrimination directive contains such an exception clause.

The closed system of exceptions in cases of direct discrimination applies to the discrimination grounds of religion or belief, disability and sexual orientation. The Framework Directive allows an exception in case of occupational requirements (Article 4(1)). A similar exception applies to churches and other public or private organisations, the ethos of which is based on religion or belief (Article 4(2)). Positive action is explicitly allowed regarding any ground of discrimination covered by the directive (Article 7(1)). With regard to disabled persons, Member States may maintain or adopt provisions on the protection of health and safety at work or measures aimed at creating or maintaining provisions or facilities for safeguarding or promoting their integration into the working environment (Article 7(2)). Article 5 contains a specific obligation to provide reasonable accommodation for disabled persons (see Section 3.5)

Differences of treatment on grounds of age, whether direct or indirect, might be justified if, within the context of national law, they are objectively and reasonably justified by a legitimate aim, including legitimate employment policy, labour market and vocational training objectives, and if the means of achieving that aim are appropriate and necessary (Article 6(1)). Even direct age discrimination can therefore be objectively justified by reasons other than occupational requirements or positive action. Article 6(1) provides some examples, such as setting special conditions on access to employment for young people, older workers or persons with caring responsibilities.

3. FORMS AND CONCEPTS OF DISCRIMINATION

All the anti-discrimination directives differentiate between direct and indirect discrimination. This distinction is important because direct discrimination is generally prohibited, unless a specific written exception can be proved. The directives which have been adopted since 2000 contain similar definitions of direct and indirect discrimination. The development of the concept of indirect discrimination meant a step towards a more substantive approach to equality, because it focuses on the effect of a rule or a practice. Substantive equality requires that further steps are taken in order to realise true, genuine equality in social conditions.[84]

Harassment, sexual harassment and an instruction to discriminate are also prohibited and defined in the recent directives.

In the following Sections, the definitions of these concepts in the Recast Directive (2006/54/EC, see Section 2.2.6), the most recent directive, will be the starting point, unless stipulated otherwise.

3.1 Direct Discrimination (Including Pregnancy)

Direct discrimination is defined in Article 2(1)(a) and occurs 'where one person is treated less favourably on grounds of sex than another is, has been or would be treated in a comparable situation.'

This definition suggests that a person who is treated less favourably should be compared with another person who is in a comparable situation. However, in cases of direct discrimination in relation to pregnancy, such a comparison is not required according to the case law of the ECJ. The Court ruled that the refusal to appoint a woman because she is pregnant amounts to direct sex discrimination, which is prohibited. The fact that there are no male candidates to whom she could be compared is not relevant if the reason for not appointing the woman is linked to her pregnancy.[85] The ECJ also ruled that although pregnancy is not in any way comparable to a pathological condition, the fact remains that pregnancy is a period during which disorders and complications may arise, compelling a woman to undergo strict medical supervision and, in some cases, to rest absolutely for all or part of her pregnancy. Those disorders and complications, which may cause incapacity for work, form part of the risks inherent in the condition of pregnancy and are thus a specific feature of that condition. The principle of non-discrimination requires that women are protected against dismissal throughout the period of pregnancy until the end of the maternity leave. Dismissal of a female worker during pregnancy for absences due to incapacity for work resulting from her pregnancy is linked to the occurrence of risks inherent in pregnancy and must therefore be regarded as essentially based on the fact of pregnancy. Such a dismissal can affect only women and therefore constitutes direct discrimination on grounds of sex. Dismissal of a female worker at any time during her pregnancy for absences due to incapacity for work caused by an illness resulting from that pregnancy is prohibited.[86]

---

[84] See on the evolution of these concepts: S. Prechal, 'Equality of Treatment, Non-Discrimination and Social Policy: Achievements in Three Themes', (2004) 41 *Common Market Law Review*, pp. 533-551.

[85] See *Dekker*, supra note 57, at paras 15-18.

[86] See in particular ECJ 8 November 1990, Case C-179/88, *Handels-og Kontorfunktionaerernes Forbund i Danmark v Dansk Arbejdsgiverforening*, ECR 1990, I-03979 (*Hertz*), at para. 15 and *Brown*, supra note 64, at paras 22-25.

3.2 Indirect Discrimination

The concept of indirect discrimination has been developed by the ECJ regarding, in particular, indirect sex discrimination in relation to part-time work.[87] The landmark case on indirect discrimination is *Bilka*, which concerned the access to an occupational pension scheme.[88] According to this scheme, part-time employees might obtain pensions under the scheme if they had worked full-time for at least 15 years over a total period of 20 years. The Court ruled that if a much lower proportion of women than men work full-time, the exclusion of part-time workers would be contrary to Article 119 (now Article 141 EC), where, taking into account the difficulties encountered by women workers in working full-time, that measure could not be explained by factors which exclude any discrimination on grounds of sex (at para 29). The measures could, however, be objectively justified if they correspond to a real need on the part of the undertaking and are appropriate and necessary to reach that aim (at para 36). The same objective justification test has been applied in many different judgments of the ECJ[89] and is now included in the definition of indirect discrimination in the most recent directives.

Indirect discrimination is defined in Article 2(1)(b) of Directive 2006/54/EC as follows:

> where an apparently neutral provision, criterion or practice would put persons of one sex at a particular disadvantage compared with persons of the other sex, unless that provision, criterion or practice is objectively justified by a legitimate aim, and the means of achieving that aim are appropriate and necessary.

There, the indirect discrimination test is as follows. The first question to be answered is whether a measure disadvantages many more persons of one sex than of the other. It is for the applicant to prove that a measure or a practice amounts to indirect discrimination.[90] In *Seymour* the Court provided more

---

[87] See for an overview E. Traversa, 'The Protection of Part-Time Workers in the Case Law of the Court of Justice of the European Communities', (2003) 19/2 *International Journal of Comparative Labour Law and Industrial Relations*, pp. 219-241 and C. Tobler, *Indirect Discrimination. A Case Study into the Development of the Legal Concept of Indirect Discrimination under EC Law*, Social Europe Series 10, (Antwerp-Oxford: Intersentia, 2005 (dissertation)).

[88] *Supra* note 42.

[89] See for an overview of more recent case law of the ECJ: C. Costello and G. Davies, 'The case law of the Court of Justice in the field of sex equality since 2000', (2006) 43 *Common Market Law Review*, pp. 1567-1616.

[90] ECJ 17 October 1989, Case 109/88, *Handels- og Kontorfunktionærernes Forbund I Danmark v Dansk Arbejdsgiverforening, acting on behalf of Danfoss*, ECR 1989, 3199 (*Danfoss*), at paras 10-16 and ECJ 26 June 2001, Case 381/99, *Susanna Brunnhofer v Bank der österreichischen Postsparkasse AG*, ECR 2001, I-04961 (*Brunnhofer*), at paras 51-62.

guidance on how to establish such a presumption or *prima facie* case of indirect discrimination.[91] When there is a presumption of indirect discrimination, the defendant has to provide an objective justification for the indirectly discriminatory criterion or practice. Indirect discrimination can be justified if the aim is legitimate and the measures to reach that aim are appropriate and necessary. The arguments put forward have to be specific. For example, in *Seymour*, the Court considered that mere generalisations concerning the capacity of a specific measure to encourage recruitment are not sufficient to show that the aim of the disputed rule is unrelated to any discrimination based on sex nor to provide evidence on the basis of which it could reasonably be considered that the means chosen were suitable for achieving that aim (at para 76).

Furthermore, the Court ruled in *De Weerd* that 'although budgetary considerations may underlie a Member State's choice of social policy and influence the nature or scope of the social protection measures which it wishes to adopt, they do not in themselves constitute an aim pursued by that policy and cannot therefore justify discrimination against one of the sexes... Moreover, to concede that budgetary considerations may justify a difference in treatment between men and women which would otherwise constitute indirect discrimination on grounds of sex would mean that the application and scope of a rule of Community law as fundamental as that of equal treatment between men and women might vary in time and place according to the state of the public finances of Member States'.[92]

3.3 Harassment and Sexual Harassment

In the directives adopted since 2000, harassment and sexual harassment (in Directives 2002/73/EC, 2004/113/EC and 2006/54/EC) are explicitly prohibited. Harassment is defined as follows in Article 2(1)(c) of the Recast Directive:

> where unwanted conduct related to the sex of a person occurs with the purpose or effect of violating the dignity of a person, and of creating an intimidating, hostile, degrading, humiliating or offensive environment.

Note that the conduct has to have both the purpose and effect of violating the dignity of a person *and* of creating an intimidating etc. environment. These are cumulative requirements.

Sexual harassment is defined in Article (2)(1)d:

---

[91] ECJ 9 February 1999, Case C-167/97, *Regina v Secretary of State for Employment, ex parte Nicole Seymour-Smith and Laura Perez*, ECR 1999, I-00623 (*Seymour*), at paras 58-65.

[92] ECJ 24 February 1994, Case C-343/92, *M. A. De Weerd, née Roks, and others v Bestuur van de Bedrijfsvereniging voor de Gezondheid, Geestelijke en Maatschappelijke Belangen and others*, ECR 1994, I-00571 (*De Weerd*), at paras 35-36.

where any form of unwanted verbal, non-verbal or physical conduct of a sexual nature occurs, with the purpose or effect of violating the dignity of a person, in particular when creating an intimidating, hostile, degrading, humiliating or offensive environment.

Sex discrimination includes harassment and sexual harassment, as well as any less favourable treatment based on a person's rejection of or submission to such conduct (Article 2(2)(a)). Harassment and sexual harassment cannot be objectively justified.

3.4 Instruction to Discriminate

The prohibition on discrimination includes an instruction to discriminate against persons on one of the discrimination grounds covered by the anti-discrimination directives (Article 2(2)(b)). This could be the case, for example, if an employer required a temporary employment agency to recruit only persons below a certain age for a specific job. In that case, both the employer and the temporary employment agency would be liable and would have to justify such age discrimination.

3.5 Reasonable Accommodation for Disabled Persons

The Framework Directive (2000/78/EC) specifies the principle of equal treatment in relation to persons with disabilities in Article 5, which reads:

> In order to guarantee compliance with the principle of equal treatment in relation to persons with disabilities, reasonable accommodation shall be provided. This means that employers shall take appropriate measures, where needed in a particular case, to enable a person with a disability to have access to, participate in, or advance in employment, or to undergo training, unless such measures would impose a disproportionate burden on the employer. This burden shall not be disproportionate when it is sufficiently remedied by measures existing within the framework of the disability policy of the Member State concerned.

This provision reflects a more substantive approach to equality, aimed at realising more equal social conditions.

4. ENFORCEMENT

In the directives adopted since 2000, the case law of the ECJ has been implemented in diverse provisions and the means of enforcement of anti-discrimination law have been strengthened.

4.1 Burden of Proof

Rules on the burden of proof have been developed in the case law of the ECJ (see also Section 3.2). With the Burden of Proof Directive (Directive 97/80/EC), this case law was integrated in legislation as far as sex discrimination was concerned in the field of pay and in employment.[93] Now the directives adopted since 2000 contain similar provisions.[94]

Article 19(1) of the Recast Directive stipulates that:

> Member States shall take such measures as are necessary, in accordance with their national judicial systems, to ensure that, when persons who consider themselves wronged because the principle of equal treatment has not been applied to them establish, before a court or other competent authority, facts from which it may be presumed that there has been direct or indirect discrimination, it shall be for the respondent to prove that there has been no breach of the principle of equal treatment.[95]

These rules do not apply to criminal proceedings, unless otherwise provided by the Member States (Article 19 (5)). Member States may also introduce rules which are more favourable to claimants.

4.2 Defence of Rights

Member States have an obligation to ensure that judicial procedures are available to all persons who consider themselves wronged by failure to apply the principle of equal treatment to them, even after the relationship in which the discrimination is alleged to have occurred has ended.[96] Organisations and associations that have a legitimate interest in ensuring that the provisions of the equal treatment directives are complied with, have *locus standi*. Such organisations, for example anti-discrimination commissions, may engage, either on behalf or in support of the complainant, with his or her approval, in any judicial or administrative procedure provided for the enforcement of the obligations under the equal treatment directives. The regular time limits in national law apply.

---

[93] Council Directive 97/80/EC of 15 December 1997 on the burden of proof in cases of discrimination based on sex, OJ 1998, L 14/6, see in particular Article 4.

[94] See Directive 2000/43/EC, Article 8; Directive 2000/78/EC, Article 10; Directive 2004/113/EC, Article 9.

[95] These rules also apply to situations covered by Article 141 and, insofar as discrimination based on sex is concerned, to the Pregnancy Directive (92/85/EEC) and the Parental Leave Directive (96/34/EC): see Article 19(4)(a).

[96] See Directive 2000/43/EC, Article 7; Directive 2000/78/EC, Article 9; Directive 2002/73/EC, Article 6; Directive 2004/113/EC, Article 8 and Directive 2006/54/EC, Article 17.

4.3 Sanctions, Compensation and Reparation

The directives adopted since 2000 stipulate that sanctions, which might comprise the payment of compensation to the victim, must be effective, proportionate and dissuasive.[97] The ECJ developed these requirements in the *Von Colson* case, which are now integrated in legislation.[98] As regards compensation or reparation when the principle of equal treatment between men and women has been breached in (access to) employment and the access to and supply of goods and services, directives further stipulate that the Member States have to introduce such measures as are necessary to ensure real and effective compensation or reparation. Compensation or reparation has to be dissuasive and proportionate to the damage suffered. The fixing of a prior upper limit cannot restrict such compensation or reparation.[99]

4.4 Victimisation

Protection against dismissal or adverse treatment in reaction to a complaint is provided for in the directives.[100] Article 24 of the Recast Directive reads:

> Member States shall introduce into their national legal systems such measures as are necessary to protect employees, including those who are employees' representatives, provided for by national laws and/or practices, against dismissal or other adverse treatment by the employer as a reaction to a complaint within the undertaking or to any legal proceedings aimed at enforcing compliance with the principle of equal treatment.

4.5 Equality Bodies

The Race Directive and the directives on the equal treatment between men and women that have been adopted since 2002, impose an obligation on Member States to appoint equality bodies.[101] The tasks of these bodies are the promotion,

---

[97] See Directive 2000/43/EC, Article 15; Directive 2000/78/EC, Article 17; Directive 2002/73/EC, Article 8d; Directive 2004/113/EC, Article 14 and Directive 2006/54/EC Article 25.

[98] *Von Colson*, *supra* note 4, at para. 28.

[99] Directive 2002/73/EC, Article 6(2); Directive 2004/113/EC, Article 8(2); Directive 2006/54/EC, Article 18. Directives 2002/73/EC and 2006/54/EC allow an exception regarding the upper limit if the employer can prove that the only damage suffered by an applicant as a result of sex discrimination in (access to) employment is the refusal to take his or her job application into consideration.

[100] See for example Directive 2000/43/EC, Article 9; Directive 2000/78/EC, Article 11; Directive 2002/73/EC, Article 7; Directive 2004/113/EC, Article 10 and Directive 2006/54/EC, Article 24.

[101] Directive 2002/43/EC, Article 13; Directive 2002/73/EC, Article 8a; Directive 2004/113/EC, Article 12; Directive 2006/54, Article 20.

analysis, monitoring and support of equal treatment. They may form part of agencies with responsibilities at the national level for the defence of human rights or the safeguarding of individual rights. These bodies have the capability to provide independent assistance to victims of discrimination; to conduct independent surveys concerning discrimination and to publish independent reports and make recommendations.[102]

4.6 Social Dialogue

Member States also have the obligation to promote social dialogue between the social partners and dialogue with non-governmental organisations or with stakeholders, with a view to fostering equal treatment.[103] The promotion of social dialogue might include the monitoring of practices in the workplace, in access to employment, vocational training and promotion, as well as the monitoring of collective agreements, codes of conduct, research or exchange of experience and good practice. The Recast Directive further stipulates in Article 21(2):

> Where consistent with national traditions and practice, Member States shall encourage the social partners, without prejudice to their autonomy, to promote equality between men and women, and flexible working arrangements, with the aim of facilitating the reconciliation of work and private life, (…) and to conclude, at the appropriate level, agreements laying down antidiscrimination rules (…).[104]

Some directives regarding equal treatment between men and women also stipulate that Member States have to encourage employers to promote equal treatment in a planned and systematic way and to provide employees and/or their representatives with appropriate information on equal treatment at appropriate regular intervals.[105] Such information may include an overview of the proportion of men and women at different levels of the organisation; their pay and pay differentials; and possible measures to improve the situation in cooperation with employees' representatives.[106]

---

[102] See further R. Holtmaat, *Catalysts for change? Equality bodies according to Directive 2000/43/EC*, European Commission, (Luxembourg: Office for Official Publications of the European Union, 2007), at: http://ec.europa.eu/employment_social/fundamentalrights/pdf/legnet/06catalyst_en.pdf (accessed 2 June 2008).

[103] See Directive 2000/43/EC, Articles 11 and 12; Directive 2000/78/EC, Articles 13 and 14; Directive 2002/73/EC, Article 8b and 8c; Directive 2004/113/EC, Article 11 and Directive 2006/54/EC Articles 21 and 22.

[104] See also Directive 2000/43/EC, Article 11(2); Directive 2000/78/EC, Article 13(2); Directive 2002/73/EC, Article 8b(2).

[105] Directive 2002/73/EC, Article 8b(3) and (4) and Directive 2006/54/EC, Article 21(3) and (4).

[106] See on social dialogue in the European Union: http://ec.europa.eu/employment_social/social_dialogue/index_en.htm (accessed 2 June 2008).

5. SOME CONCLUSIONS

For years, EU anti-discrimination law was limited to a prohibition on discrimination on grounds of nationality and sex (in relation to pay). Now, several Treaty provisions and directives have been adopted with the aim of combating different forms of discrimination on the grounds of gender, race or ethnic origin, religion and belief, disability, age, sexual orientation, part-time work and fixed-term work. Some of these directives impose far-reaching obligations on the Member States, social partners and employers. Diverse directives apply in the fields of equal pay and equal treatment in (the access to) employment and in the access to and the supply of goods and services. The scope of the different directives varies, with the Race Directive offering a broad protection against discrimination. The Sex Equality Directives cover pay, (access to) (self-) employment, statutory social security schemes, occupational social security schemes and the access to and the supply of goods and services. The material scope of the Framework Directive covering the other discrimination grounds under EU law is more limited. Areas such as the supply of goods and services, social protection, social advantages and education are not (yet) covered for the grounds of religion and belief, disability, age and sexual orientation. The part-time and fixed-term directives mainly apply to working conditions and not to statutory social security schemes. This might suggest a kind of hierarchy between the different grounds with race, ethnic origin and gender being the most suspect grounds of discrimination, which are the least likely to be upheld. It remains to be seen whether the European legislator will adopt directives offering a more extensive protection against other forms of discrimination.

The role played by the European Court of Justice in strengthening the impact of equal treatment law can hardly be overestimated. In many rulings the Court stressed the fundamental character of the right to equality. Furthermore, the development of the concept of indirect discrimination can be seen as a step towards a more substantive approach to equality. Similar definitions in the directives adopted since 2000, integrating case law of the ECJ, contribute to a better understanding of important concepts such as direct and indirect discrimination. The same is true for provisions on enforcement. European legislation, and its interpretation by the ECJ in binding judgments, has an important impact on legal provisions in the Member States and the judgments of the national courts. However, EU anti-discrimination law is also rather fragmented and complicated and this might hamper the application of the principle of equal treatment in practice. Furthermore, individuals may suffer from multiple forms of discrimination, when different grounds of discrimination are at stake (for example religion, ethnic origin and gender).[107] However, it is

---

[107] See H. Bielfeldt, *Tackling Multiple Discrimination. Practices, Policies and Laws*, (Luxembourg: European Commission, Office for Official Publications of the European Communities, 2007).

undeniable that EU anti-discrimination law offers useful legal tools to combat discrimination and interesting approaches to the concept of equality.

8

ANTI-DISCRIMINATION LAW IN THE NETHERLANDS: A SPECIFIC LEGAL PATCHWORK, NORMATIVE SYSTEM AND INSTITUTIONAL STRUCTURE

Jenny Goldschmidt

1. INTRODUCTION

Even for experts non-discrimination law in the Netherlands is a very complex issue. To get a full understanding of the law, many different national and international laws have to be consulted. Even the answer to a concrete question as to whether there is a case of discrimination or not can depend on different legal provisions. In the context of this volume it is not necessary to give a detailed description of the legal system of non-discrimination law, so I will focus on the general structure, the key concepts and the role of the Equal Treatment Commission.

This bird's-eye view intends to highlight the central questions that have to be answered when setting up a national system of non-discrimination law. The answers depend on the specific national legal, social and political context. Even although in Europe the law of the European Union plays a predominant role in the national legal systems' non-discrimination laws, the national characteristics are decisive in the choices that have been made for specific concrete problems.

The focus will be on non-discrimination law in employment, and more specifically on the civil law in force in this area, and other aspects of non-discrimination law will only be mentioned where relevant.

2. TWO MAIN SOURCES: EUROPEAN LAW AND THE CONSTITUTION OF THE KINGDOM OF THE NETHERLANDS

Dutch non-discrimination law has its roots in both European law and in the Constitution of the Kingdom of the Netherlands of 1984 (hereafter: the Constitution). This double origin explains the reason for the complex and inaccessible legal system, as the various laws and regulations both overlap and at the same time show some crucial differences.

This situation is even further complicated by the fact that other non-discrimination law can also play a role in the national legal system. The latter aspect will be dealt with only when it is directly relevant to understanding the Dutch system.

a. Implementation of European law

The first non-discrimination law was based on the European Community law as it came into force in the 1970s, described by Susanne Burri in her contribution. This means that the focus was on equal pay and equal treatment of men and women at the workplace, both in the public and in the private sectors. Gradually the scope of the European Union law has been and is still being extended to include not only many more grounds of discrimination (not only gender) but also more areas (not only work). The European Union law has been implemented in the national legal system, incorporating its specific aspects and concepts in national laws.

The laws that are based on the EU obligations are the following:

- Equal Treatment in Employment (Men and Women) Act (Wet gelijke behandeling mannen en vrouwen, WGB)
- Equal Treatment (Working Hours) Act (Wet verbod op onderscheid naar arbeidsduur, WOA)
- Sections 7:646 to 7:649 inclusive of the Civil Code (Burgerlijk Wetboek)
- Sections 125g and 125h of the Civil Servants Act (Ambtenarenwet)
- Equal Treatment (Temporary and Permanent Employees) Act (Wet Onderscheid Bepaalde en Onbepaalde Tijd, WOBOT)
- Equal Treatment (Disability or Chronic Illness) Act (Wet gelijke behandeling op grond van handicap of chronische ziekte, WGBH/CZ)
- Equal Treatment in Employment (Age Discrimination) Act (Wet gelijke behandeling op grond van leeftijd bij de arbeid, WGBL)

The European directives prescribe not only a specific normative framework, but several directives also contain an obligation to establish a specialised body to promote effective implementation of non-discrimination laws. So, the specific enforcement structure in the field of equality that exists in the Netherlands is also a direct result of the European requirements. The enforcement of the provisions that originate from other sources has been incorporated in the same structure.

b. Constitutional Dimension: Third Party Effect and Conflicts with Other Fundamental Rights

In 1984 a revised Constitution of the Netherlands came into force. This Constitution starts with the fundamental rights and freedoms, the principle of equality and prohibition of non-discrimination being the very first article. The horizontal, third party effect, has been recognized. A point for discussion at that time was how the horizontal effect had to be interpreted in practice. Essential to this perspective is the relationship between the different fundamental rights, which may in some concrete cases conflict with each other: e.g. an orthodox Christian school claims that the freedom of education and the freedom of religion mean that the school may refuse to employ a teacher because of his sexual orientation, as the philosophy of the school is not compatible with homosexuality. Which fundamental right should prevail: the freedom of education of the school or the right of the homosexual aspiring teacher not to be discriminated against because of his sexual orientation? This kind of question was considered to be too fundamental to be decided by the judiciary and thus in 1994 the Equal Treatment Act (ETA) was enacted, with the aim of regulating both horizontal effect (i.e. between private parties) of non-discrimination and the conflicts with other fundamental rights.[1] Of course this law had to be in accordance with the EU legal framework, so the main concepts and definitions from the EU system have been incorporated into the ETA as well. Moreover, the ETA has been amended several times to include amendments made to the EU legal framework and to make improvements.

Thus, the Dutch system of protection against discrimination emanates from two streams, the EU and the Constitution and, these sources being different in scope, purpose and context, the resulting laws differ too, and this creates a patchwork of legislation which is not so easy to harmonize.

At present the non-discrimination law related to employment is divided between nine laws and several ministerial decrees.[2] Although the intention is to make a unified legal system of non-discrimination law, this is easier said than done, and the realisation will probably take several more years.

Apart from the provisions in private law, the Penal Code also contains several articles that prohibit non-discrimination, but these are not included in this contribution.

c. *Other International Systems*

Although the European Community constitutes the primary international source of non-discrimination law in the Netherlands, other international laws can be relevant too. As the Netherlands has a monist system, international treaties that have been ratified are included without further legislation and the Constitution establishes the supremacy of international law. It depends on the nature of the provision at stake as to whether it is also directly applicable in a concrete case, but new laws have to be in conformity with relevant international law and the courts have to take international law into account by means of harmonious

---

[1] Equal Treatment Act 1994 (Algemene Wet Gelijke Behandeling).
[2] See also the website of the Equal Treatment Commission, http://www.cgb.nl/legislation.php.

interpretation with treaties. Thus, the European Convention of Human Rights, the various United Nations Human Rights treaties, as interpreted by the European Court of Human Rights and the UN Treaty bodies, play an essential role too.

The fact that European law constitutes a major source of anti-discrimination law in the Netherlands entails the incorporation of a very specific system of norms and concepts. Susanne Burri describes the major concepts in Section 3 of her contribution. I will avoid duplication and focus instead on the application in the Netherlands and the interpretation thereof in the practice of the specialised body, the Equal Treatment Commission.

3. OPEN OR CLOSED SYSTEM

An essential feature of part of the anti-discrimination law in the Netherlands is the closed character of the legal system of some major provisions. What does that mean? A system of non-discrimination law can be defined as either 'open' or 'closed' with reference to different aspects: the 'prohibited grounds' of discrimination, the scope of the prohibition of discrimination and the possibilities of justifying different treatment or of making exceptions to equality provisions.

a. Grounds

Although all national and international non-discrimination or equality laws refer to specific grounds that are included in the prohibition of discrimination, they do so in different ways. Compare for instance article 26 of the International Covenant on Civil and Political Rights (ICCPR) and article 13 (1) EC-treaty (EC). The first article prohibits discrimination on any ground *such as* race, colour, sex, language, religion, political or other opinion, national or social origin, property, birth or *other status* (emphasis supplied). Article 13 EC obliges the Member States to take appropriate action to combat discrimination based on sex, racial or ethnic origin, religion or belief, disability, age or sexual orientation. This provision leaves no room to add other grounds of discrimination: the list included is exclusive, while the ICCPR refers to 'any other status' and thus leaves the door open to include other forms of discrimination that are not mentioned, e.g. age discrimination. Article 1 of the Dutch Constitution has a similar open formula.

Most EU equality provisions are closed in the sense that they refer only to a restricted number of grounds, and this is the reason why the specific non-discrimination laws in the Netherlands also have a closed character and refer to a specific ground or a specific number of grounds.

b. Scope

The other distinguishing feature is related to the effect of the provision. As described Susanne Burri's contribution, the development of non-discrimination law in Europe started as early as the 1950s in the field of work and employment and was expanded only decades later to other areas, in particular 'goods and services'. This explains why most of the national non-discrimination laws also referred exclusively to work and employment, including public and private labour law.

On the other hand the purpose of the law that emanated from the equality provision in the Dutch Constitution was to regulate the third party effect of the principle of equality and thus it concentrated on the most relevant private law areas: employment and the contracts related to goods and services. State actions in cases where the State does not act as or comparable to a private party, are not ruled by these specific non-discrimination laws but fall directly under the Constitution, as the human rights provisions in the Constitution are primarily conceived as obligations of the State. Thus, the granting of a building permit to 'men only' cannot be challenged under the general equal treatment law, whereas the refusal by a department to hire a female construction worker can.

c. Exceptions

The last perspective from which a non-discrimination law can be categorised as open or closed, is the possibility to make exceptions. This is relevant in relation to the possibility to make exceptions to the legal prohibition of direct discrimination.[3] Direct discrimination, as explained by Susanne Burri, refers to cases where explicit reference to a prohibited ground is at issue: 'we don't hire women as lorry drivers'. If the same company says 'we don't hire persons who are below 160cms in height as lorry drivers', that may be a case of indirect discrimination, as the average height of women is less than that of men. Although no direct reference to a prohibited ground is made, the effect will be that fewer women are able to apply. In what we call a closed system of exceptions and justifications, exceptions are only allowed if they are explicitly foreseen in the legal provisions. Extra-legal justifications are not permitted and thus the court, or other supervisory institution, does even not consider them. The three most common exceptions to non-discrimination are genuine occupational requirements, temporary special measures and the protection of other fundamental rights. A closed system of exceptions cannot be applied in cases of

---

[3] Mark Bell, 'Direct Discrimination', paras 2.6 and 2.6.1, in Dagmar Schiek, Lisa Waddington and Mark Bell (eds.), *Cases, Materials and Text on National, Supranational and International Non-Discrimination Law*, (Oxford/Portland: Hart Publishing, 2007), pp. 269-271.

indirect discrimination, as indirect discrimination can take so many different forms that they cannot be foreseen.

4. DIRECT AND INDIRECT DISCRIMINATION

a. Direct Discrimination

While direct discrimination refers to a treatment which is explicitly based on a prohibited ground, indirect discrimination is at issue in cases where a 'neutral' criterion disadvantages persons from a specific group.

In the past, some discussion has taken place as to whether pregnancy is a form of direct discrimination (because only women can be pregnant) or indirect discrimination (because not all women are pregnant). It is clear now that discrimination because of pregnancy is direct discrimination (see also Burri, Section 3.1). This means that pregnancy cannot be used to justify any disadvantageous treatment, which implies that women cannot be denied specific allowances or remuneration by the argument that they were absent, if this absence is a consequence of their pregnancy[4].

It is important to note that in neither case is the intention of the actor relevant: the law simply forbids all forms of discrimination. Discrimination is often very closely related to stereotyped social practices and frequently people are not aware of the possible discriminatory character or effects. However, this type of behaviour is precisely what anti-discrimination law combats. Thus even unintentional behaviour can be in violation of the law. As explained in paragraph 3, a closed system of exceptions implies that, in cases of direct discrimination, no exceptions are allowed unless foreseen by law. In a recent case the Netherlands Equal Treatment Commission (ETC) ruled that the army is not allowed to grant special exemptions from missions abroad only to mothers and not to fathers with young children below the age of 5, when those exemptions are not directly related to the protection of pregnancy and the first phase of motherhood.[5]

On the other hand, when an employer publicly expresses that he will not recruit anybody from a particular ethnic or racial background, such statements are a sufficient presumption of the existence of a recruitment policy which is directly discriminatory, even when there is no identified victim.[6]

In recent case law the ECJ has further clarified the scope of the concept of direct discrimination. In the *Coleman* case, the mother of a disabled child, the care of whom was primarily provided by the mother, was treated less favourably because of that association. The Court ruled that the prohibition of

---

[4] ETC Opinion 2007/188.
[5] ETC Opinion 2008/52.
[6] ECJ 10 July 2008, Centrum voor gelijke kansen en racismebestrijding v. Firma Feryn NV, case C-54/07.

'discrimination on the ground of disability' is not necessarily restricted to the disabled person, but can also include situations like that of the mother who is associated with her disabled child.[7]

b. Indirect Discrimination

As described by Susanne Burri in Section 3.1, the ECJ has refined the concept of indirect discrimination in its case law. This is also the basis of the definition that is codified in the Directive, which has also been incorporated into Dutch law: see section 1 (1 c) of the Equal Treatment Act.

The application of the concept of indirect discrimination raises specific problems. First of all, the detrimental effect, which is the disadvantage that is caused by a neutral criterion, has to be established. Secondly it has to be investigated whether the indirect discriminatory act or behaviour can be objectively justified.

The first step requires the establishment of disadvantage or disparate impact. In some cases this can easily be done with reference to available statistical evidence: this is also the usual approach in the United States, where the concept was developed.[8] Data are compared in a relative way: what counts is the relative share of, in case of gender discrimination, women and men among the disadvantaged group. If a company has 1000 employees, among whom are 100 women, and a specific measure has a disparate effect on the 100 part-timers, among whom are 50 men and 50 women, the percentage of female workers affected is significantly larger than the percentage of male workers, and thus there is a case of indirect discrimination against women, even when the absolute number of men and women affected is the same.

However, specific statistical evidence is not always available. The ETC developed an approach whereby more general information or national statistics can be used as a prima facie assumption of proof. In these cases the defendant has to provide arguments as to why the situation in his or her organisation differs from the general one. In the case of *Seymour-Smith and Perez* the ECJ ruled that it may also be appropriate to take into account subsequent statistics to provide an indication of disparate impact.[9] This can be relevant 'if the statistical evidence revealed a lesser but persistent and relatively constant disparity over a longer period.'[10] Once the disparate impact has been established, the act or behaviour can only be justified by an objective justification in the sense of the concept as it is used in EU law, which been clarified in the case law of the ECJ, as Susanne Burri describes in Section 3.2 of her contribution to this volume.

---

[7] ECJ 17 July 2008, S. Coleman v. Attridge Law, Steve Law, Case C-303./06.
[8] Dagmar Schiek, 'Indirect Discrimination', para. 3.5.1, in Schiek *et al.* (eds.), *supra* note 3, p. 372.
[9] ECJ, 9 February 1999, case C-167/197.
[10] *Ibid* para. 61.

The ETC follows the different steps as included in the definition in the equality laws. First, it has to be investigated whether there is a proper, non-discriminatory objective for the contested measure. And secondly, the measure taken must be appropriate and necessary to that end. This is the test as it has been developed in the ECJ case law related to gender discrimination. It prescribes a very strict scrutiny test, which mainly results from the requirement that the measure must be necessary: as soon as there are alternative options, it can no longer be held necessary.

The expansion of non-discrimination grounds raised the question whether the test must be equally strict for all grounds.[11] In the *Mangold* case the ECJ ruled that the principle of non-discrimination is not only part of EC law, but is also embedded in international instruments, and the Court mentioned age in the same way as other grounds.[12] However, in the case law of the ETC there seems to be some more flexibility, in particular where age discrimination is at issue: this probably has to do with the fact that there is some support for the acceptance of a difference in the character of the various grounds, as Janneke Gerards describes it: '...even though there are many cases of unacceptable stereotyping as regards persons belonging to certain age groups, there would not seem to be a degree of social prejudice comparable to that visible with respect to race, ethnic origin, sexual orientation or gender.'[13]

In its Advice about Age Discrimination in Social Policy Plans, the ETC applies a contextual approach, by considering a distinction on the basis of age as part of a complex of policy measures taken for employees of specific age categories.[14]

Financial arguments or budgetary restraints as such can never be a sufficient justification: only when the costs would really entail a risk for the existence or seriously undermine the financial balance of e.g. a social security system would they provide such a justification.[15]

5. POSITIVE OBLIGATIONS

The equality principle as defined by Aristotle contains two obligations: the first is the obligation to treat equal cases alike; the second is to treat unequal cases unalike in proportion to their difference.[16]

---

[11] See also Schiek *et al.* (eds.), *supra* note 3, pp. 443-452.
[12] ECJ 22 November 2005, Mangold v. Helm, Case C-144/04.
[13] Janneke Gerards, 'Discrimination Grounds', in Schiek *et al.* (eds.), *supra* note 3, p. 149.
[14] Commissie gelijke behandeling, Advies inzake leeftijdsonderscheid in sociale plannen, Advies 2007/05, 14 September 2007.
[15] Schiek *et al.* (eds.), *supra* note 3, p. 453.
[16] See also: Dagmar Schiek, Lisa Waddington and Mark Bell, 'A Comparative Perspective on Non-discrimination Law', in Schiek *et al.* (eds.), *supra* note 3, p. 27.

Positive obligations as part of non-discrimination law are also embedded in the broader context of human rights law. Human rights protection includes different kinds of obligations of the State: the obligations to respect, to fulfil and to protect. The obligations to fulfil and to protect imply positive obligations to take necessary measures and to provide effective protection, against private persons as well.[17]

The positive obligations that follow from this second aspect of Aristotle's equality principle are part of anti-discrimination law as Colm O'Cinneide has explained in his contribution to this volume. However, the character of these positive obligations may differ.

a. Temporary Special Measures

The first category of positive measures, the obligation to take temporary special measures, is generally seen as an exception to the rule that equal cases have to be treated equally. Measures taken must be temporary in order to remedy enduring past disadvantages. O'Cinneide describes this possibility of preferential treatment which is anticipated in EU law and has been interpreted by the ECJ.

The ETC applies this interpretation. The criteria as developed by the ECJ entail that preferential treatment is admissible only on very strict conditions:
- the discrepancy between the available qualified personnel in the labour market and the number of women/minority group members working in that specific labour organisation must be established
- all applications must be considered objectively on their merits, absolute or automatic preference for women or minorities is not acceptable
- finally the preferential treatment has to be proportional.[18]

In practice these conditions restrict the possibility of preferential treatment and demand a solid policy from the employer, which by its nature must be temporary: preferential treatment is only allowed during the period that the disadvantage continues. On the other hand temporary special measures may be very different in character: not only recruitment but also, for example, promotion and child care facilities can be included.

b. Positive Action

Positive action is the second category of positive measures. As these measures as such do not distinguish between different (categories of) employees, they constitute no exception to the prohibition of discrimination. Positive action reflects the awareness of an employer of the existence of stereotyped practices, and entails putting policies in place to end these practices to make the

---

[17] Manfred Nowak, *Introduction to the International Human Rights Regime*, (Leiden/Boston: Martinus Nijhoff Publishers, 2003), pp. 48-51.
[18] Equal Treatment Commission, Opinion 2004-36.

organisation really neutral. Child care facilities, parental leave and facilities for different religious groups are examples of positive measures.

c. *Reasonable Accommodation*

A specific category of positive obligations is the provision of a reasonable accommodation. Although this concept is used explicitly in relation to discrimination against people with disabilities, it can be, and has been used also in relation to other grounds.

The obligation to provide a reasonable accommodation is part of the prohibition of discrimination, not an exception, and thus it is fundamentally different from a temporary special measure. The justification of the duty to provide a reasonable accommodation lies in the obligation to take relevant differences into account (and not in the enduring disadvantages from the past). This was formulated by the European Court of Human Rights (ECtHR) thus: 'The right not to be discriminated against in the enjoyment of the rights guaranteed under the Convention is also violated when States without an objective and reasonable justification fail to treat differently persons whose situations are significantly different.'[19] Of course this obligation is essential to guarantee equality to people with disabilities but it is also relevant to other groups. In 1996 the Equal Treatment Commission had already held that a car construction company had shown discrimination, because of having refused to hire a female construction worker as the company had no separate changing room and sanitary facilities for women: the ETC did not even accept the justification that steps had been taken to create the necessary facilities, but that the cost was rather high.[20]

As Susanne Burri has mentioned in her contribution to this volume, the EU Framework Directive (2000/78/EC) reflects, in article 5, this substantive approach to equality by including the provision of reasonable accommodation in the obligation of equal treatment. The Dutch Equal Treatment (Disability or Chronic Illness) Act (Wet gelijke behandeling op grond van handicap of chronische ziekte, WGBH/CZ) contains a similar provision in article 2, which says: 'The prohibition on discrimination also means that the persons on whom this prohibition is imposed are obliged to make effective modifications according to need, unless this would impose a disproportionate burden on them.' Thus, disabled or chronically ill persons are entitled to the accommodations they need, and it is up to the other party to give a justification if this is a disproportionate burden. This substantive approach of equality is in line with the new UN Convention on the Rights of Persons with Disabilities, which recognizes in the preamble (c bis) 'that disability is an evolving concept and that disability results from the interaction between persons with impairments and attitudinal and

---

[19] ECtHR 6 April 2000, Thlimmenos v. Greece, Application no. 34369/97.
[20] ETC, 3 December 1996, Opinion 1996-112.

environmental barriers that hinder their full and effective participation in society on an equal basis with others'.

In several cases the ETC has clarified the meaning of this obligation. The obligations that have been considered reasonable are, amongst others, the provision of a special PC screen for a man with bad eyesight,[21] or the provision of extra time in a written exam for a disabled student, even when this would entail additional costs for the university.[22] As a consequence of the obligation to provide a reasonable accommodation, there is a duty to investigate whether the possible barriers or disadvantages caused by the disability can be compensated for by additional measures. If there have not been any of these investigations there will be a case of discrimination. In some cases the ETC suggested that a temporary appointment (instead of a permanent contract) might be seen as a reasonable accommodation: during a probationary period it can be established whether the disability really is an obstruction which makes a proper functioning impossible. Thus, an airline could have tested whether a member of the cabin crew with diabetes could function in a proper way.[23]

An accommodation may only be refused if it imposes a disproportionate burden. This might be the case if an employer or institution for higher education were to be asked to provide private assistance, such as help to go to the toilet or to suck out wounds that produce fluids.[24]

It must be emphasized here that it is self evident that the obligation to provide a reasonable accommodation cannot replace reasonable (job) requirements, thus deafness can be an absolute disqualification for training as an emergency aid employee in a company.[25]

6. CATEGORIES OF EXCEPTIONS

In so far as the relevant non-discrimination provision contains a 'closed' system of exceptions (i.e. no possibility of a more general objective justification), an exception can only be made if it is anticipated in express terms by the law. The exceptions fall roughly into four categories: genuine (occupational) requirements, protection of (certain) members of the relevant group, exceptions based on other fundamental rights and preferential treatment. The source of the first three categories lies in the EU legal system, the last category originates from the Dutch Equal Treatment Act (ETA) one of the objectives of which was to regulate the relationship between the principle of equality and other fundamental rights. Whatever the context of an exception may be, they all have in common that they have to be interpreted very strictly (see also Susanne Burri's

---

[21] ETC 8 March 2004, Opinion 2004-21.
[22] ETC 26 October 2004. Opinion 2004-140.
[23] ETC Opinion 2006-02.
[24] ETC Opinion 2006-59.
[25] ETC Opinion 2005-60.

contribution). In section 5 above, the content and scope of the exception for preferential treatment has been described, so in this paragraph I will focus on the other categories.

a. Genuine Occupational Requirements

Section 2 of the ETA and similar provisions in specific laws concerning gender equality hold that the provisions of the law do not apply in cases where gender, race or nationality are a determining factor, i.e. a genuine and determining requirement. This rather vague exception is less open-ended than one might conclude from the text of the provision.

Genuine occupational requirements have been set out explicitly in several decrees (AMVB). In these decrees several categories have been enumerated, such as models, situations which are closely related to the privacy of clients (such as saleswomen who sell female underwear) or functions related to the education of children that demand a male or female person. An exception can never be used in a general way for all posts in an organisation. Thus, in a residential home for children with behavioural problems, because many of these children have been victims or witnesses of domestic violence by males and, as consequence, have a rather disturbed view of the male character, a genuine requirement could be made out for employing only male teachers as only a male could correct this view. However, this would only be a justification insofar as no other male carers were available.[26]

It depends on the specific ground at issue as to which requirements are accepted. Thus the exception that gender may be a genuine requirement if a specific activity aims at a particular group of women (e.g. women's shelters) might be accepted: a similar exception would not be allowed for ethnic minorities.

b. Respect for Other Rights

Respect for other fundamental rights entails some specific and some general exceptions to the prohibition of discrimination. Generally, religious offices are excluded (article 3 ETA): The Catholic Church will not be forced to appoint female priests.

Other institutions which are based on a particular religious philosophy may make demands that staff and pupils endorse or accept these foundations. However, this must not amount to discrimination on the single ground of one of the other criteria. Thus the directors of a conservative Christian school can require that the teachers actively respect that religion, but they cannot refuse to employ a homosexual teacher on the sole ground of his homosexuality because in their view homosexuality is a sin: Articles 5 (2) and 7(2) ETA.

---

[26] ETC Opinion 1995-62.

More implicit is the exclusion of the private sphere from the scope of the Equal Treatment Act, but this too is a consequence of the original intention of the law to elaborate the principle of equality for horizontal relations including the regulation of possible conflicts of (fundamental) rights. The Parliamentary history of the law makes it clear that article 7, which regulates non-discrimination in the area of goods and services, does not affect private activities. However, a strict interpretation of this provision demands that the activities really are only private.

c. Protection

Protection of individuals may be a justification for unequal treatment in the case of pregnancy or motherhood (article 2 (2)(b) ETA), or in the case of the protection of the health and safety of individuals with a disability or chronic illness (article 3 (1)(a) of the Equal Treatment (Disability and Chronic Illness) Act). Here too, a very strict interpretation is required and there are almost no cases on the subject.

Of course, the protection in the case of pregnancy and motherhood, or the fact that women enjoy pregnancy leave, must be distinguished from the prohibition on discriminating against women because of their pregnancy. Protective arrangements must never entail negative consequences, e.g. refusing specific bonus allowances to such women because they had fewer opportunities to meet the targets during their leave.[27]

7. BURDEN OF PROOF

As Susanne Burri has explained, the EU has developed a division of the burden of proof, which demands that the claimant puts forward facts or circumstances that raise an assumption of discrimination, after which the defendant has to prove that no discrimination has taken place. This division of the burden of proof had already been applied by the ETC before the EU law came into force. In practice the first step, to make a reasonable case showing discrimination, is often a difficult one. It is not sufficient that an applicant 'feels' discriminated against or 'has the impression' that her age or sex played a role. The ETC demands concrete indications. Such indications may consist of statistical information. In recruitment procedures, questions asked during the selection interview may be relevant: for example, if only women are asked about their family responsibilities.

When there is a reasonable indication, it is up to the defendant to refute the assumption of discrimination. Of course it depends on the concrete circumstances of the case as to which arguments can be relevant. The defendant

---

[27] ETC Opinion 2000-54.

may show that the selection process contained guarantees for an objective and non-discriminatory procedure, that the candidate lacked certain qualifications for promotion which others had, etc.

As a rule it can be said that the more transparent and objective the procedures are, the easier it will be for the defendant to establish that there was no discrimination. If procedures and policies are vague and confusing, there is always a risk that discriminatory aspects can play a role in decision-making. This risk is a risk for the defendant.[28] Thus, the division of the burden of proof re-emphasizes the necessity of good governance in (personnel) management.

8. EQUAL PAY

A very specific issue in equal treatment law is equality of pay. The EU Directive on Equal Pay prescribes a very specific procedure to establish equal pay for men and women, as has been explained by Susanne Burri. The ETC and its predecessors have applied the relevant provisions since 1975.[29] The ETC uses specialised job evaluation experts to establish whether two persons perform work of equal value. The gender bias of certain important job evaluation systems has also been investigated: both the job evaluation system for major parts of health care organisations and the system used at universities were proved to be biased.[30]

9. SPECIALISED BODY: THE EQUAL TREATMENT COMMISSION

After this short overview of some important concepts of non-discrimination law, we turn now to the specific machinery for monitoring its implementation and application that has been developed in the Netherlands.

The Netherlands' Equal Treatment Commission is a specialised equality body. Recent EU Directives on equal treatment prescribe the establishment of 'body or bodies for the promotion of equal treatment…'.[31] These provisions specify some rather different tasks that can be attributed to the specialised bodies: providing independent assistance to victims, conducting independent surveys, publishing independent reports and making recommendations. Other

---

[28] See also the *Danfoss* case, ECJ 17 October 1989, Case C-109/88.
[29] See: Janny Dierx, Edith Brons and Siebrand Bisschop, 'Equal Pay: Experiences of the Equal Treatment Commission', in *Equal Pay and Working Conditions, towards the uniform and dynamic interpretation of EU anti-discrimination law: the role of specialised bodies*. Report of the third experts' meeting, hosted by the Dutch Equal Treatment Commission, 23-24 June 2003, Migration Policy Group, Brussels 2004, pp. 4-17, http://www.migpolgroup.com/ multiattachments/2492/DocumentName/exp3e.pdf.
[30] ETC Opinions 1998-55 and 2006-198.
[31] See Art. 13 of the Race Discrimination Directive (2000/43/EC) and Art. 8a of the Directive on Equal treatment of men and women at work. (Directive 2002/73/EC).

possible tasks that can be assigned to a specialised body can also be thought of, such as decisions on individual complaints, and training. It seems evident that choices have to be made at the national level, such as which is the best possible structure to: monitor equality law; assist victims; see that important cases are taken to court; advise government and other institutions on non-discriminatory policies. Some roles seem to be mutually exclusive; thus it is complicated if the organisation which is supposed to deliver independent opinions and demand cooperation of the parties, is the same organisation which is part of the prosecution in criminal proceedings, for example. For this reason the Netherlands' Equal Treatment Commission can never be a blueprint for another country, but its practice can offer examples to others.

a. Historical Background and Mandate

The Equal Treatment Commission as it exists now has been preceded by several specialised equality bodies that were established in the first instance to meet the obligations emanating from the law of the European Community. The earlier bodies had a very restricted mandate, covering only specific areas (pay, working conditions, civil service) and grounds (gender). Since the 1994 new anti-discrimination legislation came into being and in these laws the competence of the ETC has been gradually expanded. However, it must be borne in mind that the Commission's power is based on this specific non-discrimination legislation. Thus, the Commission is not competent to give an opinion on cases that are not based on one of these specific laws, but e.g. on an international treaty. Of course, the Commission has to incorporate the relevant EU law in its work and the Commission interprets the Dutch law in conformity with other international legislation by means of treaty-conform interpretation. But it can only do so in cases where it is competent to hear the case. Complaints which fall outside the scope of its mandate are not admissible e.g. complaints on the admission of aliens.

b. Structure and Composition

The essential provisions on the ETC have been enacted in Chapter 2 of the ETA, sections 12-21. The Commission has nine members, amongst whom are the President and two Vice-Presidents. Alternate members may also be appointed. Whilst the full members have a contract for all or a substantial part of their working time, the alternate members have their main occupation in another organisation and perform only incidental tasks for the ETC.

The full members must meet requirements similar to those demanded of a district court judge. Roughly speaking the rules setting out the remuneration and legal status of the members, which have been laid down in the ETA and elaborated in a specific regulation, are regulated along the same lines as for the judiciary. This means that the independence of the members is guaranteed. A major difference from the position of judges is that the term for the Commission's members is fixed at six years (with an option for a second term of another three years), while a judge gets a lifetime appointment. However, during the term of appointment the members can only be dismissed or suspended after an independent investigatory procedure similar to the procedure followed for the judiciary.

The alternate members do not have to meet the same requirements, in particular they do not need to have a law degree. They are selected mostly because they have some specific added value. This can be either a specialised expertise (e.g. in equal pay, or in a specific area of employment) or skills (communication, statistics, etc). They do not receive a salary but they get a fee for their specific activities, similar to the regulation for substitute judges.

The Minister of Justice appoints the members and alternate members in consultation with the four other Ministers who are responsible for (parts of) the non-discrimination legislation. The procedure for selection is a public one, open to all, and the Commission itself is closely involved in making the proposals for nomination.

The Commission is assisted by an office under the Director, and the Commission has its own budget which is agreed every year by the Ministries responsible for the implementation of the equality legislation. The budget is based on the number of cases and other activities.

c. *The Semi-judicial Role of the Commission and Related Aspects.*

The most important task of the Commission is to investigate complaints of individuals or groups of alleged discrimination. The Commission has ample investigatory powers, which can be found in the ETA. The parties concerned have to provide all information required. Moreover, section 19(2) of the ETA provides that: 'Everyone is obliged, unless they are exempt on the grounds of official or professional confidentiality, to provide the information and documents required ... in full and in accordance with the truth, in the manner and within the time limit laid down by or on behalf of the Commission....'.

The procedure before the Commission is codified in a Regulation. After a written preliminary investigation the Commission may hold a public oral hearing to get additional information, to hear the parties and or witnesses and to discuss the case with the parties. Parties may be ordered to appear in person. In practice, the hearing is seen by the Commission as an important opportunity to explain the contents and scope of the obligations emanating from the law.

The Commission's opinion is issued after the hearing. Complaints can be lodged by individual victims, who do not need any legal representation but may be represented by organisations. Organisations representing victims can be, amongst others, interest groups, human rights organisations or trade unions. Moreover, the different equality laws also contain provisions that a request may be submitted by an association with full legal powers or a foundation which, in accordance with its constitution or statutes, represents the interests of those whose protection is the objective of the relevant law: these are the so-called group actions or class actions. The importance of this kind of action should not be underestimated. Commencing proceedings is often a very cumbersome and emotional act for individuals; organisations do not have this burden. Moreover, many discrimination cases affect groups of individuals, because they are related to collective agreements or regulations or company practices and it is more effective to challenge the total body of regulations or practices.

A final opportunity to ask the Commission for an opinion is open to a natural or legal person or competent authority wishing to know whether they have discriminated within the meaning of the equality laws: the management of a company may request an assessment of its practices or draft regulations, the workers' council may do so before agreeing to a proposal. It is clear that this kind of preventive request is very effective: the numbers of this kind of request are increasing, which is an important indication of the authority which the Commission has acquired.

The Commission's opinions are not binding on the parties, but they are considered to be authoritative and in its Annual Report of 2007 the Commission reports that 75% of its opinions have resulted in positive measures being taken by the defendant.

It must be taken into account that many individual complaints concern general measures or policies. Therefore it is relevant to mention that in 67% of these cases the measures taken are of a structural nature: they affect not only the claimant but also sometimes large groups of individuals who are in the same situation.[32] The fact that defendants have consequently taken positive measures in 75% of cases is also due to an active 'follow-up' policy adopted by the Commission. This can be seen as a positive effect of the non-binding nature of the opinions of the Commission.

After the delivery of an opinion in a case, the Commission remains in touch with the parties to monitor the implementation of the decision. Where relevant the Commission can give advice as to how to amend or remedy discriminatory practices. The Commission brings the case to the attention of relevant social partners and their organisations (trade unions, employers associations) and monitors in the same way which actions they take to adapt possible discriminatory rules and practices.

Although the Commission may formally start a court action (see section 15 of the ETA), to date priority has been given to intensive follow-up monitoring and court actions have not so far been taken. However, it is common knowledge that procedures, whether they are formal court procedures or the less formal investigations by the ETC, do not contribute to the mutual relationship between the parties. Therefore, in line with the development in civil proceedings, the Commission also makes use of alternative methods of dispute settlement. The

---

[32] Equal Treatment Commission, Annual Report 1997 (Jaarverslag), Utrecht 2008, p. 48.

Commission may refer parties to a mediator to find a solution (with an option to get an opinion if they do not succeed) and since 2007 the Commission itself has been more active after the reception of a complaint to see whether there are other effective options of handling the case. A consequence of these informal methods will be that the number of opinions decreases. In 2007 the Commission received 515 requests for an opinion and 637 files were closed: the ETC delivered 247 opinions, while other cases went to successful mediation or were otherwise settled, and some complaints were withdrawn.[33]

The fact that more and more issues have been the subject of an investigation and that the law has been interpreted in thousands of opinions of the ETC means that the body of case law provides an answer to many questions for citizens who want to know whether a certain situation is in accordance with the law: these questions can thus be answered by telephone or email. In 2007 almost 2000 of these requests reached the Commission's helpdesk which is where the public can forward them.

The relationship between the Commission and the courts has several aspects. An action brought to the Commission does not restrict the complainant's access to court. Court actions remain possible at any time (within the limits of the regular deadlines and conditions). This means that parties may go to court to enforce an opinion of the Commission if necessary. The option to do so was one of the reasons why the legislator thought that the opinions would not need binding force. When a court has to solve a dispute (part of) which has been the subject of an investigation by the Commission, the opinion of the Commission has the force of an expert opinion. In 1987 the Supreme Court of the Netherlands held that a court must give sound reasons for disagreeing with an opinion of the Commission.[34] These reasons may be related to the fact that the courts have a broader mandate than the Commission; seen in a broader context there may be other relevant arguments that play a role, apart from the non-discrimination aspect. Although there are some cases where the courts fail to make a solid argument, most courts will do so and a derivation from the Commission's opinions is exceptional. Bearing in mind that less than about 10% of the cases heard by the Commission are taken to court, it can validly be argued that the Commission's procedures avoid court proceedings and that the courts benefit from the investigations made by the Commission. In equal pay cases in particular, where the Commission will have performed a specialised job evaluation, the courts will use this in their decisions. In this context it is relevant to mention that the Commission is enabled to follow an urgent procedure, which can be finished within two weeks. This possibility is used in cases of a pending dismissal, in particular when a court case is pending, to enable the court to have the outcome of the Commission's investigation when deciding the case.

---

[33] Equal Treatment Commission, Annual Report 2007, p. 32.
[34] Supreme Court (Hoge Raad) 13 November 1987, St. Bavo v. Gielen, NJ 1989/698. See: Schiek *et al.* (eds.), *supra* note 3, pp. 919-920.

Another aspect of the relationship between the Commission and the courts is the possibility for the Commission to bring a legal action with a view to obtaining a ruling that conduct contrary to one of the equality laws is unlawful, requesting that such conduct be prohibited or that the court order the consequences of such conduct to be rectified. This can only be done with the consent of the individual affected by the unlawful act (section 15 ETA). However, to date this power has never been used by the ETC. The Commission has give priority to active monitoring policies and other informal methods. This can also be justified because victims' organisations and other NGOs may also bring a case to court: if neither the victim nor any of these organisations takes further legal action, the added interest of the Commission itself is restricted.

d. Publicity

The opinions of the Commission are published on its website (www.cgb.nl) and the Commission publishes an annual report and an annotated collection of the most important opinions of that year, edited by a board of independent experts who give their analysis of and comments on the work of the Commission and current legal developments.

In important cases the Commission issues press releases, which may generate further publicity. The President and members of the Commission are frequently interviewed in the press and in the media: this helps to disseminate information on the law. Members of the Commission and staff also contribute to the academic debate by publishing articles in legal and other periodicals. Incidentally the Commission also publishes in-depth studies on (aspects) of its work.

e. Other Tasks

The investigation of and deciding on complaints is the core of the Commission's work, not only because this absorbs most of its capacity, but also because it is this task that provides the Commission with knowledge of and insight into the practice of discrimination. Most of the cases brought to the Commission would never have become public without the accessible procedure that the Commission provides. Thus the added value of each individual complaint, often representing many similar cases, is that it unearths the enduring existence and specific character of discrimination and its different manifestations. This information is used by the Commission in the performance of its other tasks. Apart from the more secondary tasks mentioned such as the follow-up and monitoring of its Opinions and publicity, the Commission has some other relevant tasks.

First the Commission plays a role as advisor to the Government or social partners. Either on its own initiative, but also at the request of the Government or social partners, the ETC offers advisory reports on the implementation of national and international legal obligations. In 2007 the Commission published

10 advisory reports, commenting on draft legislation, on a draft policy recommendation of the Council of Europe's Commission against Racism and Intolerance, and other policy plans. Most of the advice was given on request. Similarly the Commission contributes to the reporting procedures of UN treaty bodies by forwarding its reports to the treaty bodies, sometimes in close cooperation with other organisations.

The information and experience emanating from individual investigations is also used in educational tasks. More and more the Commission is involved in education on non-discrimination at all levels of teaching and society, including primary school programmes, post-graduate courses for lawyers and vocational training for various professionals in the workforce.

The equality laws also prescribe regular evaluations to monitor the effectiveness of the law. Most of the evaluations are twofold, part made by independent experts and part the Commission's own evaluation: the experience in individual cases provides the Commission with arguments as to how to improve the legal system.

f. National and International Cooperation

The Commission works in a specific environment, which is, in part, a very particular Dutch one. The Netherlands has a long tradition of an active civic society, which (often supported by public grants, but independent of the Government) plays a very active role in combating discrimination by raising awareness, victim support, lobbying, etc. The Commission is of course also independent from non-governmental organisations but the existence of these organisations implies that certain roles can be left to them, such as the support of victims or the 'first aid' role. Moreover a network of anti-discrimination services has been established at grass-roots level, with offices run mostly by volunteers, all over the country. They can help individuals to find their way to the Commission. In turn, the Commission is involved in the education of these institutions to provide them with the necessary basic knowledge of the law.

As part of the follow-up policies the Commission maintains incidental or structural relationships with all kinds of relevant corporations and organisations, but always on the basis of independence for all parties.

In 2008 the Dutch Government decided that a National Human Rights Institution would be set up in the Netherlands, in accordance with the UN Paris Principles.[35] Together with the Dutch Data Protection Authority, the National Ombudsman and the Netherlands' Institute of Human Rights (SIM), the ETC is one of the leading partners in this process. In this context the ETC participates in the UN Network of National Human Rights Institutions.

---

[35] National Institutions for the Promotion and Protection of Human Rights, adopted 4 March 1994, G.A. Res. 48/134, UN GAOR, 48th Session UN Doc. A/res/48/134 (1994).

Internationally a network of specialised equality bodies has been set up, as described in the contribution to this volume of Ingrid Nikolay-Leitner. Here too, the ETC plays a role. Apart from this network, the members of the Commission offer contributions to conferences and expert meetings of international organisations, in particular the EU.

g. Evaluation

In its almost 15 years of existence, the ETC has developed into an authoritative institution in the implementation of equality laws. The fact that its mandate is restricted by the scope of the specific Dutch equality laws and that the opinions of the Commission are not binding can be seen as a disadvantage. However, these 'weaknesses' also entail some advantages: more possibilities for active and informal follow-up may in the long run be very effective. However, this demands a certain basic commitment to non-discrimination. Another specific feature is the position of the Commission in an active civic society: this position facilitates the potential to develop as an accessible independent expert organisation, leaving the awareness raising and victim support at the grass-roots level to others.

10. SUMMING UP: QUESTIONS TO BE ANSWERED

This short survey of the Dutch equality landscape and in particular of the role of the ETC is intended both to highlight some of the core issues of equality law and also to clarify the necessity to take due notice of the national setting. Non-discrimination law has to bring about change in established, often unconsciously persisting, patterns of dominance and subordination. The existence of these patterns is global but their manifestation and incorporation in daily life differs in different societies. Therefore, there cannot be a single blueprint for effective non-discrimination protection: national and regional circumstances have to be taken into account. The central issue is the protection of victims and the organisation of change in patterns of discrimination. The law can never be sufficient on its own, but it is necessary to give victims rights that can be the beginning of their empowerment. When setting up machinery to combat discrimination, choices will have to be made and priorities have to be chosen. Comparative information can be helpful to decide what is most suitable in the specific context. Thus, social bodies may focus on the assistance of victims or on an independent (semi-) judicial role, on taking cases to court or on informal settlement, on sanctions or on negotiations.

Some options are mutually exclusive. For the sake of equality, each society has to give the best possible answers to these matters.

9

AUSTRIAN LAW AND PRACTICE REGARDING ANTI-DISCRIMINATION IN EMPLOYMENT

Ingrid Nikolay-Leitner

1. DEVELOPMENT OF LEGISLATION

In February 2009, Austrian law in the area of equal treatment for women and men will have been in force for 30 years. In this contribution, the development of the legislation will be outlined against the background of the major international obligations. Attention will be paid to some specific features of Austrian law, including the monitoring mechanisms, with emphasis on the position, role and practice of the Austrian Specialised Equality Body.

1.1 First Steps towards Equality: the 1979 Legislation

In 1979 there was a pressing obligation to enact a provision for equal pay because of the International Labour Organisation Convention no 111, which Austria had ratified in 1973. At that time the general pay schemes (collective agreements) in Austria, negotiated by trade unions and the Chamber of Commerce, provided different levels of minimum pay for women and men. In fact this was what the ILO mainly asked Austria to change, and this is indeed what was changed during the first few years after the Equal Treatment Act was enacted.

Besides the pressure from the ILO, one of the main motives for the creation of the new law was the recognition of the fact that the market economy did not automatically proceed in the direction of more equality for women. In the first commentary to the 1979 Equal Treatment Act, published in 1981, it was stated that there was 'still a strong preference for male employees in the labour market' because of their inability to get pregnant and the possibility for men to work at night without restrictions.[1] At that time – and almost up to the year 2000 – night work by women was in principle forbidden by the law. Though the law allowed many exceptions, the general impression amongst the public and employers was that women did not work at night.

---

[1] T. Mayer-Maly, *Gleichbehandlungsgesetz* (Vienna: Manz, 1981), p. 28.

It was discussed in Austria during the preparation of the Equal Treatment Act whether the Act might create a new level of protection for women at work that might therefore reduce even further the opportunities of individual women fighting for equality in the labour market. Other experts argued that discrimination on the ground of gender was not only an individual problem of the person affected by discrimination, nor did it solely constitute an individual offence by the person who acted discriminatorily. These experts emphasized the fact that due to a general attitude in society, in many cases women's work was considered to be less valuable than that of their male colleagues was and that change would have to occur on a more general level. Many experts on women strongly doubted whether a general practice such as wage discrimination against women, which saved employers a lot of money, would ever change voluntarily. All attempts at voluntary awareness-raising, social agreements and other instruments that have been made, have only proved the importance of a legal obligation prohibiting discrimination on the grounds of gender.

The first Equal Treatment Act was short, simple and quite narrow in its scope: it stated that within an employment relationship, discrimination between women and men with regard to payment was forbidden. The legal obligation was also one of the pillars of the practical work of the Equality Body for equal treatment, the Austrian institution set up for training, legal advice and public awareness-raising in the field of equality for men and women.

The main advantage of the existence of a legal obligation, compared with a system that is based on mere agreement, is that as soon as there is a law, the problem shifts from the victim to the perpetrator of the proscribed act. Before a legal obligation existed, unequal pay was seen merely as a problem of the person being treated unfairly. She (for it was a woman in the majority of cases) had to convince the employer to pay her the same as her male colleagues. Experts could only support her with arguments in her favour, but had no effective tools. After the law came into force, the Specialised Equality Body could use the law as a tool and assist the employer to bring his practice in line with the law.

The draft for the 1979 Equal Treatment Act was also supposed to include protection against discrimination on the ground of religion or belief, ethnic origin or sexual orientation (not just gender). It is not clear why this was not finally realised in the Act. It may well be the main reason was that there was only an explicit international obligation concerning equal pay between women and men. Later international obligations – especially those of the European Union – often led to amendments of the Equal Treatment Act in Austria. Without such an international obligation, improvements in the law often could not be effected. Therefore, the overview given below includes the major international instruments that led to the enactment of national law in the field of equality between men and women. It provides a summary of the development in the private sector, however legal developments for civil servants at the federal and provincial levels proceeded along similar lines.

1.2 Chronology of Major Legal Steps towards Equal Pay and Equal Treatment for Women and Men in Austria and Their International Background

ILO 1951 The International Labour Organisation (ILO) adopts Convention 100 concerning equal remuneration for men and women workers for work of equal value.

EU 1957 The 1957 Treaties establishing the European Economic Community (EEC) included the principle of 'equal pay for equal work' (Article 119 EEC Treaty). However, this inclusion was prompted not so much by emancipation as by economic considerations. At that time, French law already endorsed women's right to equal pay, which is why France feared competitive disadvantages from a less well paid (in other words, cheaper) female workforce in other Member States (see also the contribution of Susanne Burri in this volume).

ILO 1958 Convention 111 obliges the members to eliminate all forms of discrimination on grounds of race, colour, gender, religion, political opinion, nationality or social origin, in employment or occupation.

EU 1975 The Equal Pay Directive (75/117/EEC) establishes the principle of equal pay not only for equal work, but also for work of equal value. Work is deemed to be of equal value if it makes similar demands with respect to essential criteria, such as: qualifications/skills, strain/stress, responsibility and working conditions.

EU 1976 The Equal Treatment Directive (76/207/EEC) proscribes all forms of indirect and direct discrimination on grounds of gender and marital and family status as regards access to employment, basic training, other advanced vocational training, working conditions and promotion. It applies to employment relationships in private enterprises and under public law as well as to self-employed persons.

A 1979 The first Austrian Equal Treatment Act enters into force – the 'Act on the Equal Treatment of Women and Men with regard to Remuneration' (Federal Law Gazette (FLG) No 108/1979). The separate pay scales for women and men are removed from collective agreements.

UNO 1979 The United Nations General Assembly adopts the Convention on the Elimination of All Forms of Discrimination against Women (CEDAW). Article 4 of this Convention permits temporary positive discrimination (affirmative action) to benefit women: 'Adoption by States Parties of temporary special measures aimed at accelerating de facto equality between men and women shall not be considered discrimination as defined in the present Convention, but shall in no way entail as a consequence the maintenance of unequal or separate standards; these measures shall be discontinued when the objectives of equality of opportunity and treatment have been achieved.' Article 11 of the Convention prohibits discrimination against women in the labour market.

Austria had signed and ratified the UN Convention on the Elimination of All Forms of Discrimination against Women in 1982. As mentioned above, Article 4 of this Convention explicitly holds that temporary special measures to accelerate de facto equality for women during a certain time period are not discriminatory against men. Due to this provision it was possible to include obligatory provisions for the promotion of women in the Equal Treatment Acts for the civil service including quotas which could be imposed in relation to recruitment and career prospects. This possibility is one of the few differences between the provisions in the Equal Treatment Acts for the private sector on one hand and for civil servants on the other.

In the legislation for the private sector, there are no provisions for positive action. Thus, the national law offers no more opportunities for positive action in addition to that already mentioned. This is to be regretted since the European Court of Justice's jurisdiction seems to have limited the notions of affirmative action and the promotion of women in the years following 1993.[2]

A 1982 Austria ratifies the UN Convention on the Elimination of All Forms of Discrimination against Women (CEDAW) (FLG No 443/1982).

A 1985 Enlargement of the scope of the Equal Treatment Act (FLG No 290/1985) to include the granting of fringe benefits and company measures for (advanced) vocational training. Provisions now include the principle of gender-neutral recruitment advertisements.

EU 1986 The Directive on Equal Treatment of Persons Engaged in Gainful Self-Employment (86/613/EEC) stipulates the equal treatment of women and men engaged in an activity, including agriculture, in a self-employed capacity. It also contains similar provisions concerning social security.

A 1990 New amendment of the Equal Treatment Act (FLG No 410/1990): extension of the equal treatment principle to include all aspects of working life. In particular, it includes the establishment of an employment relationship, fixing remuneration, granting of fringe benefits, basic and advanced vocational training measures, promotion and all other working conditions, as well as termination of employment. Small-scale compensation was established. A Specialised Body for

---

[2] ECJ, 17 October 1995, Case C-450/93 *Kalanke v Freie Hansestadt Bremen* [1995] ECR I-3051.
ECJ, 11 November 1997, Case C-409/95, *Helmut Marschall v Land Nordrhein Westfalen* [1997] ECR I - 6363. However, see also the more optimistic contribution of Colm O'Cinneide to this volume.

Gender Equality is appointed as a direct contact. Temporary special measures are promoted to advance the de facto equality of women and men.

A 1992 Alignment of the Equal Treatment Act with the EC directives on equal treatment (FLG No 833/1992): sexual harassment at the workplace is considered as gender-based discrimination. The principle 'equal pay for work of equal value' must also be observed with regard to collective classification schemes and remuneration criteria. Infringement of the principle of a gender-neutral job advertisement by the labour market administration and private job recruitment agencies will be punished by an administrative penalty. The amount of compensation is increased. The Act must be displayed within companies.

A 1993 The Federal Equal Treatment Act (FLG No 199/1993) enters into force. The 1979 Equal Treatment Act was not applicable to the civil service. The strict separation between labour law for the private sector and labour law for the civil service has a long tradition in Austria. Each of the nine provinces in Austria has a separate law for its civil servants, and each therefore had to construct a separate Equal Treatment Act as a part of labour law as well. This may have been one important reason why the 1979 Act covered only the private sector.

The main reason why civil servants, at the federal level, did not fall under the Equal Treatment Act until 1993 was due to the argument based on the assumption of correctness of pay schemes in the public sphere. Federal and provincial governments argued that the strict pay schemes as used in the civil service would not allow pay discrimination. The developments and cases that have arisen since 1993 revealed that this belief was wrong and that wage discrimination against women was universal.

When equal treatment legislation for the civil service finally came into force in 1993, the awareness among the general public of the necessity to combat inequalities between the sexes through the law, had increased, including the conviction that active measures are required to bring about equality. Apart from the equal treatment principle for federal employees, it also establishes the principle of targeted promotion of women in federal service.

EU 1996 The Parental Leave Directive (96/34/EC) is aimed at a fair division of duties between women and men with regard to childcare. It is the first attempt to reconcile professional and family responsibilities.

EU 1997 The Part-Time Directive (97/81/EEC) proscribes discrimination against part-time workers vis-à-vis comparable full-time workers in the same enterprise. Pursuant to the judgment of the European Court of Justice, discrimination against part-timers constitutes an indirect discrimination on the grounds of sex, because the majority of part-timers are women. The Directive on the Burden of Proof (97/80/EC) introduces rules of evidence which are more favourable to claimants.

If claimants can establish a credible case of discrimination on grounds of gender, it is up to the respondent to produce counter-evidence.

A 1998 Since its adoption in 1920, the Austrian Federal Constitution (B-VG) has expressly forbidden discrimination on grounds of sex (equality principle); the explicit commitment to the equality of women and men was added in 1998. Article 7 (2) of the Federal Constitutional Act states that: 'the Federal and Provincial governments and local authorities endorse the de facto equality of women and men. Measures to promote de facto equality of women and men, particularly by eliminating actually existing inequalities, shall be permitted.' Amendment of the Equal Treatment Act (FLG 44/1998): Regionalisation of the Specialised Equality Body.

EU 1999 The Amsterdam Treaty enters into force. This treaty of the European Union is the basis of equal treatment between women and men in the European Community.

Article 2 EC refers to the promotion of equality as one of the duties of the European Community. Article 3 ECT obliges the Community to eliminate inequalities and to promote equality between women and men. Pursuant to Article 13 ECT, the Community can take suitable measures for combating discrimination based on sex. Article 141 ECT establishes the principle of 'Equal pay for male and female workers for equal work or work of equal value'. This is in addition to the Treaty establishing the European Community, which permits so-called 'affirmative action' in the interests of equality: 'With a view to ensuring full equality in practice between men and women in working life, the principle of equal treatment shall not prevent any Member State from maintaining or adopting measures providing for specific advantages in order to make it easier for the under-represented sex to pursue a vocational activity or to prevent or compensate for disadvantages in professional careers.'

A 2001 Amendment of the Equal Treatment Act (FLG No 129/2001). Establishment of the constitutional independence of the chairperson of the Equal Treatment Commission in exercising her or his function. An application to the Equal Treatment Commission by the Ombudsman for Gender Equality has the effect of suspending the statutory deadlines for claims in court.

EU 2002 The new Equal Treatment Directive (2002/73/EC) amends Directive 76/207/EEC and contains provisions for access to employment, basic training, promotion and working conditions. Gender-related and sexual harassment are now considered an infringement of the principle of equal treatment for women and men. Article 1a stipulates active policies aimed at equality. It states that a woman is to be entitled, after the end of her period of maternity leave, to return to her job or to an equivalent post.

EU 2004 The Directive on Equal Treatment in the Access to and Supply of Goods and Services (2004/113/EC) stipulates the equal treatment of women and men in areas outside the labour market (e.g., the calculation of premiums and benefits for the purposes of insurance and related financial services). Implementation of this Directive by the Member States had to be completed by 2007.

A 2004 The new Equal Treatment Act (FLG No 66/2004) enters into force on 1 July 2004. Its first part, 'Gender Equality in Employment', implements Directive 2002/73/EC. At the same time, the Federal Act Governing the Equal Treatment Commission and the National Equality Body (Ombudsman for Equal Treatment) – GBK/GAW Act (FLG No 66/2004) enters into force. The second part of the Equal Treatment Act forbids discrimination on grounds of ethnicity, religion or belief, age or sexual orientation, while the third part bans discrimination on grounds of ethnicity in the field of goods and services, education, social protection and social advantages. The third Act taking effect at that time is the new Federal Equal Treatment Act which also forbids discrimination on grounds of ethnicity, religion or belief, age and sexual orientation in employment.[3]

2. INSTITUTIONS DEALING WITH EQUAL TREATMENT LAW

2.1. The Specialised Equality Body

The institution was founded in 1990 within the framework of the third amendment of the Equal Treatment Act for the private sector. This Act also developed the equal pay provisions, granting equal treatment throughout the scope of an employment relationship.

The main reason for the creation of a Specialised Equality Body was an almost complete lack of complaints about unequal pay, although it was quite evident that women were discriminated against in this field. Between 1979 and 1990 only 18 people had turned to the Equal Treatment Commission, which had been installed as a soft law institution at the time of the 1979 Act, to help people feeling discriminated against to complain during the course of their employment. The experts who prepared the amendment in 1990 concluded that either people did not know about the Equal Treatment Act or that it was still too difficult to complain to an anonymous commission without the support of a specialised institution, or both.

The fact that the draft of the amendment only mentions an Ombudsman as one individual person also demonstrates that only a small number of complaints were expected to reach the Specialised Equality Body. In December 1990, the

---

[3] S. Feigl, *et al*, *Your Legitimate Right,* (Vienna: Information brochure of the Specialised Equality Body, 2006).

Specialised Equality Body was established with an office of three employees. The two main tasks of the new institution were clearly stated in the law: counselling and supporting people feeling discriminated against, and providing information to the public about discrimination and equality issues. The new institution received much attention from the media and the general public. It seemed as though people had withheld their complaints until the day the Specialised Equality Body started work, especially complaints regarding unequal pay.

In the first year of its existence more than 200 complaints were received and from then on the figures increased every year. Due to this large number of complaints the new institution was quickly able to acquire unique knowledge and develop expertise about discrimination issues. For example, employers who did not want qualified women to be promoted in their enterprise very often argued that in general they would support having women at the top of the enterprise, but that the particular woman who had complained about discrimination could unfortunately not work in a team, and that their colleagues would not accept her as their boss. It was difficult to find arguments against this if you were only dealing with a single case. However, if you receive many complaints and the same arguments are used by nearly all employers, then the pattern of discrimination becomes obvious – the pattern that the individual woman who wants to be promoted is always blamed for being unable to work as part of a team.

Another big advantage for the Specialised Equality Body was that from the very beginning, although the institution was part of the civil service, it was able to act in the private sector. Therefore, their position is much easier than that of the civil service equal treatment representatives who are civil servants themselves and therefore have to act in their own professional field. It is extremely difficult to criticise the decisions of an employer who, at the same time, is making decisions about your own professional career.

From 1990 (private sector) and 1993 (civil service) until 2004, the Specialised Equality Body only dealt with equal treatment cases on discrimination between women and men. The institution became quite well known to the public and respected among employers. While beforehand many employers, especially in the private sector, had considered equal treatment as something they might or might not concede to women, they now learned that the Equal Treatment Act was as authoritative as any other Act in Austria. A large part of the counselling concerning gender during the past twenty years has been about unequal pay. Remarkable progress has been made in the field of access to work for women, and with regard to working conditions. Complaints about discrimination in relation to promotion are still infrequent. Most of the complaints that reach the Specialised Equality Body always were, and still are, about sexual harassment at work although this is also the field in which awareness-raising was extremely successful. While at the start of the Equality Body's activities, sexual harassment was seen mostly as a minor problem of hypersensitivity among some women, now many employers co-operate with the Equality Body to prevent harassment, which is considered to be one of the decisive barriers for women at work.

Detailed information about complaints to the Specialised Equality Body can be found in the biannual reports for the National Assembly, published on the webpage www.gleichbehandlungsanwaltschaft.at.

2.1.1 Enlargement of Mandate under the Equal Treatment Act in 2004

In the framework of the 6th amendment to the Equal Treatment Act in 2004 for the private sector, the scope of the competencies for the equality body has been enlarged. Since that time, anybody who feels discriminated against in the workplace on the grounds of gender, ethnic origin, religion or belief, age or sexual orientation can turn to the Ombudsman for counselling and support.

Furthermore, people who feel they have been a victim of discrimination in the field of education, social protection or social advantages because of their ethnic origin, can ask for support. As well as this, people who feel discriminated against in the area of access to and the supply of public goods and services are able to bring a claim. In this area, ethnic origin is so far the only relevant ground. The pending 7th amendment of the Equal Treatment Act came into force on the 1st of August 2008. Since then, complaints in areas other than work are also possible on the ground of gender.

2.2. The Equal Treatment Commission

The Specialised Equality Body is not supposed to be impartial, in the sense that its purpose is to offer the best possible support for victims of discrimination. However, the role of the Equal Treatment Commission is that of an impartial, independent body, which should thoroughly examine a case that is brought forward by an individual, with or without the support of the equality body, and give an opinion as to whether the Equal Treatment Act has been violated or not. As opposed to court decisions, the opinions of the Equal Treatment Commission are not binding.

There are two main reasons why the legislators of the Equal Treatment Act designed such a soft law institution. One reason was to make it easier for employees to raise a complaint against their employer while still being employed. The other idea behind the composition of the Commission, in which mainly social partners are represented, was the hope that in many cases reconciliation or joint dispute resolution could take place and solve the specific discrimination problem. The background to this way of thinking fits in with the long tradition of social partnership in Austria in which negotiation is a basic principle. It was anticipated that employers would comply voluntarily with the law as soon as they recognised that discrimination took place in their enterprises.

In the period between 1979 and 1990 the few cases brought before the Commission were in fact reconciled in negotiations between the social partners, the representatives of employers and the representatives of employees. They reached agreement after each side accommodated the views of the other. When in 1991 the experts from the Office of the Ombudsman started to take part in the procedure of the Commission, a completely different approach was adopted. Equal treatment was no longer to be negotiable, in the sense of there being a possibility of compromise. Instead, there was a necessary benchmark of compliance with the Equal Treatment Act i.e. equal treatment where discrimination would not be tolerated, as opposed to violation of the Equal Treatment Act.

With the 2004 amendment of the Equal Treatment Act the Commission was split up into three chambers. One of the chambers is still competent to deal with gender issues and the co-ordination of the work of the senates. One of the other two is concerned with discrimination in employment and occupation on the grounds of ethnic origin, religion or belief, age and sexual orientation, with the final one dealing with ethnic discrimination in other areas of life.

2.2.1. The NGOs

Since the extension of the grounds of discrimination, as provided for in the law of 2004, non-governmental organisations also play a role in the procedure of individual complaints against discrimination. There are strong and successful NGOs in Austria, most of them working against discrimination on one of the several grounds. Until 2004 there was no pressure from women's NGOs to take part in the procedure before the Equal Treatment Commission. They relied on the Ombudsman in matters of equality law, and in cases where women felt discriminated against and turned to an NGO, they would be referred to the Ombudsman.

However, organisations in the field of discrimination on the ground of sexual orientation or ethnic origin had started to challenge the discriminatory situation earlier by taking individual cases to court. When these grounds were included in the scope of protection under the Equal Treatment Act, these organisations were prepared to take part in the procedure before the Commission as well.

Since 2004 there have been three provisions on NGOs in the law. (1) In the provision on the examination of particular cases in one of the chambers of the Equal Treatment Commission, the law states that a person affected by discrimination is entitled to be represented in proceedings instituted before the Commission by a person enjoying his or her confidence, in particular by a representative of one of the organised interest groups or a non-governmental organisation. The Chamber must call in a representative of a non-governmental organisation nominated by the person affected. (2) Meetings of the chambers are confidential and non-public, but the chair can call in external experts in an advisory capacity. These experts very often also come from NGOs. (3) A specific association of NGOs, the Claimant Association for the Enforcement of the Rights of Victims of Discrimination, can join litigation in court for the enforcement of rights under the Equal Treatment Act as a third party.[4]

Non-governmental organisations in the fight against discrimination on the grounds of ethnic origin and sexual orientation also play a significant role in promoting equal treatment in society. The Centre for Work against Ethnic Discrimination (ZARA), for example, publishes an annual monitoring report, on incidents of discriminatory behaviour with regard to ethnic discrimination in all fields of society.[5] NGOs in the field of sexual orientation have been very strongly engaged in the struggle for the recognition of homosexual marriage. Since the law to date does not cover protection against discrimination with regard to access to goods and services and social protection for victims on this ground, homosexual couples do not have the same rights as heterosexual couples concerning, for example, rental agreements and social security.

In the field of gender equality NGOs were rather hesitant with action concerning equal treatment law, except for specialised lawyers' organisations like the 'Austrian Association of Women Lawyers', which concentrated on legal advice in the course of legislation and on public statements concerning women's issues and law. This situation changed after the entry of Austria into the European Union, a step that opened up access to the budget for carrying out transnational projects concerning special topics within the framework of gender equality. Since then projects on equal pay, mentoring, gender mainstreaming and the promotion of women, especially targeted at employment in engineering and qualified positions in the field of technical expertise, have become quite common.

2.3. Networking of Equality Bodies on the EU Level

Austria's entry to the European Union also entailed participation in networks of the rising number of member states. Many equality networks have a theoretical character, i.e. they are not involved in daily policies or practices. Thus, an EU network of experts exists for gender law and there is a network of independent experts concerning the implementation of anti-discrimination law in the member states. The members of these networks report to the relevant institutions of the European Union on the progress of implementing the existing law and on the gaps that still remain. This helps the Union to locate the need for new provisions, including new directives which subsequently have to be implemented in the other member states. EU institutions also receive independent information on

---

[4] Federal Law on the Equal Treatment Commission and the Specialised Equality Body, Section 12 (2), Section 14 (4); Federal Act Governing Equal Treatment, Section 62.

[5] ZARA (Zivilcourage und Anti-Rassismus-Arbeit), *Rassismus Report (Einzelfall-Bericht über rassistische Übergriffe und Strukturen in Österreich)*.

defaults in member states which can then be discussed, criticised or even become a matter of formal legal procedure against a member state.

In 2002, equality bodies in various member states, together with the Migration Policy Group, as the Network of Specialised Equality Bodies, started the project 'Towards a uniform and dynamic Implementation of EU Anti-Discrimination Legislation: the role of specialised bodies', supported by the EU under the European Community Action Programme to Combat Discrimination.

For the first phase of the project, up until 2004, the network only had seven partners (six specialised bodies from Sweden, Belgium, the Netherlands, Ireland, Denmark and Austria), one observer (the UK) and the Migration Policy Group as an additional partner. The main activity during this time was the arrangement of expert meetings on specific topics in the field of anti-discrimination law, such as: how to prove discrimination; how to reach both the goal of equal treatment for all victims of discrimination and the goal of gender equality; equal pay; sanctions and remedies; methods of strategic enforcement; and on the issue of whether single strand bodies (competent for all discrimination grounds) or single ground bodies (competent for one or a few grounds) might be the more or the less effective way to combat discrimination through the support of individual victims and information for the public.

Representatives from specialised equality bodies in all member states were invited to the expert meetings, and the intensive discussions on all topics contributed to the development of the network.[6] In particular, the last issue mentioned, namely which kind of specialised body would be the most effective, caused a lot of internal discussion. When the network started, there were a few countries with a long tradition of Ombudsman-type institutions in the field of gender, and some other countries that had started anti-discrimination practice and litigation on the grounds of ethnic discrimination. The majority of the Ombudsman/equality institutions at that time were single-ground institutions. The Equal Treatment Commission (Commissie Gelijke Behandeling) in the Netherlands, the leading partner in the project, was an exception, being competent for all grounds from the 1990s onwards.

Very soon after the start of the network, it was absolutely clear that the situation would be as heterogeneous in the rest of the fifteen member states. Moreover another ten countries were about to join the European Union, who were required to establish a specialised body from the very start, as this was prescribed in the Race Directive of 2000 and the Revised Second Equal Treatment Directive on equal treatment of men and women. The members of the network decided to be as comprehensive as possible, and invited all specialised bodies and also decided to accept more than one partner organisation per country. On the other hand, from the very beginning the network tried to ensure

---

[6] The reports of these expert meetings have been published and are available at the website of the Migration Policy Group: see http://www.migpolgroup.com/topics/2078.html.

that its members met standards with regard to their mandate and their independence. Independence from government institutions as well as from the private sector is one of the two pillars of specialised equality bodies, which distinguishes them from other institutions working in the field of equality and anti-discrimination within government structures. The other pillar is the mandate of specialised bodies, based on the law and comprising not only legal advice but also support for victims and the right to inform the public freely.

Since 2005 the network has had the title EQUINET. For the time being it comprises 30 member institutions and one with observer status. An overview of the status, mandate and resources reveals a rather inhomogeneous picture.[7] However, there is a clear tendency towards one comprehensive specialised body per country, with the competence to advise and support victims of discrimination on all grounds mentioned in the law of the European Union.

Detailed information on the status of member organisations, mandate, personnel and budget is to be found on EQUINET's webpage; see: www.equineteurope.org.

3. PRACTICE AND MAIN PROBLEMS IN THE APPLICATION OF THE EQUAL TREATMENT ACT IN AUSTRIA

3.1 General Experience: Case Management and Counter-Arguments

Starting an individual legal procedure against an employer is never easy for somebody who wants to stay within the enterprise, and no aspect of labour relations causes such turbulent conflicts as issues concerning equal treatment. This is still true in 2008, and was all the more so in 1991 when the first clients of the Specialised Equality Body began their legal actions.

As mentioned above, unequal pay was a frequent complaint at that time. Often women were very openly discriminated against, as demonstrated in the following case that was considered by the Equal Treatment Commission in 1992. The issue in question was whether paragraph 2(1) 2 of the Equal Treatment Act permitted a practice where male semi-skilled workers were automatically put on a higher pay scale than female semi-skilled workers, who were put on the lowest wage grade. This practice allowed for male employees to earn substantially more for the same or equal work. The rationale given for granting the male employees a higher wage grade was that men have to support their family, and previous experience had shown that they were not prepared to work for as little money as women. The Commission considered that automatically implementing this pay discrepancy between men and women, without clear grounds for maintaining the

---

[7] An overview of the profiles can be found on the website of the Migration Policy Group: http://www.migpolgroup.com/infopages/2116.html and at www.equineteurope.org.

distinction, constituted discrimination regarding the rate of pay. As a result, the employer was directed to end the practice which discriminated against women.

It is often argued that preferential treatment for men, such as occurred in this case, is justified because men would otherwise leave the company. However, according to a decision laid down by the Equal Treatment Commission prior to 1991, this is not a valid argument. In that case, they stated that unequal treatment of men and women on the basis of the labour market situation or the generally greater mobility of men is not justified in material terms. Indeed, the Commission expressly stated at the time that pay differentials in particular, arising from men's generally greater mobility contravene the equal treatment principle. There is also no legal basis to the argument that men have to support a family. Current family law in fact states that both spouses are equally obliged to contribute to supporting the family.

Despite the difficulties in bringing legal proceedings against an employer, traditionally there was less pressure to abstain from (legal) action when a number of women undertook a legal procedure simultaneously. However, even then similar threats were issued: 'The company would no longer hire women at all; male colleagues would lose money because of the need to meet the demands of women; and – last but not least – the company would move to another country and all employees would lose their jobs.' However, the experience of the Equality Body shows quite clearly that no employer ever actually had the intention of no longer hiring women. It seems that the real motive behind unequal treatment is to save money at the expense of women and this practice still continues, even though it is implicit and less open.

Another argument against equal pay for women sounds much more threatening: 'equal treatment will be brought about by downgrading men's pay'. However, at least in Austria, it seems unlikely that this will actually happen because of the strong position of men in the labour market and the wide range of employees organised in trade unions with the right to negotiate collective agreements that not only apply to their members but to all workers in a certain trade or industry. Although trade unions represent male as well as female workers, it was always perfectly clear that equal treatment for women and men would not be a target that could be achieved quickly and as a matter of course by cutting down men's pay. An example may help here. In the 1990s a big trade union redistributed a small part of the yearly increase of pay in favour of unskilled workers, the majority of them being women. This action helped to close the pay gap in that specific sector – but when the negotiations for the following year started trade union negotiators found themselves confronted with heavy pressure from their young skilled workers, nearly all male, who argued that this time they had to be favoured to balance the injustice of the previous year. The gender pay gap was therefore re-opened in the next year.

Another threat used against claims for equal pay is that enterprises which have the possibility of moving their production, especially to low pay countries, do not hesitate to shift production. Here too, experience showed clearly that this decision to move is made irrespective of attempts, for example, by the workers' representatives in the enterprise to achieve equal pay for women and men.

The most remarkable change in the 18 years of activity of the Specialised Equality Body is not the narrowing of the gender pay gap. The gap is still wide open and cannot be closed solely by individual litigation. Only the arguments to justify the gap have changed and unequal pay is incorporated in the salary system in a less visible and open way. The most remarkable change is that in 2008 hardly anyone still considers unequal pay for women to be acceptable. The argument openly used in the 1992 case that a man has to earn more to support his family, now sounds old-fashioned and out-dated. The consensus is that women's work should be valued equally with men's work. Every employer agrees with this fact, and this should be regarded as a notable success. Still, in such a situation it can be even more difficult for an individual woman to insist that she is discriminated against with regard to pay. This is because many employers are fully convinced that an equal pay policy is in effect in their enterprise and see it as a personal attack if one of their employees denies this.

3.2. Procedure to Support Victims of Discrimination in Practice

Since it is still such a contentious matter to raise a claim in the field of equal treatment, the Specialised Equality Body follows a set routine as soon as a person feeling discriminated against turns to the institution and the institution's experts also assume that this might be a case covered by the Equal Treatment Act.

The most important procedure, the counselling procedure, is reflected in the scheme below.

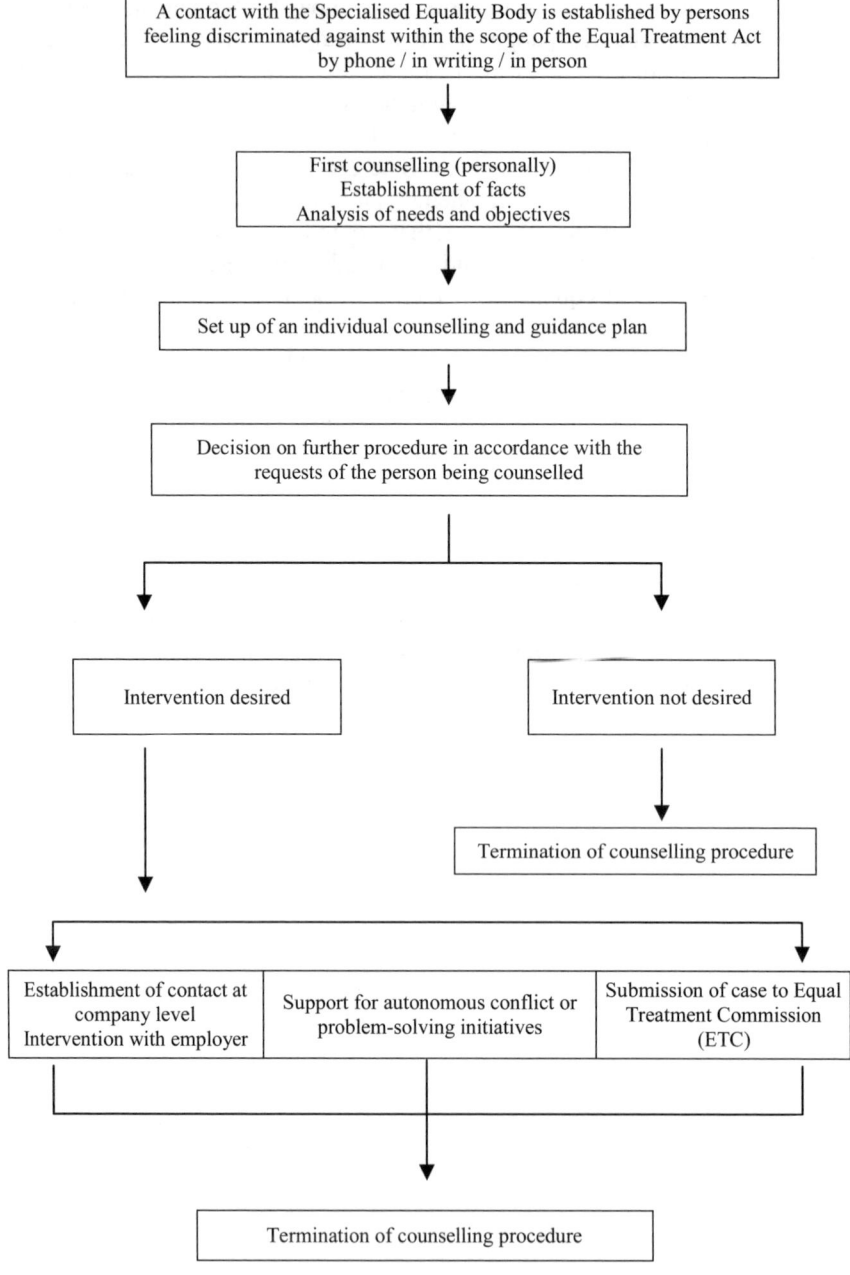

A lot of complainants in all fields of employment turn to the Specialised Equality Body to get information about their rights and to gain a better insight into the background of their payment or treatment to know whether they are discriminated against or not. Again, particularly a woman who is discriminated against with regard to pay, is often faced with the situation that her managers, colleagues and trade union representatives try to convince her individually that she might earn less than male colleagues, but that this fact definitely has no connection to discrimination at all. Therefore, the expert at the Equality Body is sometimes the first person to investigate whether there could be a case of discrimination instead of simply denying it. This prima facie investigation can also be extremely important for victims of discrimination in cases of sexual harassment, age discrimination or discrimination on the ground of ethnic origin in the field of access to goods and services.

Some complainants are even satisfied with just recognition of possible discrimination and want neither intervention nor to file a case. But the majority of persons turning to the Specialised Equality Body want support while they conduct negotiations with their employer or other institutions in which discriminatory behaviour has occurred. There are no formal requirements for the action of the Specialised Equality Body under the jurisdiction of the Equal Treatment Act. Very often it is a phone call or an official letter from the Equality Body that initially informs the employer or institution about the legal provisions and the entitlement to damages for the victim of discrimination. Sometimes the experts at the Equality Body negotiate a settlement with compensation. In any case the negotiations follow the basic principle of the Equality Body that the complainant has to decide the steps he or she wants to undertake. The Equality Body provides full legal information but does not initiate any legal steps without the consent of the complainant. Even if the experts are fully convinced that discrimination has taken place they refrain from action if the victim decides not to undertake legal action. This principle is as much for the reassurance of the clients as the fact that nobody has to pay anything for the counselling and support of the Equality Body. Also important is confidentiality, which is the other basic principle of the work of the Equality Body. Confidentiality and a free procedure are also legally provided when the service of the Senates of the Equal Treatment Commission is required.

If the Specialised Equality Body's negotiations in a case are not successful, or if a person who feels discriminated against decides to forward his or her case to the Commission from the very beginning, the Equality Body can pass on the case and the Commission has to institute a confidential procedure within a month. As previously mentioned, this is also possible for persons feeling discriminated against by other institutions and NGOs. The procedure before the Commission may require a year or more, which is a heavy burden for complainants. But on the other hand the result is much more official, especially since the complainant is not bound to preserve confidentiality with regard to the result of the opinion the Commission has given.

Many complainants want an opinion of the Equal Treatment Commission before they undergo the risk of a court procedure. A court procedure is necessary anyway to decide about any financial entitlement and compensation. If there is an opinion of the Commission and a court wants to decide differently, it has to give reasons. Only a few court cases in the field of equal treatment law are decided in Austria every year; about 50 procedures take place before the Equal Treatment Commission and about 5000 persons turn to the Specialised Equality Body for counselling and support. These figures show quite clearly that it will not be possible to eliminate discrimination solely through individual negotiation and litigation. General and structural measures are necessary for a measurable development.

The significance and major asset of the work of the specialised soft law institutions, through their work with cases, is to get the attention and raise the awareness of the public and of political leaders in all parts of society about discrimination issues. Cases, examples and stories make discrimination visible and understandable. It is the courage and the persistence of persons who individually insist on equal treatment and therefore turn to the Equality Body and the Commission, together with experts, that help to form a society in which discrimination regrettably still takes place but at least is judged and sanctioned.

10

COMPARATIVE STUDY ON POSITIVE ACTION IN LAW AND PRACTICE

Colm O'Cinneide

1. INTRODUCTION

Positive action is a concept of great importance in the context of anti-discrimination law. It involves the use of special measures to assist members of disadvantaged groups in overcoming the obstacles and discrimination they face in contemporary society. Different types of special measures may be used to achieve this purpose. Employers may give preference to women or members of disadvantaged ethnic minority groups in selecting candidates for employment and for promotion. Government agencies or employers may provide special training, assistance and advice to members of disadvantaged groups. Universities may reserve or 'set aside' special places in their classes for members of minority groups. Governments may introduce laws that require private and state companies must have a certain number of women on their board of management.

Sometimes described as 'affirmative action' in the United States, positive action is widely used in Europe, North America, Africa and India to benefit different groups. Many national parliaments have passed laws requiring the use of positive action. Positive action in favour of women is common in the EU. So too is 'affirmative action' to assist Afro-Americans and other disadvantaged minority groups in the United States. Special measures are in place in South Africa and the United Kingdom (UK) to help members of African and Asian ethnic groups to overcome the obstacles that they may face in accessing employments, social services and the political process. In India, there are extensive positive action systems in place which are intended to assist members of lower castes and severely disadvantaged social groups. Many countries have positive action measures in place for disabled persons, including special employment arrangements. European Union (EU) legislation permits the use of special measures to combat the disadvantages faced by members of under-represented groups. International human rights law permits and may even require the use of positive action in certain circumstances. Therefore, the legitimacy of using positive action is now widely established.

However, the use of positive action can sometimes cause controversy. At times, members of majority groups have used legal or political methods to challenge the use of special measures to assist disadvantaged groups. Often, these challenges are brought by individuals who argue that the introduction of special measures to assist disadvantaged groups discriminates unfairly against them. Measures giving preferential treatment to disadvantaged groups in employment have proved to be particularly controversial. As a result, a variety of legal controls have developed in different states which attempt to clarify when positive action can be used. This paper discusses a) why positive action has become an important element of anti-discrimination law and policy; b) what type of measures are used as part of positive action initiatives; and c) the legal controls that exist in this complex area of law. Particular reference will be made to the law of the European Union, the United Kingdom and the United States to develop key arguments.

2. THE LIMITS OF ORDINARY ANTI-DISCRIMINATION LAW

To understand why the use of positive action may be necessary, it is useful to understand the nature of the disadvantages that affect women and members of other groups which are under-represented in employment and other areas of social life. Sometimes, direct discrimination may take place, where a women or a member of another disadvantaged group is not employed or promoted or selected for a benefit because of their gender, ethnic group or social status. Indirect discrimination may also exist, where the application of apparently neutral and fair criteria to distinguish between individuals may have a disproportionately negative impact upon members of a disadvantaged group which cannot be justified. Both these forms of discrimination can have very bad consequences for members of disadvantaged groups, who often face social exclusion and the denial of equal treatment as a result.

Consequently, anti-discrimination law usually prohibits both these forms of discrimination. Individuals are encouraged to bring legal actions if they have suffered direct or indirect discrimination, and offenders are punished through the civil law by the imposition of damage awards and other forms of legal remedy. By imposing this prohibition on such forms of discrimination, anti-discrimination law has been very successful in many countries, and in particular in Europe and North America. It has altered the behaviour of many employers and public bodies, changed social attitudes towards disadvantaged groups and prevented many forms of discrimination.[1]

However, it is also important to understand that using anti-discrimination law to eliminate the disadvantages faced by women and other under-represented groups may only be capable of bringing about a limited amount of social change.

---

[1] For an analysis of the effectiveness of anti-discrimination law in the UK, see B. Hepple, M. Coussey, and T. Choudhury, *Equality: A New Framework: Report of the Independent Review of the Enforcement of UK Anti-Discrimination Legislation,* (Oxford: Hart Publishing, 2000), para. 1.33.

Discriminatory attitudes are often deeply embedded in society. Anti-discrimination law prohibits direct and indirect discrimination: however, it cannot stop discrimination where there is no clear evidence that discrimination has occurred, or where individuals are not willing to complaint about the negative treatment they have suffered. Even if an individual may wish to complain about discrimination, the financial and social pressures to conform may be so great that the individual may decide not to proceed with the case.[2]

If there is a lack of individual complainants willing to bring an action in particular areas of economic activity or social life, then anti-discrimination law may have very little impact in those particular areas. For example, there have been problems with sex discrimination for some time in the huge financial services industry in London. Female employees of leading investment banks have often complained of sexist attitudes and resentment of pregnant workers taking time off.[3] However, until recently, very few cases of sex discrimination were brought in relation to gender equality issues within the City of London financial services sector. This has begun to change, with some female investment bankers receiving very large damage awards (including awards of over one million UK pounds sterling) for sex discrimination. However, victims of discrimination still appear slow to come forward with complaints, due to social pressures.

In addition, individuals complaining of discrimination may have great difficulty in establishing a clear case under anti-discrimination legislation. This is particularly true when it comes to indirect discrimination, where the law is complex and proving facts may be difficult. This can discourage use of anti-discrimination law.[4] Even if an action is successful, the remedies that an individual can obtain may be limited to redressing the immediate wrong: often, wider changes to how an organisation works, which may benefit more persons than just the individual victim who brought the discrimination case, will not be required under anti-discrimination law. This can seriously limit its impact.[5]

However, deeper problems may also exist. The views and expectations of employers, public bodies and other organisations will often be shaped by dominant social assumptions and stereotypes. Employers may have a clear idea of how a 'normal' employee is supposed to look and behave: this may result in candidates from dominant social groups being selected in preference to less obvious candidates who may be equally as qualified. Organisations may look for potential employees to be from similar backgrounds as the senior managers of

---

[2] See S. Fredman, *Discrimination Law,* (Oxford: Oxford University Press, 2001), p. 165. See also S. Fredman and E. Szyszczak, 'Interaction of Race and Gender', in B. Hepple and E. Szyszczak, *Discrimination: The Limits of the Law,* (London: Mansell, 1992), pp. 214-26.

[3] See the Fawcett Society, *Sexism in the City,* (London: Fawcett Society, 2007).

[4] See N. Bamforth, M. Malik and C. O'Cinneide, *Discrimination Law: Theory and Context,* (London: Sweet & Maxwell, 2008), Chs. 6 and 7.

[5] S. Fredman, *supra* note 2, pp. 170-73.

the organisation: in this way, the dominance of particular social groups will be 'replicated', with other groups being left out in the cold. A man from a dominant ethnic group who is also from traditionally successful socio-economic background will often succeed where a woman or a person from a more disadvantaged background will not: this is a problem in most human societies.

Disadvantaged groups may also lack the social capital and access to networks of influence that members of dominant groups may possess.[6] For example, members of ethnic minorities, or persons with disabilities, or those from particular socio-economic backgrounds may find it difficult to access top universities as a result of educational and cultural barriers: this in turn may make it very difficult for those groups to access good jobs or enter positions of influence. Assumptions, expectations and stereotypes about how women and members of under-represented groups behave and act may cause them severe disadvantage, often in subtle ways that will not make it possible to bring a case under anti-discrimination law. For example, in European states, an employer might assume that a Muslim woman from a traditional religious background would not wish to do particular types of work, or to meet with men in certain circumstances, and decide not to employ her: as a result, she might lose out on the opportunity to prove her ability just because of casual assumptions and stereotypes.

Other problems may exist. Disadvantaged groups often suffer from neglect by central government and local authorities, often caused by lack of understanding of their specific needs, and the failure to take into account their particular circumstances. This neglect is often due to the limited participation of members of these disadvantaged groups in decision-making processes.[7] This problem can occur in both the public and private sectors, and can unfairly limit their opportunities to participate. For example, the lack of persons with disabilities at senior decision-making levels within most public and private organisations has lead to the needs of disabled people being ignored in most societies for a long time. Also, where there are very few women and members of disadvantaged groups participating in particular areas of social activity, this can result in these areas becoming very unwelcoming to potential entrants from unusual or new backgrounds. The experience from North America and Europe is that it is difficult for minorities or women to enter into areas of employment or social activity which are completely dominated by men or members of dominant groups. The jokes, customs, practices and behaviour of those already in the organisation or involved in the activity in question may deliberately or unconsciously exclude newcomers.

---

[6] For the idea of 'social capital', see P. Bourdieu, 'The Forms of Capital', in A. Halsey, H. Lauder, P. Brown & A. Stuart Wells (eds.) *Education: Culture, Economy and Society*, (Oxford: Oxford University Press, 1997), pp. 46-58.

[7] See S. Fredman, *supra* note 2, pp. 22–23.

There also may be a lack of 'role models', i.e. successful individuals from disadvantaged groups participating in particular activities or organisations, or employed in senior positions. If such 'role models' exist, this can encourage members of disadvantaged groups to enter the organisation or activity in question. British and American universities often have special policies which encourage and support members of disadvantaged groups to register as students, in the hope that this will encourage other members of such groups also to enter university. However, if no such 'role models' exist, this may severely discourage individuals from disadvantaged groups attempting to enter what will often appear to be hostile or alien environments.

All of these factors explain why discrimination and disadvantage may persist in societies which have strong anti-discrimination laws. Collectively, they are often described as 'structural' forms of inequality, because they involve underlying social structures rather than individual acts of discrimination. Alternatively, the term 'institutional discrimination' is also sometimes used, as many of these factors relate to how institutions work and the influence played by the culture of public and private institutions.

The existence of these structural or institutional factors helps to explain why 'ordinary' anti-discrimination law will not always succeed in eliminating discrimination and disadvantage. As already discussed, anti-discrimination law has had great successes in Europe and North America over the last forty years, in particular in the context of gender equality. However, the primary focus of such law is on securing equal treatment for individuals. Structural forms of inequality often cannot be addressed using anti-discrimination law.[8]

This also explains why it is often necessary to take special measures to promote equality and to remove the disadvantages faced by some social groups. Women, disabled persons, ethnic minorities and other disadvantaged groups face many obstacles: giving preferential treatment to these groups in certain circumstances may assist them to overcome these obstacles. Also, disadvantaged groups may also suffer from a long history of discrimination and social exclusion. This can mean that they lack education, employment and state support, which may keep them in poverty or poor socio-economic conditions, which can make their disadvantaged position worse. This cycle can be very difficult to break. Social policy in Europe is increasingly directed towards finding ways of combating social exclusion.[9] As part of this policy development, it has become apparent that achieving progress requires that special measures are taken to ensure socially excluded groups are able to participate in decision-making by public authorities, as well as in education, employment and other important areas of social life. Without such participation, social exclusion will

---

[8] *Ibid*, pp. 7–11. See also J. Squires, *Gender in Political Theory*, (Cambridge: Polity Press, 1999).

[9] See H. Collins, 'Discrimination, Equality and Social Inclusion', (2003) 66/1 *Modern Law Review*, pp. 16-43.

remain a persistent problem. Active steps to promote greater equality are required.

3. WHAT IS POSITIVE ACTION?

The term 'positive action' can describe a wide variety of policies and initiatives. Sometimes positive action is understood as meaning preferential treatment for minorities, women and other disadvantaged groups. Giving preference to candidates from disadvantaged groups may be an important part of any positive action policy. However, positive action strategies can take a variety of forms, which may not always involve the use of preferential treatment.[10] Any well-designed positive action strategy will probably attempt to make use of several different forms of positive action. Different strategies may use different forms of positive action at different times, depending upon the nature of the disadvantages at issue and the relevant socio-economic and political context in question.

A broad definition of positive action could therefore include all measures which seek by means of positive steps to alter existing social practices so as to eliminate patterns of group exclusion and disadvantage.[11] Within this wide definition, Christopher McCrudden, Professor of Human Rights Law at the University of Oxford, has identified five basic categories of positive action.[12]

Category 1: Eradicating Prohibited Discrimination

The first category consists of positive measures to eradicate discrimination, which involve organisations taking active steps to identify and put an end to any policies which cause discrimination. In practical terms, this type of positive action will often involve the use of regular reviews of how an organisation selects its employees, conducts promotion and does its business. The aim of these measures is to put a stop to any discrimination which is taking place, or which may take place in the future. The organisation may change its employment policy, or how it consults with its workers, or how it provides goods and services to the public. These measures often help to eradicate direct and indirect discrimination: however, they may do little to eliminate the more complex problems of structural or institutional discrimination.

---

[10] C. McCrudden, 'Rethinking Positive Action', (1986) 15 *Industrial Law Journal*, pp. 219-243.
[11] This broad definition is adopted from C. Bell, A. Hegarty and S. Livingstone, 'The Enduring Controversy: Developments on Affirmative Action Law in North America', (1996) *International Journal of Discrimination and the Law*, pp. 233- 234.
[12] C. McCrudden, *supra* note 10.

Category 2: Purposefully Inclusive Policies

The second category involves the use of polices and practices which do not give preferential treatment to disadvantaged groups on the basis of their gender, ethnic origin or other specific distinguishing feature, but instead use general criteria as a basis for giving special assistance. For example, public authorities may provide special measures to assist unemployed persons back into work, or give special support to schools in a particular area which has many poor families. These policies may however indirectly benefit disadvantaged groups: for example, polices in the US which give special assistance to schools with a large proportion of immigrant or poor children will mainly benefit the Afro-American and Hispanic minority groups.

Governments often make use of such policies when they do not wish to be seen as giving special treatment to certain social groups. However, their disadvantage is that their general nature means that they may not benefit the groups most in need of special assistance. For example, in the UK, different ethnic groups have different social problems: the British Pakistani community (who come originally from Pakistan and who are overwhelmingly Islamic in religion) have particular problems arising from anti-Muslim prejudice and low numbers of their female population participating in employment that other ethnic minorities, such as the British Indian community (who usually come from wealthier backgrounds and from a variety of religious backgrounds) do not.[13] General measures aimed at poorer communities, or in schools in particular areas, might not address the specific problems faced by the British Pakistani community.

Category 3: Outreach

The third category involves the use of 'outreach' programmes. These are strategies which public or private bodies put into effect with the aim of attracting more applications from disadvantaged groups for employment, promotion or entry into training or educational courses. This could include the use of targeted advertising, the establishment of special links with community groups, schools and ethnic minority organisations, and careful presentation by the body reaching out to disadvantaged groups to ensure that it is seen as open to diversity and applications from individuals from disadvantaged groups. Public bodies may also establish special outreach programmes to make sure that the health, transport, welfare and educational services that they provide are being used by disadvantaged groups. For example, public authorities in London, which is a very diverse and multi-cultural city, provide information on how individuals can

---

[13] See the statistics as to comparative disadvantage among the UK's minority groups contained in *Fairness and Freedom: The Final Report of the Equalities Review Panel* (London: Cabinet Office, 2007).

access the public services in a wide variety of languages, including both Mandarin and Cantonese.

Other forms of outreach could involve the 'setting aside' or reservation of places at particular stages of the recruitment process (such as ensuring that a woman is always interviewed for every vacancy or promotion opportunity), or providing special forms of training for members of disadvantaged groups. For example, the UK Home Office, the central government department in charge of policing, immigration and internal security, has established a special scheme under which employees from ethnic minority groups are given special training in how to apply for senior positions within the department.[14] Special targets have also been established for senior management, who are encouraged to ensure that a certain proportion of senior staff come from minority backgrounds, with some success.[15] The advantage of such outreach and development schemes is that they can compensate for the disadvantages and obstacles faced by members of disadvantaged groups: their weakness is that such schemes can encourage participation by disadvantaged groups, but cannot guarantee it, or ensure definite results.

Category 4: Preferences

Fourthly, giving preferential treatment of members of disadvantaged groups in employment (and at times in education) is an important category of positive action. A variety of ways may exist for giving preference to individuals from disadvantaged groups in recruitment, promotion and selection for senior management. In some countries, it is possible to reserve posts or positions for women, disabled persons or members of a particular minority group. Alternatively, a person's gender, ethnic background, disability or any other personal characteristic which links them to a disadvantaged group may be a factor which can be taken into account in recruitment and promotion decisions. For example, a company may decide that it does not have enough women in senior management: as a result, it may decide that a person's gender can be taken into account when interviewing candidates, and if two or more candidates are more or less equally qualified for the post in question, then preference can be given to a female candidate. This is known as applying preferential treatment as a 'tie-break'. Preferential treatment can also involve taking a candidate's link to a disadvantaged group into account as a 'plus-factor', i.e. it acts as a positive factor in favour of a candidate, which takes its place among the other factors that apply.

---

[14] See House of Commons Debates (*Hansard*), 3 November 2005, col. 1253W.
[15] See *Employment Monitoring Report 2006/07* (London: UK Home Office, 2007), available at http://www.homeoffice.gov.uk/documents/employment-monitoring-report.pdf (last accessed 15 May 2008).

The considerable advantage that preferential treatment has over other types of positive action is that it usually guarantees a successful outcome. Often, preferential treatment is introduced when other forms of positive action have failed, because it is effective. For example, in Norway, years of positive action using alternative strategies has resulted in a considerable degree of gender equality throughout society. However, women remained very under-represented at the highest level on the management boards of private companies and public bodies. Therefore, in 2003, the Norwegian Parliament passed legislation that established that if companies did not take steps to ensure that their boards of management were made up of 40% female members within two years, companies would be legally required to implement this quota or face legal sanctions. The Parliament acted on its threat in 2006 after this target was not reached by many private companies, requiring all company boards to meet this quota by 2008 or else be fined or dissolved.[16]

The disadvantage with preferential treatment measures, which may be compulsory and imposed by legislation (with as the Norwegian law) or voluntary (as is more often the case in Europe and North America), is that it can provoke backlash in the form of legal and political challenges. Individuals from non-disadvantaged groups often allege that this form of positive action constitutes discrimination against them. Preferential treatment may also widen the gaps between different groups, increasing resentment and hostility, and may also be abused. (See the discussion below on the justification for positive action.)

Category 5: Redefining Merit

The fifth category of positive action identified by McCrudden consists of attempts to 'redefine merit', that is, to examine and redefine the criteria that employers use for filling posts (or that educational institutions use for selecting students) in such a way as to ensure greater participation from disadvantaged groups. Often, the manner in which the desired qualifications for a post are defined by an employer will exclude many potential applicants from under-represented groups. For example, an employer may decide that a post involves very long and irregular hours and assesses candidates on the basis that they must be able to work such hours. This may often disadvantage many female applicants, who may have child care responsibilities, and other applicants who care for older family members. However, this requirement may not actually be necessary: perhaps the work-load for the post could be rearranged or adjusted in some way? Current conceptions of 'merit' may mask stereotypical assumptions and ignore other ways as to how a particular job could be performed.

---

[16] For more information, see the comprehensive outline of the legislation available (in English) at the website of the Norwegian Ministry of Children and Equality, http://www.regjeringen.no/en/dep/bld/Topics/Equality/rules-on-gender-representation-on-compan.html?id=416864 (last accessed 12 May 2008).

It may therefore be possible to reconceptualise what qualities are required for many posts, and to redefine our concepts of 'merit' in a way that opens up employment and education to members of disadvantaged groups. In the US, as discussed below, the Supreme Court has recognised that having a diverse student body can improve the educational experience of students.[17] As a result, universities now may take the ethnic and socio-economic background of a student into account in admission decisions and treat membership of an under-represented group as a positive factor, on the basis that admitting more members of under-represented groups into the student body will improve its diversity and therefore the overall standard of education.

It may also be the case that being from a disadvantaged group may be a positive reason for appointing someone to a particular post. For example, for Western countries concerned about Islamist terrorist attacks, it is useful to have Muslim police officers, who may understand the background political context and work with Muslim minority communities in a better way than would other police officers. Therefore, being Muslim may be treated in some countries as a positive personal characteristic in recruiting members of the police and security services.

Having a certain proportion of senior figures in government and in elected bodies from disadvantaged groups may improve decision-making. Therefore, many European states in particular have reserved places in elected assemblies for members of particular ethnic groups, or require political parties to select a certain number of female candidates.[18] Some countries consider that the social imperative of combating the exclusion faced by disadvantaged groups is so compelling as to justify requiring very extensive inclusion of members of disadvantaged groups within education and employment. For example, both the Indian Constitution and subsequent legislation passed by the New Delhi Parliament make positive action in favour of the 'disadvantaged castes' within India society a legal priority. A certain number of seats in the federal and state legislatures are reserved for candidates from lower castes, as are places in the leading Indian universities and in the public service.[19]

---

[17] See *Grutter v Bollinger* 539 US (2003).

[18] See C. O'Cinneide and M. Russell, 'Positive Action to Promote Women in Politics: Some European Comparisons', (2003) 53 *International Comparative Law Quarterly*, pp. 587-614.

[19] See Articles 14-17 of the Indian Constitution: see also Constitution (Scheduled Tribes) Order 1950; Constitution (Scheduled Castes) Order 1950; Scheduled Castes and Scheduled Tribes Orders (Amendment) Act 1976; Constitution (Sixty-Fifth Amendment) Act 1990.

4. HOW AND WHEN POSITIVE ACTION IS USED

Positive action strategies can therefore take a variety of forms, often combining elements of several or even all of these different categories. Many of these forms of positive action have been used by different countries at different times. The use of such special measures often predates the introduction of anti-discrimination law. For example, many European and North American states introduced employment quotas and reserved particular posts for disabled persons in the aftermath of the First and Second World Wars, because of the very large number of seriously wounded survivors of both wars.[20]

Other forms of positive action measures were introduced initially in the USA in the late 1960s and early 1970s to remedy the wide-spread segregation of the Afro-American community. Many of these 'affirmative action' measures were originally introduced by court order in order to provide a remedy for direct or indirect discrimination.[21] However, the use of positive action measures in the USA expanded beyond their use as remedies in discrimination cases. A range of positive action measures are now used, and form a key part of the post-1960s drive to remove segregation and to ensure equality of treatment for Afro-Americans and other disadvantaged groups.

Examples of such positive action measures include the use of preferential treatment to benefit particular disadvantaged groups in university admission procedures. Preferential treatment for Afro-American and other under-represented groups is also common in awarding public sector supply contracts and in recruiting staff in the public sector and armed forces. There is ongoing political controversy about the use of preferential treatment, which is discussed in the next section. However, the strength of support in the US for the use of positive action can be seen in the support for such measures expressed by leading US politicians, as well as the armed forces and leading US business corporations, in the arguments submitted to the US Supreme Court in the case of *Grutter v Bollinger*.[22]

Within the EU, there is a wide diversity of approaches to the use of positive action. Differences exist not only between different member states, but also within member states in how positive action is used to address different types of

---

[20] See L. Waddington, 'Reassessing the Employment of People with Disabilities in Europe From Quotas to Anti-Discrimination Laws', (1996) 18 *Comparative Labour Law Review*, pp. 62-101.

[21] US legislation permits courts to issue 'consent decrees', where discriminating companies agree to take positive action measures to remedy the damage caused by their discriminatory policies. The US Justice Department under the Violent Crime Control and Law Enforcement Act 1994 may enter into consent decrees with municipal police departments alleged to have engaged in a 'pattern or practice' of conduct that infringes upon the civil rights of its persons as afforded by federal state and local laws. See 42 USC 14141 (Su IV 1998).

[22] 539 US (2003).

disadvantage.[23] Certain general pan-European trends can be detected. Generally, EC law permits, rather than requires, the use of certain forms of positive action (see below). Thus what form positive action takes in each country is decided by the member states themselves, rather than by the EU.

National laws usually permit more extensive positive action to be used to benefit disabled persons than for any other form of disadvantage: this reflects the extensive use of employment quotas in the post-war period.[24] The use of 'strong' forms of positive action, including preferential treatment, is relatively common when it comes to ensuring greater gender equality. For example, many German states have introduced 'tie-break' requirements that women be given preference where more than one candidate can satisfy the recruitment criteria for posts in the public service. These measures largely came about because of the influence of a major expert report which advocated that the German public service should become a 'model' of employment equality.[25]

In France, a failure to ensure a fair representation of women in the lists of candidates selected by political parties for elections can result in the loss of state funding. A variety of measures have been introduced in other European states to either permit or require political parties to take positive action measures in selecting female candidates.[26]

In contrast, positive action outside the gender and disability context is less common. In the UK, public authorities are subject to 'positive equality duties', which require them to monitor the impact of their policies on disadvantaged groups and to take action to remove obstacles to equality of treatment.[27] Other forms of positive action directed towards removing the disadvantages faced by minority groups are also increasingly common in the public and private sectors.

In Northern Ireland, a part of the UK which has been subject to severe inter-religious and ethnic violence between Protestant and Catholic minorities, a set of 'fair employment duties' have been imposed upon all private and public sector bodies who employ more than a fixed amount of employees. These duties require employers to monitor how many Catholics and Protestants are employed in their workforce and to take measures to remedy the under-representation of any group. These 'fair employment duties' have had considerable impact in improving the

---

[23] See the discussion on the differences between member states when it comes to positive action on the grounds of ethnic origin in D. Caruso, 'Limits of the Classic Method: Positive Action in the European Union After the New Equality Directives', (2003) 44 *Harvard International Law Journal*, pp. 331-386.

[24] For an account of the use of quotas for disabled persons, and the problems inherent in such schemes, see L. Waddington, *supra* note 20.

[25] N. Colneric, 'Making Equality Law More Effective: Lessons From the German Experience', (1996) 3 *Cardozo Women's Law Journal*, pp. 229-250. See also D. Schiek, 'Sex Equality after *Kalanke* and *Marschall*', (1998) 4/2 *European Law Journal*, pp. 148-166.

[26] See C. O'Cinneide and M. Russell, *supra* note 18.

[27] See C. O'Cinneide, 'Positive Action and the Limits of the Law', (2006) *Maastricht Journal of European and Comparative Law*, pp. 351-365.

position of the historically disadvantaged Catholic minority.[28] The Northern Irish measures have generated better results than many other types of positive action approaches used elsewhere.[29]

In some states, private employers may be required to adopt positive action measures if they wish to tender for public sector contracts. In the US in 1961, President Kennedy introduced this form of positive action, requiring government contractors not only to abstain from unlawful discrimination, but also to increase the numbers of racial minorities in their workforces. Later extended by Executive Order 11246, these 'contract compliance requirements' are enforced by the US Office of Federal Contract Compliance Programs and apply to about 300,000 private sector contractors.[30]

This form of positive action has also been applied (in various forms) in Canada,[31] Australia,[32] and South Africa, where positive action in the aftermath of the racism of the previous apartheid state is common.[33] In the EU, recent modifications to the rules which govern how public bodies can make contracts with private companies for supplies and services have increased the ability of public bodies across Europe to use similar 'contract compliance' measures.[34]

Another important form of positive action should also be mentioned. Various 'mainstreaming' policies or 'diversity strategies' have been implemented in the EU by public authorities. It can be unclear what 'mainstreaming' means: the word is prone to a variety of interpretation.[35] However, it has been defined by the Council of Europe as the incorporation of a concern with achieving equality in all public sector policies at all levels and at all stages in policy making.[36] McCrudden has identified two main components of effective mainstreaming: 'impact assessment', which examines the impact of public policies on disadvantaged groups, and 'participation', which encourages

---

[28] See C. McCrudden, R. Ford, and A. Heath, 'Legal Regulation of Affirmative Action in Northern Ireland: An Empirical Assessment', (2004) 24/3 *Oxford Journal of Legal Studies,* pp. 363-415. Note also that the Police (Northern Ireland) Act 2000 requires that 50% of persons recruited to the NI Police Service as police trainees or support staff are to be Roman Catholics: these measures are intended to overcome the historic under-representation of Roman Catholics in the Northern Irish Police Service.

[29] See H. C. Jain, P. J. Sloane and F. M. Horwitz, *Employment Equity and Affirmative Action: An International Comparison,* (London: M.E. Sharpe, 2003).

[30] See further B Hepple, M. Coussey and T. Choudhury, *supra* note 1, p. 65.

[31] Employment Equity Act 1995.

[32] Equal Opportunity for Women in the Workplace Act 1999, amending and consolidating the Affirmative Action (Equal Employment Opportunity for Women) Act 1986.

[33] *Supra* note 31.

[34] See C. O'Cinneide, *Taking Equal Opportunities Seriously,* (London: Equality and Diversity Forum, 2003), Part VIII.

[35] See T. Rees, *Mainstreaming Equality in the European Union,* (London: Routledge, 1998).

[36] See *Gender Mainstreaming: Conceptual Framework, Methodology and Presentation of Good Practices,* Final Report of Activities of the Group of Specialists on Mainstreaming (EG-S-MS (98), (Strasbourg: Council of Europe, 1998).

the involvement of these groups in decision-making processes.[37] Mainstreaming as a strategy has attracted support from the UN, the EU, the Commonwealth Secretariat, ILO and OECD in recent years.[38] Almost all of the EU states, as well as the EU institutions, have implemented gender mainstreaming programmes of varying degrees of effectiveness and ambition. There have been also some limited attempts to mainstream disability issues into EU law and policy, but there has been no comprehensive cross-ground programme of equality mainstreaming.[39] Mainstreaming does clearly have great potential as a positive action strategy. However, a major problem with mainstreaming policies is that the implementation of effective mainstreaming often only happens when all the necessary ingredients of political good-will, organisational capacity, strong leadership and expert advice are in place.[40] This reflects a recurring experience in discrimination law: equality initiatives often have little impact in the absence of a clear legal framework regulating their use and strong political support.

In general, positive action measures can take different forms. Sometimes they are required by law. At other times, they can be introduced voluntarily by public or private bodies, if national law permits this. There is no fixed formula for automatic success.[41] Different measures have very different impact in different contexts. For a positive action strategy to be effective, it should be designed for the particular environment within which it will be applied, and have clear justifications, goals and targets.[42]

5. CRITICISMS OF POSITIVE ACTION

Experience from Canada, the Netherlands, the USA, Australia, the UK and elsewhere has shown that the success of positive action policies often depends upon the extent to which the justification and purpose for such measures is

---

[37] C. McCrudden, 'Mainstreaming Equality in the Governance of Northern Ireland', (1999) 22/4 *Fordham International Law Journal*, p. 22.

[38] See e.g. the discussion of mainstreaming in the Global Action Platform for Action that was agreed at the UN Fourth World Conference on Women in Beijing in 1995: *Global Platform for Action – Beijing*, (New York: United Nations Publishing, 1995). For a very comprehensive account of mainstreaming initiatives and best practice, see F. Mackay and K. Bilton, *Learning From Experience: Lessons in Mainstreaming Equal Opportunities*, (Edinburgh: Scottish Executive Social Research, 2003).

[39] See J. Shaw, *Mainstreaming Equality in European Union Law and Policy-Making*, (Brussels: European Network Against Racism, 2004).

[40] See J. Rubery et al, 'Gender Equality Still on the European Agenda – But For How Long?', (2003) 34 *Industrial Relations Journal*, pp. 477-97.

[41] See G. Stephanopoulos et al, *Affirmative Action Review Report to the President*, (Washington DC: White House, 1995), Parts 3 and 4.

[42] See J. S. Leonard, 'What Promises are Worth: The Impact of Affirmative Action Goals', (1985) 20 (1) *Journal of Human Resources*, pp. 3-20.

understood by the population at large.[43] Positive action measures are often be attacked, misunderstood or challenged through the courts or the political process. At times, positive action is regarded by some as involving unfair 'special treatment' for particular groups, or as an unjust manipulation of the normal rules of society. Sometimes, positive action is accused of being 'discrimination in reverse', on the basis that by giving special treatment to some groups, other groups are treated unequally and lose out in their turn. Where these criticisms of positive action become widely accepted, than courts, legislatures and policy makers often become reluctant to permit the use of special measures to assist disadvantaged groups.

Many forms of positive action do not require any particular justification. This is particularly true of policies which aim to root out prohibited discrimination, or to eliminate polices and practices which unfairly disadvantage particular groups. However, other forms of positive action can cause some conceptual difficulties, as they may involve preferential treatment for certain disadvantaged groups.

Also, positive action may involve the use of a factor such as a person's ethnic group or gender or religion to define the groups who receive special assistance. However, most of anti-discrimination law is concerned with trying to eliminate the use of these factors as a way of distinguishing between different people. As a result, positive action is sometimes criticised for using ways of classifying people which anti-discrimination law generally attempts to eliminate.

For example, when Afro-Americans are given preferential treatment in admission systems for US universities, some opponents of positive action argue that the use of their race and ethnic origin to identify Afro-Americans as a group requiring special assistance is not justified. They argue this on the basis that such forms of positive action involves the use of distinctions based on race and ethnicity which US anti-discrimination has spent decades attempting to prohibit. Also, opponents of positive action often suggest that the use of special measures to help disadvantaged groups maintains social distinctions between groups and contributes to the fracturing of society along religious, ethnic, racial and social lines.[44] Some critics also argue that positive action is a form of unhealthy 'social engineering', where governments attempt to change society using artificial and counter-productive policies.[45]

In contrast, supports of positive action argue that special measures are necessary to correct the structural discrimination aced by disadvantaged groups. The argument is also made that the use of positive action is justified by the goal of achieving real and substantive equality for all in society: the special treatment

---

[43] See the discussion in the various essays in C. Agocs (ed.), *Workplace Equality: International Perspectives on Legislation, Policy and Practice*, (Hague/London: Kluwer Law International, 2002).

[44] See B. Barry, *Culture and Equality*, (Cambridge, MA: Harvard University Press, 2001).

[45] See M. Abram, 'Affirmative Action: Fair Shakers and Social Engineers', (1986) 99/6 *Harvard Law Review*, pp. 1312-26.

of disadvantaged groups compensates for and redresses the persistent inequalities to which they are subject.[46] Supporters of positive action also argue that positive action need not in any way undermine the quality of job performance or of employees, if applied properly.[47]

Much of this debate centres round the question of the legitimacy of the use of 'suspect' characteristics such as ethnicity and gender to decide who benefits from positive action. At first glance, the standard approach of anti-discrimination law should be to treat equality as involving a right to have decisions that affect the individual taken without reference to particular personal characteristics such as race, sex and so on. This has been described as an 'anti-classification' approach: it assumes that anti-discrimination law should aim to eliminate the use of particular forms of suspect distinctions.[48]

However, supports of positive action often counter these arguments by suggesting that the use of positive action is justified where the lack of participation by disadvantaged groups in important areas of social activity may contribute to the social exclusion of these groups. This is sometimes known as the 'anti-subordination' approach, as it approves of the use of positive action where necessary to remedy the subordination of disadvantaged groups within society.

Positive action is also sometimes justified on the basis that it ensures greater social 'diversity', or compensates for 'past injustice'. Both these two particular rationales for positive action are questionable. Attempting to use the concept 'diversity' to justify special treatment for particular groups runs the risk of opening the door for every social group to make a claim for support. Arguments based on 'past injustice' may fail where no clear link exists between the past discrimination and the current individuals or groups making the claim. In general, the argument that positive action can provide an effective remedy for group disadvantage may be the strongest case in its favour.

The argument can also be made that it makes little sense to treat positive action as being equivalent to unfair discriminatory measures that attack the dignity of disadvantaged groups. Elizabeth Anderson has criticised the argument that states must refrain from using 'suspect' characteristics and adhere rigidly to the anti-classification principle. She argues that anti-discrimination law is built around the idea of stopping the use of 'suspect' classifications in a negative or

---

[46] See e.g. R. Dworkin, *A Matter of Principle,* (Cambridge, MA: Harvard University Press, 1985); G. Ezorsky, *Racism and Justice: The Case for Affirmative Action,* (Ithaca, N.Y.: Cornell University Press, 1991).

[47] H.J. Holzer and D. Neumark, 'What Does Affirmative Action Do?', (2000) 53 *Industrial and Labour Relations Review*, pp. 240-66.

[48] J. Balkin and R. Siegel, 'The American Civil Rights Tradition: Anticlassification or Antisubordination?', (2004) 58 *U. Miami L. Rev.* pp. 9-33.

harmful manner.[49] Anderson concludes by discussing the use of positive action to correct the disadvantages faced by Afro-Americans in the USA.

> There is no contradiction...in using race-conscious means to eradicate the causes of race-based disadvantages. Surgery is often needed to repair knife wounds.[50]

Another leading US academic, Professor Owen Fiss, has similarly argued that 'affirmative action' measures that aim to break down what he describes as 'caste' patterns of disadvantage and subordination should not be treated as discriminatory measures requiring special justification, but rather as special remedial measures.[51] The leading UK academic in this area, Professor Sandra Fredman, has similarly argued that the use of positive action is legitimate and does not involve discrimination at all. She suggests that such types of positive action can be necessary to break down structural forms of indirect discrimination, and can therefore be conceptualised as a *remedy* for discrimination.[52]

In South Africa, equality legislation prohibits 'unfair discrimination' rather than 'discrimination' and defines inequality not in terms of making classifications upon suspect grounds but as constituting a denial of dignity and the imposition of harmful and demeaning burdens upon particular groups. Therefore, positive action that uses 'suspect' ways of classifying people, such as their race, will be fair where it is directed towards removing group disadvantage and is objectively justified. Section 15(2) of the Canadian Charter adopts a similar approach.

Other theories have suggested alternative means of justifying positive action. The British Professor Hugh Collins has suggested that the goal of achieving 'social inclusion' for all groups in society justifies positive action.[53] Others, such as the Canadian philosophers Charles Taylor and Iris Marion Young, have argued for special measures to accommodate the different groups in society.[54]

All of these arguments in favour of positive action are based around the central idea that positive action is a useful method of promoting full equality in practice for disadvantaged groups.[55] However, even strong supporters of positive

---

[49] E. Anderson, 'Integration, Affirmative Action and Strict Scrutiny', (2002) 77 *New York University Law Review*, pp. 1195-1271.
[50] *Ibid*, p. 1270.
[51] O. Fiss, 'Groups and the Equal Protection Clause', (1976) 5 *Phil & Pub Aff*, pp. 107-177, p. 126.
[52] See S. Fredman, *supra* note 2.
[53] H. Collins, *supra* note 9.
[54] See I. M. Young, *Democracy and Inclusion,* (Princeton, N.J.: Princeton University Press, 2000).
[55] Research has shown in a number of different public and private sector contexts that concentrating upon complying with anti-discrimination norms alone yields limited results: patterns of inequality and exclusion are extremely difficult to break down unless positive action is taken. See H. C. Jain, P. J. Sloane and F. M. Horwitz, *supra* note 29.

action often accept that the use of positive action should have to be shown to be objectively justified and only be maintained for the minimum period necessary to achieve its goals. There may be important instrumental reasons for this. Even positive action measures that set out to remedy disadvantage may lack a firm rational basis, or be manipulated to support special interests or cliques, or may unduly penalise others outside of the disadvantaged group in question. There may be an interest in not causing unnecessary tensions between different social groups. All of these reasons indicate why it is necessary to examine the impact of positive action measures, and to maintain some legal controls on their use.

Some states maintain tight controls on the use of positive action, preferring a 'formal equality' or 'anti-classification approach', where the use of positive action is kept to a minimum. Other states adopt a 'substantive equality' or 'anti-subordination' approach, which is much more welcoming to the use of positive action. The trend in most North American and European states is towards the greater use of positive action measures, as it is in India, South African and elsewhere. International human rights law also increasingly recognises the importance of positive action, while often requiring that the use of special measures to assist particular groups be temporary in nature and kept under review. This position is also adopted by many states.

6. EU LAW AND POSITIVE ACTION

EU equality directives as interpreted by the European Court of Justice (ECJ) permit the use of positive action in certain circumstances.[56] The case of *Kalanke*, which was the ECJ's initial decision on the use of preferential treatment as a form of positive action, concerned a regulation of the Bremen state government which gave automatic priority to a woman over an equally qualified man in recruitment to ranks within the government service where women were generally under-represented. This regulation was challenged by an opponent before the ECJ on the grounds that it was incompatible with EC law's prohibition on sex discrimination.[57] Article 2(4) of the Equal Treatment Directive 1976 provided that 'this Directive shall be without prejudice to measures to promote equal opportunity for men and women, in particular by removing existing inequalities

---

[56] Mark Bell has argued that a 'patchwork of models' of equality has developed within EU equality law and policy, made up of three main strands: the standard anti-discrimination approach, a newer attachment to substantive equality, and a desire to manage diversity. See M. Bell, 'The Right to Equality and Non-Discrimination', in T. Hervey and J. Kenner (eds.), *Economic and Social Rights under the EC Charter of Fundamental Rights: A Legal Perspective,* (Oxford: Hart Publishing, 2003), p. 91.

[57] ECJ, 17 October 1995, Case C-450/93 *Kalanke v Freie Hansestadt Bremen* [1995] ECR I-3051.

which affect women's opportunities…'[58] However, the ECJ considered that the use of this type of preferential treatment for female applicants was a departure from the general principle of equal treatment on the grounds of gender. The Court was concerned that the manner in which the regulation gave automatic reference to women over men in certain circumstances appeared to involve direct sex discrimination against men. Therefore, despite the fact that the regulation was intended to remedy disadvantages faced by women as a result of past discrimination, the ECJ held that the regulation fell outside the scope of permissible positive action.

This judgment by the ECJ was subject to strong criticism by NGOs, academics and some politicians.[59] However, the ECJ in subsequent decisions has shown a greater willingness to accept the use of positive action.[60] In the case of *Marschall*,[61] the ECJ took the view that the positive action at issue in this case was compatible with the gender equality principle. This case involved another regulation passed by a German state government, which made provision for female candidates to be given preferential treatment in recruitment to the state government service, but only where the men and women candidates affected have been individually assessed and found to have equivalent qualifications. The ECJ considered that the requirement for individual assessment of each candidate meant that women were not receiving automatic preference over men, as the possibility existed that a man could always show that he was a superior candidate to others and deserved to be appointed. Therefore, the Court held that principle of gender equality was not breached.

This more permissive approach was also adopted in the case of *Badeck*. Here, another German state law required that preferential treatment for women in the initial stages of recruitment prior to the actual hiring decision: for example, places were reserved for female candidates at the final job interviews. However,

---

[58] This was supported by Recommendation 84/635/EC that encouraged the Member States to adopt positive action policies to promote a better balance between the sexes in employment. The decision in ECJ, 13 December 1989, Case C-322/88 *Grimaldi v Fonds de Maladies Professionnelles* [1989] ECR 4407 confirmed that the Recommendation was an interpretative guide to Art 2 (4).

[59] The Commission proposed an amendment to the Equal Treatment Directive along the following lines: 'Possible measures shall include the giving of preference, as regards access to employment or promotion, to a member of the under represented sex, provided that such measures do not preclude the assessment of the particular circumstances of an individual case.' This amendment was subsequently rejected. See COM (96) 88 final, and (97/C 30/19) OJ C.30/57 30 January 1997.

[60] See C. Tobler, 'Positive Action under the Revised Second Equal Treatment Directive', in AFFA and EWLA (ed.) *L'égalité entre femmes et hommes et la vie profesionnelle; Le point sur les développements actuels en Europe*, (Paris: Dalloz, 2003), pp. 59-92 for an excellent analysis of this gradual shift in position.

[61] ECJ, 11 November 1997, Case C-409/95, *Helmut Marschall v Land Nordrhein Westfalen* [1887] ECR I – 6363.

the ECJ decided that these requirements did not involve giving women automatic preference over men and so this form of positive action was acceptable.[62]

After the *Marschall* and *Badeck* decisions, the ECJ appears to have established that positive action to compensate for past disadvantages is permissible when used to distinguish between more or less equally qualified candidates, provided that an opportunity for individual merit assessment is always available. The provisions of the Race Equality,[63] Framework Equality[64] and revised Gender Equality Directives,[65] all agreed since 2000, now give wide scope to member states to use positive action. Article 141(4) of the EC Treaty as inserted by the Treaty of Amsterdam[66] makes express provision for the use of positive action. Article 23 of the EU Charter of Fundamental Rights also recognises the legitimacy of positive action.[67] These provisions establish that positive action is permissible when it is used to compensate for specific disadvantages faced by particular groups.

The new shift towards a greater embrace of the substantive equality approach can be seen in the ECJ decisions in the cases of *Schnorbus*[68] and

---

[62] ECJ, 28 March 2000, Case C–158/97, *Badeck v Landesanwalt beim Staatsgerichtshof des Landes Hessen* [1999] ECR I – 1875.

[63] See Article 5 Council Directive 2000/43/EC implementing the principle of equal treatment between persons irrespective of racial or ethnic origin: 'With a view to ensuring full equality in practice, the principle of equal treatment shall not prevent any Member State from maintaining or adopting specific measures to prevent or compensate for disadvantages linked to racial or ethnic origin.'

[64] See Article 7(1) Council Directive 2000/78/EC establishing a general framework for equal treatment in employment and occupation: 'With a view to ensuring full equality in practice, the principle of equal treatment shall not prevent any Member State from maintaining or adopting specific measures to prevent or compensate for disadvantages linked to any of the grounds referred to in Article 1.'

[65] See Article 3 of Directive 2006/54/EC of 5 July 2006 on the implementation of the principle of equal opportunities and equal treatment of men and women in matters of employment and occupation: 'Member States may maintain or adopt measures within the meaning of Article 141(4) of the Treaty with a view to ensuring full equality in practice between men and women in working life'. See also Article 6 of the Council Directive 2004/113/EC of 13 December 2004 implementing the principle of equal treatment between men and women in the access to and supply of goods and services.

[66] See Article 141(4) EC Treaty: 'With a view to ensuring full equality in practice between men and women in working life, the principle of equal treatment shall not prevent any Member State from maintaining or adopting measures providing for specific advantages in order to make it easier for the under-represented sex to pursue a vocational activity or to prevent or compensate for disadvantages in professional careers.'

[67] See Article 23(2) of the Charter: 'The principle of equality shall not prevent the maintenance or adoption of measures providing for specific advantages in favour of the under-represented sex.'

[68] ECJ, 7 December 2000, Case 79/99, *Julia Schnorbus v Land Hessen* [2000] ECR I-10997.

Briheche.[69] In these cases, the Court accepted that wide discretion should be given to states in deciding how to us positive action measures to remedy the disadvantages faced by women. In the case of *Lommers,* the ECJ considered that a child care scheme which gave priority to women was compatible with the principle of gender equality, on the basis that the child care scheme in question was intended to address the under-representation of women.[70]

However, in the cases of *Abrahamssohn*[71] and *EFTA Surveillance Authority v Norway*,[72] the ECJ confirmed that giving automatic preference to females would remain a violation of the principle of gender equality. This case-law continues to cause some difficulties. The ECJ has not yet clarified what exactly constitutes giving automatic preference to women. This means that the position of the Court on positive action remains ambiguous and uncertain. This lack of clarity may at times discourage the use of certain forms of positive action in member states, as governments can be reluctant to risk a negative decision by the ECJ.

Some experts have suggested that the ECJ should give member states even more discretion when it comes to the use of positive action on the grounds of ethnicity or religion.[73] However, this suggestion remains controversial. Some experts have expressed fears that member states may use positive action measures to give unfair advantages to some religious groups. There are also concerns that such positive action measures may be used to protect religious organisations against the requirement to respect the principle of gender equality and now the right to equality on the grounds of sexual orientation. Therefore, there may be a case for retaining some legal controls on the use of positive action: member states should perhaps be required to show that preferential treatment is objectively justified as necessary to reduce disadvantage and under-representation.[74]

In general, the EU's experience of positive action has been that it is an essential policy tool for addressing problems of disadvantage. However, there is a need for legislation and consistent court decisions to clarify when preferential treatment in particular can be used. Also, it appears to be better if public and private bodies are given flexibility and a margin of discretion in how to apply positive action measures. Attempts to control the use of such measures can result

---

69 ECJ, 30 September 2004, Case 319/03, *Briheche v Ministre de l'Intérieur*, [2004] ECR I-8807.
70 ECJ, 19 March 2002, Case C-476/99, *Lommers* [2002] ECR I – 2891.
71 ECJ, 6 July 2000, Case 407/98, *Abrahamsson and Andersson v Fogelqvist* [2000] ECR I-5539.
72 Case E-1/02, 24 January 2003. See the discussion of this case by C. Tobler, 41 *Common Market Law Review* (2004), pp. 245-260.
73 See D. Caruso, *supra* note 23.
74 P. Skidmore, 'The EC Framework Directive on Equal Treatment in Employment: Towards a Comprehensive Community Anti-Discrimination Policy?', (2001) 30/1 *Industrial Law Journal*, pp. 126-132.

in uncertainty and a lack of clarity. However, it may be useful to maintain some legal controls in place, in particular to require that positive action measures be shown to be objectively justified and not misused or manipulated.

7. POSITIVE ACTION IN THE UK

EC law controls the extent to which member states can introduce positive action measures. However, the member states can choose whether or not to make use of positive action strategies: there is no express obligation in EC law to do so. The UK has historically avoided the use of certain types of positive action measures: successive UK governments have been reluctant to introduce forms of preferential treatment, except in the special and difficult context of Northern Ireland (see above). However, in recent years, public and private bodies in the UK have increasingly made use of a wide variety of positive action strategies.[75] Recent legislative reforms now require public authorities to take some forms of positive action. In addition, proposed new legislation will make it easier for public and private bodies to take positive action measures.

In general, the UK's anti-discrimination legislation, much of which predates the equivalent EU legislation, prohibits any unequal treatment on the grounds of race, ethnic or national origin, nationality, disability, sexual orientation, gender, religion or belief, and age. This has been interpreted as prohibiting most forms of preferential treatment, as this is defined as a form of discrimination, even though it is done for positive reasons.[76]

The exceptions permitted to this general prohibition of preferential treatment are limited. Sections 37 and 38 of the UK Race Relations Act 1976 (the 'RRA') allows employers to provide special training and 'encouragement' to members of disadvantaged ethnic minority groups. This permits 'outreach' initiatives to encourage members of disadvantaged groups to apply for employment or promotion within an organisation. Such outreach initiatives are now widely used in the public and private sectors. However, measures that gave automatic preferment or substantial advantages to minority candidates remain unlawful, for now. Section 35 of the RRA permits the provision of special services in the form of education, welfare, training and other benefits to address the special needs of particular minority groups. This permits a wide range of positive action measures: many UK public authorities have special polices in place to assist disadvantaged groups, especially recently arrived migrant communities. However, there remains considerable uncertainty as to what types of positive

---

[75] See L. Barmes, 'Promoting Diversity and the Definition of Direct Discrimination', (2003) 32/3 *Industrial Law Journal* 200. See also L. Barmes and S. Ashtiany, 'The Diversity Approach to Achieving Equality: Potential and Pitfalls', (2003) 32/3 *Industrial Law Journal*, pp. 274-296.

[76] H. Slater, 'Making a Positive Difference: A Legal Guide to Positive Action', (2002) 111 *Equal Opportunities Review*, pp. 12-17.

action to assist members of disadvantaged ethnic groups are lawful and which are not.[77]

A similar position applies across all of the other equality grounds. For example, section 47 of the UK Sex Discrimination Act 1975 (the 'SDA') again only permits special measures to train and "encourage" women. Section 49 of the SDA also permits very limited positive action by trade unions, employer organisations and professional bodies, who can reserve positions on their representative bodies for women.[78] The Sex Discrimination (Election Candidates) Act 2002 also permits preferential treatment by political parties in selecting candidates for election.[79] However, in general, UK legislation has restricted the ability of public and private bodies to give preferential treatment to members of disadvantaged groups. The major exception is the Disability Discrimination Act, which permits preferential treatment for disabled persons.[80]

However, many private and public sector organisations have in recent years introduced various positive action measures to encourage more participation in employment and other areas of social life from members of disadvantaged groups.[81] However, many of these positive action measures exist in a legal grey zone. Any measures that could be interpreted as giving preferential treatment to members of disadvantaged groups run the risk of being declared by the courts to be unlawful.[82] Greater clarity and coherence are required.

The recent report of the Discrimination Law Review, an internal government assessment of the existing strengths and weaknesses of UK anti-discrimination law, concluded that greater scope for positive action should be permitted in UK law.[83] It appears likely that legislation will soon be introduced to make this reform. This proposal makes sense, especially as much greater scope for positive action already exists in Northern Ireland, a part of the UK, as already discussed above.

Also, as also discussed above, various positive equality duties have now been imposed upon UK public authorities, which require them to take active steps to eliminate discrimination and to promote equality of opportunity for disadvantaged groups, through 'mainstreaming' and other positive action

---

[77] See L. Barmes, *supra* note 75.
[78] See M. Russell, *Women's Representation in UK politics: What can be done within the law?*, (London: The Constitution Unit, 2001).
[79] See C. O'Cinneide and M. Russell, *supra* note 18.
[80] See S. Fredman, 'Disability Equality: A Challenge the Existing Anti-Discrimination Paradigm?', in A. Lawson and C. Gooding, *Disability Rights in Europe*, (Oxford: Hart, 2005), pp. 199-218.
[81] For a discussion of the strengths and problems of 'diversity management' strategies, see L. Barmes and S. Ashtiany, *supra* note 75; J. Wrench, 'Diversity Management Can Be Bad For You', (2005) 46/3 *Race and Class*, pp. 73-84.
[82] See L. Barmes, *supra* note 75.
[83] See *A Framework for Fairness: Proposals for a Single Equality Bill for Great Britain* (the Discrimination Law Review), (London: Department for Communities and Local Government, June 2007), paras 4.44 - 4.57.

initiatives. These duties have been praised as a new and effective policy response to problems of inequality. They are an ambitious attempt to make equality issues a core concern for public authorities: under these duties, which are legally enforceable, public authorities are required to take positive action measures to combat disadvantage. However, it remains unclear which positive action measures public authorities can adopt in implementing these duties. Therefore, it makes sense to reform the law to permit more flexibility for both public and private bodies in using positive action.

An interesting debate also exists in the UK as to whether the positive duties imposed in Northern Ireland on private employers should be extended to all private employers throughout Britain. An independent expert review of UK anti-discrimination law recommended in 2000 that positive duties be imposed upon British employers to take measures to promote equality of opportunity in their employment practices.[84] However, in the recent Discrimination Law Review, the UK government decided not to adopt this approach.

8. THE US EXPERIENCE WITH AFFIRMATION ACTION

The Equal Protection Clause of the US Constitution requires federal and state authorities not to discriminate. Any use of 'suspect' forms of classification, such as a person's race or gender, has to be shown to be clearly justified.[85] As in the UK, this restriction on the use of such forms of classification also applies even they are used for the purposes of assisting disadvantaged groups. Therefore, the use of preferential treatment to assist Afro-Americans will be unlawful unless it can be shown to be clearly justified.[86] Other forms of positive action are more acceptable.

Affirmative action practiced by private or public employers and unions is subject to similar review under Title VII of the Civil Rights Act of 1964. In general, the US courts give more flexibility to the use by private sector bodies of preferential treatment measures than is given to public authorities.[87] Also, where positive action measures are introduced to remedy existing discrimination, the courts are again are willing to permit the use of preferential treatment.[88] The US

---

[84] B. Hepple, M. Coussey and T. Choudhury, *supra* note 1, paras 3.37-3.50.

[85] The use of race or ethnic origin to differentiate between individuals will be subject to 'strict scrutiny' by the US courts: see *Brown v Board of Education of Topeka* 347 U.S. 483 (1954). For the less strict standard applied in gender cases, see *Craig v Boren* 429 US 190 (1976). For the much weaker standard applied in age discrimination cases, see *Massachusetts Board of Retirement et al v Murgia* 427 U.S.307 (SC).

[86] See the famous decision in the case of *University of California v Bakke* 438 U.S. 265 (1978).

[87] See *United Steelworkers of American v Weber* 443 US 193 (1979).

[88] *Johnson v Transportation Agency* 480 US 616 (1987).

Supreme Court in the case of *Sheet Metal Workers v EEOC*[89] clarified that employers and unions could voluntarily adopt positive action measures (including preferential treatment) to undo the legacy of past discrimination: the Court also confirmed that under the Civil Rights Act 1964 US courts could also require discriminating employers to implement positive action measures.

In assessing the lawfulness of positive action measures, the US courts assess both the purpose of the positive action measure used and the means it employs. When the 'strict scrutiny' test is applied, as will be the case when public bodies use preferential treatment measures, there must be a compelling government interest in achieving the aim of the measure in question, and the means employed to achieve this aim must be 'narrowly tailored', i.e. use preferential treatment to the minimal degree possible.[90]

This analysis is similar to the 'objective justification test sometimes employed by the European courts. However, the US case-law has controversially established that the fact that a group suffers discrimination and disadvantage in general in society cannot by itself justify the use of preferential treatment measures, even if it may justify other forms of positive action.[91] This has tended in practice to limit the use of positive action measures.[92] However, the courts have been willing to accept the use of preferential treatment and other forms of 'strong' positive action measures in university admission policies where such measures promote 'diversity'.

Originally applied by Justice Powell in his judgment in the case of *University of California v Bakke*, this approach was confirmed by the Supreme Court in the recent case of *Grutter v Bollinger*.[93] The Court upheld the University of Michigan Law School's affirmative action programmes which gave bonus points to applicants if they came from an under-represented group, on the basis that this was done to promote the diversity of the student population and also because the Law School's admission system permitted each applicant to be examined on their own merits. However, the Supreme Court confirmed in the even more recent decision of *Parents Involved In Community Schools v Seattle School District No. 1*[94] that the 'strict scrutiny' standard would still continue to be applied to the use of distinctions based on race, even if these distinctions were for the purposes of implementing positive action measures. This has produced a complex case-law, which has been criticised as too restrictive.[95] It could be argued that the US, with the UK and the EU as a whole, should give public and private bodies greater flexibility in adopting positive action measures.

---

[89] 478 US 421 (1986).
[90] *Adarand Constructors Inc v Pena* [1995] 515 US 2000.
[91] See *supra* note 86.
[92] See in particular E. Anderson, *supra* note 49.
[93] 539 US (2003).
[94] 551 US (2007), 28 June 2007.
[95] E. Anderson, *supra* note 49.

9. INTERNATIONAL HUMAN RIGHTS LAW

International human rights standards appear to permit the use of positive action measures, which may at times be required to be implemented to make the right to equality meaningful for all. Article 26 of the International Covenant on Civil and Political Rights (the ICCPR) provides that '[a]ll persons are equal before the law' and that States Parties 'shall . . . guarantee to all persons equal and effective protection against discrimination on any ground'. In its General Comment 18 on the ICCPR, the UN Human Rights Committee (HRC), which is charged with interpreting the Covenant, stated that '[not] every differentiation of treatment will constitute discrimination, if the criteria for such differentiation are reasonable and objective and if the aim is to achieve a purpose which is legitimate under the Covenant.'[96] At paragraph 10 of the General Comment, the HRC expressly recognised the need for positive action:

> [T]he principle of equality sometimes requires States to take affirmative action in order to diminish or eliminate conditions which cause or help to perpetuate discrimination prohibited by the Covenant. For example, in a State where the general conditions of a certain part of the population prevent or impair their enjoyment of human rights, the State should take specific action to correct those conditions. Such action may involve granting for a time to the part of the population concerned certain preferential treatment in specific matters as compared with the rest of the population. However, as long as such action is needed to correct discrimination in fact, it is a case of legitimate differentiation under the Covenant.

This General Comment therefore clarifies that positive action is fully compatible with the right to equal treatment, and may actually be required in certain circumstances to give effect to this right.[97] This logic is also adopted in Article 4(1) of the Convention on the Elimination of All Forms of Discrimination Against Women ('CEDAW'), which states that:

> Adoption by States Parties of temporary special measures aimed at accelerating de facto equality for men and women shall not be considered discrimination as defined in the present Convention, but shall in no way entail as a consequence the maintenance of unequal or separate standards; these measures shall be discontinued when the objectives of equality of opportunity and treatment have been achieved.

The same article also provides that 'special measures... aimed at protecting maternity shall not be considered discriminatory.' Articles 2(e) and 3 of CEDAW go further and impose a strong positive obligation upon States Parties

---

[96] General Comment 18, para. 13, p. 28 (1994).
[97] In General Comment 23 the HRC recognised that (in para. 6.2) that 'positive measures by states may also be necessary to protect the identity of a minority and the rights of its members to enjoy and develop their culture and language and to practice their religion, in community with other members of the groups.'

to take active steps to secure equality for both sexes. Article 5(1) CEDAW illustrates the breath of this requirement, with its obligation upon states to 'modify the social and cultural patterns of conduct of men and women, with a view to achieving the end of prejudices ...and all other practices which are based on the idea of the inferiority ...of either of the sexes or on the stereotyped roles for men and women.' Article 7 of CEDAW makes clear that such 'temporary special measures' may be used to secure equality of political representation.

Other international instruments take a similar position, including the UN Conventions on the Elimination of Racial Discrimination ('CERD') and the Rights of Persons with Disabilities ('CRPD'). The ILO Discrimination (Employment and Occupation) Convention (No. 111) classifies special measures for those needing special assistance as falling outside the definition of discrimination. A series of UN policy documents have also adopted similar views, such as the Beijing Declaration of the Fourth World Conference on the Rights of Women and the 1995 Copenhagen Declaration.

For another example, the European Court of Human Rights has interpreted the European Convention on Human Rights as recognising the legitimacy of positive action measures, if they can be objectively justified. In the *Belgian Linguistics* case, the Court made clear that positive action is not incompatible with Article 14, finding that 'certain legal inequalities tend only to correct factual inequalities'.[98] In *Thlimmenos v Greece*, the European Court of Human Rights held that discrimination might arise if states 'without objective and reasonable justification fail to treat differently persons whose situations are significantly different'.[99]

Therefore, there is a broad consensus that international human rights law permits the use of temporary and proportionate positive action measures, and even may impose certain obligations upon states to use positive action.

10. CONCLUSION

Positive action is a very important tool in the fight against discrimination and disadvantage. It involves the use of special measures to assist disadvantaged groups in overcoming the structural forms of discrimination that limit their opportunities to participate in society. Different forms of positive action may be used in different circumstances: there is no fixed formula. It is important to have legal controls in place to regulate the use of positive action and to encourage public and private bodies to make use of special measures to assist disadvantaged groups. However, experience from the EU, the UK and the USA indicates that if legal controls on the use of positive action are too restrictive, this may impede its

---

[98] ECtHR, Application Nos. 1474/62, 1677/62, 1691/62, Judgment of 23 July 1968, (1967) 1 EHRR 252.
[99] ECtHR, Application No. 34369/97, Judgment of 6 April 2000, (2001) 31 EHRR 15.

effectiveness. Positive action should not be seen as a departure from the principle of equal treatment: instead, when applied in a proportionate manner, positive action can play a vital role in ensuring substantive equality of treatment for the disadvantaged.